Date: 3/22/19

A Taste of Naples

Big City Food Biographies Series

Series Editor

Ken Albala, University of the Pacific, kalbala@pacific.edu

Food helps define the cultural identity of cities in much the same way as the distinctive architecture and famous personalities. Great cities have one-of-a-kind food cultures, offering the essence of the multitudes who have immigrated there and shaped foodways through time. The **Big City Food Biographies** series focuses on those metropolises celebrated as culinary destinations, with their iconic dishes, ethnic neighborhoods, markets, restaurants, and chefs. Guidebooks to cities abound, but these are real biographies that will satisfy readers' desire to know the full food culture of a city. Each narrative volume, devoted to a different city, explains the history, the natural resources, and the people that make that city's food culture unique. Each biography also looks at the markets, historic restaurants, signature dishes, and great cookbooks that are part of the city's gastronomic make-up.

Books in the Series

New Orleans: A Food Biography, by Elizabeth M. Williams

San Francisco: A Food Biography, by Erica J. Peters

New York City: A Food Biography, by Andrew F. Smith

Portland: A Food Biography, by Heather Arndt Anderson

Chicago: A Food Biography, by Daniel R. Block and Howard B. Rosing

Kansas City: A Food Biography, by Andrea L. Broomfield

Rio De Janeiro: A Food Biography, by Marcia Zoladz

Madrid: A Culinary History, by Maria Paz Moreno

The Food and Drink of Sydney: A History, by Heather Hunwick

A History of the Food of Paris: From Roast Mammoth to Steak Frites,
by Jim Chevallier

The Food and Drink of Seattle: From Wild Salmon to Craft Beer,
by Judith Dern, with Deborah Ashin

A Culinary History of Taipei: Beyond Pork and Ponlai,
by Steven Crook and Katy Hui-wen Hung

The Food and Culture of Miami: From Sun and Sand to Surf and Turf,
by Kimberly Wilmot Voss

A Taste of Naples: Neapolitan Culture, Cuisine, and Cooking, by Marlena Spieler

A Taste of Naples

Neapolitan Culture, Cuisine, and Cooking

Marlena Spieler

ROWMAN & LITTLEFIELD
Lanham • Boulder • New York • London

Published by Rowman & Littlefield
An imprint of The Rowman & Littlefield Publishing Group, Inc.
4501 Forbes Boulevard, Suite 200, Lanham, Maryland 20706
www.rowman.com

6 Tinworth Street, London SE11 5AL, United Kingdom

British Library Cataloguing in Publication Information Available

Library of Congress Cataloging-in-Publication Data
Names: Spieler, Marlena, author.
Title: A taste of Naples : Neapolitan culture, cuisine, and cooking / Marlena Spieler.
Description: Lanham, Maryland : Rowman & Littlefield, [2018] | Series: Big city
  food biographies series | Includes bibliographical references and index.
Identifiers: LCCN 2018019320 (print) | LCCN 2018021971 (ebook) |
  ISBN 9781442251267 (electronic) | ISBN 9781442251250 (cloth : alk. paper)
Subjects: LCSH: Food—Italy—Naples—History. | Food habits—Italy—Naples—
  History. | Cooking, Italian—Neapolitan style. | Naples (Italy)—Social life and customs.
Classification: LCC TX360.I8 (ebook) | LCC TX360.I8 S65 2018 (print) |
  DDC 641.300945/731—dc23
LC record available at https://lccn.loc.gov/2018019320

Printed in the United States of America

Contents

Big City Food Biographies—
Series Foreword

Cities are rather like living organisms. There are nerve centers, circulatory systems, structures that hold them together, and of course conduits through which food enters and waste leaves the city. Each city also has its own unique personality, based mostly on the people who live there but also on the physical layout, the habits of interaction, and the places where people meet to eat and drink. More than any other factor, it seems that food is used to define the identity of so many cities. Simply say any of the following words and a particular place immediately leaps to mind: bagel, cheesesteak, muffuletta, "chowda," and cioppino. Natives, of course, have many more associations—their favorite restaurants and markets, bakeries and donut shops, pizza parlors, and hot dog stands. Even the restaurants seem to have their own unique vibe wherever you go. Some cities boast great steakhouses or barbecue pits; others, their ethnic enclaves and more elusive specialties like Frito pie in Santa Fe, Cincinnati chili, and the Chicago deep dish pizza. Tourists might find snippets of information about such hidden gems in guidebooks; the inveterate flaneur naturally seeks them out personally. For the rest of us, this is practically unchartered territory.

These urban food biographies are meant to be not guidebooks but rather real biographies, explaining the urban infrastructure, the natural resources that make each city unique, and most importantly the history, people, and neighborhoods. Each volume is meant to introduce you to the city or reacquaint you with an old friend in ways you may never have considered. Each biography also looks at the historic restaurants, signature dishes, and great cookbooks that reflect each city's unique gastronomic makeup.

These food biographies also come at a crucial juncture in our culinary history as a people. Not only do chain restaurants and fast food threaten the existence of our gastronomic heritage, but also we are increasingly mobile as a people, losing our deep connections to place and the cooking that happens in cities over the generations with a rooted population. Moreover, signature dishes associated with individual cities become popularized and bastardized and are often in danger of becoming caricatures of themselves. Ersatz versions of so many classics, catering to the lowest common denominator of taste, are now available throughout the country. Our gastronomic sensibilities are in danger of becoming entirely homogenized. The intent here is not, however, to simply stop the clock or make museum pieces of regional cuisines. Cooking must and will evolve, but understanding the history of each city's food will help us make better choices, will make us more discerning customers, and perhaps will make us more respectful of the wonderful variety that exists across our great nation.

Ken Albala
University of the Pacific
Series Editor

Preface

How did I ever come to write this book? I'm not Neapolitan or even Italian American. I haven't spent years living there. But when I come to Naples, I feel at home. And I get really excited about my next meal.

I got to Naples in a round-about way, via the northern town of Verona, famous for Romeo and Juliet. I was visiting the Rana pasta family (I am in love with their artichoke ravioli). Giovanni Rana, founder of the company; his son, Gian Luca; and a handful of their friends were tapping the edge of a Parmigiano wheel to pry it open. Suddenly, one of the cheese-popping guys leaned over to me, out of the blue, and asked, "Have you ever been to Napoli?" He continued, "I'm from Napoli. It is a place like no other. You must go as soon as you can. I have a feeling it's for you." He went on to say that whether aristocratic or poverty stricken, Neapolitans are all the same: they run down to the beach, rejoice in the sea, eat spaghetti with tomatoes—then the big cheese popped open, and our conversation was over.

Coincidentally, not long after, I was at a dinner in London in which dessert was a big airy babà. This cake, light as a cloud and bathed in sweet rum, made me swoon. Manuela Barzan and Michele Lomuto, waving at me from the other side of the table, had carried it on their laps on the plane from Naples. When they saw how much I was enjoying it, they exclaimed on behalf of the Naples Chamber of Commerce, "You must come meet Mennella, the baker!"

So it seemed I was on my way, but I was still nervous. I had been to Naples long ago, and while I swooned over the pizza and fell in love with the home-canned tomatoes sold in the streets, my best friend had her wallet cut from her handbag on a bus so artfully that she didn't notice it was gone until it was too late. A few days later, I was held by the police for a short while (gulp)—maybe a few minutes, but it felt like forever—and I never even figured out why. So, yes, I was intimidated.

Did I fall in love with Naples the second visit, when we ate (accidently and un-likely, I know now after many, many return trips) one mediocre meal after another? No, I did not. Not at first, that is. On the last day, however, there was a huge power blackout. Everyone—including me—was worried about finding a nice, hot cup of coffee. Trudging from this cafe to that one, I ended up on the Capri ferry since it had its own generator and was cranking out *cappuccini*. To me, as well as to those around me, it seemed the sensible thing to do. I began to think, *These might be my people*. Though I returned home that afternoon, it was on that boat, surrounded by caffeinated Neapolitans, that I fell in love.

The next visit, my third, was the charm. Walking down the plane's stairway onto the tarmac, I felt the gods and goddesses walking with me. Looking ahead, I saw Vesuvio in the background; I was energized but not overexcited. I breathed in the air: it smelled warm, nearly tropical, with an overlay of car exhaust.

I looked around and saw this vibrant, boisterous Mediterranean ode to life. From that day forward, the (often conflicting) aspects of Naples revealed themselves: cultured, noble, opulent, and poverty stricken; wide boulevards and narrow alleys; mansions and tenements; garbage overflowing the dumpsters. Crossing the street was as death defying as in Cairo thanks to the traffic. Gazing at the perky people surrounding me, I bought a *sfogliatella*, sat down, and took a bite. A big, fat joyful bite. It was so unbelievably delicious. I felt at one with all the other *sfogliatelle* eaters (and pizza eaters, and pasta eaters, and gelato eaters).

After that, I spent years visiting Naples frequently, consulting for the Naples Chamber of Commerce. Although I was an outsider, homes and restaurants opened their kitchens to me. Most kitchens are never far from Nonna's cooking, even if only the memory of Nonna. I felt my own grandmother next to me, even though my Ashkenazi grandmother had never set foot in Naples. But the love of cooking, of feeding family—even cutting the onion in her hand rather than fancy-schmancy on a cutting board—it was the same. But it's not only nonnas who keep tradition alive through cooking; there are nonnos (grandfathers), too, and uncles and aunts: they are stirring the spaghetti, simmering the sauce; Uncle Vito takes us to his fields to see tomatoes growing; Chef Mimmo wants to show us how he makes his mamma's *linguine alle vongole*.

With each meal and visit, this outsider became privy to the food knowledge of insiders. There, in the kitchen, as the culinary story of Napoli unfolded, I learned of their food culture and how it grew, their history—of agriculture, geo-graphy, and attitude—interweaving to create this seemingly simple (yet surpris-ingly complex) cuisine.

I yearned to share it, because when *you* go to Naples, I want the food to sing to you. Knowing its background story makes it sing more sweetly. And if you don't go, cooking the dishes still can bring huge pleasure to your food life.

It wasn't exactly a cookbook I wanted to write; it was a love letter to the people and their food traditions, generation passed to generation, the particular joy that is the Neapolitan way. And in fact the Neapolitan way, that unique attitude and style, has its own term: *Napoletanità*.

I know from experience that everything—art, music, food (even pizza)—is enhanced by knowledge, so I sought to learn more. Each time a new aspect unveiled itself to me—a morsel of history, a joke, a legend—everything tasted better for it. Even the most delicious dish is more satisfying—more succulent, if you will— when understood through its onion-like layers of culture and history.

Since I'm not Neapolitan, I felt uniquely unqualified to write with authority about someone else's cuisine. As a Neapolitan, you *know* which way is best: the way your Nonna or Mamma makes it. Without my own Neapolitan traditions, I spent a lot of time learning from others: chefs, cooks, artists, *pizzaioli*, pasta makers, cheese makers, any and everyone who lifted the lid to let me see what was going on in their pots.

Then I realized—lightbulb moment—that it was precisely *because* I am on the outside looking in that I can see things with greater objectivity—without the nostalgia of my Nonna's ragù or my Mamma's pasta e fagioli. I can appreciate the many layers and aspects of a dish or regional variation, tasting with objectivity instead of familial loyalty. I could admire and appreciate it from the outside, if you will, painting a culinary biography rather than looking in the mirror and scrawling a family food self-portrait.

Everything spoke to me: the sense of family, the arguing, loving, interacting, lively families. The devotion of friends loud and joyous, the love of arguing—have I mentioned this?—unquenchable, generous hospitality, cheerfulness even in the face of adversity, light-filled optimism juxtaposed with the heavy burden of depression—in Naples I found that everything was emotional. And everything, especially the food, reflects this emotionally charged state of life.

The place, the people, the food—I fell hard and deep for it all, especially the way of eating. At the same time, I saw that visitors didn't always understand what was on the table and why. As a result, they came away feeling at least slightly negative. Why was this like this, unlike the rest of Italy? To really appreciate Neapolitan food life, its best to understand how it evolved, the people to whom it is so important, and what makes it the way it is.

You may know Italy very well, having traveled it countless times; you may summer in Tuscany, winter in Cinque Terre, and follow the fashions of Milano, but

Napoli . . . Napoli is a world of its own. To start, you might need an interpreter. (And not just figuratively—UNESCO has declared the Neapolitan dialect its own full-fledged language.)

How to untangle the many layers of Neapolitan food culture so that it makes sense? Many food customs may not be obvious to foreigners, no matter how well they know Italy, or even to other Italians. I began to feel like an unofficial food tour guide of Naples no matter where in the world I was: Invite me to dinner, and I'll make spaghetti with tomatoes! It will be a revelation!

When you glimpse why and how it all became that way, the understanding can impart a sense of belonging. Suddenly you understand the suffering and pleasures, the triumphs and defeats, the disasters and joys—all that has led to what's on your plate. If locals tell you this is never eaten with that, listen to them. Simply by sitting down at the table, you suddenly belong to the tribe.

That knowing look when you reach up into a tree and then slip a just-picked lemon into your handbag while walking down the street in Sorrento, and your buddy exclaims, "*Ah, lei è una Napoletana!*" (Ah, I see you are a Neapolitan!) Or when you mention Naples to a Neapolitan in a faraway place, and their eyes glaze over with warmth as they motion with their hands the *portafoglio* (the folding of the pizza to eat in the streets) or drift off dreamily muttering about fresh mozzarella or the dark coffee. At that moment it feels as if you are family.

The food of Naples and Campania, the *Mezzogiorno*—the midday sun (another name for the south of Italy, including Sicily)—is the food that those who would become Italian Americans ate and still eat, albeit fused with American cooking and culture: red sauces, spaghetti, lasagna with ricotta, big fat meatballs.

For a number of years, I became, for lack of a better term, a culinary interpreter working with Manuela Barzan and the Naples Chamber of Commerce accompanying chefs to demonstrations, describing to the audience what was being cooked, how, and why. I worked on festivals and celebrations with food themes and went back and forth to Naples at the drop of a hat. Sometimes we traveled abroad introducing authentic ingredients: fresh buffalo mozzarella, San Marzano tomatoes, good olive oil.

And so, though I am not Italian in the least, I became a de facto long-distance Napoletana (the name residents of Naples give themselves). It was as if, finally, the nerves of the place hit the receptors of my brain: it all clicked. Napoli was like the family I longed for, or perhaps had as a child when meals together mattered. The Neapolitans—they liked each other, they hated each other, they sang, they held each other, they were just so indefatigably alive that I fell into step.

Then I was hit by a car, and everything stopped during the years it took me to recuperate. I was unable to taste or smell, write, or even think clearly. When I recovered, I realized that this was the book I wanted to write. Returning to Naples after years was, of course, emotional. It had changed, I had changed, and yet, still weak and vulnerable, I felt Naples's vitality, and it inspired my own.

The big piles and bins overflowing garbage throughout the city streets were gone. In their place were recycling containers: one for plastic, one for glass, along with one garbage can. Napoli was recycling, and oh so conscientiously. If Naples could remake itself, then perhaps I could, too.

I found myself interacting with everyone; even the smallest thing—buying a metro ticket, a pizza, a container of dog food—requires interaction, a conversation. Of course, it's a little intimidating when one is used to the reserve of other, less gregarious places. I gave myself a day to acclimate; then I dove right in. I felt my blood pumping more energetically and my mind slipping into gear. Neapolitans, I realized, notice everything. They notice, and they might just comment on it. You might be shocked at first. How many times have people asked how old I am? (Why? I don't know.) Do I have children? Am I married? Can I cook? Do I like peaches? Pizza? Naples? What was at first strange soon became endearing, even hilarious. And I answer, honestly, because—why not? Adults of all ages want to speak with me—with you—and so do children. You don't have to say a word: just smile and nod and listen.

One of the backdrops to life in Naples is the fresh food sold everywhere—to eat at a little table set on the pavement, to gobble up right there, to take home and cook. In alleyways, silvery jumping fish and sea creatures in shells are sold from tiny tables, oh so fresh. Boxes of fresh fruit are arranged beautifully. Baskets and buckets are lowered into the street from apartments several floors up to exchange goods with money to pay for them. You see these everywhere in the *centro storico*—it's normal.

That's when I learned that if you've lost your mojo, you might find it there in the cobbled streets, or along the sea, or in a marketplace, or in a pizzeria. I did (and pretty much in all those places).

And so I felt horrified when I heard snobby attitudes echoed about Naples: "Oh, the north is so chic, Tuscany and Piemonte divine, Umbria so green." It's all true. And Rome *is* eternal.

I even had a colleague who, when I invited her to an event in Naples, replied, "No thank you; I prefer the north." She had, of course, never been to the south. It is possible that she would not enjoy it; she was far too uptight. To appreciate Napoli, Campania, I was beginning to realize, one must open his or her heart. Knowledge opens you up to all that ignorance hides. What a joyous discovery was my little Napoli! Why would people look down on her? I began to feel very protective.

Devoted Italian American food blogger Peter Francis Battaglia pointed out plaintively in a private interview, "The food of Naples suffered in the United States (and to a degree, still does) from the same problem as 'ethnic' food today: the assumption that this cuisine couldn't be excellent or of high quality because it was/is considered cheap (and of a poor immigrant class)." Even in recent decades Italian food of the north was considered classier than that of the south. It went further: a whole generation of southern Italian immigrants on America's shore suffered from racism, prejudice, and bigotry after escaping a poverty-stricken land of hunger. They were considered second-class citizens, and their food, though delicious, was considered lower class.

Fourth- and fifth-generation Italian Americans, many of whose origins were Neapolitan, forgot their ancestors, never knew the "old country," didn't realize that what they know as "red sauce cooking" has an amazing history extending thousands of years, a cuisine as rich and varied as that of, for example, Paris or Beijing.

If you are the children or grandchildren or great-grandchildren of these immigrants, I want you to go to Campania, to the delicious culture in your DNA. In fact, I want to take you all by the hand, trattoria to trattoria, beach to cafe to pizzeria, to revel in the atmosphere, and I want to say, "Look! Isn't it gorgeous? It is yours."

As an outsider invited in, I realized that I was in a particularly excellent place to write about the food life of Naples. Unfettered by family, traditions, and prejudice toward "Nonna's ragù" or "Mamma's lasagna," I could objectively appreciate it all.

A few years ago, the legendary cookbook author Paula Wolfert encouraged me to continue learning from cooks in their kitchens and bringing their culinary culture to my readers. I was touched and flattered. This is what she has spent a lifetime doing; no one could so it as well as she. Certainly not me.

I wondered if books about food cultures were still relevant, with the internet, YouTube, even food travel television. I mean, anyone with a smartphone can whip out a video of Zio Giuseppe making rigatoni or Nonna simmering her Genovese. I didn't think anyone needed food writers observing in kitchens any longer.

But Paula was right, and I cannot thank her enough for the encouragement. It is not enough to make a video or to show people whizzing through the country (even picturesquely on motor scooters), eating this, cooking that, then zipping off again. To go into their kitchens—peering into pots, watching Nonna make pasta, Uncle Vito stir ragù, the baker offering both a warm smile and a big fat babà—is to enter their stories and, with it, emotion: happiness, sadness, personal history, regional history. Life comes alive as you inhale the steamy aromas of the kitchen. And to share this? How privileged I am.

Note: Because this is such a personal portrait of Napoli's food life and because the observations and conversations contained herein are mine, mistakes or misrepresentations are accidental, regretted, and mine alone.

Acknowledgments

None of this would be possible without Manuela Barzan, who, along with Michele Lomuto and the Naples Chamber of Commerce, opened the doors of Naples and welcomed me in. We worked together on film festivals and book festivals, baking celebrations, and extravaganzas of everything edible (and potable).

To Alan, Leah, Jonathan, Gretchen, and Mondo—amazing, marvelous Mondo.

To Judy Witts Francini, my Tuscan buddy who led me through the streets of Naples, pointing out so much that I would have missed without her (including the actor Peppe Zarbo). To Julia della Croce, my Italian sister, and to the beautiful (inside and out) Sonia Carbone, a quintessential Napoletana, always ready to drop everything and tell me the stories of Neapolitan food life that only a native would know.

To Albert Sapere and Gennaro di Testa for mozzarella magic; to Paolo and Danilo Ruggiero and the whole tomato-loving family in Sarno; and to Beatrice Ughi, native Napoletana and U.S. importer of beautiful Italian artisanal foods.

To Mary Jo Schleicher and Renee Espinoza, as well as their kids, Ace and Josie, and to Shelly Butcher, Faith Kramer, Annie Levy, Jonell Galloway, Katy Hui-wen Hung, Robyn Eckhard, Carolyn Phillips, Barbara Berry, Jeni Markowitz Clancy, Johanna Saffari, and the late Josephine Bacon.

To Alexandra Sofis, my Greek sister, and to dear Brita Rosenheim and her lovely Maureen and Emmanuelle. To Susie Morgenstern, who writes like a soulful angel for the children of France.

Tia Keenan, my *sorella* in cheese; the late Gareth Jones, who loved Italy deeply; and Vicky Primhak for lemons from her tree in Procida.

To Merisi Vienna, Faith Willinger, Claudia Esposito, Francesco Strazzanti, and Kristina Gill, photographer and coauthor of the book *Tasting Rome*. And to Clark Wolf: "Only dance." There is only one thing better than being in Napoli, and that is being in Napoli with Clark.

Ken Albala, an incredibly patient editor, food experimenter, and noodle soup artist. To Suzanne Staszak-Silva for commissioning and kindly waiting for this book. To Patricia Stevenson, senior production editor, and to Erin McGarvey, the copyeditor whose careful, heartfelt editing helped coax my words into a clear(er) manuscript.

Daniel Young, who loves Naples as much as I do, and to Michele and Charles Scicolone, Napoletane Flavia Vitale, Barbara Castaldo Lajnvas, and Duly Torrecilla Peckmann. To Joe Casale, in honor of his childhood summers on the isle of Capri with his Caprese Nonna, and to writer Lisa DePaulo and blogger Peter Francis Battaglia for their Italian American tales of *pizze* and love for their Campania heritage.

Thank you to the legendary Barbara Fairchild and to Nick Fox of the *New York Times* editorial board, a brilliant editor (and also a maestro at making egg creams), who, along with Pete Wells, assigned and worked with me on a variety of articles. I also thank former colleagues at the once-great *San Francisco Chronicle* food section, for which I wrote many columns about Neapolitan adventures.

Giuseppe Di Martino, a passionate believer in the goodness of Gragnano pasta and its world ambassador. Ros Martin, who, along with Tony Smith, came with me to Naples to make great radio: BBC Radio 4's *The Food Programme*, which sent me to Campania to report on the tomato harvest. To Paolo Ruggiero of Gustarosso and to Antonio Mennella and his amazing babà, whose first bite put my passion in motion and led me to Naples.

Karen Morss and her San Francisco Bay–area Lemon Ladies Farm, sweet, fragrant lemons, grown with love. She takes mail orders!

Gioia Gatti Moreno and Mirella Menglides, of New York's Italian Trade Association. Friend and colleague Antonietta Kelly from London's Italian Trade Association. A big thank-you to pastry chef and cookbook author Nick Maglieri for kindly sharing his recipe for *sfogliatelle*.

To inspiring writer Bee Wilson, whom I first met long ago in Italy.

We had such fun in Naples, didn't we? Eric Burkett, Deborah Grossman, Priscilla Martell, Erica Bauermeister, Julie Powell, Molly Wizenberg, Francis Lam, Andrea Rademan, Enid Goldstein, Scott Hocker, Janet McCracken, Rose Levy Barenbaum, Kiri Tennenbaum, Winnie Yang, and Stanley Tucci, who, along with Julie Powell, previewed *Julie and Julia* for the Islands in the Bay Food and Film Festival. To Giorgio di Fiore, whose taxi service, FioreTransfer, is like a magic carpet. To Chef Wan and his television crew from Malaysia: filming his food and travel TV show in Naples and Capri was so hilarious that a decade later I am still laughing.

Thank you to Maria Teresa Caiazzo and Valentina Santonastaso of Pasta Di Martino communications, for the careful editing help with Neapolitan spelling, grammar, traditions, and so on.

To Melody Elliot Koontz, who once came to Las Vegas with the Napoli gang; to Sam Jacobs for Sophia Loren's charming cookbook *Come Eat with Me* (1977); and to Roberto Caporuscio, for his New York–based, soulful Neapolitan pizza.

To Edouard Cointreau; his son, Eduardo Cointreau; his daughter, Florence Cointreau; and the whole Gourmand family. Their annual cookbook awards, which honor food and wine books in their original languages from all over the world, make Earth a more understanding place. If there were a world peace prize for cookbooks, Gourmand would surely win.

Laura Sevrin, Jonell Galloway, Michelle Brachet, James McIntosh and Thomas Ernst, Anya von Bremzen, Betsy McNair, Bruno Brunetti, Michelle Kemp-Nordell, Ofer Vardi, Chef Marco Pozzobuon, and dear Emily Pozzobuon.

Sergi Kashuba, Nic Baker, Maria Luisa Müller, Judy Joo, Kerrie Lynam, and the wonderful George, Amy Sherman, Sue Kreitzman, Lisa Lerner Schmier, Trish Kelly, Rosa Rajkovic, and Marcy Smothers (a.k.a. "Polpetta"). And a huge thanks to Paula Wolfert for a lifetime of Mediterranean inspirations.

1

❖ ❖

Introduction

If Rome Is Italy's Heart, Then Naples Is Its Soul

Edgy, scruffy, loud, Napoli is a place of contrasts. Many mutter knowingly, "The sacred and the profane." It is the best place, it is the worst: the kindest and cruelest, earthy and elegant, rich and poor. Seething, voluptuous, infectiously in love with life. Neapolitans feel it in their bones, see it in their streets, read it in their literature, battle it day to day in their most inner, expressive, Neapolitan soul.

The *centro storico*, the historical center of Naples, has a population density close to Hong Kong's. Living quarters are cramped; life percolates in the streets; people sit on balconies watching the "show."

Washing colorfully strung across narrow alleyways like banners or celebration bunting. Vespas whizzing around with fashion-devoted teenagers or even with whole families: Mamma, Papà, and a bambino or two—maybe even the family dog. Men are stylish, women of all ages, too. I gaze at these exotic creatures and think that I never could hope to be as fashionable and vivacious—they must be a different species completely! But then I see little old nonnas tending pots of herbs or cooking pasta, and I see a different side of Naples, that of the Mamma, the nurturer. Neighbors gather in hidden courtyards, tiny *piazzette*, or anyplace near the sea, cooling off as the day's heat lifts, gossiping, admiring the view, and just sharing humanity.

At the long beautiful seafront lined with mansions and grand hotels, its rocky beaches for sunbathing and swimming, Naples gives a sigh of relief and forgets the warren of dirty, dark cobbled streets, the rundown apartment buildings in nondescript neighborhoods. To be there feels wonderful, just to glance at the sea, the sky, the islands. Mount Vesuvius fills the heart with a sense of—for lack of a better word—joy. Only five miles from the city, Vesuvius gives all Neapolitans—no matter their class or socioeconomic level—a sense of unity, a sense of community, of the incredible luck of being surrounded by such natural beauty while also living in the shadow of a force of terrifying destruction.

In Naples, ones takes pleasure from the senses, gratefully, especially food and sociability. Neapolitans cram as much life into each day as possible, each moment, because—well, remember Pompeii?

And know that your heritage reflects both contrasts: a warren of dirty cobbled streets or rundown apartment buildings, areas of industrial ugliness, but also the long, beautiful seafront of rocky beaches for sunbathing and swimming, grand mansions, charming, picturesque, winding alleyways, and great civic spaces of *grandi piazze* and public monuments. And know that the insane traffic prevents no one from being a part of the life of the street. If you are Neapolitan, rich or poor, the city and culture is yours.

The views alone are beautiful, uplifting, dreamy. Gazing at the sea, the sky, Mount Vesuvius lifts the heart. For Neapolitans, it is an everyday joy.

Mythology claims that the coast was inhabited by beautiful mermaids called Sirens who lured sailors to their deaths on the rocks. Many say that the city of Naples herself is like a Siren: seductive and dangerous, once she has you charmed, you never want to leave.

One of the legendary mermaids, Parthenope, was spurned by Odysseus. In a fit of despair, she threw herself into the turbulent sea around the Li Galli islands off the Amalfi Coast. Her body washed up on the shore of what became the city of Naples. The original name of the city was Parthenope, remaining so until the Greeks established Neapolis (now Naples). You see Parthenope's name everywhere: streets, restaurants, businesses. Parthenope is never forgotten.

Naples is, despite its fascinating history and cultural wealth, intimidating. People are put off from visiting by stories of street crime—although these days Naples is far safer than many other cities, my own included. Neapolitan food has so much to offer: a Mediterranean clarity, a glimpse into the soul and history of this ancient land. Even for those who might think they know about the food, there is so much to learn. Even for Italians, even for Neapolitans, even for Neapolitan chefs—always so much more to learn!

Some people think they know it all already: pizza, pasta, red sauce, right? A famous American food writer from a top newspaper stated that he knew everything about Neapolitan food, so he didn't need to come in person, despite my encouragement. He would stay in Florence, thank you very much. He later visited Naples for a short stay—a few days?—and published a meh recipe or two. All of America read it and thought that this was what real Neapolitan food was. Heartfelt Naples and her vibrant food life deserve better.

Neapolitan wisdom suggests caution: pickpockets are highly skilled professionals. Yet the hospitality of the people means that gifts are pressed on you, your plate is heaped with delicious things, and no one ever wishes for a cup of coffee he or she cannot afford. The *caffè sospeso* is the concept of sharing, anonymously. *Sospeso* has extended into other areas of Neapolitan food life; during summer gelato makers have gelato *sospeso* so that no child goes without ice cream.

Even for those who have just arrived, this spirit is contagious. On a bench under a shady tree in Piazza Carità, I watched several young European backpackers putting together their lunches on a shady bench. A beggar—small, old, wizened—approached them with his hand outstretched. He was not shy; he was determined. One of the backpackers nodded to him and finished making a big panino full of ham and cheese and all good things. Then the backpacker broke his sandwich in half, giving the beggar the bigger half. The young man was still hungry, you could tell, but he was also satisfied. "People here are so kind and friendly," he told me. "I want to give something back to the culture around me." It was his second day in Naples.

Sotto questo cielo non nascono sciocchi ("under these skies no fool is born") is a quintessential Neapolitan proverb. As friendly, cheerful, and openhearted as Neapolitans are, this is the other side: they are not fools; they are observant; they watch; they keep alert to the situation at hand.

But life in Napoli can be difficult; it can require creativity just to get by. There is, of course, after much muttering about how impossible it is, always a way. Their sense of humor is endlessly creative, sometimes slapstick, and sometimes more ironic than the famous British sense of humor. History bequeathed Naples many gifts, and one—though not exactly a welcome gift—was difficulty. Can we depend on others? Not always. Sometimes not at all. Neapolitans developed a survival culture. Known as *arrangiarsi*, it is the ultimate plan B, the ability to look at a situation and realize that if plan A doesn't work out, you devise another. And why stop at making life simply bearable when it can be joyous? Maybe you don't need to stick to the rules—do whatever works. Something always will.

When your plane lands in Naples, look out the window to your left, or wait until you descend the stairs onto the tarmac. There, not so far in the distance (only five miles)—almost as if you could reach out and touch it—is Mount Vesuvius (referred to by locals simply as Vesuvio).

Vesuvio has much to do with everything about Naples. We all know the story of the destruction of Pompeii due to its eruption in 79 BCE and how modern-day fruits and vegetables taste sensational because of the lava-enriched soil. How, almost wherever you go in the Naples area, there is Vesuvio, looking majestic and beautiful. But don't be lulled into thinking that this magnificent capless mountain is benign. Hardly! All residents of Napoli have a designated safe place and escape route in the event of a major eruption.

But the possibility of impending—or not so impending—volcanic doom goes a long way toward explaining the temperament of the people. They are, like their weather and their mountain, extreme. They are warm or frightening and usually funny. They like to sing. They know life is hard, but they are alive, and by this fact alone they are triumphing!

Italy's third-largest city, with a population of four million, Naples is seen as the capital of Italy's south. The climate is quintessentially Mediterranean along the coast, but inland—which can be hilly, mountainous, or flat plains—winters get cold, and sometimes there is even snow. Its region, Campania, is divided into five provinces: Napoli, Benevento, Avellino, Caserta, and Salerno. Stretching from Napoli south to Sicily, the regions of southern Italy, though unique from a food perspective, relate to each other. Campania shares mozzarella and exquisite tomatoes with Puglia. Calabria and Napoli share a love of hot pepper in varying degrees, as well as lemons. Napoli and Sicily share the love of arancini, fresh ricotta, cannoli, and gelato. Greens, bread, olive oil—these are all things that the entire area shares, part of the south's identity.

Naples has a cuisine so unique for a city and region, so distinctly its own, that you could call it a national cuisine.

The city of Naples (or Napule, in the Neapolitan language/dialect) is divided into thirty *quartieri* (neighborhoods) and *rioni* (districts), each with its own personality, though not as hyper-organized as Paris's *arrondissments*. The funicolare, the metro, and streets, so fascinating that you want to keep walking, make getting around the city almost a pleasure (unless you're driving). The town is relatively compact, with only a few main streets like Via Toledo and Via dei Tribunali, large boulevards that link neighborhoods: leafy well-heeled Vomero, shopping destination Chiaia, or Naples's *centro storico*, the historical center of the city. Rione Luzzatti is said to be the backdrop to Elena Ferrante's novels—even in what perhaps could be called a slum, the food is important and delicious.

Singing breaks out spontaneously here, there, wherever crowds gather—even the train station and the gates of the university! Groups meet to tango in the Galleria Umberto I, which is looking a lot perkier these days. There is a boutique hotel at the top, where one can breakfast overlooking the galleria. Never mind the McDonald's and other international brands. Naples has seen everything come and go; it all passes, but Naples endures.

The glittering grandeur of its past left a backdrop for everyday life: majestic palaces, ruins, grand buildings, churches and cathedrals, crumbling baroque in faded hues of yellow and rose. The former royal buildings are now mostly museums that are open to the public such as the spectacular Museo Cappella Sansevero, whose stairs you can descend to visit the skeletons who lie deep underground. Or walk through the garden and gaze at the tiles of the Majolica Cloister (from 1739) at Santa Chiara and feel your heart sing.

There is still pride of the personally crafted. Small workshops and ateliers where craftsmen and artists create much of life's accoutrements by hand: the *presepe*, of course, and jewelry, art, fashion designers, and shoes (those who have read Elena Ferrante's *Those Who Leave and Those Who Stay* will remember Cerullo's shoe store and creations). There are antiquarian book shops, handcrafted perfumes, and sacred art. Little votives, the charm-like figures of various body parts, are to hang in the church in honor of a particular prayer of healing—an arm when praying for someone with a broken arm, a heart to help heal heart problems.

There is even a term, *genio Napoletano*, referring to the type and number of geniuses born in Naples.

Because Naples—and all of Campania—is so food obsessed, it is full of small, personal, individual food shops specializing in cheese, handmade chocolates, marmalades and honey, breads, and of course pastries, wine and limoncello. There are shops dedicated to kitchen wares, which are nearly impossible for me to pass without buying a plate, a coffee mug, something bright and cozy and *molto Napoletano*.

The whole city is dotted with countless palaces, convents, churches, monasteries, and museums. Peer into the courtyard of Palazzo dello Spagnolo and gasp at the elaborate rococò staircase. Tiny shops line the narrow streets and many, probably most, people prefer to shop at them, along with the street markets such as Porta Nolana and Pignasecca, Naples's oldest street market. There are few covered markets in Naples, but Mercatino La Toretta is worth knowing. Located in the Mergellina district, just a few blocks from the American embassy, it's a great combination of permanent market stalls and shops with fresh fruits and vegetables, salame, cheeses, meat, poultry, and fish (fresh and frozen). There's a shop devoted to breads, an *enoteca* for wine, and a chocolate store for the happiness of your soul. The outlying areas—small towns that are part of the larger metropolis—are almost like suburbs.

Art is a part of life. Street art splashes walls at every turn—is nothing left ungraffitied in Naples? Illustrated, hand-painted signs proclaiming such wisdom as *"mangiare bene per vivare meglio"* (eat well to live best) are created in little workshops throughout the city, ready for restauranteurs or shop owners to purchase and put on their own walls. Sometimes when I look up and see balconies festooned with plants, curious albeit everyday items, graffiti, clotheslines linking buildings together, laundry flying high over the streets, I think, *This is* all *art*.

You know you're in the south because people are physically affectionate. Men touch men. Women touch women. Everyone touches. They pat arms and shoulders and hold hands.

Neapolitans are known to be superstitious. When an item has gone missing from your home, it could well be 'O Munaciello, also known as the little monk, an old man/young child spirit that haunts houses at night and moves your things around. He also brings good luck, and his generosity knows no bounds. You may meet him, but you will not know it because he will be in disguise. One always must be open to meeting him. If you *do* meet him, even if you don't know it, *Na bona furtuna*—it is your good fortune. Charms of the little monk—a gnome-like creature dressed in monk's garb—are sold for good luck. With the little monk close to you, all will be well.

Pulcinella, a masked, hunchback character from the Commedia dell'Arte street theater, is an endearing prankster who appears in old theater and puppet shows and is known for always being hungry. He has, shall we say, a strong streak of matters gastronomical, though some might call it greed. He especially loves pasta. You'll see figurines of both Pulcinella and the little monk, as well as what looks like whole red chile peppers (which are actually horns) or *corni*, designed to ward off the evil eye and bring good luck. When you are Neapolitan, you maybe believe in luck, and even if you don't, you think, "Well, it won't hurt."

Rich or poor, the art of eating beautifully is alive and well in Naples. Eating well is not reserved for only the rich or young or beautiful; it is for everyone, part of the national (and by national, I mean Neapolitan) psyche.

Life in Naples is not calm, so don't come hoping for the easy life. Chaos, yes, but also soul. Empathy. Singing. Food. Sex. Naples is so sexy you don't even need sex to be so sexy. It's like an all-over miasma of lovely feelings without the bother of the act itself. Beauty is more strongly felt, emotions more fiery. Good can be blissful, and bad, evil incarnate. Napoli is nothing if not intense contrasts.

Traffic lights? Well, yes, Naples has them, but they are more of a suggestion than a requirement. Two cars squeeze through lanes supposedly only wide enough for one car; if wide enough for two, you'll have a third vehicle sneaking its way in between. Motorbikes with whole families perched on them are the norm rather than the exception. Crossing the road is as scary and death-defying as it is in Cairo or Beijing.

Mark Twain was stunned, even in his days when there were few cars on the streets: "How people aren't run over every day is a mystery." Yet while you dodge speeding Fiats and swarms of *motorinos* buzzing manically around you, only a few steps away an elegant waiter crosses the street balancing his tray: breakfast cappuccino and espresso, a basket of *sfogliatelle*, a glass of orange juice. Despite the insanity of traffic, he makes it to the other side of the street without hurrying, without spilling a drop.

Avoiding traffic? Take the subway! Naples's new subway system is useful, convenient, and beautiful. Subway line 1 is the art line, with the stations displaying more than two hundred works of contemporary art. Toledo station is like a dream, a seaworthy, free-form design that carries you along with the excitement of creativity and beauty until you reach your train. The trains are often crowded, but when they are not, a sing-along and dance fest can break out. It happens, maybe not every day, but this is Napoli. It happens.

Toledo station is amid so many delicious eating experiences that passing through the station en route to your next meal is another part of the sensory pleasure. When you get to Dante station, Bar Mexico is to your left, and to your right eventually you'll find Via dei Tribunali, with its profusion of *pizzerie*, legendary pizzerias.

In Spaccanapoli—the Spanish Quarter—the laundry that hangs in the sun from window to window and sometimes across the street between tiny tenement-like apartments is almost like exterior design—bright banners of colors and shapes. Along the shore, on Via Partenope, crumbling palazzi of baroque splendor are interspersed with elegant hotels. Castles and churches speak of aristocratic pasts; yet around the corner are dark cobbled alleyways. Across the bay the bucolic little islands hover on the water: jet-set Capri, tiny Procida, rustic Ischia.

One can't mention Naples, not even the food, without mentioning soccer. The local team, S.S.C. Napoli—short for Società Sportiva Calcio Napoli (Naples Soccer Sporting Society)—has an almost religious devotion. Its light blue banners and donkey mascot are all over the city, not only near their stadium in Fuorigrotta. When Napoli plays a home game, it is insane—the audience is excitable. When they win, it is ecstasy.

The shadow of the Camorra, a loose-knit group of organized crime families sometimes referred to as the Neapolitan Mafia, may haunt the city, but few people speak openly about them (a good practice to follow). When Roberto Saviano wrote a tell-all book about the Camorra called *Gomorra* (followed by the movie *Gomorra*), most found it shocking. They felt the shadow, but most Neapolitans prefer to walk in the sun. Let's not think about that, okay? In recent years much has been done to lift the shadow.

The towering block of housing projects and desolate small rural towns (which nonetheless offer delicious food), the stunning architecture, breathtakingly beautiful sea and stretches of both rocky and sandy beaches, castles, and museums are all inhabited by characters from Central Casting.

For spiritual support through catastrophes such as famine, earthquakes, war, and drought, Naples has about fifty-six official patron saints, none more venerated than San Gennaro (Saint Januarius in English), a bishop who was beheaded at the Solfatara di Pozzuoli. His blood is preserved in silver containers. For more than six hundred years he has been commemorated in a ceremony in which his dried blood turns to liquid.

Among the other Neapolitan saints is soccer star Diego Maradona. When he led Naples to soccer sovereignty (twice!) over Italy's north, shrines to Maradona popped up throughout Naples, which are tended by devoted residents.

No one in Naples is Italian: they are always Neapolitan. I find myself, shortly after arrival, being absorbed into the city, talking with my hands, leaving no cheek unkissed, arguing when required, smiling, and occasionally dancing and singing. Inhaling the perfume of basil, closing my eyes in delight as I bite into a summery tomato or fat, juicy mozzarella, Italian words (with a Neapolitan accent) taste delicious coming from my mouth like a musical miracle.

Gesticulating, exclaiming, and conversing excitedly, I'm always surprised to see that I haven't turned into a Napoletana, I feel so much the part. The mirror says no: my eastern European genes are visible. Looking closer, though, I notice my smile is livelier, I tilt my head listening, argue good-naturedly about—well—whatever seems right at the moment, feel more generous toward the world than I usually do. I am a nicer, more thoughtful person: this is Neapolitan Marlena. Oh, and suddenly I'm very interested in pastry.

Naples is sometimes called *la città dalle mille contraddizioni* (the city of a thousand contradictions), for things here are not clearly cut, and if they are, there is always an exception. And if there is an exception, we must discuss it thoroughly, then argue, and then perhaps come to the exact opposite conclusion.

Food is spoken of as *poesia*, poetry—*emozione* (emotion) above all. Do you hear such talk elsewhere? Other places seem to be mostly hype about the latest food trend. In Napoli, you suddenly remember how wonderful southern Italian food is. Pasta, pizza, eggplant parmigiana, baba au rhum, mozzarella all can be made in other places—even made very well—but eating it in Naples is experiencing the original. It's like visiting Egypt and seeing the mummies, pyramids, and papyrus paintings. It is all familiar from modern interior decor, clothing, paintings, fabrics, and films; yet here are the originals, the designs that came about through unique genius and vision. What we see elsewhere are just echoes of these stylized images. So too is it with a beautiful Neapolitan pizza, ball of mozzarella, or plate of pasta. It is the original.

Giuseppe Di Martino refers to that one dish that is closest to most Neapolitans' hearts as *la Devozione*. Each bite holds the story of Naples, reminding you of where you are. Eat it without cheese, as locals do—they will love you—and you will understand the tomato—and Naples—even more. My restaurant motto in Naples is "When in doubt, order the spaghetti with tomatoes." It will always be terrific.

When you land at the airport, glance to the left as your plane glides in. There you will see the volcano. Wherever you find yourself in the environs of the city, look around: there it likely will be, reminding you, overlooking the city and the bay, so beautiful, so deadly. If the sprawling metropolis goes about each day as though it is the last, this is why.

Knowing that at any time your world can drown in fiery lava and ash lends urgency to life. And if it doesn't erupt, well, there could always be an earthquake! So how can you face each day *without* living life to its sensation-filled fullest? And how can you say no to babà, pizza, a plate of pasta al pomodoro? How can you say no to seconds, when that volcano could make tomorrow a moot point?

Neapolitans are generous, energetic, and perhaps a bit melodramatic or hotheaded sometimes. And oh, do they love to talk: it is a city of talkers in a country of talkers. Occasionally it is time for no talk at all, simply a facial expression worth a thousand words.

This is the Neapolitan way of life: a people so passionate about eating well that, frankly, eating with them is inspiring and life enhancing. Before you know it, you're surrounded by musicians and singing choruses of "Funiculì, Funiculà." It might sound cheesy, but when you are in its grip, nothing feels as authentic and wonderful. Life is meant to be felt deeply. We are here such a short time that we must grasp each and every moment.

Neapolitans seem to crave human interaction. The word "conviviality" doesn't even come close. I often get hungry for human interaction, too, but I can keep up only so long; the Neapolitans just keep going. Long after I'm too tired to think and just want to curl up quietly under the covers, my companions will still be eating and drinking and carrying on. I honestly don't understand how they do it. Sometimes I look at Neapolitans and think, *Where does your energy come from? What is your superpower? Don't you ever just want to chill and do nothing?*

No one refers to Napoli and means only the city, especially culinarily; it is a way of describing the whole area, for the foodways of Campania have long fed the city and vice versa. As excitable and energetic as the city is, its surrounding countryside is quiet, bucolic, and peaceful, as calm as a watery dream. These two natures are intertwined at the table. Naples's food life emerges from the whole region. Look at a map and you'll see: here are the buffalo, there the cows, here the sheep, cheese, and cured meats—here, here, and there. This is where the grapes grow for wine, and tomatoes with their love for the volcanic soil of Vesuvio grow abundantly in this area. Olive trees dot the countryside; their oil used in *everything*. I'm not sure there would be a cuisine without it.

The city's vastness and urban sprawl can overwhelm, however. You head out of town into endless sprawl, industrial towns, high-rise apartment blocks and bleak neighborhoods, and dusty streets occasionally interspersed with beautiful towns here and there. Along the coast, just when you think you'll spend the rest of your life driving through Naples, the road enters a tunnel. Bursting out the other end, you are in the most beautiful place imaginable. Palm trees frame your view of the sea, beaches, and resorts on one side of the cliffside road leading down to the sea; on the other, small villages climb into the hills with hotels and restaurants. Castellammare di Stabia, Vico Equense, Sorrento, a string of beautiful beaches in between beautiful villages and towns, with lemon gardens terraced along the hillsides. Amalfi, Positano, Ravello, the islands Ischia, Procida, Capri, they form a strand of beautiful jewel-like resorts and towns and villages: welcome to *la dolce vita*!

Could anyplace be more different from the tense urban grit of Naples? It's so amazing that each time I travel this path, I want to break out laughing with joy when we exit the dark tunnel into the sun and lemon trees and beaches.

And one more important thing: Time does not mean the same thing to Neapolitans (or anyone from Italy's south) that it does to northerners. If you keep showing up on time, someone will explain this to you.

Because Naples's music is like its food—from the heart, a big, warm embrace of life—here is a sidebar about Neapolitan songs.

Canzoni Napoletane: The Neapolitan Songs

Greek mythology tells us that music was born in Naples, daughter of the sun and Sirens. It's easy to believe, because music is everywhere. People sing to themselves in the street as they go about their business of living; people sing to others in the street and pass the hat. People even sing at the table after a meal. Walking down the street, you might hear music, someone singing, playing an accordion, while in the noble palaces are concerts of great opera.

Si nun si canta se more is a Neapolitan proverb that means "If you don't sing, it's because you're dead!"

Although I say that everyone sings, I mean everyone except the world-famous opera star Enrico Caruso. Though born in Napoli and celebrated the world over, his 1901 performance in Naples's opera house, San Carlo, drew vehement criticism. He had suffered a throat hemorrhage and was emotionally devastated and refused to ever sing in Naples again. He sang in San Francisco, soothing its citizens through their earthquake ordeal in 1906 while there on tour, but never again in Naples. He died at Hotel Vesuvio overlooking il Castel dell'Ovo, and the hotel named its restaurant for him.

Canzoni Napoletane: The Neapolitan Songs (*continued*)

The twentieth century gave the world a new way of enjoying music: the invention of voice recordings meant that people could listen to music without being at the same location, together. Suddenly the whole world was falling in love with Neapolitan songs such as "'O sole mio," "'O surdato nnammurato," "Santa Lucia," "'E Spingule Francese," Totò's "Malafemmena," and, of course, "Torna a Surriento" (written on the balcony bar area of Sorrento's Tramontano Hotel and said to have been popular in Mao's China).

"Jamme, Jamme!" cries the expressive Neapolitan song, "Funiculì, Funiculà"— a traditional folk song, I believed, and so did many others. In fact, both Richard Strauss and Nikolai Rimsky-Korsakov heard the song in the streets and, thinking it a folk song, included it in their own works. Strauss was actually sued and had to pay royalties.

It is not, as it turns out, a folk song at all. This is what I was told: In the late 1880s, a cable car was engineered to climb from the lower parts of Napoli to its higher sections, and all the way up to Vesuvio. But passengers were frightened, and tour companies were worried that it would keep clients away. To reassure them, a song was commissioned as an advertisement, to reassure all of its safety.

But what if I was told wrong (which looks very likely)? Campania mythology and stories are engaging, but Wikipedia tells us that the song was composed in 1880 by Luigi Denza (with lyrics by Peppino Turco) and presented at the famous Piedigrotta festival that same year. It quickly sold more than a million copies.

One hears singing everywhere. An accordionist may serenade you in a restaurant (especially on a Saturday night) or at a gathering place of sightseers; at the train station someone might start a sing-along.

Recently I saw the grumpiest guy transformed by traditional Neapolitan songs that suddenly played on the radio. He joined in, singing to himself, his spirits lifting as he did. For a little while afterward, he was no longer grumpy. It was a joy to watch.

And since nothing could be more Neapolitan than a song about coffee, here you go: "Na'tazzulella 'e cafe" sings about the meaning of coffee, pastries, and enjoying life. To paraphrase, "Without coffee, what would it mean to be Neapolitan? Without *sfogliatella* or babà? These are not just everyday habits—they are a way of life, so full of pleasure that you may need to close your eyes with each sip and bite."

2

La Storia
Naples's Culinary History

Knowing the past helps you understand (and appreciate) the present. Each dish you eat today tells the story: all three or four thousand (at least) years of it. The vivid flavors of Naples didn't just spring up and evolve cleverly in the kitchen.

Its past is in its DNA; many Neapolitans are descendants of ancient times. The city itself is one of the few European cities dating from ancient origins, never destroyed.

Naples has endured centuries upon centuries of foreign occupation, natural disasters, poverty, plague, catastrophic earthquakes, World War II, and, every so often, Vesuvio. You would think that this was enough to crush even the strongest of souls, but no. Naples is vibrantly, energetically, richly, alive. Especially at the table.

History offers snippets of information, but connections must be ferreted out, excavations must be conducted, surviving texts must be discovered, translated, and studied. Before we start, I must tell you that in scurrying through vast piles of research, I found names and dates that didn't match, as well as many, many conflicting versions of the same events. I tried to choose what makes the most sense, but I cannot truthfully vouch for complete accuracy. No one can. Even the written word can be misleading: Who wrote it? When? Why? Therefore, I apologize if my dates or events do not correspond with others: one of us may be right, or we both may be wrong. It's a tricky little dance through whatever records are available.

ANCIENT TIMES: THE BEGINNING AS WE KNOW IT

The area we know as Campania has been inhabited since the Neolithic period. The original peoples were from three groups: the Osci, Aurunci, and Ausoni. They spoke Oscan language, part of the Italic language family. Another Oscan tribe, the Samnites, migrated from central Italy into Campania, and being more aggressive than the Campanians, they easily conquered Capua and Cuma, one of the most prosperous and fertile areas of the Italian Peninsula.

The area was explored by the seafaring Phoenicians, then settled by Greeks, developed by Romans, and occupied by so many nations you could get whiplash trying to follow the goings-on. Invaders included Etruscans, Normans, Hohenstaufen, dozens of successions of French kings (Anjou), the Spanish (Aragon), Germans, and the Holy Roman Empire. Ironically, rather than impoverishing the culture, each ruling nation enriched it. Layer after layer helped form—over the years, decades, centuries, and millennia—a unique cultural personality.

Many of today's iconic Neapolitan foods date back to the most ancient of times. The traveling, trading Phoenicians, for example, brought rabbits to Ischia (and to the other Mediterranean islands they traveled between). Today Ischia's most famed dish is braised rabbit, *coniglio all'Ischitana*.

The Phoenicians were great picklers, too. Very likely it was in the Phoenician kitchen that the fish sauce *garum* (also known as *colatura di alici*) originated. The Greeks embraced pickling fish and making sauce when they came to power; soon each Greek port had its own recipe.

The earliest traces of Greek civilization in what is now Campania were around 2000 BCE. The scattered colonies came to be known collectively as Magna Grecia. Its people spoke Greek, practiced Greek culture, and dominated the area for centuries until the Romans conquered. The ancient Greeks were fond of the region, its weather, landscape, and fertility. They felt it was a land that soothed life's burdens.

By 750 BCE, Cuma was a Greek trading station; 550 BCE saw the building of the Temple of Hera and Greek city of Poseidonia, named after the god of the sea, now the magnificent ruins in Paestum. An exciting project under way regarding food and history research of Paestum is a joint endeavor between the government department for antiquities and Giuseppe Di Martino of Pastificio Di Martino. They have hired an archeologist to work on-site, researching the foods of ancient Paestum, with an eye toward replicating their food as it was perhaps three thousand years ago. They have also inaugurated food events on-site for the exploration and experience of tasting modern-day cuisine linked with its past.

Greek rule never made it as far as the Sarnese area around Mount Vesuvius; instead, the region was ruled by Etruscans. The Etruscans were a mysterious people who didn't leave a lot of information behind about who they were, though many believe that the Etruscans were perhaps descendants of the Hittites, who spread out from their Middle Eastern empire after its collapse.

The Samnites in the area fought the Roman Republic during the period around 340 BCE in skirmishes known as the Samnite Wars. In the first, Rome won rich pastureland of northern Campania and extended its presence. From 280 to 275 BCE, Rome fought Greece in the city of Maleventum (bad wind). First colonized by the Romans, it was ruled at times by the Samnites and Longobards. The Romans won the city back from Greece and renamed it Beneventum (good wind; modern-day Benevento). Prospering, it became the second city in southern Italy, with Capua as the first. The iconic Benevento Christmas torrone is a Samnite confection.

In 216 BCE, the bustling town of Capua allied with Carthage against Rome in the Second Punic War, isolating it from the rest of Campania, which remained allies of Rome. In 211 BCE the Capuans, who had resisted the invaders with their imposing walls, were starved into submission by Rome, which gained even more of what is now Campania.

While much of Campania was a center of Hellenistic civilization, Roman rule created a Greco-Roman culture. Both Greeks and Romans supported olive cultivation for oil and grape growing for wine.

The Greeks were fond of fish and mollusks, meat, goat cheese, and high-alcohol wines, according to various archeological finds. The Romans brought richer, even more indulgent food habits.

It's possible that a fire-baked flatbread was a precursor to modern pizza. Local Roman soldiers stationed in the far reaches of the Roman Empire in what is now Israel returned with a fondness for the local hot flatbreads eaten by the Jews (likely matzo). A traditional Naples Christmas confection, *struffoli* (balls of crisp, fried, toffee-covered dough), likely originated in the Greek culture (Magna Grecia), since the word is derived from Greek, meaning "round," and the technique is similar to Greek pastry making.

THE BIRTH OF NAPLES

Between the ninth and eighth centuries BCE, Greek sailors from the island of Rhodes founded the city known as Parthenope. Named after the mermaid of local mythology, the city was founded on the spot where her body supposedly washed ashore. Around this time, people from Euboea in Greece, known as Cumaeans, began to establish colonies in the area. Greek traders founded a colony on the island of Megaris, a beautiful spot just off the coastline (today taken up entirely by Castel dell'Ovo).

A century or two after, in the seventh century BCE, Cuma decided to establish a new city, Neapolis (*nea*: new; *polis*: city), adjacent to Parthenope. The older parts of the city were called Paleopolis, whereas Neapolis became the modern-day Napoli (also known as Naples). Precisely why Cuma expanded at this time is not known, though it had recently thwarted an invasion attempt by the Etruscans. Perhaps they felt a need for a more solid presence in the area.

Neapolis grew and grew, thanks in large part to the influence of the powerful Greek city-state Syracuse in Sicily. Eventually, the new and old cities on the Gulf of Naples merged to become a single inhabited area with a flourishing cultural life.

Samnites captured the area in the fifth century BCE; then in the fourth it was conquered by the Romans. By the end of the fourth century BCE, Campania (with the exception of Naples, which remained Greek—for a while) was a full-fledged part of the Roman Republic.

The Romans valued its lush rural areas, pastures, and fertile growing regions. This kept them supplied with lavish ingredients for which Roman banquets were so famous. The Romans loved eating. I've often thought—when faced with the third pasta of the meal—that the ancient Romans bequeathed today's Neapolitans their brilliant appetites.

When Rome rose to power, the Romans took over making fish sauce from the Greeks, though after the collapse of the Roman Empire, production of *garum/ colatura di alici* ceased except for the area of Campania in the tiny town of Cetara, as well as another nearby town. From at least the third century, *garum* was the number-one seasoning in the Roman Empire; now it is a specialty condiment. Any savory dish referred to as "Cetarese" has either anchovies or *garum/colatura*— or both.

Greco-Roman culture was maintained throughout the Roman era. With the exception of Naples—which kept the Greek language, lettering, and customs—much of Campania adopted Latin as its official language and Romanized its alphabet.

Pasta established its character during the Roman Empire. An obligation of wheat-growing areas (now known as Gragnano, named after the grains that grew there) was supplying Roman soldiers with grains. Spoilage and bugs were an issue, so they started grinding the grains, turning the resultant meal/flour into a paste, which was more digestible than whole, raw grains. Then they discovered that it could be made into thin flatbreads and eaten in soup—more digestible still and so tasty. (Pasta was still eaten this way into the thirteenth century, when dough began to be cooked directly in liquid.)

Roman emperors Claudius and Tiberius (the latter remembered especially for his excesses) enjoyed the luxurious playground of Campania's coastline and islands. All of Rome's rich and powerful flocked there.

Some retired there, such as Lucius Licinius (a.k.a. Lucullus), who settled on the island of Megaris after a career in the army and politics. He lived in a grand, opulent villa with fish ponds and manmade islands jutting into the sea at what is today the site of Castel dell'Ovo. Lucullus devoted himself to life's pleasures, especially gastronomy, and is perhaps most famous for his quote: "Tonight Lucullus dines with Lucullus." Dining without guests one evening, he was presented with a modest meal. He was outraged! That a grand meal is not just for company but also for oneself is amazingly prescient even for modern times. We should feed ourselves as carefully, as mindfully, even (or especially) when dining on our own.

Another late-life Neapolitan was the Latin poet Virgil (70 BCE–19 BCE). Parts of his epic poem *The Aeneid* are located in Campania. It was his actions that gave Castel dell'Ovo (Castle of the Egg) its name. Legend tells that Virgil buried an egg in the ground, declaring that when the egg broke, disaster would befall the city, which was already growing around it. (Update: Although Naples has seen its share of disasters, no one has yet found the broken egg.)

It was a period of relative calm with culture and entertainment—the good life.

I hate to tell you this, but I must, and you know it anyway: The beautiful ruins of amphitheaters scattered throughout the Roman lands were once home to terrible, bloodthirsty encounters of both humans and beasts. No one won. The oldest amphitheater, dating from 80 BCE, was located in the wealthy, fun-loving city and seaside resort of Pompeii.

Pompeii's atmosphere was lively, its hot mineral baths said to be beneficial. At the time of Vesuvio's eruption, Pompeii was just digging itself out from an earthquake in 62 AD. People were optimistic, blissfully unaware of what Vesuvio was capable. Rebuilding their town and vibrant economy was supreme. It was something like the Wild West.

Along the coastline on the Cumaean Peninsula in the Phlegraean Fields (Campi Flegrei) was another mineral springs and coastal resort, Baiae (Italian: Baiae; Neapolitan: Baia), named after Baius, the helmsman of Odysseus's ship in Homer's *Odyssey*, said to be buried nearby.

Baiae had problems with volcanic movements; yet they are what created the hot mineral waters for which Baiae became so famous. (It is still an active volcano area with occasional tragedies.) In the bathhouses of ancient Baiae, sulfurous springs filled pools and a complex system of chambers channeled underground heat for saunas. Doctors often prescribed these healing baths to their patients.

Marius, Lucullus, and Pompey all frequented Baiae. Julius Caesar had a villa there, as did Nero. Hadrian died there. With large swimming pools, a domed casino, and rampant hedonism, the elite considered it superior to Pompeii, Herculaneum, and Capri. Baiae was, however, so notorious for its corruption and scandal that Seneca the Younger wrote about it in "Baiae and Vice."

The town was first administered by nearby Cuma, became imperial property under Augustus, and then later became part of Port Julius, the base of the western fleet of the Imperial Roman Navy.

It was all downhill from there: sacked by Barbarian invaders, again by Muslim raiders, then finally devasted by nature. What was left became rife with malaria, leaving the once glamorous resort deserted. Meanwhile, seismic activity was busy burying it underwater. (Note: At Campi Flegrei, you can tour the submerged past of Baiae, either floating over it in a glass-bottomed boat or swimming through the ruins of statues and buildings—it is magical. The Piscina Mirabilis is also available to visit, though visitors must call ahead.)

By this time, Campania had a fairly large Jewish population in Pompeii and Pozzuoli. A fresco in Pompeii shows an olive press (wedge press) still used today by the Berbers, likely a remnant from when Jews and Berbers crossed paths trading throughout the Mediterranean. The artichokes now so beloved by all of Italy were at the time eaten only by the Jewish community, most likely brought to Campania from the Eastern Mediterranean, where they are thought to have originated, though some say they originated in North Africa. Pliny the Elder called artichokes "monstrous productions of the earth." But when the Jews fled the south of Italy, local affection for the thistle remained, as it does to this day. The fleeing Jews, who ultimately ended up in Rome, created a fried artichoke, *carciofi alla Giudia*, which remains one of Rome's great specialties.

Meanwhile, life was good—*if* you were rich. All who dined at Augustus's banquets at his villa overlooking the sea (at what is now Punta di Posilippo) agreed that the moray eels (some say lampreys) raised in the villa pond were delicious. This was more than a gastronomic comment, however, as it referred to the villa's previous owner, Publius Vedius Pollio, a man famous for his cruelty. Once, at the table, Augustus witnessed Pollio decree that a slave be fed to the eels. His crime? Breaking a goblet. Demanding all the goblets, Augustus paid for them; then he had them broken. Pollio was stunned and the slave freed. Henceforth, this incident served as a strong lesson in ethics, condemning this evil practice.

CATASTROPHIC ERUPTION OF VESUVIUS

Then, one morning in 79 AD, Vesuvio awoke, violently erupted, and destroyed the cities of Pompeii and Herculaneum, along with the hillsides and fields, burying all with an epic explosion of molten lava cascading down the mountain. When it hit the Bay of Naples, it formed huge, porous lava rocks. Toxic gases sprang from the ground, settling in the air. The snowfall of ash made breathing impossible.

The sheer destruction of so many and so much is still stunning to imagine. Pliny the Elder, a scientific scholar, was surveying the area at this time, carefully taking notes and making observations about the strange geological occurrences prior to the volcano's eruption. He survived the initial eruption but was killed by the poisonous gas fumes.

Their catastrophe was a gift to the future, however, through volcanic enrichment of the soil and preservation of everyday life in the ruins, including what people ate. Carbonized bread was found in the ruins—a hard, black, flattened loaf of not unappealing bread. So far, about six loaves have been discovered. There are frescoes of fruit baskets lush with figs and pomegranates and cave paintings of hunting. A mosaic of fish is on display at the Naples National Archeological Museum. The remains of thirty-three bakeries have been excavated in Pompeii, including one much like a pizzeria; you can see its oven, which bears a strong resemblance to modern-day pizza ovens. An excavation at Oplontis in the Villa Poppea shows a fresco of a cake, though we do not know its exact ingredients.

Ash-buried Herculaneum was discovered before Pompeii, but due to the difficulty of excavation, archeologists left it alone. When Pompeii was unearthed in 1750, archeologists focused on that site instead, a shame for Pompeii, which no doubt lost much due to crude archeological methods. Using less invasive techniques and advanced technology today, excavations are less destructive. The Pompeii Food and Drink Project is an opportunity for noninvasive fieldwork in the ruins of Pompeii. There is no digging; instead, participants do research with lectures, observations, photography, and so on.

Due to better excavation techniques, Herculaneum (Ercolano) is in a more pristine state with minimal destruction. For a startlingly lifelike portrait of everyday life in both Pompeii and Herculaneum, visit the interactive museum in Ercolano, where the past is re-created visually with holograms and other means. It is like a portal to that far-off time.

What was ancient Roman cooking like? Apicius tells of a predilection for sweet and sour flavors, which hints of a link to Jewish and Arabic influences, likely from Sicily, where there was a large population of both groups. The inclusion of raisins in savory dishes, such as today's *pizza di scarola* (endive focaccia), *braciole al ragù* (meat rolls in ragù sauce), or Neapolitan meatballs, likely originated there. Arabs were the first to embrace sugar, and, combined with vinegar, *mosto cotto*, or citrus juice, influenced Sicily's (caponata, anyone?) predilection for sweet and sour. Naples also was influenced but less so than Sicily.

Campania's *pastiera*, a citrus and spiced cheesecake-like pie studded with tender cooked wheat berries, is an ancient dish. According to mythology, the goddess Parthenope emerged from the sea singing sweetly. The locals brought her gifts of ricotta cheese, eggs, sugar, and spices, along with wheat berries. Upon her return to the sea, she gave the food gifts to the local gods, who turned them into cake. The modern incarnation of *la pastiera* comes from the convent tradition of Neapolitan cooking, specifically the nuns of San Gregorio Armeno, who began baking what we know as *pastiera* around 1600.

The wheat grains themselves symbolized fertility and a return to spring after the winter. Pagan rituals of fertility celebrated around the spring equinox originated with the cults of Artemis, Cybele, and Ceres and included symbolic foods. Christianity came to Campania with the arrival in Napoli of the apostles Saint Peter and Saint Paul and several martyrdoms.

THE DECLINE OF THE ROMAN EMPIRE

With the decline of the Roman Empire, its last emperor, Romulus Augustulus, was imprisoned in 476 AD near Castel dell'Ovo, Naples, dying there around 500 AD, during which time the area entered a period of uncertainty.

During the Gothic Wars in 543, Totila briefly took the city for the Ostrogoths. In 536, the Byzantine general Belisarius took the city by surprise from the slopes of Vesuvio, entering via the aqueduct. Naples aligned with the Italian center of Byzantine power, the Exarchate of Ravenna. It's possible that coffee and rice came to what is now Campania during its Byzantine era.

A rebellion ensued in 615 AD, however, and by 638 the area was created as a duchy; then it was elevated to independent duchy in 763. Greco-Roman culture continued in Naples, but under Duke Stephen II Naples's allegiance switched to Rome rather than Constantinople, putting it under papal rule.

Local contenders for the ducal throne feuded between 818 and 832 until Theoctocitis was appointed without imperial approval. Because it was without imperial approval, it was later revoked and Theodore II took his place. However, he was driven from the city by a popular uprising and replaced by Stephen III, who was too self-obsessed to be a legitimate ruler.

By 840, the Duchy of Naples gained complete independence, returning, after the capture by Pandulf IV of the Principality of Capua (a longtime rival of Naples), to direct control by the Lombards for a brief period. After three years, the culturally Greco-Roman-influenced dukes were reinstated.

In 902 AD, the Neapolitans defeated the Saracens on the Garigliano River. By the eleventh century, like many territories in the area, Naples hired Norman mercenaries, Christian descendants of the Vikings, to fight their rivals. Duke Sergius IV hired Rainulf Drengot to battle Capua. By 1137, the Normans controlled previously independent principalities and duchies such as Capua, Benevento, Salerno, Amalfi, Sorrento, and Gaeta. It was in this year that Naples, the last independent duchy in the southern part of the peninsula, came under Norman control.

At one point Naples was threatened by Sicard of Benevento. Benevento was in many ways separate from the rest of Campania, reflected to this day in, among other things, its cooking (onions *and* garlic rather than one or the other). In 1140, the last ruling duke of the duchy, Sergius VII, surrendered to Roger II Trusbart, who had proclaimed himself king of Sicily seven years earlier. This saw Naples (and smaller independent states in the area) joining the Kingdom of Sicily. Naples was now a second-tier city to Palermo, Sicily's capital. During this time, Spanish, French, and Aragonese cultural influences were introduced to Campania.

After a period of time as a Norman kingdom, the Kingdom of Sicily passed to the Hohenstaufens, a powerful Germanic royal house of Swabian origins. Naples valued education—the University of Naples, founded by Federico II, is the oldest state university in the world—leading it to become the intellectual center of the kingdom. By the end of the Middle Ages, Naples's neighbor to the south, Salerno, was known throughout Europe for its medical school, which combined ancient Roman, Greek, and Arab medicine.

In 1266, conflict between the Hohenstaufens and the papacy led to Pope Innocent IV crowning Angevin dynasty Duke Charles I as king. Charles moved the capital from Palermo to Naples, where he resided at the Castel Nuovo. Much of Naples's Gothic architecture stems from this era.

The Sicilian Vespers in 1281 and 1282—a massive riot that left two thousand French dead and the kingdom split in half—left Sicily vulnerable. The Crown of Aragon took over, establishing a separate Kingdom of Sicily, while Naples officially continued to be known as the Kingdom of Sicily (for those who have wondered about the name "the Kingdom of the Two Sicilies" given upon reunification in the 1800s).

Then, in the 1300s, the French Anjou dynasty of Naples took Sicily, making Naples its capital. Frederick III was recognized as king of the Isle of Sicily, while Charles II was recognized as the king of Naples by Pope Boniface VIII. In 1309, Roberto d'Angiò was proclaimed king of the Angevin Kingdom of Naples. A building campaign of great monuments transformed the city, including Castel dell'Ovo, which today is one of the symbols of the city.

Alfonso I conquered Naples after his victory over the last Angevin king, René, reunifying Naples and Sicily for a brief time.

A major earthquake hit the area in 1349, but Naples survived with minimal damage and continued to grow, ruled by a succession of occupiers, including Spain, Austria, the Bourbons, and, briefly, a Jacobin republic.

In 1442 Alfonso V of Aragon conquered Naples and made it the capital of Aragon. The new dynasty, with its links to the Iberian Peninsula, enhanced commerce in Naples. As it grew in importance, Naples attracted Pisan and Genoese merchants, Tuscan bankers, and celebrated Renaissance artists such as Boccaccio, Petrarca, and Giotto. (Unfortunately, the frescoes Giotto left behind in Castel Nuovo were destroyed by earthquake.) Boccaccio wrote of Naples, describing it as "desolute" and setting it as a backdrop to parts of *The Decameron.* He also wrote a love story about a noblewoman and the king set in Naples.

The Ottomans tried (and tried and tried) to reconquer but were firmly rebuffed. In 1494 it became obvious that the Ottoman Turks could not win when Naples allied with the Habsburg Empire and Aragon, both strong naval powers.

Charles VIII was able to bring it under the control of the French, though, allowing the Neapolitan King Frederic to remain on the throne. However, under the control of Louis XII, King Frederic was taken prisoner to France in 1501. Four years later, Spain won Naples at the Battle of Garigliano, and Naples became part of the Spanish Empire, although France attempted to take it back in 1529.

Spanish and French rule brought class snobbery to Campania. In food it created a defining difference between the cuisine of the aristocrats and that of the poorer classes. The former was characterized by elaborate, more cosmopolitan dishes and expensive ingredients, including meat. The poor ate what was cheapest and what could be grown locally (that is, cereals and vegetables). These foods were embellished over the centuries and influenced by aristocratic cuisine, so that today traditional recipes of the poorer classes have often acquired excellence and finesse while preserving simplicity of ingredients.

SPANISH RULE

Spanish viceroys were appointed to Naples to rule the area directly. Most were ineffective, and life continued as it had been. Then, in September 1532, Pedro Alvares de Toledo (Pietro di Toledo) arrived on the scene.

He started by building a castle in Baiae, though the city was nearly deserted and in ruins. With the goal of making the south of Italy invulnerable, old city walls throughout the area were expanded and an entire new seawall was built. Fortresses were modernized, grand buildings constructed, naval shipyards enlarged. Don Pedro planned the square grid of streets lined with multistory buildings, barracks to house the Spanish soldiers. At the time, this grid design was considered unique.

That area is known today as the Quartieri Spagnoli, the Spanish Quarter—a colorful, evocative heart of the past with narrow cobbled streets, laundry hanging from windows, alleyways so steep they are paved in stone steps. Many Spanish soldiers stationed there were greatly influenced by it, such as Miguel de Cervantes, who went on to write *Don Quixote*.

Don Pedro was responsible for considerable social, economic, and urban progress not only in the city of Naples and its surrounding area but also throughout the southern Italian kingdom. Unfortunately for its citizens, he ruled harshly.

He closed the Accademia Pontaniana in 1542 and declared death the punishment for petty theft. He broke up land holdings by bringing feudal barons and now landless peasants from the countryside into the city; the population swelled to 200,000, second in Europe only to Paris.

Worse, Don Pedro supported the Inquisition. Already active in Sicily, it forced Jews and Moors to convert, flee, or face execution. Most Moors headed south to North Africa, where they had a huge influence on culture, whereas the Jews went north to the rest of Italy and beyond.

To his great disappointment, Don Pedro was never able to institute the Inquisition in Naples. When he announced his plans for it in 1547, rioting was immediate, as it had not escaped the landowners that in Spain the Inquisition confiscated the property of the wealthy. Emperor Charles V ordered Don Pedro to back down. To further calm the people, he sent Don Pedro to Siena to handle a local problem. While in Florence visiting one of his daughters, however, he died unexpectedly.

His impact on the city of Naples remains huge, a heritage of buildings, structures, and the Spanish Quarter. Now you need not wonder for whom Via Toledo was named.

Through the marriage of his youngest daughter, Eleanor of Toledo, to the Grand Duke Cosimo I de' Medici in 1539, Don Pedro's descendants included Bourbon kings of France and Spain; Habsburg-Lorraine emperors of the Holy Roman Empire, Austria, and Austria-Hungary; grand dukes of Tuscany; several Stuart kings and queens of England and Scotland; kings of Italy from the House of Savoy; and other noble families. One of Don Pedro's direct descendants was Diana, Princess of Wales, whose son, Prince William, Duke of Cambridge, is the future king of Great Britain.

Naples became Europe's second-largest city after Paris. A class of merchants and craftsman grew, contributing to the general wealth and style of the city. The lavish Palazzo Reale remains a symbol of Bourbon reign.

By 1606, baroque painter Caravaggio established his studio in Naples. Baroque architect Cosimo Fanzago from Bergamo moved there as well, and in 1631 Vesuvio came to life again, destroying settlements in the area, though not the city itself.

As always, the poor did their best to survive and the rich did their best to enjoy life—in this case, they ate chicken, a true luxury at that time! We can surmise this from Neapolitan artist Massimo Stanzione's painting (ca. 1635) depicting a well-dressed woman in everyday clothing posing in the marketplace with a chicken.

Chicken was not eaten often by the poor and didn't become a major part of Neapolitan cuisine. Sometimes you find it in a soup, to which you will perhaps add a little pasta. You might eat it when you are ill, or you might eat a more lavish version on a national or religious holiday. Sometimes chicken is roasted with lemons, potatoes, and rosemary, and lately I've seen some wonderfully juicy chicken burger patties. Some say that Neapolitans don't eat much chicken because they prefer more flavorful meat. Maybe, but also because traditionally chickens were kept for eggs, which are abundant in Neapolitan cuisine. A frittata in the evening, a light fluffy dessert, or a raw egg and glass of red wine in the morning. When you eat a chicken, it lays no more eggs.

The Neapolitan Republic was created in 1647 and then suppressed. By 1650, its population reached 450,000. But nothing lasts for long; in 1656 the plague rattled its saber of death. At least three quarters of the city's population perished. It was a major blow to life as all knew it. Mass graves were organized, and the remains of this sad city of souls can be glimpsed today in subterranean Naples and in cemeteries such as Cimitero delle Fontanelle.

In 1707, Austria conquered Naples. Although still recovering from the plague, its population was once again growing, and it became a center for the arts. Caravaggio, Rosa, and Bernini were among its population. Writers and philosophers flocked there as well.

A revolution led by a local fisherman named Masaniello saw the creation of an independent Neapolitan Republic, but, alas, after only a few months Spanish rule returned. By 1714, the Spanish lost Naples as a result of the War of Spanish Succession, and the Austrian Charles VI took over, ruling from Vienna and sending viceroys to manage locally as the Spanish had done previously.

However—Are you still with me? Would you like to lie down for a few minutes?—the War of the Polish Succession saw the Spanish regain Sicily and Naples, now recognized as independent (under a cadet branch of the Spanish Bourbons in 1738 under Charles II) by the Treaty of Vienna.

In 1747, German archeologist Johann Joachim Winckelmann arrived in Naples to study the drawings, statues, stones, and ancient papyrus scrolls of Paestum, Herculaneum, and Pompeii. He influenced King Charles III of Naples to enact Europe's first modern laws of archeological site protection and preservation, which has been important to the area's heritage.

One of Naples's most lavish architectural symbols is the opulent, massive Reggia di Caserta. Built in 1750 by Italian architect Luigi Vanvitelli, it is a baroque jewel surrounded by grand gardens with waterfalls and fountains, stone sculptures, and rolling greenery. So magnificent that many say it rivals (or even exceeds) the majesty of Versailles, and it is happily open to the public.

To visit is an uplifting experience for its beauty, history, and attitude of cherishing local treasures: Consorzio di Tutela, the governing body for *mozzarella di bufala* production, excellence, and control, has its office in this prestigious location.

Vanvitelli also helped create many of the neoclassical palaces in which the nobles of Naples vacationed, now known worldwide as Ville Vesuviane.

During the reign of the Bourbons in Naples (considered by historians the city's most gilded age), the phrase "See Naples and die" was coined. Naples was wealthy, with opulent palaces, and the third most populous European city after London and Paris. Some credit the phrase to Johann Wolfgang Von Goethe, who visited Naples (and wrote sensuous love poems about and to his future mistress) from 1786 to 1788. In his writing, he expressed the sad possibility that one might die before experiencing the epic beauty and magnificence of Naples. The phrase caught on, whomever its author might have been. Later, after Naples developed a reputation for being dangerous, the saying jokingly meant the opposite: if you dare to come to Naples, you might die!

During the time of Ferdinand IV, the French Revolution made its way to Naples. Horatio Nelson, an ally of the Bourbons, arrived to warn the city in 1798. Ferdinand was forced to retreat and ended up in Palermo, where he was protected by a British fleet. The French revolution divided the population. Naples's lower classes (the *lazzaroni*) were pious and royalist, favoring the Bourbons. They fought the Neapolitan pro-republican aristocracy, and civil war ensued.

The republicans conquered Castel Sant'Elmo and proclaimed a Parthenopaean Republic, secured by the French Army. A counterrevolutionary religious army of *lazzaroni* under Fabrizio Ruffo had great success against the French, who surrendered the Neapolitan castles and were allowed to sail back to Toulon. Ferdinand IV was restored as king.

After only seven years, Napoleon Bonaparte conquered the kingdom and installed Bonapartist kings, including his brother Joseph Bonaparte. The Bonapartists, supported by the Austrian Empire and allies, were defeated in the Neapolitan War, and Bourbon Ferdinand IV once again regained the throne.

The Congress of Vienna—Austria, Russia, Prussia, and Great Britain (the countries that defeated Napoleon)—in 1815 redrew the map combining the kingdoms of Naples and Sicily and balancing spheres of influence to avoid future conflict. In 1816 they named Naples its capital.

Culturally and socially, beautiful Naples thrived. Often the last stop on the Grand Tour, throngs of well-heeled, well-bred, often British tourists decamped seeking culture, history, and artistic inspiration. Devised in the 1660s, the Grand Tour was considered a profound necessity for the education of the wealthy classes, usually upon leaving Oxbridge. (The Grand Tour came to an end in the 1840s with the rise of modern rail transport and mass tourism such as Thomas Cook Tours. Naples was the first city on the Italian Peninsula to have a railway, opened in 1839.)

Poet and writer Giacomo Leopardi lived in Naples, the School of Posillipo and the School of Resina dominated local painting, and the first Italian ballet school was established in Teatro San Carlo, where opera legends Bellini, Rossini, Verdi, and Donizetti, among others, worked. Sciences also thrived: the first public aquarium and marine life research center opened, the Astronomic Obseratory of Capodimonte was founded in 1816 (now hosting the Italian Laboratory of Astrophysics), and in 1841 the first volcano observatory was founded.

UNIFICATION

The Italian Peninsula had been, throughout its centuries of history, a collection of many small, separate, independent states, republics, dukedoms, principalities, papal states, and city-states. Between some there was much interaction; between others, not so much: each spoke its own languages or dialects, so they often didn't understand each other. Some were often at war with each other. Throughout the "boot" of Italy, each tiny place remained tightly aligned with its own foods and culture.

Politically, everything changed with unification, but culinary traditions remained loyal to their region and still do to this day. This is why what you eat in Venice is not what you eat in Rome, Tuscany, and certainly not Naples. The only thing people can agree about, even if they don't eat pasta regularly, is that it's wonderful.

Giuseppe Garibaldi, considered the founding father of modern Italy (along with Giuseppe Mazzini and Camillo Benso Conte di Cavour), insisted that the pasta of Naples played a crucial role in the unification of the republic. In 1860, Garibaldi and his men marched throughout the area in an effort to liberate the Kingdom of the Two Sicilies and the Papal States. He found that there was only one thing his soldiers could all agree upon: pasta. They loved it.

His soldiers were from diverse areas of what would become Italy; many had never tasted pasta before (especially the dried durum wheat pasta of Campania). Despite not speaking the same language, they were joined by pasta: the way it made them feel—full and strong—and how delicious it was. Somehow the pasta was both physical and spiritually unifying. Pasta also played another role: According to an oral history of the Risorgimento, *spaghetti alla carbonara* referred not only to a pasta dish or to the men who work with coal—the *carbonari*—but also to a secret society that tried to overthrow the Italian government.

Life in Naples in the early twentieth century was difficult because the people were poor and hungry. Even before the wars, families would live seven to a room with barely enough food to survive. Then Vesuvio erupted. Again. Does it ever stop? Not so far.

The poor cooked whatever ingredients they could get—simply eking out enough food to survive felt like an act that defied the odds. If one couldn't get fava beans or peas, why not cook pasta with their empty, discarded pods? With access to a chicken, perhaps from a cousin in the countryside, then eggs may be available to top a plate of pasta. The poor even ate weeds to stay alive. After World War II, no one wanted to see such foods again. Weeds such as purslane, once a traditional salad green, were such a food, as is spaghetti with fried eggs. Each bite was a bad memory reminding the citizens of that awful, hungry time.

During World War II, Naples and Campania were more heavily bombed than any other Italian area. Although the Neapolitans did not rebel against Italian fascism, Naples was the first Italian city to rise up against German military occupation. *Le quattro giornate di Napoli*, the four days of Naples, refers to September 27–30, 1943, in which the people rose up against the Nazis, who were threatening to deport all young local males. Naples had had enough, and the people flung themselves into action, keeping the Nazis so busy that the Allies were able to get a toehold in the area and turn the tide of the war locally.

Salerno became the temporary capital of the Kingdom of Italy, with King Victor Emmanuel III living in a mansion on its outskirts. In September 1943 Salerno was the scene of heavy war destruction, Operation Avalanche. This paved the way for liberation by the Americans and Allies on October 1, 1943.

The bombing of the region's infrastructure stopped the Nazis, but it also made getting food extremely difficult. The occupying Allies tried to provide food for all. At first they were only able to offer one hundred calories a day, since food couldn't make its way through the usual channels, and a black market sprang up. It is thought that perhaps a third of the goods from the Allies was stolen and sold illegally.

As usual, the wealthy had more options and were able to get away down the coast to Sorrento or to the countryside where food was more accessible. But the poor were very hungry. They ate what they could get their hands on, finagling food in whatever ways they could.

As if 1944 hadn't punished Italy enough, Mount Vesuvius erupted. Again.

Nonetheless, the eternal against-all-odds optimism of Naples continued as it always had and as it does today. As infrastructure was repaired, food became available, and the people were happy to be able to fill their stomachs after so many years of hardships.

Then came the giddy boom years heralding hope and the era of *La Dolce Vita*. Special funding from the Italian government helped improve the economy, and grand landmarks such as Piazza del Plebiscito were repaired, cleaned, and revitalized. The symbol of Naples's rebirth, however, was the rebuilding of Santa Chiara. Destroyed during an Allied air raid, the magnificent majolica, with its delicate painting of yellow lemons, green leaves, and twisting vines on the sleek tiles located in the courtyard of a complex of church buildings, is, once again, upliftingly beautiful.

All of Naples began to regenerate; the austerity of the war and its aftermath faded. People were enjoying their new lives and especially their new way of eating. There were new foods advertised—modern foods, commercial foods, processed foods. Science suggested that the way to eat now was to give up old-fashioned olive oil for modern margarine and to eschew vegetables, beans, and pasta for more meat.

But cultures lose their traditions at their own peril, especially foodwise. Not only was pleasure and tradition under attack, but weight problems and health concerns also arose. In the 1950s, along came the "discovery" of the Mediterranean diet! The traditional diet was found to be a healthy (possibly the healthiest) way of eating— as most Neapolitans always knew—and American epidemiologist Ancel Keys told it to the world. There were problems with his work, but ensuing decades of study confirm the benefits of the Mediterranean diet: Olive oil! Fish! Vegetables and fruit! Even coffee, wine, and chocolate—all healthy in moderation!

In the 1960s and 1970s, political activism originating in France affected all of Italy (as well as Europe and the United States) but was primarily concentrated in the north. Campania was not greatly disrupted; it would, however, benefit from the resulting welfare laws gained from the strife.

The 1980 earthquake in Irpinia destroyed whole areas, and many were killed. In rebuilding, those who had left returned. This was especially true for the young people who had traveled to the north or to other parts of the world seeking a better future. They revived the communities from which they once fled, opening restaurants and revitalizing culture, as traditional ways were overlaid with the more modern and exotic influences brought back from afar. Pop artist Andy Warhol created two famous paintings of the earthquake: *Fate Presto* and *Vesuvius*. The originals are on exhibit at Terrae Motus in Reggia di Caserta.

Even now, more than a century after unification, with a national language and national media, Italians still claim loyalty to their own neighborhoods, villages, towns, islands, or cities (known as *campanilismo*). This is especially true in the south—and Naples is the historic capital of the south.

Because Naples was, for so long, its own kingdom, its history separate from the rest of Italy, there's a feeling that its brilliance has been overlooked by the north.

That, with the Risorgimento, it has lost out and is now looked down upon. The north got the economic, political, and cultural riches, along with investment in infrastructure, and the south got—garbage in the streets?

Do Neapolitans harbor resentments? Of course. It's a thorn in their side, something that has been, in their eyes, unfairly done to them. This little chip on the shoulder fuels many a grudge better fought on the soccer field than in the streets. They can battle it out in a soccer game while remaining a united nation—more or less.

Still, the impression exists that Neapolitans are resentful, northerners haughty. Yet when the people of Campania are stereotyped as "lazy" or "slow," I bristle along with the Neapolitans and protest! From my own observations, no one works harder than the citizens of Campania. To be honest, I don't know where they get the energy.

The first half of the twentieth century was difficult. Education was viewed as a luxury well into the 1960s, and most could not afford to take the exams in order to proceed to high school, let alone university. This further drove a wedge between classes, since those who could afford to continue their education learned to speak Italian and those left behind spoke only dialect. Opportunities smiled on those who spoke Italian.

In the streets, Naples had a dodgy reputation. Crime frightened tourists away; there was garbage in the streets and corruption on so many different levels. Neapolitans were sick of it, but what could they do?

Antonio Bassolino had an idea. As mayor of Naples from 1993 until he became president of Campania in the early 2000s, he was responsible in large part for Naples's cultural renaissance. Looking around, he saw dust, filth, and decay, and he felt that Naples deserved better. It deserved to have its humanity back, its street grandeur, its magnificence, and, most of all, its "good vibes." It deserved to be cleaned and renewed; its people needed to feel pride again. Mayor Bassolino felt that art—both viewing it and creating it—gave people a sense of hope and comfort and elevated the soul. He therefore set about on a program of arts, music, culture, and community, with the deeply held belief that making Neapolitans feel good about themselves again would reduce crime and give the people—especially the young—a sense of belonging and of being appreciated. And he was so right: with less crime, street life blossomed, interaction became vivacious once again, and crime continued to drop. In my own personal observations of Naples over the years, the two biggest dangers I've experienced are crossing the street and eating too much!

In 1993, Naples's first Metro line opened, easing the way Neapolitans got around. Anyone who has ever driven in Naples knows how challenging it can be. Along with the funicolare, buses, and the *circumvesuviana*, a train connecting the region of Vesuvio that includes Sorrento, Sarno, and Striano, the Metro helped to foster a sense of belonging to the people of the entire city, regardless of economic and social class. And the stations are visually so exciting, especially line number 1.

Today there's interest in and a renewal of local culinary traditions based on examining the past as well as reacting to foreign styles. A resurgence of pride in Monzù cooking resulted in a large event in 2016 honoring the Monzù of the past and the "modern" Monzù, inheritors of the tradition. And pizza is enjoying new excitement and respect among chefs for its artistry and creativity.

The Risorgimento in a Nutshell

The Risorgimento took decades (about six) to result in a unified Italy. Though not strictly Neapolitan history, Naples figured prominently in the Risorgimento and was hugely affected by it. To understand the history of the food, we need an overall sketch of what was going on.

In 1820, the Spanish king Ferdinand VII was forced to deal with an uprising of troops headed for South America in Cadiz, Spain. This was the first of many revolutionary demonstrations that spread across Europe during the first half of the 1800s. In Italy, the revolution began in Sicily (including Naples) against King Ferdinand I of the Two Sicilies, who was forced to make concessions and promise a constitutional monarchy. This success inspired Carbonari in the north of Italy to revolt as well, and in 1821 the Kingdom of Sardinia gained a constitutional monarchy as a result of the Carbonari uprising.

The Holy Alliance was not pleased and decided to intervene, sending an army to crush the revolution in Naples in 1821. The king of Sardinia called for Austrian intervention, and, because the Austrian forces were larger and better armed, the Carbonari revolts collapsed, their leaders fleeing into exile.

Meanwhile, in what is now Italy, the liberals demanded a constitution like the Kingdom of Sardinia and the Kingdom of Two Sicilies. Unfortunately, the monarchs asked for Austria's help in defeating the nationalists and revolutionaries. Austria obliged, and the monarchies were fully restored to power.

A second wave of revolutionary fervor in 1831 spread from Modena to Perugia, this time including the aristocracy and bourgeois. This, too, Austria quashed, once again reinstating the reign of monarchs. In 1833, there were more revolts, this time by the political society La Giovine Italia (Young Italy), aimed at creating a unified republic. It was suppressed, people were arrested, and others went into exile abroad (among them Giuseppe Garibaldi, who headed to South America to fight for Uruguay's independence).[1]

A new wave of nationalist revolts revived in 1841 and was suppressed, with more arrested and some killed. Some asked: Why not unify under the rule of the pope?

The Risorgimento in a Nutshell (*continued*)

Meanwhile, in 1844, the Risorgimento decided that Rome would be the capital of an Italian republic. Without enough support, however, this movement, too, was violently suppressed.

The election of Pius IX in 1844 brought new hope to Italy's moderates, though the nationalists continued to revolt and fail, resulting in more chaos and more deaths.

In 1847, all of Europe was in crisis, and the Italian peninsula was no exception. Food costs rose, and the people grew frantic. Each state reacted differently. The Papal States, Tuscany's grand duchy, and the Kingdom of Sardinia reacted with moderation, but other states reacted more severely. In the Kingdom of Two Sicilies, all attempts at revolution were violently suppressed.

In 1848, a wave of revolutionary sentiment spread from Paris to Berlin to Vienna and soon reached the Italian duchies, weakening Austria's power in Italy. In 1849, the reactionary armies defeated the constitutional and republican governments established in the last twenty years. Austrian armies were defeated in Lombardy-Venetia, Parma, Modena, Bologna, the Marche region, Romagna, and Tuscany. Louis Napoleon Bonaparte (a.k.a. Napoleon III) invited the French army back from exile, to Rome, joining forces with the pope.

Meanwhile, the Kingdom of Sardinia's ties with the Catholic Church weakened. Pope Pius IX returned to Rome. Garibaldi was exiled to New York City; another revolutionary, Giuseppe Mazzini, fled to London.

In February 1851, British statesman William Ewart Gladstone visited the prison in Naples where Giacomo Lacaita, legal adviser to the British embassy, was imprisoned as a political dissident by the Neapolitan government. Gladstone deplored the prisoners' condition, and in April and July he published two letters to the Earl of Aberdeen against the Neapolitan government, followed by "An Examination of the Official Reply of the Neapolitan Government" in 1852, which is believed to have contributed to the cause of the unification of Italy in 1861. French writer Alexandre Dumas lived in Naples for two or three years, reporting on the situation for foreign journals. In this, he, too, was involved with the unification. He also based several of his historical novels in Naples.

Allied with France and Great Britain, in 1855 the Kingdom of Sardinia entered the war against Russia, sending its soldiers to Crimea. The Savoy monarchy was concerned about diplomatic support from the French and British to help Italy resist Austria. In the meantime, cholera reached epidemic levels and thousands of people died.

The democratic movement, now under Mazzini, failed in 1857, marking the end of his leadership. The Italian National Society was established to reach out to democrats and moderates, freeing Italy from the Savoy monarchy. The Kingdom of Sardinia severed its alliance with Austria and amassed its soldiers on the Lombardy-Venice border.

The Risorgimento in a Nutshell (*continued*)

In 1858, Napoleon III was the target of a failed assassination attempt by an Italian nationalist. Rather than damage the alliance between France and the Kingdom of Sardinia, however, this attempt convinced the French emperor to back the nationalists, which Count Cavour, prime minister of Piedmont, had urged for a long while. Cavour and Napoleon III signed a secret agreement to join forces against Austria. Still in exile in London, Mazzini wanted nothing to do with it.

Napoleon III and Victor Emmanuel II agreed in 1859 to form an alliance against Austria, and the Second Italian War of Independence—also called the Franco-Austrian War, Austro-Sardinian War, or simply Italian War—broke out.

Once Lombardy was freed from Austrian rule, Tuscana, Parma, Modena, Romagna, Marche, Umbria, and the provisory governments joined the Kingdom of Sardinia. Fearing a military attack by Prussia, and concerned about the surprising revolutionary activities in central Italy, Napoleon III signed an armistice in Villafranca with the Austrian emperor Franz Joseph, playing a crucial role in Italian unification.

Garibaldi gathered his ragtag army, and "the Thousand" marched from Sicily north, gathering and uniting each region they passed through. Success in defeating the Bourbon army was theirs in three months. Victor Emmanuel II, however, prevented the Thousand from entering Rome, which was under the protection of the French.

On October 21, 1860, Naples joined a united Italy under King Victor Emmanuel II and the Savoy monarchy. Except for Rome and Venetia, the Italian peninsula was now (mostly) united; the House of Savoy allowed the Second French Empire to annex Nice from the Kingdom of Sardinia in exchange for French support of its quest to unify Italy. Consequently, the Niçois were excluded from Italian unification, and the region has been part of France ever since.

In 1861 the Bourbons lost the last battle with Garibaldi's forces in Gaeta. The Italian state proclaimed Victor Emmanuel II the king of Italy at the first Italian Parliament in Turin on March 17, 1861. On March 27 Rome was declared its capital, though it wasn't even officially a part of the new nation.

In the south, in a wave of anti-Savoy sentiment, former Bourbon soldiers roamed the countryside, joined by groups of peasants and bandits who were unhappy about the unification.

Garibaldi organized an expedition to conquer Rome, but he was stopped by the Italian army in the Calabrian mountains of Aspromonte and injured in the attack. Meanwhile, Italian unification continued despite the skirmishes of brigandage (now supported militarily by the Bourbons and the clerics) that continued in the south. A united Italian common monetary currency was established.

In 1863 the Italian parliament proclaimed martial law in the south, enabling extra force to be used against these vigilantes. The situation by now verged on

The Risorgimento in a Nutshell (*continued*)

civil war, which took ten years to subdue and resulted in thousands of arrests and executions.

French troops gradually retreated from the Papal States in 1865 in response to the Italian government's renouncement of Rome as its capital. France agreed to transfer the capital from Turin to Florence instead.

In the Austrian-Prussian War of 1866, Italy became allies with Prussia to liberate Venetia, still under Austrian rule. The third war of independence broke out, which Prussia won, annexing Venetia to Italy. Although Garibaldi defeated the Austrians in Trentino following orders from the king, he was forced to withdraw because the war had already ended. However, Garibaldi could not forget about making Rome the country's capital. In 1867, he attempted to conquer it with an expedition of volunteers. The pope was protected by the French, who stopped the expedition at the gates of Rome.

France declared war on Prussia in 1870 and withdrew its troops from Rome. The Italian government took advantage of this situation and sent its soldiers to the city. On September 20, they occupied Rome, and the city fell, marking the end of papal rule there. Latium/Lazio was annexed to the Kingdom of Italy, and finally, in 1871, Rome was made the capital of Italy, with the pope serving as spiritual leader.

It wasn't until 1954, however, when Trieste was returned to Italy from the former Yugoslavia, that Italy assumed the composition and shape that it has today.

---

1. If you are British, you might ask, "How did the Garibaldi biscuit come about and why is it called Garibaldi?" The Garibaldi biscuit (Britspeak for cookie) was named after Giuseppe Garibaldi, created in honor of a visit to South Shields (near Newcastle) in England in 1854. The confection, produced by Peek Freans, was a thin layer of squashed raisins or currants sandwiched between two thin cookies, quite reminiscent of the classic Eccles cakes. The Garibaldi biscuit has been an iconic food ever since. Its counterpart in the United States, made by the Sunshine Biscuit Company, was popular for many years, even after Sunshine was bought by Keebler, which added a chocolate version. When Kellogg's bought Keebler, however, it discontinued the entire line.

THE THREE THREADS OF *LA CUCINA NAPOLETANA*

The magic spark that unites all of the elements of *la cucina Napoletana* is the joy of the table. That is its essence, but it comes together in a way that is uniquely, distinctly Neapolitan. Naples has three distinct culinary traditions that combine to form the culinary palette and outlook of the Neapolitan table. As three strands of gastronomical tradition and history, they weave together to create one united cuisine.

Cucina Povera

When most people think of the food from Italy's south, they think *cucina povera*, rural ingredients such as pasta, vegetables, legumes, cheese, fish, crustaceans, mollusks (along the coast) and hunted meat and fowl (inland) prepared simply with olive oil and often tomatoes.

Cucina povera results from life's difficult conditions: the heat of the summers, lack of rain, political unrest. Those who lived there knew poverty and hardship and consequently developed a cuisine in which nothing is wasted. Inventiveness is kindled in the face of scarcity.

Lest you dismiss it as "food of the poor," think of the ingenuity and enthusiasm that goes into creating luscious dishes from humble ingredients and stretching them to feed the whole family. Faced with starvation, the people of Campania created delicious meals from a handful of ingredients. Lentils ladled over toasted country bread, beans with spaghetti, and cabbage and pork soup were something to enjoy, not just means of survival.

Ricotta cheese was made from the tiny bits of curds floating in the whey after cheesemaking. After the arrival of the tomato, *cucina povera* flashed with the brilliance of that scarlet fruit—it enhanced everything. The food of the *contadini* and *lazzaroni* (the farmers and the city's blue-collar workers) was as colorful as Naples street life itself: red tomatoes, green peppers, yellow lemons. Street food—pizza, pasta—was part of the unique cuisine of Naples.

And typical of the way class distinctions are obscured in Naples, many wealthy people today who can afford to eat the finest, most expensive dishes prefer spaghetti with tomatoes or bread topped with tomatoes and olive oil. It has the taste of home, of their childhood, rich or poor. Embellish it with caviar, with truffles, with gold—such dishes can get no better than they already are.

Monzù

As *cucina povera* celebrates the "food of the poor," the Monzù tradition could be called the "food of the rich," since it came to Naples from the luxurious cooking of the French chefs of aristocratic households.

During the era of the Kingdom of the Two Sicilies (Sicily and Naples), the Spanish viceroys and the French Bourbons imported great chefs to prepare the foods suitable for grand courts and aristocratic houses. The aristocrats preferred a richer, more elaborate cuisine than what was eaten by the residents of Campania in part because it was a statement of class, status, and station in life.

These were eventually referred to as Monzù (or Monsù), possibly a mispronunciation of the French word *monsieur*, which is how the chefs would have been addressed in French-speaking kitchens. Their way of cooking was complex, refined, and elaborate. They preferred pale colored dishes in shades of beige and light brown that showed off the cream, cheese, and other rich foods of the upper classes. Used to cooking for royalty and aristocrats, the chefs often found that they lacked the ingredients to practice their culinary traditions. Meat, certain vegetables, and dairy foods were scarce. They continued to whip up the fashionable presentations of the era, such as roasted peacock with its plumage or a grand ballotine of many meats stuffed with other meats (a sort of a highfalutin' turducken), but they also used local ingredients to create dishes in the French tradition. *Timballo* comes to mind; instead of using meat in the multilayered molded concoction, the Monzù used pasta. They rarely used pasta in everyday food—you wouldn't have been served a plate of pasta and sauce in one of the grand houses—but pasta became an important part of their elaborate culinary constructions. The Monzù chefs created a strong link between the grand cuisine of France and to the food that ordinary folks were—and are today—eating.

Stuffed peppers, *gateau di patate*, eggplant parmigiana, *sartù*, savory vegetable tarts, babà, and béchamel all came from this influence of cooking. Another dish of the French occupation is "Russian salad," potatoes dressed with mayonnaise and garnished with shrimp and pickled vegetables. Russians call this dish *Salat Olivier*, which most likely came to Naples by French chefs who had worked in the grand houses of Russian aristocracy. And the French pastry known in English-speaking countries as a napoleon was named not for the French emperor, but rather for a pastry of Naples. *Larousse Gastronomique* does not mention the napoleon, though it describes a similar cake as *gateau Neapolitain* (a round pastry-and-custard concoction rather than the individual *sfogliatelle* pastries or the rectangular napoleons of today). Nothing links the pastry to Napoleon, nor was there a connection to France, so it's likely that napoleons evolved from *sfogliatelle* and the mispronunciation of "Neapolitan." (In Italy, the pastry is known as *mille foglie*, meaning a thousand layers; in France it is *mille-feuille*. The rest of the world thinks napoleons belong to Napoleon and has forgotten its link to the city of its origin.)

Le Cucini dei Conventi

The third culinary thread of *la cucina Napoletana* is *le cucini dei conventi*, the kitchens of the convents and monasteries of the Catholic Church. With their huge vegetable and fruit gardens and mission of providing food and shelter to travelers, pilgrims, and those in need, the network of convents and monasteries helped to spread the popularity of many dishes. Pastas, omelets, and a variety of dishes were created in the convents; the word *prete* (priest) in a dish's name hints at its convent origins.

Many of Naples's iconic pastries originated in medieval convents, baked by nuns for religious fests, family celebrations, and visiting prelates. The good sisters rose early and baked by candlelight to prepare for early morning customers who awaited their cakes, hot from the oven. Sometime around the year 1700, a sister at the Santa Rosa convent in Conca dei Marini mixed together some flour and ricotta cheese and filled the crisp pastry with it, fashioning it to resemble a monk's hood—or perhaps it was a seashell shape, a popular rococò design motif of the culturally and artistically sophisticated region. The recipe may have been passed beyond the walls of the cloister by a nun to her nephew, because sometime later this pastry appeared in the the fashionable pastry shops of Via Toledo in Naples, called *sfogliatelle*. Or perhaps the pastry originated in Croce di Lucca monastery and made its way to Via Toledo by a different route.

The hospitality of feeding was a lightbulb moment for me. Knowing that many dishes originated in the convents and monasteries, I long wondered how they could become such defining characteristics of *la cucina Napoletana*. I asked myself how it happened, and then the light went on: hospitality, of course! Travelers eating at the convents and monasteries brought home to their own tables (and towns and villages) the tastes of the dishes they ate there, and eventually such dishes became fully part of Napoli's food life.

La Cucina Napoletana (and La Cucina Italiana) and the Jewish Community

So many of the vegetables and specialties that we think of as classically Italian had their roots in the Jewish kitchen. Zucchini are widely used, the largest ones fried with vinegar and fresh mint (*alla scapece*). Zucchini flowers were first made popular by the Jewish community as a way of using something that might otherwise go to waste. And so pretty. So light. So versatile (*sciurilli*). Even today they are prepared the same way: dipped into a batter and fried until crisp (sometimes filled with fresh white cheese).

The Jewish community of Naples—both the kingdom (i.e., much of the south) and the city—was once large in number and strong in influence upon the culture and food.

In 161 BCE, Judah Maccabee sent a delegation to make a treaty between Judea and Rome, leading to the beginning of Italy's Jewish community. Soon Jews began settling in Rome and the south. Some were merchants migrating from outposts of the Roman Empire; others were brought back as slaves after the conquest of Jerusalem. Fennel, an Italian favorite, was possibly brought to Italy's south with the first Jews from Judea, so common was it in ancient Israel.

La Cucina Napoletana (and *La Cucina Italiana*) and the Jewish Community (*continued*)

The earliest and largest colonies of Jews were in the ports along the Bay of Naples. Pompeii, Herculaneum, and Stabia were towns with a large Jewish presence, as was Sicily and Sardinia.

When the region was conquered by the Byzantines, the Jewish community of the south continued to thrive though they had fought on the side of the Goths. In 1159, when Benjamin of Tudela visited the city of Naples, he noted the presence of about five hundred Jewish families in Naples. Capua had a long Jewish history and three hundred families. Salerno had its own Jewish quarter, with many of the six hundred Jewish families involved in the medical school.

In 1288, however, the Kingdom of Naples issued an expulsion order. Any Jews remaining after 1293 were forced to convert. Benevento was a center of Jewish crafts and boasted a yeshiva, but in 1288 Dominican priests spread anti-Jewish sentiments and they were expelled. Though allowed to return in 1617, in 1630 they again were expelled, never to return.

Amalfi was home to Jewish merchants, many in the silk trade and dying industry. The history reads familiarly: they, too, were expelled. By 1541, there was no longer a Jewish community in Amalfi.

In 1492, King Ferdinand of Naples welcomed Jews fleeing Spanish persecution. Alas, three years later, the French conquered the kingdom of Naples, and the persecution resumed. In 1510, Spain once again controlled Naples, expelling the Jews—unless one paid 300 ducati to stay. By 1535, the last Jews in Naples were gone.

Jews were allowed to return to the Kingdom of Naples in 1735; in 1831, a small group settled in the city. The Rothschild family purchased Villa Pignatelli in 1841 for use as a Jewish center to help the new residents settle. But the community didn't grow in great numbers. By the 1920s there were around 1,000.

It is believed that Rome has the largest ongoing Jewish community in the world. Jews who originated there (or came to Rome from the south of Italy by expulsion order) are called Italkim, not Sepharadim or Ashkenaim. Later Ashkenazi from the north and east fled the pogroms associated with the Black Death in 1348, the French expulsion in 1394, and then Spain.

Artichokes had long been eaten by the peasants, but it was the Jews who first appreciated them and brought them to the Neapolitan table. From the south they brought their love of artichokes to Rome's ghetto, where *carciofi alla Giudia* is one of Rome's most beloved specialties. Fennel, eggplant, and pumpkin were considered "vile" food of the Jews by the famous culinary commentator Pellegrino Artusi. Jews fleeing Spain to the Kingdom of Naples brought Sephardi foodways. Marinating and salting fish were Jewish crafts, as was the art of frying fish, learned from their years in Iberia. It appears that in Naples, where

La Cucina Napoletana (and *La Cucina Italiana*) and the Jewish Community (*continued*)

frying is an art, the skill was introduced by the Jews. Chocolate spread from the New World to Spain, then throughout Europe after the expulsion.

Under Muslim rule of Sicily from 831 to 1061, Jews particularly thrived, especially professionally and businesswise, and embraced Arabic tastes and ingredients. When the Jews were forced to flee, it had become part of their own culinary repertoire. The classic Neapolitan combination of raisins and pine nuts in savory dishes such as meatballs or spinach is thanks to Sicily's Jewish and Arab populations.

The expulsion decree affected only Sicily at first, so the Jews migrated north. But the Inquisition followed—though never put into effect in Naples—and soon the Jews were forced to flee again. The Jewish community decided that it couldn't keep wandering region to region upon the whim of the rulers and moved en masse to Rome.

The Roman Jewish community absorbed the Jews of the south, and many of their descendants are still a part of the Jewish community of twenty thousand or so. This relocation brought many Sephardic (often Arab-sounding) dishes from Sicily and Naples (i.e., the south), which ended up in the Roman culinary lexicon. The Jewish communities of the south never recovered their population nor communities. However, at Pasticceria Boccione, likely the last remaining kosher bakery in the Roman ghetto, you'll find a little culinary remnant: pizza Ebraica (Hebrew or Jewish pizza). In addition to the ricotta and cherry tarts and chocolate biscotti, pizza Ebraica has been baked by the Limentani family for about two centuries. It's what people come to the shop to eat, even Pope Benedict, who sent an emissary followed by a thank-you note because he loved the cookies so much. I say cookie, because pizza Ebraica is not a pizza at all, but rather a large flat pan of bar cookies. The word *pizza* once referred to any pie—sweet or savory—and in some places it still does. A big flat pan of sweet pastry richly studded with raisins, pine nuts, almonds, and candied citron, pizza Ebraica is said is to have been brought to Rome in the sixteenth century from the southern Jewish communities fleeing the Inquisition. The word *Ebraica* means Hebrew, referring to anything Jewish.

The southern combination of sweet and sour likely layered the Arab's fondness for sweets with anything savory and sour. When the Jews went north, they took this preference with them, adding raisins and almonds to meatballs, fish, spinach, *focacce* of bitter greens, not only to sweets and confections. I have seen the same combination in Morocco, where many of the Arab community fled.

Jews migrating to Naples as part of the expulsion brought with them Sephardi foods. Spanish Jews, having fled to the New World, kept their European

La Cucina Napoletana (and *La Cucina Italiana*) and the Jewish Community (*continued*)

connections and established businesses importing New World foods, among them tomatoes, peppers, potatoes, corn, pumpkin, and chocolate. Although Europe was a culinary beneficiary of the expulsion, food writer Gustavo Arellano writes in the *New Yorker* that many food historians think that flour tortillas were brought to the New World by crypto-Jews and Muslims fleeing the Inquisition in the seventeenth century (January 13, 2018).

In 1848, the Risorgimento saw Jews emancipated throughout what is now Italy. In the north, Jewish life flourished; the south never rebuilt its Jewish culture or its population.

In the years leading up to 1938, most Jews thought of themselves as Italian first, and Jewish second, partaking wholeheartedly in Italian culture. Then Mussolini's Italy turned against its Jews (see the film *Garden of the Finzi-Continis*). Even near Naples, there was a concentration camp (Campagna). Though not itself a death camp, cattle cars transported its occupants to Poland. Between 1942 and 1943, fifty Jews were hidden by villagers in the area of Caserta and saved from German deportation. After World War II, the Jewish community of Naples numbered between six and seven hundred, and many moved away, often to Israel. Today, the city's Jewish population is only about two hundred; yet remnants of Stars of David and Hebrew writing are visible here and there on historical buildings. At the Naples synagogue in Palazzo Sessa on Vico Santa Maria a Cappella Vecchia, there's a commemorative plaque to honor its deported Jews. Recently, however, a movement has arisen whereby various communes (local governments) open synagogues or centers to welcome back Jews. We'll see.

3

Sea, Sun, Sky, and Volcanic Soil
The Fresh Things That Grow There

Campania doesn't need a farm-to-table movement—eating has always been this way. A plate of tomatoes, a handful of olives, a bowl of roasted artichokes—at its heart, *la cucina Campana* is a garden of infinite variety and exquisite quality. When you taste such things—tiny wild strawberries, sweet perfumed melons, aromatic grapes for both table and wine, almonds, walnuts, and hazelnuts, artichokes from Paestum and Procida, San Marzano tomatoes from around Vesuvio—you might exclaim, "Amazing!" If you were Neapolitan, you might, on taking your first bite of a particularly good apricot, tomato, or melon, gasp, "*Il miracolo!*"

Then you might think: well, of course, it tastes amazing—I'm surrounded by gorgeous views, everyone is charming, and chefs and cooks are utterly devoted to their craft—and chalk up that dazzlingly bright flavor to your imagination. But it's not your imagination. Bite into a flat peach (*pesche tabacchiera* because of its similarity in shape to a tobacco or snuff box): white or yellow fleshed, uniquely aromatic, sweet, and juicy. You are excused if you gasp with pleasure. Or a round peach, plump and almost mango-like in intensity.

Melons are extraordinary: watermelon (*anguria* or *cocomero* in other regions) and cantaloupe (*cantalupo*, named after a small town in the north of Italy). Not long ago I was staying in the Spanish Quarter and heard cries, or perhaps announcements, coming from a loudspeaker on a small truck. At first I thought perhaps it was political and wondered if there was an upcoming election. But one night I came upon a truck on one of the cobbled streets that had stopped and the passengers were imploring people to buy the melons they had grown and picked on their farm. I bought a big yellow-skinned, white-fleshed, honey-tasting melon and headed home with my evening plan in place: knife, plate, melon.

Greens taste . . . greener: bitter greens more bitter, basil more fragrant, the garden proudly following the seasons of the year. You might miss being able to get everything all year long, but oh, the flavor of what is grown in season, right there! Why? For one thing, the hot, intense, southern sun, though it can be foe as well as friend of the field. The soil is incredibly rich and volcanic, a result of Vesuvio's lava flow, which left behind the minerals that now extravagantly nourish the earth. The devotion of the farmer is crucial: choosing traditional seeds, nurturing the plants, harvesting in the heat of the sun.

Neapolitans are so hardworking that I often worry about them: Don't they get exhausted? How can they keep going? But they do. They know it is expected, needed. The pleasures of the table are so important and so close to their hearts, to their very beings. It is considered *normale*.

Could you imagine Neapolitans getting as sociable and vivacious gathering around microwave dinners, bottled salad dressing, and frozen pizza? Me neither.

Since its almost impossible separate Neapolitans from their love of tomatoes, let's begin there.

TOMATOES: NAPLES'S CULINARY SUPERSTAR

Pick up a tomato; admire how round, red, and bright it is. Then you bite: its skin against your lips, your teeth; then it bursts. Tangy tomato water bathes your mouth, and you begin to chew the flesh. Some people don't like the seeds. For me, they are the best part of a raw tomato, each seed covered with a layer of geléed juice. Eating a ripe tomato, whole, from your hands, is one of life's great pleasures.

Tomatoes, if they are well grown, are good everywhere—sometimes even great. In Campania, though, they are special. Minerally, sweet, tangy, juicy, and so very, very, very *tomatoey*. I have heard tomato love described as a religion, as a cult. I have also heard Neapolitans say, "Of course I *love* tomatoes; I am Neapolitan!"

The tomato was one of the New World foods unleashed on the world by Christoforo Colombo's voyage. But where did it originate? Central or South America is the general agreement; they still grow wild in Ecuador and Peru. A few years ago, I tasted a yellowish, reddish wild tomato in the Peruvian highlands. In that first bite of the ancient fruit I could taste the promise of what the tomato would become. As I chewed, I imagined the tomato traveling, changing with the seasons, the soil, the weather, and those who planted it.

It was cultivated first in ancient Aztec Mexico around 700 AD. The English word *tomato* and the Spanish *tomate* both came from *tomatl*, the Nahuan language of the Central American Aztecs.

Following the Spanish colonization of the Americas, in the huge exchange of fruits and vegetables (chiles to Asia, paprika to Hungary, chocolate to Europe) that transformed the diets and cuisines of the world, the tomato came to Europe. Arriving in the 1500s, it was named *pomo amoris* (love apple) and *pomo d'oro* (golden apple), which suggests that at least some of the first tomatoes were yellow in color.

The earliest recorded mention of the tomato by a European was by Venetian Pietro Andrea Mattioli, a doctor and naturalist who in 1544 recommended eating them with salt, pepper, and oil. They were still considered too dangerous to eat in the northern parts of Europe, but they were so attractive that gardeners—especially the British and Florentines—planted them for beauty and decoration.

One of the reasons for their fear was that the fruit—*solanum lycopersicum*—belongs to the nightshade family (as do eggplant and potatoes, which were also slow to be accepted). Potato leaves and green potatoes contain solanine, which is toxic. Tomato leaves were thought to be harmful but are now accepted as safe and in fact give a fresh tomato fragrance when added to certain dishes. And eggplant? We'll get to that later.

There was another reason not to eat tomatoes, however. At that time, the wealthy in northern Europe ate from flatware and plates made of pewter, which has a high level of lead. When acidic foods such as tomatoes came into contact with pewter, lead leached into the food. People sickened, and some died, but they didn't realize that the cause was the interaction between the tomato and eating utensils—they just noticed that those who ate tomatoes got ill. The poor ate from utensils of wood—who could afford pewter? Seeing no ill effects from tomatoes, they continued eating them. This was the main reason that tomatoes were eaten only by poor people until the 1800s, especially Italians. Except for Naples, which was the exact opposite.

In Naples, the tomato was adored by the rich, who did *not* use pewter utensils. In fact, the earliest cookbook with tomato recipes was published in Napoli in the late seventeenth century, though rumors circulated that the recipes themselves were Spanish. By the end of Bourbon reign (and reunification) in 1861, both aristocracy and *contadini* were eating everything tomato.

For anyone who was still concerned, an English newspaper published a story in 1864 claiming that research showed the tomato to be not only edible but also healthy.

Although most tomatoes eaten in Campania are sweetly, juicily ripe, sometimes Neapolitans enjoy green tomatoes in their salads and sauces. I used to wonder how they could enjoy such a tart thing; wasn't a green tomato abrasively sour? Having almost always had a tomato garden, I would try to enjoy my green tomatoes as they do in Napoli but almost always gave up and made green tomato chutney instead. Later, I discovered that green tomatoes in Napoli are mild and refreshing, their slight acidity giving a delicious edge to anything cooked or eaten with them. Suddenly I understood the affection for these tangy, refreshing green tomatoes.

The industry of preserving tomatoes originated in nineteenth-century Naples. They are canned whole and peeled (*pelati*), chopped, and made into *passata* (pureed, strained tomatoes) as well as *concentrato* (tomato juice/puree reduced to a thick, smooth, intensely flavored paste). These days manufacturers sometimes cut corners by exporting the tomato paste and mixing with water at its destination.

Sometimes tomato *conserva* is made, slowly cooking tomatoes for a long time until they turn into a dark, smooth, reddish paste. *Estratto di pomodoro* is one of the oldest ways of preserving the tomato: skinned, seeded, pureed ripe tomatoes spread on a large board and covered with a light cloth to dry. Stir several times daily with a wooden spoon until the mixture is dark red and the consistency of a dry paste; then roll into balls and cover with olive oil.

Cut into halves, sprinkled with salt, and dried in the sun until slightly chewy— nothing is quite like a sundried tomato. Riding from Napoli to Puglia the first time I visited Italy, I saw what seemed like endless bedsprings topped with a carpet of tomatoes cut open and drying in the sun. Nearly every house had a tomato-covered bed outside; the mystery was solved when I tasted one of these intensely savory, chewy dried tomatoes.

The San Marzano

The San Marzano tomato is a type of plum tomato differentiated from others by its long, narrow shape and sharp little point at the tip. It is a fragrant, fleshy tomato, with fewer seeds than most and bright red skin that peels off easily (and must be harvested only by hand).

Though some claim the Spanish introduced the San Marzano to Campania in the early sixteenth century, il Assessore all'Agricoltura della Regione Campania (the Campania Region Agriculture Department) says otherwise. It claims that the first seed of the San Marzano tomato came to Campania in 1770 as a gift from the Kingdom of Peru to the Kingdom of Naples. It was planted in the area that is now the commune of San Marzano.

It thrived in the Campania soil and became the most beloved of tomatoes, gaining great popularity in the 1960s and 1970s, when tomato canning and exporting was expanding. But in the 1980s, the San Marzano was struck by a series of problems—among them plant health—and the cultivated area and production of the tomato was reduced and nearly disappeared.

The result was almost a complete loss of the San Marzano, but the San Marzano tomato preservationists are heroes. They worked to bring the tomato back, and in 1996 they achieved the DOP (protected designation of origin) label from the European Union for processed (i.e., canned) foods. Today the well-being and preservation of the San Marzano is entrusted to the consortium for the protection of San Marzano tomatoes, which researches, oversees, and advises on all aspects of these tomatoes.

One of the heroes of the San Marzano is the Ruggiero family, which has been cultivating San Marzanos since 1910 under the name Gustarosso. They fought hard for not only the survival of the San Marzano but also its DOP designation (much like Champagne is to sparkling wine or Roquefort to blue cheese). "Growing in other parts of Italy means that even with the most traceable of seeds, they can't be San Marzanos," explains Paolo Ruggiero. "The San Marzano has specific growing areas, mostly in the Sarnese-Nocerino countryside, as well as the Acerrano-Nolana area in the province of Naples."

Paolo's father, Eduardo Ruggiero, has dedicated his whole life to the preservation of this precious tomato as president of both the Dani Cooperative and the Consorzio DOP San Marzano. He supervises the entire production process, supplying the farmers with plants and providing them with technical assistance throughout the transplanting, growing, and harvesting phases. Rules for DOP labeling also include breeding of seeds and the distance between plants. Sustainability is crucial as well.

Another family of tomato crusaders is the Regas, owners of Strainese and Rega brands, who own a small plot in the Sarnese Nocerino. The Regas have long been growing such tomatoes and were active in establishing a DOP for San Marzanos. Visiting the Strainese farm at harvest, I saw family members of all ages working in the hot weather during the throes of harvest time.

I had been under the impression that the San Marzano was a tomato better for cooking than for eating raw, but when I mentioned this to Paolo Ruggiero as we chatted in the fields, he disagreed. Though uniquely excellent for canning, "the San Marzano is best raw, not cooked, so you can taste all its organoleptic properties."

The flavor of the San Marzano is often described as bittersweet. When I visited during the harvest in Sarno, a farmer handed me a tomato and a shaker of salt. Tasting it raw made the connection in my brain between raw tomato and those in the can. Now I understood them: meaty textured, not too juicy or seedy, super umami, with just enough sweetness to put it in perfect balance. It tasted like it wanted to meet a pizza.

Most San Marzanos are raised on small farms linked together as a cooperative. The Dani Coop is such a cooperative, consisting of about a hundred farmers in the

Agro Sarnese Nocerino, a small area south of Napoli, the fertile valley to the south-east of Vesuvius in the provinces of Avellino and Salerno, where the village of San Marzano is located. The tomatoes are tended by centuries-old cultivation methods, including manual spring water irrigation and hand harvesting.

The farms are small, in the shadow of Vesuvius; many of the farmers are in their fifties or older. In the heat of the sun, one holds a sun umbrella while the other picks, periodically changing places. The Gustarosso label reads, "Grown by grandparents."

The harvest usually starts in August and continues until the end of September and sometimes later. They are picked seven or eight times—sometimes even more—because they are picked only when ripe. Another reason for hand harvesting.

Tomatoes in Jars

My first visit to Napoli started with tomatoes. Fresh off the train, darting across a huge street, dodging scary traffic, I wondered what I had gotten myself into. I was ready to go back to the train station and get outta there!

Catching my breath, I noticed a stand in front of me, and then another down the street. And another. Everywhere I looked, I saw people standing behind folding tables piled high with pyramids of jars, each filled with tomatoes.

Even though I didn't have a kitchen and wasn't yet a cook, I was born a tomato lover. I bought a jar, and when I got to the youth hostel, I couldn't figure out what to do first. So I sat down and opened the jar. There was a basil leaf, just one, lying on top of the tomatoes so elegantly. Tomatoey perfume wafted up, and I started eating. At this point, my memory becomes one of those technicolor moments when the scratchy gray of old films and the sepia-tinted past burst into bright color.

I'd always eaten ripe raw tomatoes out of hand, but eating them canned, straight from the jar, seemed daring, even odd. But they smelled so good. I dug in, forking up pieces of tomato, chewing my way through thoughtfully, relishing their sweetness, deep flavor, and ever-so-slight tanginess. When the tomatoes were gone, I drank the juicy tomato water. I was entranced. Who knew canned tomatoes could be like this?

Years later, when I returned to Napoli, I returned to the street looking for the tomato people. They were nowhere in sight, so I asked around. "No, it is a shame. They are now finished." Meaning we don't do it that way any longer.

But the tomatoes that are now commercially canned or put up by friends were as good, the enthusiasm just as intense. And I realized that it wasn't just the rosy memory of a young person coming of age and discovering her sense of self via a jar of preserved tomatoes: uh-uh, no. The tomatoes really *are* that good.

Is It Real or Is It Fake?

Last year I tasted canned San Marzaninos—tiny, cherry-sized San Marzano-like tomatoes. They were marvelous! Thinking they might be a new best thing in San Marzano world, I asked Paolo Ruggiero. "No," he explained, it is a hybrid and so cannot have a DOP certification, adding, "A tomato can be delicious, but if it doesn't meet the San Marzano list of specifications, it can't be a real San Marzano. . . . If you [see a] San Marzanino DOP, it is a fake."

But if there are so many excellent tomatoes growing in the region, why choose San Marzano? One reason, with canned tomatoes especially, is that San Marzanos offer a level of consistency. They have specific levels of sugar and acid and are packed without other ingredients such as basil leaves or flavorings. This makes their taste pure and authentic, perfect for pizza and other tomato sauce dishes. Chefs can add whichever herbs or other ingredients they like, but the tomato sauce is about the tomatoes. It's important to know what to expect when you open the can.

Because of San Marzano's cachet, there's a huge international market in mislabeling, charging higher prices for lesser tomatoes sold under the San Marzano name. It is fraud, cheating the customer, appropriating the San Marzano name, and stealing the Neapolitan tradition. Each time mislabeled tomatoes are eaten, it contributes to developing a taste without its backdrop of authenticity, which is especially important in transmitting culinary culture to the next generation.

In the United States, most of the canned tomatoes—more than 95 percent—are wrongly identified as San Marzano, complete with fake DOP labels. Customers pay top price for such products but miss out on the authentic experience of tasting the true products.

How do you make sure that the canned tomatoes you buy really are San Marzano? The label must say these magic words: "Pomodoro San Marzano dell'Agro Sarnese Nocerino D.O.P." It must also display the logos of both the Consorzio and the DOP. The Consorzio also assigns unique numbers to each can, which appears something like this: "N° XXXXXXX."

However, some labels read correctly but have been printed elsewhere, *not* in Italy, which means they, too, are fake. So how to tell? It's always good to trust your canned tomato merchants, as they likely know the manufacturer—information that a supermarket shelf is unlikely to provide. In the United States, Gustiamo, an online Italian grocer that sells the most exquisite of authentic products, agrees. Also, with San Marzanos, look at the price. If they are cheap, they are not San Marzanos. Real San Marzanos are not cheap.

The Consorzio notes that San Marzano tomatoes can be imported to the United States only in cans that are labeled peeled, whole, or *filetti* (though this is less common). If you see the words *puree*, *sauce*, *chopped*, *diced*, or *organic* (which is not regulated by the Consorzio) on the labels, they cannot be San Marzano. Canned tomatoes from any other part of Italy are hybrids, as are the tomatoes used in tomato paste. None of these would be true San Marzanos.

To acertain whether your San Marzanos are real or faux, regardless of what the label says, send a photo of the label to the Gustiamo website, and the president of the Consorzio will assess it.

Risotto Bianco con Pomodori (White Risotto Topped with Tomato Sauce)

Serves 4

So simple, yet so wonderful: a white cheesy risotto topped with tomato sauce. You can make it vegetarian by omitting the sausage.

3–4 ounces spicy sausage or pancetta, diced (confession: I often use a Spanish chorizo for its flavor and availability)

2 tablespoons olive oil

1 medium-large onion or 2 small onions, chopped and divided

1 can San Marzano tomatoes and their juices (a little more than a cup in volume, slightly under a pound in weight; if tomatoes are in season, by all means use about 1½ pounds of fresh ripe tomatoes, diced)

salt and pepper to taste

a small handful of sweet basil leaves

2 quarts, approximately, of broth of any kind (vegetable, chicken, beef, etc., or water plus a bouillon cube), about 8 cups

3 tablespoons butter (or olive oil, as desired)

2 cups arborio, *carnaroli*, or other risotto rice

2–3 ounces of cheese: pecorino, ricotta salata, provolone, or Parmesan, diced finely

Cook the sausage or pancetta in olive oil with half the onions, slowly until softened and just starting to brown. Increase the heat and add a cup of water, stirring and cooking a few minutes as it makes a nice broth; then add the tomatoes, salt, and pepper. Cook over medium-low heat for about ten minutes. Add the basil, and then set it aside while you prepare the rice.

Heat the broth in a saucepan and keep it warm.

Lightly sauté the remaining onion without letting it brown in the butter (or olive oil), then add the rice, stirring and coating each kernel. When each rice kernel is gilded with the golden oil and onions, slowly pour in a cup of the simmering broth while stirring. The rice will absorb the liquid almost immediately.

Risotto Bianco con Pomodori (White Risotto Topped with Tomato Sauce) *(continued)*

Keep stirring and add another cup of broth, increasing the amount of liquid as the rice cooks. It should take fifteen to twenty minutes for the rice to be al dente. Whatever you do, *don't overcook!* The rice should be slightly underdone, as it will continue cooking while it sits.

Add the diced cheese, stir thoroughly, and cover, letting the rice finish cooking. It will be quite soupy, but the liquid will absorb as it sits.

Reheat the tomato sauce over medium-high heat, letting it reduce and become quite intense.

Stir the risotto, distributing the melted cheese throughout the rice. Taste for salt and pepper, and serve in warmed bowls, each portion topped with hot tomato sauce and garnished with a sprig or two of basil.

Other Tomatoes of Campania

Besides the famous San Marzano, more than three hundred varieties of tomatoes are grown in Italy, most in Campania. There are Corbarino cherry tomatoes, yellow cherry tomatoes, Crovarese tomatoes (a type of Corbarino), *pomodorino del piennolo*, and on and on. . . .

These, too, are grown by families and harvested together in big festive gatherings. At Nobile, Strianese, and many other tomato farms, families and friends come together each year to pick the tomatoes, pack them, and send them on their way.

Pomodorino di piennolo are a hanging bunch of small, oblong tomatoes with a tiny tip at the bottom. Grown around Vesuvio, they are characterized by intense flavor and perfume. Five different varieties of tomatoes are used for hanging bunches: Fiaschella, Lampadina, Patanara, Principe Borghese, and Re Umberto. Principe Borghese is also used for making dried tomatoes. To make the hanging bunches, the tomatoes are harvested before complete ripeness and threaded onto a hemp string into bunches called *schiocche*. Though usually red, yellow tomatoes can be presented like this as well. Hanging in the open air, they keep fresh for long periods of time, even into the winter. As they hang, their flavors intensify as they dry slightly. *Piennolo* tomato bunches are such a delicacy that they are sold in wooden gift boxes to send to family and friends all over Italy.

The grape (a.k.a. baby plum) Crovarese, the luscious cherry *pomodorino di Corbara*, and Corbarinos are prepared in the same manner as the *pomodorino di piennolo*. Originating in the hills of Corbara on the slopes of the Lattari Mountains in the province of Salerno, they are grown using traditional methods, without irrigation, which results in a firm, tasty tomato. As the climate changes, this, too, may change. No one knows yet.

I thought I knew yellow tomatoes from my home state of California, but these yellow tomatoes were a revelation to me. They aren't as acidic but rather more umami. Yellow tomatoes are currently popular on pizza. Gustarosso produces a delightful jarred yellow tomato, Lucariello.

The cherry tomatoes of the entire region—*pomodori ciliegino*—are super sweet, juicy, uber-tasty cherry tomatoes. Fabulous in salads, sandwiches, soups, pasta, and pizza. What could be more Neapolitan?

Striano, just a few stops from Sarno on the little Circumvesuviana train, has many excellent DOP tomatoes. As in Sarno, Striano tomatoes are a family affair, with everyone getting together each year to harvest and can.

The Pomodoro di Sorrento is a fleshy, firm, large round tomato, light red with green coloring similar to the *cuore di bue* (oxheart), from which it is likely derived. Sorrento tomatoes came directly from the New World in the early twentieth century when the Sorrento shipowners, ferrying their lemons to the Americas, returned with the seeds. It is a salad tomato, best enjoyed raw.

Each tomato canning company might have its own methods, but all are linked by their love of tomatoes. "Tomatoes are my life!" exclaimed Tommaso Cisale, the perky, elfin, production manager of CALISPA brand preserved tomatoes and vegetables. We were at a harvest party where wine flowed, poured by white-jacketed waiters, and a long table was covered with innumerable tasty, canape-sized, tomato-based goodies. As Tommaso opened yet another tin to taste a different batch, he added that he has worked his whole adult life—forty years—with tomatoes.

The guy near him animatedly joined the conversation, expressing his own love of tomatoes; he turned out to be the owner of CALISPA, Nobile di Leo. The appreciation of tomatoes was so intense among guests and staff alike; truly, it was the most sincere party I have ever been to.

Fare la Butteglie: Bottling Tomato Passata

When bottling tomatoes, Neapolitans work with the glee and delight of the people who have just discovered this miracle, even though they have been doing it their whole lives, as have their parents and grandparents before them. The tomato sauce they bottle today seasons their lives—and their meals—throughout the coming year. This usually takes place just after Ferragosto, the holiday that ushers in summer vacation, when everything closes and Neapolitans gather with family and friends. The tomatoes are ripe, the family and friends are there to help, the timing is perfect.

The weather is very hot when it's time for this big, messy job, so everything is done outside. First the tomatoes are picked (or purchased) and given a cooling bath. While the tomatoes are bathing, everyone has coffee. Are there any tomatoes not ripe enough for canning? Let's eat them in a sandwich of country bread with olive oil! After the coffee drinking, snacking, and digesting, boiling water is poured over the rest of the tomatoes to loosen the skins. While they cool, perhaps another coffee? Maybe this time with a pastry? Then it's time to peel, endlessly peel—even the kids work at peeling tomatoes. Uncle Vito or Nonno Peppe gets out his wine in the hopes of making the job easier. Then the tomatoes are cut, cooked, pureed, strained, and poured into bottles. Sometimes a tomato or two is cut into wedges and stuffed in as well. Capped tightly, they are layered into a pan and set to boil over a fire, sometimes with a potato or two on top of the filled bottles, which weigh down the bottles and, when tender, indicate when the puree is done.

It's important to have a supply of wonderful preserved tomatoes, because they are always good and often what you want to eat. Even when a ferocious heat wave strikes and you can barely lift a fork to your mouth, eating tomato sauce makes you feel better.

All who took part in the tomato-fest come away with jars and jars and jars of tomato, enough to keep them tomato sauced throughout winter. Whoever couldn't make it that day is on the tomato list: Aunt Assunta, who had trouble with her feet this year and couldn't come herself; Uncle Beppe, who got stuck on the motorway; and others who couldn't make it for canning day.

And with the leftovers? Sometimes you run out of jars—for this, you cook pasta! It's a party!

Pummarola

EVERYDAY TOMATO SAUCE USING CANNED TOMATOES

So many think that a lot of ingredients, a long cook time, Italian heritage, and secret herbs are needed to make a proper red sauce (just like homemade!), so they buy a jar of sauce. Wait! Stop. Please stop. Don't do it, even if the label says "all natural" or "old country taste."

Please forgive me. I'm not usually this bossy, but we're talking about the taste of Napoli here. When you find yourself in the supermarket reaching for that jar of ready-made pasta sauce (ragù, etc.), just put it down.

Instead, open a can of tomatoes (or slice up some fresh cherry tomatoes if they are in season) and squish them through your fingers like an Italian mamma or whirl them through a blender. Heat the mixture through for maybe ten minutes, or until it thickens a bit, and there you have a nice, bright-tasting tomato sauce. A little onion sautéed in olive oil *or* garlic, a pinch of red pepper flakes, and a basil leaf or two is fine, but don't overdo it: this sauce is about *tomatoes*.

Pummarola (continued)

BASIC NEAPOLITAN TOMATO SAUCE USING FRESH TOMATOES

Neapolitan tomato sauce is basically pureed tomatoes, fresh or canned, cooked down to whatever consistency you wish. I always found that certain canned tomatoes need a pinch of sugar. When I asked Neapolitan friends about this, they said, "No, you don't need sugar." Then I realized that Neapolitan tomatoes—whether San Marzano or one of the other great DOP tomatoes—are so sweet and less acidic that they don't need sugar. Tomatoes from other places sometimes do.

Nothing could be more Napoletano than this basic sauce, except this sauce without onion, only tomato. *Pummarola* is Napoletano dialect for "tomato."

Any Neapolitan sauce of tomatoes may be referred to simply as *la salsa* because tomato sauce is the sauce; it's what Neapolitans eat.

2½ pounds ripe tomatoes, quartered or chopped roughly	1 small onion, chopped
Salt to taste	Olive oil
	A few basil leaves

Combine the tomatoes with the salt and onion. Cover and cook slowly for about half an hour, stirring every so often to keep them from burning on the bottom.

When tomatoes are cooked through and the mixture is sauce-like, remove from stove. Use as is or puree through a sieve or whirl with a blender, food processor, or stick blender. This sauce can be the basis for any dish calling for a basic tomato sauce. Or place it in a jar or other container with several basil leaves on top and cover with a slick of olive oil and a lid. Keep in the refrigerator for up to two weeks, no longer, or in the freezer for up to six months.

Scarpariello: A few big spoonfuls of grated pecorino stirred into tomato sauce is very Neapolitan and adds a delicious dimension to simple tomato sauce. Toss it with gnocchi, *fettuccelle*, *paccheri*, or any chunky pasta.

Filetti: The word *filetti* seems old fashioned these days and is used less and less; a more modern way of describing a quickly cooked sauce of tomato pieces would be "*sciuè, sciuè*" (Quick! Quick!).

Heat a clove or two of halved garlic and/or a little chopped onion in a tablespoon or two of olive oil, then add lots of quartered, peeled tomatoes (about 14 ounces if using canned tomatoes). Cook until soft (but not pureed) into a sauce. Add salt, pepper, or pinch of red pepper flakes to taste.

FRUITS AND NUTS

The fresh things of Campania are so full of flavor that at first bite you wonder how it is possible. A melon may taste so ripe and sweet that it's as if it made a pact with the sun. When you take a bite, you can only sigh with pleasure.

The vegetables and fruit follow the seasons, absorbing the sun's rays with great joy. Naples sometimes has rain, even occasionally snow, but the sun is never far away. And the vegetables taste as if they know this.

Fruits

Some of the special local fruits include fico Bianco del Cilento DOP (figs), kaki Napoletano IGP (persimmons), albicocca Vesuviana IGP (apricots), Pagani and Sorrento oranges, Ciliegia della Valle dell'Irno and della Recca cherries, and wild cherries used in maraschino liqueur or jarred in syrup as Amarena, which are divine.

But also there are the tiniest wild strawberries, perfumed and sweet, and melons so intense you can't imagine wanting cake for dessert when you could have melon (though melon gelato is sublime). Once upon a time, the sweetest, most juicy watermelon (*'o mellone*) was sold in slices in little street shops called *mellunari*—now sadly gone.

Pears and peaches are grown with great care and, like all of the fruits of Campania, truly exceptional. The *percuoco* and *perzeca* are sweet and delicious. Sometimes ripe peaches are sliced into a glass of red wine, a cooling afternoon *merendina*. When tiny and green, the peaches may be pickled.

Juicy, sweet, and fat Catalanescas, a table grape from the area around Vesuvio, were brought by the Spanish. Though they thrived in Campania soil, their name reflects their origin.

The Annurca apple is a Campania native that has earned the IGP (protected geographical indication). An ancient apple, the Annurca is recognizable in frescoes of Pompeii. Pliny the Elder, Roman naturalist from the first century AD, observed that the apples were buried and aged in sand and straw. Today they are still treated this way. The name Annurca comes from *mala orcula* ("bad hereafter") because the apples originated in Pozzuoli, and hell was believed to be located in the area.

A smallish to medium apple, it is juicy, firm, crisp, and sweet with just the right amount of tanginess and a lovely aroma. Its skin is streaked red with a brownish area near its stem. My introduction to the Annurca was watching a group of Neapolitans gather around a box of the apples, gleefully taking one, biting into it, chewing happily. No other apple, no matter how delicious, compared. This apple is seasonal and tastes like life in Campania. Even today the Annurca is grown only in Campania.

Mostly green when harvested, they develop their red color while ripening on mats of straw (or wood shavings, pine needles, etc.) in the sun, where they are carefully turned regularly by hand for twenty to fifty days. Ripening off the tree prolongs the season.

Most of the Annurca orchards are in Benevento, Campi Flegri, Avallino, and Caserta. A homey dessert, especially for Sunday lunch, is Annurca apples roasted with honey and cinnamon. I like to make crostata and add a little bit of fresh rosemary to the apples. Not traditional, perhaps, but tasty.

Nuts

Campania is said to have the longest history of hazelnut cultivation in Italy. The name for the province of Avellino is derived from the old word for the hazelnut tree, *avellana*. (The new name is *nocciola*.) Frescoes in Herculaneum show how important hazelnuts were in everyday life. In the Kingdom of Naples at the end of the seventeenth century, special offices were set up to measure the nuts for export, especially to France and Holland.

Nocciola di Giffoni IGP and Nocciolo Mortarella Campania are the two most cherished types of hazelnut in Campania. Though the toasty little nuts are occasionally found in savory dishes or eaten out of hand, most are used in chewy nougat, chocolate Gianduiotto, brittles, cookies, cakes, and pastries.

Walnuts, or *noce di Sorrento*, have been grown in Campania since at least the first century AD. Paintings from the ruins of Pompeii and Herculaneum show the presence of walnuts. Although they are not used in many dishes, they are enjoyed simply, especially after a big meal at Christmastime. Unripe, they are steeped in alcohol to make a delicious liqueur called *nocillo*.

Almonds are eaten in so many things in Campania: kneaded into a peppery dough and baked until crisp for taralli (a savory cookie) or made into crunchy toppings or ground into a paste for sweet things. *Torta Caprese* (either dark chocolate or lemon and white chocolate) is based on ground almonds, not flour—irresistible. And there's an old-fashioned traditional drink called *latte di mandorla*—almond milk—which is as fragrant as walking through a blossoming almond orchard. Mennella's Gelato on Via Toledo makes a luscious gelato as lyrical as poetry.

Pistachios are hugely popular these days in Naples and surroundings, usually coming from Sicily. Suddenly green pastes are everywhere: savory on sandwiches or sweet in almost anything.

Pine nuts also come from Sicily and are especially popular in dishes with Sicilian provenance, such as baked goods, cooked greens, or the famous Neapolitan meatballs with raisins and pine nuts. Since Naples and Sicily were once part of the same kingdom, it makes sense that certain ingredients are embraced across borders.

BEANS, LEGUMES, CHESTNUTS

The *fagiolo di Controne* is a delicious whitish, round or egg-shaped bean with tender creamy flesh and a delicate skin that doesn't interfere with the pleasure of bean eating.

We know little about its origins—only that it has long been grown in the Albruni Mountains. It is grown mainly on small farms in the commune of Controne, a small village about fifty miles outside Salerno.

The beans are harvested at the end of October, dried on cloths for a few days, and then shelled and stored in cool, well-ventilated places. The best place to buy them is at Controne's "bean fair" in late November, which also offers tastings of traditional dishes.

Cicerale are a particularly delicious tiny chickpea, grown since the year 1000 near Agropoli, in the hills of a little village called Cicerale. Not far from Paestum, and the Cilento and Vallo di Diano National Park, it is a green and rustic land that gives the Cicerale a distinctive flavor, dense texture, and high potassium content. They are good cooked in *pasta con ceci*, with braised wild boar, or simply stewed with aromatics and ladled over garlic-rubbed toast with a splash of olive oil. Use *ceci di Cicerale* along with preserved tuna from Cetara, local olive oil, lemons from the tree outside your window, and a little chopped white onion from Pompeii. A traditional village recipe is *cicci maritati*, chickpeas stewed with fava, peas, beans, lentils, and cereals such as wheat and corn in a hefty soup.

Pasta con Ceci (Pasta Cooked in Chickpea Broth)

Serves 4

Classic Napoli *pasta con ceci* is another soup often made with *pasta mista*, a mixture of different sizes of pasta. The mixture is a celebration of frugality and gives a different texture (and thus taste) to each mouthful. *Ammiscata* is the name for *pasta mista* in Neapolitan dialect.

It should be thicker than a soup and soupier than a pasta dish. There's a lot of leeway for the cook: if you like it thicker and more like pasta on the plate,

Pasta con Ceci (Pasta Cooked in Chickpea Broth) *(continued)*

decrease the liquid accordingly; if you like it soupy, this is a good balance. Add another cup or so of liquid if you prefer it soupier.

4 tablespoons extra virgin olive oil, plus extra for drizzling
3 whole cloves garlic, peeled
Half of a mild to medium-hot fresh red chile, seeds removed, left in a chunk
About 12 slices air-dried, peppery or garlicky (or both) salame

4 cups cooked chickpeas with their cooking liquid
Several small sprigs fresh rosemary
1 cup chicken or other broth (or water mixed with bouillon cube)
Approximately 12 ounces mixed pastas or another hearty pasta such as *laganelle* or *candele*, broken up
Salt and pepper to taste

Place the garlic and chile in the olive oil to warm through, taking care not to let the garlic brown.

Add half the cooked chickpeas.

Puree the remaining chickpeas with their liquid and add to the pot. Cook together about ten minutes.

Add the rosemary sprigs and the broth and bring to the boil. When it begins to bubble and boil, add the pasta to the pot.

Reduce heat to medium so that it doesn't burn on the bottom, and cook over medium to medium-high heat, stirring every so often, until the pasta is no more than al dente.

Taste for salt and pepper and serve each bowlful with a drizzle of olive oil.

Variation: Tiny shellfish such as squid, especially grilled, are delicious with pureed chickpeas; add a handful when the pasta is nearly al dente.

Chestnuts are eaten in savory dishes rurally, especially soups, vegetables, and game; they are made into sweet confections, and they are roasted on the street, especially in the city. Marrone di Roccadaspide (IGP), Castagna di Serino (DOP), and Castagna del Vulcano di Roccamonfina (IGP) are three types of the chestnuts that have grown in Campania since around the twelfth or thirteenth centuries.

LEMONS

To understand how important lemons are to the area, just look at a rack of postcards for the Sorrento and Amalfi Coast and the islands of Capri, Ischia, and Procida. The beautiful vistas, seascapes, beaches, and plates of food are surrounded by lemons, lemons, lemons.

Local people are emotionally attached to "their" lemons; few families in the region of Sorrento or Amalfi do not have at least a few lemons trees to call their own. No matter how steep the slope they are growing on, they are visited, cared for, and cherished. Like the tomato, lemons are a fruit Napoletanos consider not only a part of their heritage but also a part of themselves, a part of their identity. Once, walking in the lemon tree–covered hills above Sorrento with several local women, I reached up and grabbed a golden yellow fruit, and then popped it into my pocket. My friends laughed, saying, "You are a real Napoletana!"

Lemon trees provide beautiful, fragrant fruit, and gorgeous landscapes, but they also help preserve the soil from erosion and instability. A variety of lemons have proliferated and evolved from earlier ones, each with its own characteristics: from tiny to massive, from sweet and juicy to those eaten for their peel and pith. In Campania, the world is full of lemons and all the more beautiful for it.

Amalfi Lemon Fritters

Serve these doughnut-like fritters with either raspberry jam or lemon marmalade, if desired. You could even fill a syringe or pastry bag and squirt jam into each fritter.

2 cups white flour	2 teaspoons vinegar
1 envelope dry yeast (about 1¾ tablespoons)	Zest from 1 organic, unwaxed, fragrant lemon, grated or
¼ cup sugar	chopped
1¼ cup lukewarm water	Oil for frying
1 egg	Confectioners sugar for dusting

Mix the flour with the dry yeast and sugar; then stir in the lukewarm water, mixing well. Add the egg, vinegar, and lemon zest, and set aside.

Heat the oil to smoking; it is ready when a cube of bread dropped into it sizzles and turns golden right away.

Using two large spoons, create dollops and gently slip each into the hot oil, dropping them in very near to the oil rather than too high, so it doesn't splash and injure you. When golden on the bottom side, turn them over, and cook on the other side.

Remove from hot oil with a slotted spoon or wire mesh, and place on absorbent paper or a wire rack to degrease.

Serve sprinkled with confectioners sugar, if desired, and raspberry jam or lemon marmalade.

Variation: Adding raisins or sultanas (golden raisins) soaked in grappa to the dough is more Venetian than Neapolitan, but it is delicious, so Neapolitans love them this way as well.

According to Campania's department of agriculture, it is likely that lemons originated in northern India and were brought to Campania in the first century BCE by Jews "for whom [they] had a ritual value." The lemon is portrayed in mosaics and paintings from Pompeii, a part of life in the Neapolitan area since ancient times. (Interestingly, Pompeii had a large Jewish presence.) This clearly predates speculation that the lemon made its way to Campania via Amalfi from Sicily, where Arab traders had introduced them, though both stories are likely true. The citron was an important fruit in Judea, where King Simon Maccabeas chose to depict it on his coins in 142 BCE. According to Theophrastus, by the fourth century BCE citrons were being cultivated in southern Italy, including Sicily and Corsica.

In Amalfi, documentation of the lemon dates from the eleventh century onward. The medical school of Salerno recognized the health benefits of lemons and recommended their medicinal use. The lemons of Maiori, near Amalfi, were quoted on the New York Stock Exchange at the beginning of the twentieth century.

The first specialized lemon groves on the Sorrento Peninsula were created by Jesuit priests, who grew the Femminello Ovale lemon between Sorrento and Massalubrense in 1600. This lemon, in time, differentiated to become the cultivar known as the Ovale di Sorrento, Massese, or Massalubrense lemon and has earned IGP recognition.

The Ovale di Sorrento, named for its oval shape, has been a part of the area's landscape for centuries and was granted the IGP in 1999. Mostly grown on steep, terraced hillsides, the lemon trees are canopied with a protective netting or straw mat called *pagliarelle*, an ancient technique that helps protect them from cold coastal winds.

Bright yellow in color and medium large in size with juicy, tangy flesh that is pale in color, they have a beautiful fragrance. Harvested by hand from October to February, the Sorrento lemon is the same type as that grown in Capri.

The Sfusato Amalfitano lemon, the most common on that coast, helped earn UNESCO heritage site status. Before lemon trees, the region was planted with mulberry trees for the silk trade. When silk declined, mulberry trees were replaced with lemons.

The Sfusato is a medium-large lemon with a rough, thick, pale yellow skin. Its flesh has few seeds and is juicy, tart, and delightfully sweet in fragrance. Recent studies at the Federico II University of Naples show it to be one of the richest lemons in vitamin C. It shares many growing characteristics with its Sorrento siblings: harvest season, terrace cultivation, and straw mats protecting them from the elements.

Take a walk through the main street of Amalfi, past the main church, the shops, and restaurants to the very end of the street. On your left is the paper-making museum. Across the way is the lemon farm of the Aceto family (ironically, their name translates to "vinegar"). The farm starts at the end of the street, stretching around and up into the surrounding hillsides of La Valle dei Mulini.

The Aceto family started growing lemons in a small plot in Ravello in 1825. Post–World War II, they were the largest growers and exporters of lemons on the Costa Amalfitiera. In 1989, Luigi Aceto set up a cooperative for Sfusato Amalfitano, the typical lemon of the area. When I spoke with him, we sat in the shade of a canopy of lemon trees. "I was born in the lemon orchard," he said with a smile, gesturing to the trees all around. "Sometimes I think that instead of blood in my veins, I have beautiful lemon juice," adding, "Some consider me '*il poeta dei Limoni*,' the poet of all things lemon."

Polpettine di Vitello, Pollo, o Tachino, al Limone (Little Lemony Meatballs)

Serves 4

These are good with ground turkey or chicken, though veal is more traditional.

4 slices rustic bread, preferably stale	Zest of 1 lemon
Equal parts water and milk, to cover the bread	1–2 tablespoons chopped flat leaf parsley
1 pound lean ground turkey, veal, or chicken	Salt and pepper to taste
3–4 cloves garlic, chopped	Flour and a small amount of oil for browning
8 heaping tablespoons fresh grated Parmigiano	Juice of 2 lemons
1 egg	4 cups of arugula leaves

Place the bread in a bowl, and add the water and milk to cover. When soft, about five to ten minutes, squeeze the bread of its excess liquid; then place in a larger bowl to mix with the other ingredients.

To the soaked bread, add the ground turkey, garlic, Parmigiano, egg, lemon zest, parsley, salt, and pepper. Mix with a fork or your hands until well combined.

With a spoon, scoop a large, walnut-sized ball of the meat mixture, and then plop it into a plate of flour. Using your hands, pick up the mixture and roll it into a ball shape. Repeat using all of the meat, adding more flour if needed.

Heat a small amount of oil in a heavy frying pan, preferably nonstick. When the oil is hot and shimmering on the surface, gently add the meatballs, taking care not to splatter oil or break the meatballs apart. Cook over a medium-low heat, turning every so often until they are evenly golden and lightly browned.

Squirt with the lemon juice, continue cooking a minute or two as it evaporates, and serve on plates either garnished or tossed with the arugula.

Like the rest of the islands and coastline, Procida is famous for and oh-so-proud of its lemons. There are a number of lemon cultivars on Procida, but one is especially unique: "the bread lemon," *il limone di pane*. Huge golden orbs—they can be seven to ten inches long—with a thick layer of pith (which isn't as bitter as ordinary lemons), an intense aroma, and only a small amount of pleasantly acidic juice. It is the basis of the island's special dish: *limone al piatto*, or *insalata di limone*.

The first time I encountered a bread lemon, I was disappointed when I cut into it: mostly pith with a tiny amount of flesh. I asked as politely as I could, "What is with the lemon?" "It's a bread lemon," I was told, enthusiastically, happily. "You know, for salads."

Suddenly these massive lemons, huge and mostly pith, took on new importance. Though their flesh is sweeter than other lemons, they have little juice. Then the aha moment: its pith wasn't a drawback—it was its reason for being. Delicate in both taste and texture, the pith is the bread for which the lemon is named.

I have wondered whether the huge lemons of Procida are any relation to the citrons of Calabria, which is a province bordering Campania. Calabria is a world source for ritual citrons for the Jewish festival of Sukkot. Rabbis come from far and wide to supervise the harvest. Could these citrons be related to the bread lemons of Procida?

Whether the Procida lemon is a really a citron or just a big bread lemon descended from the Femminello lemon, evolving and developing its own characteristics, there's bad news: the trees are disappearing from Procida and Ischia. Newer types of lemon have more to offer—more juice, for one thing—and locals are trying to save this unique citrus biodiversity and heritage.

For centuries the Procida lemon was grown by families. After World War II, there was an increased demand for lemons, so more families and businesses planted trees. The lemons are eaten not only fresh but also as the basis of other dishes such as limoncello and the "national" dish, *insalata di limone* (raw lemon salad).

Procida (and Ischia) lemons flower twice a year: in April for summer fruit and in June for October fruit. The autumn/winter fruit has a smoother skin and is smaller than the big, fat summer lemon that is so iconic and characteristic of its type.

I find it curious that the same fruit is used so differently in neighboring lands, Napoli, and its neighbor across the sea to the east, Greece. In ancient times the two were linked as Magna Grecia. Both lands—Campania and Greece—share the culinary love of olive oil, tomato, and lemon, but in Greece lemon is the main flavoring ingredient in almost everything: soups, meats, and sauces, often beaten together with eggs (in Campania, the egg lemon sauce does exist but primarily for Easter roast meats).

In Naples, lemon is squirted onto fried food and roasted fish and added to salads and rich dishes such as lemon risotto and lemon pasta, as well as endless cakes, sweets, granitas, and pastries. If you go to the Amalfi Coast or Sorrento and don't eat lemon cake or *delizie al limone*. . . . Well, it's unlikely in any event, so don't even countenance such a sad thought.

Savory, grated lemon zest is appearing on pizzas more and more; lemon zest is made into a creamy sauce for pasta and sprinkled onto fish, chicken, risotto, yellow tomatoes, anchovies, and basil. The yellow of the tomatoes and the yellow emotion of the lemon zest is quite fashionable at the moment. Lemon zest/peel, preserved in sugar syrup, is divine, especially for the sweet baked goods of Christmas.

Other citrus grows in the area, of course. I was pleased to find rare finger limes being cultivated on a farm in Valle dei Mulini; perhaps they will take off in restaurants. I hope so: they are as fragrant as makrut lime with the texture of caviar, amazing on the succulent oysters and briny raw seafood of the coastline.

Limoncello

The most famous Campania food product made from lemons is limoncello (or *limuncell*, as the Campanians call it). Handed down generation to generation in the home kitchen, almost every family along the coasts and islands has long made limoncello for their own consumption. A friend told me that as children they made limoncello at school, learning chemistry and math from the process.

In recent years, however, as tourists began flocking to the area in the early 1960s, limoncello became *the* drink to sip on warm evenings at the café or for aiding digestion after a trattoria dinner. Soon visitors began asking where to buy this drink, and its commercial life was born. Now it is sold all over, especially at the airport.

Homemade limoncello is better, though, as countless Napoletani agree: No matter how many companies make excellent versions commercially, people still make limoncello at home. Lemons grow everywhere, and there's something satisfying about making this traditional homemade drink instead of buying it.

To make limoncello, start by peeling off the zest only (no white pith) and infusing it in pure alcohol, then straining and combining it with a sweet syrup. Sometimes milk is added for a creamy limoncello; sometimes the liqueur is made from oranges (*arancello*). Many lemon farms make limoncello and host tastings; some rent out their properties, old-fashioned grand houses with amazing views, as venues for happy events.

Limoncello (*continued*)

Everyone's recipe is different. Some marinate the lemon zest for months, others for days. Some add lemon juice to the sugar syrup; some don't. Some use more sugar, some less. Some limoncellos are more bitter than others (it depends upon the lemons themselves).

I like this version because it includes lemon juice as well as zest and is almost lyrical in fragrance and delicacy: not too strong or sweet, I just want to keep sipping.

3–5 lovely unwaxed lemons   1 cup water
1 bottle grappa or neutral spirit   2 cups sugar
    such as 151-proof Everclear   Juice of one large lemon
    (if using spirit, dilute with water
    to half its potency)

Using a paring knife, remove zest from the lemons and place the zest in a crock or large jar with whatever alcohol you choose. Alternatively, you can use a lemon zester, which peels long, thin ribbons of zest without the bitter pith. Using a zester results in a shorter steeping time, since the zest has more surface area.

Cover the lemon and alcohol tightly and steep for one to two months in a dark place. I usually steep for about a month and a half, but it depends on the lemons, the alcohol, and the weather. Sometimes I steep for a month, and then add thin peels from another lemon a few days before decanting, finishing, and bottling. This seems to add freshness. Warmer weather and higher alcohol content hasten the infusing.

Prepare two bottles by washing and sterilizing. Use a dishwasher if you like, or simply pour boiling water in the bottle along with something metallic like a metal skewer or a long knife to conduct the heat and prevent the glass from breaking.

Make a syrup by heating together the water, sugar, and lemon juice. Stir until the sugar dissolves; then remove from heat and allow to cool.

When cool, add the syrup to the lemon-steeped alcohol for several hours or up to a day.

Strain, using a sieve or strainer, into the bottles using a funnel. (This recipe makes about a bottle and a half of limoncello.)

Seal each bottle and store in a cool place until ready to drink. I like to keep mine in the freezer, where it gets cold and syrupy, but doesn't freeze.

My favorite summer cocktail is basil steeped in limoncello. Crush a small handful of basil leaves with your fingers, place in glass, and add limoncello. Drink immediately or refrigerate—it gets better and better the longer it sits. I suggest about three days.

VEGETABLES

In Campania, like all of Italy, it is the vegetable dishes that give contour to the meal, that fill it out with their colors and freshness—hence the word for this vegetable course: *contorno*. Plates and platters don't come garnished like in French cuisine; rather vegetable dishes are somewhat stark on the plate. You choose the vegetables you want to accompany your meal: salads, braised vegetables in season, fried potatoes.

There are so many vegetable dishes in Campania, so many traditional vegetable dishes. Many can be first courses, antipasti, or even main courses. Neapolitans love their vegetables. I was once at an olive farm in the Castera countryside in which the family was hosting a lunch of local specialties. "We love our vegetables," said the grandfather. "Maybe once a week or even once a month we eat a little prosciutto or other rich foods, but every day, *this*" (and here he gestured to all of the vegetable dishes on the table) "this is what we eat every day."

Neapolitans usually like their green salads simple, light, and refreshing: lettuce and radicchio leaves, some tomato, thinly sliced onion and fennel. Often the tomatoes served in an *insalata mista* are not completely ripe, firm and slightly sour instead of sun-drenched sweetness; it's considered more refreshing this way. To make a classic Napoli salad of simplicity, toss in a bowl a head of butter lettuce with maybe a little radicchio; be sure the greens are crisply fresh. Add half a thinly sliced mild onion, half a bulb of fennel thinly sliced, some tomato wedges, and toss together with a little acid: lemon juice or wine vinegar. Add a little more salt than you think you need, and when you serve it, dress it with olive oil. Black pepper is optional.

Depending on where you are and who makes the salad, it might come piled with a handful of savory anchovies, olives, olives, and more olives, artichoke hearts, egg wedges, peppers, and/or capers. We're well beyond simplicity now, but you get the picture.

Almost every vegetable grows in Campania, all eaten in season throughout the culinary year. Vegetables are, after all, the most important part of *la cucina Napoletana*.

Here are a few of the specialties.

Artichokes (Carciofo di Paestum IGP)

Artichokes were adored by both Greeks and Romans, most likely brought to Campania with the Jews from the eastern Mediterranean. It's likely that they reverted to wild at some point after their arrival. They weren't noted as growing in Campania until the ninth century. Others say that the vegetable came to Italy/Campania with the Arabs, perhaps to Sicily via Spain or directly from North

Africa. In Campania and Sicily, the artichokes thrived. The first real documentation of artichokes came in the early 1400s, though a century earlier its cousin the
cardoon was popular.

Documents from the Kingdom of Naples show that the artichoke has been cultivated in the area of Salerno since the nineteenth century. They likely were planted
in the areas adjacent to the temples of Paestum by farmers in the Neapolitan area
who brought their artichokes from the gardens in Schito, near Castellammare di
Stabia (now famous for its artichokes), to the fertile Sele Plain. There, the artichoke
evolved into the Tondo di Paestum (Paestum Round).

The Salerno area accounts for 90 percent of the artichokes grown in Campania.
Local folk medicine attributed many therapeutic properties to the artichoke, including a medicinal wine to cure the liver: combine a liter of white wine and several
big handfuls of artichoke leaves to macerate for five days; strain and bottle; then
drink a glass or two each day.

In season you can find artichokes roasting on the streets of Napoli and in restaurants throughout the area. If they are on the menu, don't hesitate—just order them.

The island of Procida is an island of lemons, yes, but it is also an island of artichokes. So many people have urged me to visit near the end of April during the
sagra dei carciofi, or artichoke festival. I have heard rumors of all the good things
there are to eat: parmigiana of artichokes, pasta with artichokes, stuffed artichokes,
frittate, and raw salads.

Other Vegetables

The arugula of Napoli is so strongly flavored that I get a shiver of pleasure down
my spine thinking about eating it (in a salad with a big ball of mozzarella). Its
leaves are thin and spindly, its flavor so fresh that it slaps you with it. Eat it as a
salad or with mozzarella, prosciutto, pizza. It's just wonderful arugula.

Cauliflower is at its best in early winter—a perfect time for its Neapolitan reason
for being: *insalata di rinforzo*, the Christmastime salad of pickled vegetables. Cauliflower braised with tomatoes and olive oil makes a fabulous pasta sauce. If eaten
without the pasta, it makes a great *contorno* or vegetable side dish. And cauliflower
makes the *best* fritters.

The celery of Campania, especially if homegrown, is particularly flavorful. A
tiny bit in a sauce will rewire your brain regarding the way you feel about celery.

Lettuce—often *incappucciata*, a local, crispier variety of iceberg—is usually
mixed with carrots, fennel, fresh onions, and slightly unripe tomatoes for an everyday *contorno*. It sounds ordinary, but it is so refreshing because each ingredient
is so good.

Eggplant, or *melanzane*, is so much a part of local food culture that it seems as if it has grown there forever, sprouted from Neapolitan earth. But, like the tomato, that's not the case at all.

Also like the tomato, people were afraid of the eggplant. They named it *melazane*, which translates as "insanity apple" (*mela*: apple; *zane*: insanity). (Meanwhile, over in the New World, that fear didn't exist. They looked at the vegetable and thought, *It's shaped like an egg; let's call it eggplant!*)

The Arabs first brought eggplant to Spain and Italy (most likely Sicily or the Kingdom of the Two Sicilies first). No doubt it was the relationship of the Two Sicilies that spread the use of the eggplant from the Arabs to the Jewish community of the island of Sicily to Naples. In the sixteenth century, large colonies of Jews who had lived in Sicily since Roman times were forced to flee the expulsion. More than thirty-five thousand Jews fled north carrying the vegetables and seeds they couldn't imagine living without.

Knowing how quintessential a vegetable the eggplant is in Campania, it took a surprisingly long time to catch on. As Antonio Frogoli declared in Rome in 1631, it was only "eaten by people of lowly status . . . or Jews." Artusi concurred, famously stating that eggplant was "vile" because it was eaten by Jews. Then along came agronomist Vincenzo Tanora in 1644, who reflected that one should pay attention to what the Jews ate, because the laws of Kashrut made Jews quite careful (shall we say finicky?) about their food. Until then eggplant had been thought to be dangerous; taking the stance that, since Jews ate it, it must be safe changed everything. Eggplant is now one of the most beloved vegetables throughout Italy.

The traditional type of eggplant grown in Campania is the *melanzana cima di viola*, a long oval fruit with gleaming, dark purple skin, tender flesh, and few seeds. Grown in the Acerrano-Nolano and Sarnese-Nocerino countryside, it is harvested from May until the end of December. The Neapolitan eggplant is very similar—it looks like *cima di viola* on the outside but is harvested for a shorter season: from the end of September until the end of November.

Neapolitans eat it fried, stewed with tomatoes, cooked with chickpeas, tossed with spaghetti, or served with swordfish and *paccheri* sauced with marinara. Of course, it's the star of their *melanzane alla parmigiana*.

The oldest way of preserving eggplant is *sott'olio*, lightly pickled and covered with oil. It's simple to make: Cut up, sprinkle with salt, and leave for a few hours. Cook in brine with white wine vinegar until tender but still chewy. Squeeze dry, and then add garlic and oregano. It's a very old recipe still adored by Napoletani. They are good in sandwiches, especially roasted pork, with bread as *merenda del cafone*, "peasant's snack," or with a strong provolone cheese as part of an antipasto.

And on the Amalfi Coast, eggplant is the basis for a layered chocolate dessert.

Spaghetti con le Melanzane (Fried Eggplant with Spaghetti)

Serves 4

I can't sing the praises of eggplant enough. When I found that Napoletani felt the same way, it was simply another reason to love them. You can use other pastas in this dish, preferably local shapes to keep the dish tasting of Campania: fettuccine or *fettuccelle, paccheri* (large tubes), or *mezze maniche* (short, large tubes) are all good choices, though spaghetti would be my first choice, followed by *paccheri*, with both shapes offering the essential taste and texture of Napoli.

1 large eggplant or 2 small to medium ones, cut into bite-sized cubes	1 large can (1 pound, 12 ounces) San Marzano tomatoes, whole with their juices
Salt to taste	Pinch of sugar
4 tablespoons extra virgin olive oil	Large pinch of dried oregano, crumbled
1 onion (or 1 large or 2 small shallots), diced	1 pound spaghetti, preferably from Gragnano
1 clove garlic, slivered	Freshly grated pecorino cheese (optional)
Pinch of chile flakes	
Handful of sweet basil	
½ cup dry white wine (optional)	

Toss the diced eggplant with several good pinches of salt. Set aside for about fifteen minutes; then pat dry with a paper towel.

Meanwhile, make sauce. Lightly sauté the onion (or shallots) and garlic with the chile flakes, basil leaves, and a pinch of salt in two or three tablespoons of olive oil over medium-low heat until onions are softened. Raise the heat to high and pour in the wine, boiling until the liquid is reduced by about half.

Reduce the heat to medium, add the tomatoes and their juices, a pinch of sugar, and the oregano leaves. Cook, stirring occasionally and breaking up the tomatoes with a wooden spoon, while you prepare the eggplant and spaghetti.

Heat a tablespoon or two of the olive oil in a heavy frying pan and add the eggplant. Let it brown, turning it occasionally but taking care not to break up the cubes. When the eggplant is browned in parts and just cooked through, remove from heat and cover.

Now cook the pasta. Bring a large pot of salted water to the boil and add the spaghetti. Cook until it is softened but not yet al dente; in other words, it should have a crunchy interior when you bite into it. Drain, reserving a cup or so of the cooking water.

Add the drained spaghetti to the pan of simmering tomato sauce and toss to coat well. Cook together, tossing as you cook and adding some of the cooking water. If the sauce is too thick, add more water; if too thin, add less. Taste for salt and pepper and season accordingly. The spaghetti is ready when the sauce is thickened and the pasta is just al dente. Do not cook any further than this!

Arrange spaghetti and sauce on a platter, pour the eggplant on top, and serve freshly grated pecorino cheese alongside.

With its sweet aroma and licorice-y, anise flavor paired with a celery-like crunchy texture, fennel is a delicious vegetable. Eaten raw in simple green salads, it is invigoratingly strong; cooked in soups or with almost anything else, it is mild and delicate. In the springtime, it's often served with peas or other young vegetables of the season.

Friarielli (broccoli rabe) is one of my favorite vegetables, the bitterness of the greens deeply satisfying bathed in a miasma of garlic, chile, and olive oil. Neapolitans claim the *friarielli* as theirs alone, not eaten outside of Campania. I tend to side with the Neapolitans on this. *Friarielli* may well be turnip greens, but growing in Campania, they have morphed into something special and uniquely local.

Eat at them in a vegetable antipasto or paired with local sausage. They are wonderful stuffed into a crisp, savory *sfogliatelle* or spooned onto bread, perhaps with a few olives or some provola cheese melted on top.

The history of eating *friarielli* goes back to the time of imperial Rome. And locals apparently ate them as enthusiastically during the Middle Ages as they do now: the Salerno medical school warned about getting indigestion from eating too much *friarielli*. They are in season in winter, though they may appear at other times throughout the year since they grow easily. There is seldom need for chemicals, so they are often organic. They are also high in antioxidants.

I have developed quite a *friarielli* dependency. After yearning for them for too long, one year I arrived in Naples during the season and decided to buy a nice bagful the day before I left. I was dreaming happy dreams when I filled a plastic bag with leaves, leaves, and more leaves. By the next day I'd be winging my way home to Britain. For once, I didn't mind. I had my *friarielli*—a massive bag of it—and was ready to eat my fill. By the time my *friarielli* was eaten, I reasoned that I would be over the hump of missing Naples and ready for my next Italian adventure.

However, I was involved in an adventure already, though I didn't yet know it. While I and my traveling buddy, baking guru Rose Levy Beranbaum, happily ate lunch, my *friarielli* sat in the hotel room in its bag. As we set about walking the city and enjoying our last day there, as we went to dinner, as we inhaled the spirit of deliciousness, style, and Italian chic that is Napoli, my *friarielli* sat in its bag. And who knew what happens when *friarielli* sits in its bag?

Apparently everyone in Naples knew except me. When I returned to my hotel room, the elevator doors opened to the most ghastly smell imaginable. I thought the hotel was having a problem with the sewers or the garbage situation in Naples had taken a turn for the worse. I wondered whether the drains were clogged and spewing horrible stuff. Regardless, it was intolerable and smelled even worse the closer I got to my room. I opened the door and was unable to breathe—even an open window with the sea breeze from the bay did not help things.

I trotted down to the ever-so-elegant lobby. "Oh please," I said, irritated yet polite. "I can't stay in this room. The hotel must have a problem somewhere."

The clerk looked at me tolerantly, glancing from his colleagues to the maid, then back at me. He didn't quite know how to break it to me, though they had figured out the problem already. "Take me to your room," he said. "I can perhaps show you what the problem is."

I opened the door to a smell that was worse than ever. "I have nothing here that could smell bad; all I have is *friarielli*."

"Ah, Signora Spieler, the *friarielli*, it is so delicious and so healthful to eat, but something bad happens to it when it sits in a plastic bag." Somewhat astonished that anyone might be unaware of this, he continued, "Did you not know this?" (Years later, I think Rose is still laughing.)

Note: Another bitter green of Campania with no silly story such as mine is the tiny bitter brassica, *cima di rapa novantina*, a broccoli top harvested at only ninety days old.

HERBS (*ERBE*)

Rosemary grows wild on the hillsides, as does fragrant thyme. Sometimes you'll find sage, and the dried seeds of fennel are an important seasoning, along with hot pepper flakes. But the main herbs that you'll find supporting the dishes and giving them their identity are sweet basil, oregano, marjoram, mint, and flat leaf parsley. In season, borage abounds. Its pretty purple-blue flowers often decorate salads or are scattered on top of thick lentil soup.

Sweet basil usually is combined with tomatoes, especially for pasta or pizza. You know it's there, its sweet aroma unfettered by other herbs or spices. Oregano, usually used dried but sometimes fresh, is one of the iconic flavors of the south: a sprinkle over a tomato-slicked pizza lets you know it's there—and that you are there, and that the pizza (oh, the pizza) is there for you. It is great in pickled vegetables (*sott'olio*). Mint is used fresh, often in salads or in marinated dishes: fresh, sweet, perky. Eating it is a revelation—that's how fresh it tastes.

But what is always a surprise to visitors is how much flat leaf parsley is used. Who would think of parsley as being such a supporting actor in Naples's theater of cuisine? Yet flat-leaf parsley has so much fresh flavor, and the parsley grown in Campania is, like most things that grow there, extraordinary. People attempting to explain the intoxicating flavors there need only to look as far as parsley.

PEPPERS (PEPERONE)

Peperone papaccella Napoletana is a pepper uniquely Neapolitan. Large, round, ribbed, and squashed at the ends, it grows only in the area. They are traditionally eaten green, though they turn red or yellow when ripe and are harvested from June until the end of December.

In the past, *papaccella* primarily were preserved in vinegar. These days, they are also used whenever fresh peppers are used. They are a rediscovered food star. When pickled, however, they are sensational, especially when used in cooking: with potatoes and meat (bacon, pancetta, and pork), with salt cod or eel, or preserved in oil like eggplant. The pickles are good as part of an antipasto at any time of year. In winter, when country people butcher pigs and preserve their meat, they eat pickled peppers with fried liver and cooked pig's blood.

Peperonata Napoletana/Puparunata Napulitana (Braised Red and Yellow Peppers with Tomatoes)

Eat this as part of a vegetable antipasti, with grilled fish or steak, stuffed into a frittata, tossed with pasta and meatballs, or spoon onto a roll for a sandwich. They are so delicious, I could go on forever.

Peeling the peppers before cooking them with the other ingredients gives this dish its unique finesse. For its delicate character, the peppers are best peeled by parboiling, though roasting or grilling blisters the skin and is easier. However, the smoky aroma changes the dish, so my advice is to boil or bake them for this recipe. Even if all the skin is not loosened and removed, it gives a purer pepper flavor.

6 peppers, 3 each red and
  yellow
¼ cup extra virgin olive oil
3 cloves garlic, sliced
2 small or 1 medium-sized white
  onion, peeled and cut into thin
  wedges, strips, or slices
Salt to taste

1 cup canned, diced tomatoes in
  their juices or 2 cups diced fresh
  tomatoes
1–2 tablespoons capers or 2
  tablespoons caper berries, stems
  removed and berries sliced
1–2 tablespoons fresh oregano leaves,
  coarsely chopped

To peel the peppers, plunge them whole, with stems, into boiling water. Cover for thirty seconds to a minute; then turn them over and repeat. Remove peppers from the hot water and place in a bowl. Cover and cool.

When cool, remove stems and seeds. Using a paring knife, peel the skin from the flesh. Start peeling where the skin is blistered and pulled away from the flesh. It doesn't need to be perfect—a little skin may remain. Cut the peeled peppers into strips and set aside.

Heat the olive oil over medium heat until warm. Add the garlic and cook a moment, then add the onion and continue cooking a couple more minutes. When the onions are softened, add the peppers with a pinch of salt and continue to sauté, stirring for a minute or two.

Add the tomatoes, cover, and cook over medium-low heat for about twenty minutes. Add the capers and oregano, cook another ten minutes or so, covered, then taste for salt.

Although the Neapolitans fell in love with the tomato unreservedly early in its European arrival, they were less sure about the potato. Well, they were sure they didn't want to eat it. Since there was little demand, it was inexpensive. Since it was cheap, eating it became a sign of abject poverty.

In 1949 W. H. Auden wrote to Igor Stravinsky saying that the Neapolitans thought he was crazy because he ate potatoes not due to poverty but because he actually liked them.

Though *patatine*, French fries, are eaten happily, as are roasted potatoes with meat, most Campanian potato specialties disguise the spud by mashing it with cheese, ham, and butter for *o 'gattò* or by mixing it with flour for potato gnocchi. About half of the potatoes planted in Campania are new potatoes: small, tender, with thin skin and delicate flesh (especially the yellow-fleshed varieties). These are so tender and delicious in salads or roasted along with fish or meat.

Patate con Due Peperoni (Countryside Potatoes with Two Types of Peppers)

Serves 4 as a side dish

The crumbly, tender potato flesh blends deliciously with zesty garlic, olive oil, and two types of peppers, including some of the briny pickle-y sort. Napolenta Sonia Carbone described it to me, and I've been preparing it ever since. It pairs well with simple roasted or grilled meat.

1–1½ pounds creamy fleshed, waxy potatoes, whole and peeled

6–7 cloves garlic, thinly sliced or coarsely chopped

3–4 tablespoons extra virgin olive oil, or more as desired

3–5 mild pickled Italian peppers, preferably round cherry peppers, thinly sliced or chopped

1 roasted red pepper or 2 small red piquillo peppers, thinly sliced or coarsely chopped

Salt and pepper to taste

Boil the potatoes in lightly salted water until just tender; drain and keep warm.

Warm the garlic in the olive oil in a heavy frying pan until it is just fragrant and lightly colored, then add the peppers and heat through. They will smell divine!

Coarsely break up the potatoes into chunks with a fork, then pour the sizzling hot peppers over the potatoes and gently toss together. Serve immediately.

ZUCCHINI AND SQUASH

It's almost as if zucchini—as well as other squash—wants to grow in Campania, as it grows easily, lushly, and abundantly bathed by the hot dry sun. Since it is easy to grow, it is inexpensive to purchase and has long been considered food for the poor. During times of real poverty, zucchini might be all there was to eat, but it is so versatile that it contributed a huge number of recipes to *la cucina povera*.

All socioeconomic groups love zucchini these days: such a refreshing and tasty vegetable, and so versatile, too. It can be layered with cheese, shredded and tossed into pasta, sliced into a frittata, and simmered in soup (especially the *minestra di Pasqua* at Easter made with young zucchini). They are great grilled or fried and splashed with a little vinegar in a *scapece*. They also can be prepared *sott'olio*, as a pickle. There are always several types of zucchini dishes in the vegetable antipasto when it is in season.

If you grow them yourself, you have the bonus of *fiori di zucca* (see below), but also the stems and leaves, called *tenerume*. Add them to soups such as minestrone of vegetables and beans or cook with other vegetables in a sort of *ciambotta*.

Zucchine alla Scapece (Browned and Marinated Zucchini)

Sleek, browned slices of zucchini dressed with a hit of vinegar, garlic, hot pepper, and mint. Eat right away or make ahead. Either way, it is delectable, wonderful to fork up as a summer antipasto.

The word *scapece* is Neapolitan dialect, some say for the Latin *ex apicio* (the legendary cook Caelius Apricius, author of *De Re Coquinaria*, who is said to have prepared this vinegar seasoning for the first time), but others say it's an abbreviation of the Spanish word *escabeche*, meaning pickled, a culinary remnant from the days of Spanish rule. This makes sense, because it is eaten in various guises throughout Calabria and all of the south, including in Sicily, where sugar is added for a sweet-and-sour effect (a culinary souvenir from Arab inhabitants).

You want the slices thin and dry before frying. They are still delicious when limp, but crispness depends upon the moisture in the air and the vegetable itself. In Italy's south they are left for a few hours to dry on a tray (covered with a light cloth for insect protection) under the strong sun.

2½ pounds small to medium zucchini	2–3 tablespoons fresh mint leaves, chopped
Extra virgin olive oil for frying	Pinch or two of hot red pepper flakes
1–2 cloves garlic, sliced or chopped	Salt to taste
Wine vinegar to taste	

Zucchine alla Scapece (Browned and Marinated Zucchini) (*continued*)

Cut the zucchini into thin rounds (about ⅛-inch thick). If your zucchini are young and fresh, cut them and proceed. If they are a bit older and perhaps bitter, sprinkle them with salt and set aside for twenty minutes or so; then rinse, pat try, and proceed.

Heat the olive oil in a pan (preferably a nonstick pan); then brown the zucchini slices, taking care not to crowd the pan. You may need to do this in several batches so that the zucchini browns rather than wilts and gets soft. Toward the end of their browning, add the garlic.

Remove the zucchini from the pan, drain on paper, and then sprinkle with the vinegar (just a little bit, a few teaspoons at the most—you don't want to drown the zucchini). Add the mint leaves, red pepper flakes, and salt. Toss well and allow it to marinate for an hour or two. This may be prepared days ahead of time if desired and stored in the refrigerator.

Large, delicate, and the color of sunshine, *fiori di zucca*, or squash flowers, are as tasty to eat as the fruit. The most common way of cooking them is usually battered and fried; even more enticing is stuffing them with ricotta before frying. The crisp, light batter protects the gossamer texture of the flowers, and when you take a bite, it's all about the crunch of the delicate coating paired with the fresh, light vegetable (and hopefully creamy ricotta) inside.

Zucca lunga di Napoli (*cocozza zuccarina*), a big, long, green-skinned, orange-fleshed winter squash similar to Hubbard squash, is a particularly delicious pumpkin. They are large, sometimes weighing more than sixty pounds. The agricultural department says that squash has always been a part of the local culinary traditions, but since pumpkin eating was spread by the Jews from Sicily north throughout the rest of Europe after the Spanish expulsion, I credit the Jews. Regardless, this squash is a delicious, important part of local cuisine.

Thinly sliced, fried, and eaten with vinegar, garlic, chile, and parsley, they are divine; diced, they are marvelous in soups and minestrones; and thinly sliced and sautéed with garlic and chile flakes, they are delicious tossed into a spaghetti *aglio e olio*.

Its seeds are toasted, salted, and eaten after Sunday lunch or at any informal gathering.

Roadside Stands

When you see fruits and vegetables at a roadside stand, it's never a bad idea to stop. You'll get some great fruits and vegetables at a good price, hear a story, and likely come away with a recipe or two.

Maybe you're driving on the narrow, winding road between Amalfi and Vietri—a road that doesn't provide a lot of room to pull over to the side. But there, at a curve in the road, is a three-wheeled mini-truck (an Ape, pronounced ah-pay, meaning "bee"). A man stands next to the truck, which is piled high with the huge lemons and bright red tomatoes of the area. The man, browned from the sun, grew and picked them, and he is now standing in the sunshine on the road, overlooking the deep blue sea, selling them. They are, predictably, fragrant and delicious and beautiful.

There's a guardrail to protect you from the sheer drop, so why not turn back to the truck and start tasting tomatoes? The lemons are so good, you can eat them whole. I can't buy enough, and my husband—not the biggest tomato lover in the world (ditto for lemons)—wonders how we will get through so many. My inner Californian laughs at such an idea—I know that tomatoes for breakfast, lunch, and dinner a few days in a row is not a hardship, only a delight. The lemons will last until we reach home in the United Kingdom. The farmer smiles as I admire, munch, and purchase his tomatoes and lemons; then he tucks a few extras into the bags, and we head back onto that twisting, scary cliffside road.

Or perhaps it is autumn in Mondragone, a seaside town though a somewhat nondescript part of Caserta, where, up and down the not-too-picturesque main drag, people stand behind wooden boxes resting on folding tables or the tailgates of trucks. It's porcini, I'm told, picked themselves. I pay as they weigh some out for me.

And Campania-grown garlic is beautiful. It is fragrant and fresh, sweet and pungent, and smells and tastes of garlic without being offensively strong. It is simply extraordinary. I wrote this as I ate my way through two bouquets of garlic that I bought from a man on Via Pignasseca. It was during the terrible Lucifero heatwave in August 2017. The man with the garlic was so downtrodden. No one was buying his garlic. "It's hard work to grow," he said to me. He was almost crying. I bought two bunches just because. I didn't need garlic, but this guy needed to sell it and had worked hard to grow it. I wanted to see him a little happier with life. But when I opened a head and tasted a clove, it was I who was happier with life. Truly, it's the loveliest garlic: fragrant but not offensive, strong but not overpowering—garlic as the allium gods and goddesses meant it to be.

SELVATICI: **WILD THINGS**

Though a lesser part of modern Neapolitan *cucina*, wild things have traditionally been gathered and eaten for health, for the joy of the hunt, and also for the intense flavors concentrated in these uncultivated leaves. And they are free.

Yet, for many, the days of poverty are best forgotten—after all, look at all the wonderful foods we grow (and buy) now!—and interest in wild greens has diminished. But for others, especially the grandmothers and grandfathers, these wild things are necessary to digest, to protect, to gather the goodness from the earth.

Wild asparagus was beloved by Greeks as well as Romans. The best was said to grow on the volcanic island of Nisida in the gulf of Pozzuoli. Apicius recorded recipes for asparagus but doesn't specify whether it's wild or cultivated, so we are unsure whether it was being cultivated then, though he does instruct long boiling before saucing and seasoning. Ensuing centuries and rulers didn't appreciate asparagus as they did other vegetables. Perhaps the heat of the southern sun prevented its domestication? In any event, wild asparagus is cherished on the modern-day Neapolitan table but as a special dish, perhaps foraged by Uncle Peppe or Nonna.

Wild arugula tastes intense, like an entire bowlful concentrated into a few small, spindly leaves. Both wild and domestic arugula are important to Neapolitans. It is found tucked into sandwiches and garnishes almost everything, especially mozzarella. Arugula is easy to grow and reseeds itself until the cultivated little garden patch is full of arugula gone wild.

I've found wild asparagus in olive groves, wild fennel on country roads, and purslane on a tomato farm (the farmer considered them weeds!). Wild things grow here, there, everywhere: dandelion leaves, rosemary, sage, spinach, nettles, wild fennel, cactus, and arugula. The island of Capri is covered, in season, with wild marjoram, often used instead of fresh oregano. And beautiful borage, both wild and cultivated, with its cucumber-ish taste, is eaten sprinkled over lentil soup and salads and mixed into cod fritters.

Pasta and *cucina Napoletana* guru Giuseppe Di Martino tells of his uncle preparing arugula and purslane salad with great joy. "But the word for purslane in the original Parthenopean language is *pucchiacchella*, which, for Neapolitans, is considered rude and naughty and definitely not something you want to say loudly, especially in a mixed group or in public."

Old-time Napoletani remember purslane and wild arugula being sold together in bunches, in the streets, foraged from the countryside. A low growing, sprawling weed, purslane has small, juicy, paddle-shaped leaves and sturdy, often red-tinged stems growing from the middle of the plant. It also has the highest level of omega-3 fatty acids of any vegetable—almost as much as fish. In Sicily there is a *ferragosto* salad called *purciddona* similar to the Naples's *puchilla.*

But people stopped eating purslane after World War II, associating it with times of hunger, a wild plant eaten to survive. In the prosperity that followed the war, purslane fell out of favor, considered "poor people's food." There was no longer any need to eat "weeds."

However, a new generation, without negative associations, has become interested in many old/new foods. And so purslane became a chic little green again, served by modern restaurants redefining their cooking styles. Cookbook author Michele Scicolone told me that in the lovely little Amalfi Coast town of Praiano, she ate a salad of purslane and other wild greens alongside an assortment of fried tidbits. The chef said they were trying something new, which makes me realize that nothing is new, even though we might think it is.

To make the Neapolitan *puchilla,* toss together a bowlful of half purslane leaves and half young arugula (or more to taste). Remove the purslane paddles from the stems, and add a handful of chopped raw onion and thinly sliced spicy, crisp, fresh radishes. Dress with salt, olive oil, and a few drops of vinegar or lemon juice to taste.

Two other vegetables that grow wild in profusion in Campania are not eaten. The first is grape leaves; after much research, I have come to the conclusion that they are not used for cooking because there are so many other interesting leaves to eat. The other is cactus, which grows wild everywhere. Though everyone dotes on its fruit (*fico d'India*), they don't eat the green paddle-shaped cactus leaves so adored in Mexico. I asked around, but the consensus was that no one eats it. Then I opened Elizabeth Minchilli's wonderful blog, *Eating My Way through Italy* (also a book): a photo, taken on the island of Ponza (not far from Campania), showed a platter of *la parmigiana* made of cactus instead of eggplant; Elizabeth said it was delicious.

Funghi is Italian for fungus, also known as the wild mushrooms that most Italians look forward to searching for whenever weather conditions are just right. The mushroom varieties are numerous, as well as deeply delicious, but can be deadly. Each area of Italy has its own *funghi,* and Campania is no exception. Porcini—edible boletes—are by and large the most coveted, but there are more delicious mushrooms to gather.

The important thing to remember is that wild mushrooms need to be gathered *only* by those who know what to look for. If you are not an experienced mushroom gatherer, you *must* to hook up with someone who is. Never eat wild mushrooms without vetting them; the same goes for wild greens.

WATER

Because of Campania's volcanoes (live and defunct), the area is rich with hot springs and other varied water sources. Some are delicious, some strong and sulfurous, and most are considered healthful. Available in bottles is both Ferrarelle (light and delicately sparkling, from the now-extinct Roccamonfina volcano) and Lete (light and so refreshing). If I'm not having a beer with my street pizza, I'm having local water. The water from Terme Grand Telese is quite sulfurous but said to have great healing properties. Many other areas have abundant waters, such as Ischia, famous for its springs and spas.

FROM THE SEA

Sorrento and Massa Luberense host a type of prawn, the Parapendalo (*Pleisonika narval*), also known as Nassa shrimp. A pink shrimp with firm, sweet flesh, it is relatively common in the western Mediterranean. In the area it is served at its most delicate—that is, raw—and though tradition indicates a squirt of lemon, many say, "No, eat the flesh as it is—sweet and fresh." If sautéed, add just a little salt and pepper.

The Nassa shrimp lives in dark underwater caves, which makes it difficult to catch with nets, so fishermen use a traditional tool made of woven myrtle and rush. This device, called a creel, is large and round with a narrow entryway that makes it easy to trap the shellfish attracted by its bait. Creels are handmade by fishermen in winter, when fishing is impossible. Catching these shrimp is a difficult task, a local craft, and the creel delivers a smaller yield than other methods. As a result, new generations are not attracted to this traditional life.

To encourage this ancient technique, which is at the heart of many fishing villages and a great help in keeping the balance of sea life in check, the Punta Campanella Nature and Marine Reserve encourages the use of creels in the area. They are biodegradable, which is good for the ecology of the sea, and repairing them encourages comradery as fishermen sit around the harbor or beach, chatting while mending their creels. The creels definitely contribute to the revitalization of the fishing community.

The local Slow Food Convivium is creating a presidium to help support the local fishermen by acknowledging their role as "sea sentinel." An active group of coast fishermen helps to prevent illegal fishing.

Keeping fishing sustainable is a high priority for the good of the people, for the good of the sea and all of the creatures that live in it. Laws are made and broken (as they are the world over). The problem in Campania is not huge industrial fishing ships, as elsewhere, but the independent fishermen in unregistered boats who haul up from the sea whatever they wish, regardless of the situation. For instance, since 1988 it has been illegal to harvest sea dates (*datteri di mare*) because it destroys their habitat and depletes their numbers. Yet people fish for them and sell them. It's a shame.

The types of fish in an area define not only the cuisine but also the life of the locals. It is sad to accept that fish are disappearing; they have always been part of life. And when a species disappears, it upsets the ecology of the entire ocean. For example, the inundation of jellyfish all over the world: swimmers are stung, beaches are clogged with them, and it's getting worse. This is because their predators—bluefin tuna, for example—and their competitors for food are disappearing. The result is a population explosion.

The way to help is simply to pay attention to what fish you eat in Italy and in the rest of the world. There is no single fixed list of sea creatures to avoid; it changes as marine biologists learn more and as the sea changes. Online lists are updated continually; check Monterey Bay Aquarium and Slow Food websites for what is sustainable in Campania.

Linguine o Spaghetti alle Vongole (Pasta with Clams)

Serves 4

Pasta with clams is one of the most iconic dishes of Campania. When you visit Napoli, you'll find it everywhere, presented with great pride. The *vongole veracce*, local clams, really are fantastic—and that Neapolitan spaghetti or linguine—mamma mia!

You can cook this with mussels instead of clams, a variety of seafood in place of clams, or with a portion or two of cooked beans—beans and seafood are a delicious local combination, especially with pasta. Instead of spaghetti, enjoy the clam sauce with *paccheri* or *calamarata*, the big fat tube pasta so beloved in Naples.

5 cloves garlic, 2 cut in half, 2 thinly sliced, and 1 finely chopped or grated
¼–⅓ cup olive oil
Pinch red chile pepper flakes, if desired

1 pound largish clams
1 pound small clams (known as *verace* in Naples; if small clams are not available, use double the large clams or substitute mussels)
Salt and pepper to taste

Linguine o Spaghetti alle Vongole (Pasta with Clams) (*continued*)

2 pints grape or cherry tomatoes (in Napoli it would be the tiny *piennolo* or another small, sweet tomato)
2 tablespoons olive oil
⅓ cup dry white wine
1 pound linguine or spaghetti
Several tablespoons chopped flat-leaf parsley

Cut one pint of tomatoes into halves and leave the rest whole.

Warm the two sliced garlic cloves in about half the olive oil with a pinch of red pepper flakes, if desired. When the garlic begins to smell fragrant, add the clams (or the clams and mussels). Cover and cook over a medium heat for about ten minutes or until the shells open. Discard unopened clams or mussels.

In a saucepan, heat the halved garlic cloves and red pepper flakes in the remaining olive oil until fragrant and lightly sizzling. Add the tomatoes, white wine, and salt, and cook over medium-high heat until the tomatoes become thick and sauce-like—about fifteen minutes. Set aside and keep warm.

Meanwhile, bring a large pot of salted water to the boil and cook the linguine or spaghetti until just short of al dente.

Drain, reserving a cup or so of the pasta cooking water.

Add the linguine or spaghetti to the clams/mussels and their liquid in the pan. Over medium heat, finish cooking the pasta, adding a little of the cooking water as you go, as well as the chopped/grated garlic, salt and pepper, and a drizzle of olive oil.

Toss the cooked tomatoes with the spaghetti and clams. Sprinkle generously with parsley and serve.

Whole roasted branzino (also known as *spigola* or European sea bass) is light, yet savory, with a delicate texture. A little garlic and parsley is good, a little salt and tomatoes, a drizzle of olive oil, but not so much that it distracts from this exquisite fish. Stuffing it with lemon is too wonderful.

To roast a whole branzino, have it gutted and scaled with the head and tail attached. Your fish should weigh between one and one-and-a-half pounds. Wash it, pat it dry, and place it on a baking sheet. Heat the oven to 475°F. Chop a few cloves of garlic with a handful of flat leaf parsley and a big pinch of salt. Rub it into the cavity of the fish; then add a single layer of sliced lemon to fill its insides. Arrange leftover lemon slices on the baking sheet and scatter with tomatoes. Sprinkle fish and tomatoes with a pinch of fresh or dried oregano, and then lavish it with olive oil. Place the fish in the hot oven to roast for fifteen to twenty minutes. Cut the cooked fillets from the bones before serving.

4

A Napoli si Mangia Così

The Iconic Products of Naples— Cheeses, Wines, Oils

A *Napoli si mangia così* is a Neapolitan proverb that translates to "in Naples we eat like this."

What it means is this: "We turn the beautiful local milk into cheese, grapes into wine, olives into oil." Also, "We appreciate our local foods, we eat with joy, this is who we are."

Where else exists a term describing loyalty to local products? In Napoli, it is *campanilisimo*. There's even a term describing loyalty to local cheeses: *formaggisimo*.

Campania is emphatically locavore; after all, what grows there is so full of flavor, why would they want to eat anything else? There is one huge exception: coffee.

COFFEE

Like so many foods (and people and ideas) that come from afar, in Napoli coffee is transformed. When the raw (green) coffee beans arrive in Campania, you might say they go native: roasted deliciously dark, prepared short and strong. Of the foods shaped by local character, let's start with coffee—because, after all, that is how most of Napoli starts (and often ends) the day.

Napoli . . . dove il caffè è una cultura: Naples, where coffee is a culture, proclaims the package of celebrated local coffee roasters, Passalacqua. Around the world, people love coffee, but in Napoli it is not just a drink—it is a way of life. Some say that Neapolitan coffee culture has developed so many distinctive qualities, rituals, and traditions that it is even more diverse and complicated than its pasta!

Italians are said to drink three or four cups of coffee a day, but who can count how many cups Neapolitans drink? From the early morning foamy cappuccino, *caffè latte*, or macchiato, through the endless stream of tiny espressos that follow throughout the day. I sometimes ask myself: When are Neapolitans *not* drinking coffee?

Having a coffee in Naples has a social element to it, no matter the time of day or night. Whether with a friend or family, chatting to the barista, or alone, there's a pleasant, solitary well-being that is, in a strange way, a sociable moment.

Neapolitans are adamant about how to drink coffee: which type at what time. It's not a question of right or wrong from a vantage point of cultural arrogance or fashionability; rather, it's a way of looking out for those who might not know what is healthy and what is not. (Healthy according to local beliefs, which is everything if you are local and mystifying if you are not.)

For instance, Neapolitans drink milky coffee—cappuccino or *caffè latte*—only in the morning—but that's it until the next day. Never order a cappuccino after lunch or dinner when asked whether you'd like coffee—and don't even *think* of ordering one *before* a meal. The waiter will not sneer at you or look down his nose; most likely, he will just refuse to serve it to you. Not because it is uncool or un-Neapolitan, but simply because he considers it *dangerous* (to the stomach). As for drinking a cappuccino or other coffee before or during a meal (are you insane?), I don't recommend it.

When my British husband, who is dedicated to his milky coffees and doesn't drink wine, tried to order a pre-lunch cappuccino, the waiter nearly burst into tears, so worried was he about my husband's digestive health: "It's not healthy. He will not digest his meal. He will have a stomachache." We called a Neapolitan friend to intervene and explain that he would be okay: "He is British and used to this. We will take full responsibility for his safety."

Finally the cappuccino appeared, carried by a very worried but resigned waiter. It was beautiful and milky, and my husband sipped it happily. The poor waiter was in a nervous state throughout the meal, however, glancing surreptitiously at my husband out of the corner of his eye for any worrying signs. "I was ready," the waiter told me later. "The hospital is just around the corner."

Coffee beans come from a plant belonging to the genus *Coffea* of the Rubisceae plant family. Italy's coffee culture dates back to the sixteenth century, when the first beans arrived in Venice on one of the trading ships from in the Middle East, likely originating in what is now Ethiopia (or perhaps Yemen) when a goatherd noticed his animals were particularly frisky after eating specific berries.

Venice's Caffè Florian was Italy's first cafe, but soon Milano and Trieste were under the spell of coffee, too, and Naples was not far behind, catching coffee fever by the late 1700s. A widely read pamphlet authored by a gastronome named Pietro Corrado helped spread the word, including in his booklet a song praising coffee as the drink of hospitality, friendship, and good wishes.

When Naples met coffee, it was love at first bean, and soon Naples was the coffee capital of the south. King Ferdinand IV's wife, Maria Carolina of Austria, queen of Naples and Sicily, is said to have served coffee at her lively, culture-rich royal court gatherings, circa 1768. Soon dedicated coffee-drinking establishments began popping up, places for highbrows, aristocrats, and intelligentsia to meet and discuss ideas.

Throughout the troubles of the 1800s into the twentieth century, drinking coffee was soothing, invigorating, reviving. For those who couldn't go to *caffes* to drink, families roasted their own beans on the street just outside their front doors over open fires; sometimes they sold coffee as well.

It is generally agreed that espresso was born in Naples thanks to the invention of a steam-driven coffee-making machine. Some disagree, claiming that espresso was invented in Torino (Turin) in 1884, since that was where the first machine was patented. The steam-driven coffee machine made the grand *caffè* possible.

Espresso is not a particular coffee bean or type of roast, but the brewing method to make a strong coffee very fast with very hot water forced through the grounds at high pressure. This is the Neapolitan espresso: dark, fragrant, with that bitter edge, its foam so creamy and dense it almost tastes sweet. To your barista, it is his or her craft, art, reason for being.

A Neapolitan espresso starts as a *ristretto*—the first expression of steam through the beans resulting in a strong extract of coffee pleasure, stronger than in the rest of Italy. It has a creamy texture and low acidity and is topped with its own foam.

Your cup will be hot; often they are kept submerged in boiling water when not in use. The belief is that the heat and cleanliness let the flavor of the coffee come through more clearly. I keep mentioning cleanliness: it's not germaphobia, but rather the aromatic volatile oils from the coffee beans, which can taste rancid if they are not washed away between brewing.

The menu is as follows: Espresso is a short shot freshly made. Cappuccino consists of espresso with frothed, steamed milk, its name referring to the creamy brown color of the drink, the same as the robes of Cappuchin monks. *Macchiate* means "stained," just a tiny splash of milk or foam on top of an espresso, and a *caffè latte* is an espresso with lots of hot milk. It is never abbreviated as "latte," because latte means milk; order one, and that's what you'll get: a glass of milk.

To order a coffee with a shot of alcohol added, order *caffè corretto*, or "corrected coffee." Although Neapolitan coffee is strong, the process of brewing it results in a lower caffeine level.

The *caffè* life may have begun among those of "high society," but, Naples being Naples, it soon spread throughout all classes. Sit, sip, eat rich pastries, and engage in the Neapolitan sport of people watching. You can stand at the bar, too. There's always someone to watch (and interact with).

The history of Naples's *caffè* bars—the small, family-run, ever quirky, warm-hearted places where you know you'll get a wonderful coffee (and who knows what else)—is surprisingly modern. Until around the late 1920s and early 1930s, the only coffeehouses were grand cafés, Gambrinus being the most important. The grand cafés were opulent and luxurious, with chandeliers, huge mirrors, comfortable tables and chairs, and formally dressed waiters. The cafés offered an island of gentile peace in the midst of the busy city, a place where businessmen could discuss finances and intellectuals could discuss philosophy and the state of the world while indulging in coffee and pastries. Of course, such establishments were by their nature frequented only by those who were well off. Who else had either the time or the money?

After World War II, as life returned to normal, milk and dairy shops, which didn't have a lot to sell, began making coffee and serving drinks. Eventually they turned into local *caffè* bars, as small and simple as the grand cafes were large and luxurious. Many *caffè* bars added sandwiches, granita, and other dishes to their coffee and pastries. Now the *caffè* was no longer a preserve of the aristocracy; all classes could enjoy. Many of these local *caffes* are still family run, in the same location for decades. This is the coffee-drinking life of Napoli, rooted in the 1950s and 1960s.

And what a coffee-drinking life it is. You may dash into a *caffè* bar and down a short, sharp shot of espresso *al volo*, meaning that you drink it quickly, standing up. As that strong dark coffee enters your system, it brings a brief few moments of pure pleasure and propels you into the rest of your day.

Wherever you take coffee, you'll be served a glass of water alongside the *tazzina* (a tiny cup used for espresso). Drink it before your coffee—it is meant to clear your palate for the coffee pleasure to come. Drinking the water afterward could worry the barista that perhaps the coffee wasn't good, so you are rinsing your mouth to be rid of the taste.

Oh, and takeout? Here it doesn't mean a big cardboard cup full of coffee to carry away; it means someone at the *caffè* runs to your business or home with a tray filled with coffees. You'll see them scurrying about, darting through chaotic traffic without spilling a drop.

Barmen may be friendly or severe, some even may be fatherly, but it is a serious profession, not something baristas do on the side until they get their big break in films or publishing. Indeed, the role of a barman/barista is an important one in a Neapolitan's life. The barista knows what you like—whether it is to drink quietly or to engage in conversation—and is someone you trust.

The basics of espresso are simple, but the signature drinks express the artistry of the barista. Neapolitans like their espresso sweet, and traditionally sugar may be added by the barista. If you want it unsweetened, just request it. (Some bars, of course, serve it unsweetened.)

Ending a meal without a coffee? Why would you want to, when the coffee helps digest, prolongs that feeling of satiated bliss, and recharges you for wherever you are headed next?

Neapolitans are very exacting about their coffee. The blend of beans—called *miscela*—gives each *caffè* (and home) its coffee's unique character. Although the rest of Italy prefers arabica, Neapolitans prefer robusta, which is cheaper, has more body, and is more bitter (and about 50 percent more caffeine). A classic Neapolitan espresso combines different types of both beans, to the barista's taste.

The degree of roasting is crucial: How dark do you desire? Neapolitans like their beans dark but not to the point of being oily and nearly black. Neapolitans refer to the most important aspects of a wonderful coffee as the "four Ms," which refers to the *miscela* (blend), *macchina* (coffee machine), *macinatura* (the grind, the grinder, and its state of cleanliness), and *mano* ("hand," referring to the barista's skill). Sometimes the four Ms become the *five* Ms by separating the grinder from its state of cleanliness, thus making two categories out of one. Many baristas adjust their grind according to the daily temperature and humidity.

In America, coffee styles change constantly: dark roast coffees give way to a new wave of lighter roasts; the milk is self-serve, with varying fat levels, or even made from nuts, oats, or soy. But novelty for its own sake grows old fast; there is always the new next big thing. This makes me appreciate the sincerity of Napoli's coffee culture even more; one of the great comforts of *caffè* life is its security, predictability, comfort, and sense of belonging.

In Napoli, the aim is to produce good, solid espresso honed by years of dedication and attention. Popularity comes not from the number of tweets or Instagram posts, but rather from the generations of customers devoted to drinking delicious coffee. When I leave Naples, I often take coffee beans home, but even with a Neapolitan coffeepot, it's just not the same. I think it needs the local water.

The hourglass-shaped Moka stovetop espresso maker is the iconic symbol of home coffee throughout Italy; indeed, what home is without one? No couple enters matrimony without one. Invented by Francese Morize in 1819, then redesigned by Alfonso Bialetti in 1933, the little pot is fabulously designed, making a strong, concentrated espresso. Alfonso's son, Renato, redesigned and marketed the Moka into a symbol of Italian coffee worldwide. When Renato Bialetti died at age ninety-three, his three children honored him by placing his ashes in a large replica of the coffeepot and burying it.

Whereas nearly every household in Italy has a Moka pot, these days the Napoletana *caffettieres* are found only in Naples. Called *cuccuma* and also known as La Napoletana, it is the most recognizable symbol of Naples' coffee-making life.

Some say it was invented in Naples in the seventeenth century, modeled after an earlier coffeepot invented by the French Archbishop Jean-Baptiste de Belloy. The *cuccuma* was once used throughout Italy but was overtaken by the Moka, which is quicker and easier. When the Moka came on the scene promising espresso at home just like in *il caffè bar*, it was an Italian's dream come true.

In Napoli, though, the *cuccuma* has regained favor over the Moka, not only for its coffee but also for its iconic design. Southern Italian Riccardo Dalis re-created the classic design for Alessi, starting research in 1979 and going into production in 1987. Since then, its modernist beauty has earned international admiration.

Unlike the Moka espresso pot, which uses steam, the Napoletana uses gravity. The *cuccuma* produces coffee that is smooth, rich, and beautiful, somewhere between an espresso and drip. (I must confess that I have been known to wake up in the morning, singing to myself about "my little cuccumella." I also pack it in my suitcase for travel.)

Naples is a great place to buy coffee miscellany because it is so important to Neapolitans: long shelves are lined with a zillion sizes and shapes of Mokas and *cuccumas*, roasting pans, and grinders. Sometimes a *cuccuma* will have a tiny figurine of Pulcinella on top or a red *corno* on the spout (the red chile lookalike is said to scare away the evil eye). I bought my simple *cuccuma* at Pignasecca Market. It was the cheapest I could find and makes beautiful coffee.

Making coffee in a *cuccuma* demands a bit more attention than either filter or Moka pot espresso. It uses a finer grind than the Moka—said to facilitate more aroma and full-bodied flavor—and it demands its ritual. The more often you make it, the better you get at it, and the better the coffee becomes.

Looking like a tall, rather narrow cylinder with a handle and spout, the *cuccuma* consists of three parts: a bottom, which you fill with water; a middle filter, which is where you spoon the ground coffee; and an upside-down pot with spout on top.

You fill the bottom (which becomes the top when you flip it over) with water, place the filter inside and spoon in coffee grounds, and twist on its cap. Next, place the part with the spout on top, upside down, then the whole thing on the stove.

Don't turn the heat up high—keep it low to medium. Keep the handle away from the flames (it can melt). When the water boils, steam comes out of the tiny hole in the bottom, and it is ready to flip. It doesn't take long, depending on the size of the pot. You get used to your own pot.

Taking care, and using oven mitts, remove the pot from the heat. Grab both handles, using both hands to keep the pot together, and flip it over. Now the hot water will work its way down through the coffee grounds.

The pin-sized hole that releases steam and lets you know when to turn sometimes spouts hot water when flipping, so take care to avoid getting scalded or burned. Sometimes the *cuccuma* needs a little tap (or a slightly harder smack) against a hard surface to start the flow of water. If it is flowing well, it doesn't need it.

Now the magic happens: Hot water filters through the coffee grounds (and it takes longer than you would think; each *cuccuma* is different and brewing time varies according to size). As the water passes through, it trickles into the pot, the part with the spout. Once the water has dripped through, the pot is served at the table with the spout upward, ready to pour. A small cone called a *cuppetiello* is often used to cover the spout while it is brewing. It is said to hold in the coffee's aroma. Though some feel that exposing the grounds to the intense heat of the stove results in a bitter coffee, I personally prefer it this way.

Until the 1970s, it was a joyful tradition to end the big Sunday family meal with coffee made using a huge *cuccuma*, which could serve ten or twelve people. Nothing eases digestion more than a strong (albeit tiny) cup of *caffè Napoletano*. The joy of its arrival reminds me of a friend's comment: "It comforts us from our sadness that the meal is ending." A Neapolitan coffee after a meal gives that feeling of happiness despite the tragedy of the meal's end.

Inviting someone for a coffee homemade in the Napoletana is a gesture of caring. When author Elena Ferrante has a character offer to make coffee in her Napoletana for another character, you can feel the tenderness. You think (or at least I did), "This person is so human—she is trying her best to be kind."

Naples used to have hundreds coffee roasters, small and big, artisanal or nearly so, each with a clientele so devoted that it can veer on religious-like veneration. Most of the coffee roasters have moved out of the city of Naples to the Sorrento Coast and beyond. A number of years ago I visited Caffen Coffee Roasters, and as the beans were roasting in constant motion, being turned gently over for just the right amount of heat, I thought that nothing had ever smelled so good.

Some *caffès* do their own roasting—though less and less these days—and some Neapolitans prefer roasting their beans at home. In the not-so-distant past, most coffee beans for home use were bought raw, green, then roasted and ground at home. An elderly friend remembers the families in his area roasting the beans outside the kitchen door in the street. Some still roast their own beans; it is another way of making the coffee your own.

The barman might ask whether you want your coffee Neapolitan style, meaning short, strong, and sweet. (I say "barman," but it could be either man or woman. The non-gender-specific "barista" is used, too, a word coined not by hipsters in the trendy cafes of Brooklyn but in Italy during Mussolini's reign of facism.) Napoli *caffes* often have their own secret formulas for *zucchero-crema* or *cremina di caffè*, a mixture of sugar and espresso used to sweeten and give body to their espresso drinks. Even if you don't ordinarily take sugar in your coffee (I don't), give it a try. So delicious! But a bit bitter without the sugar.

Many *caffes* have signs announcing that sugar is added unless patrons specifically request no sugar (without sugar is *senza zucchero*, or you could say *amaro*, meaning bitter). And yet rules are made to be broken. As a Napoletana expressed when we were drinking our coffees, "Sweet coffee is delicious, and it leaves you with the taste of sweet. Without sugar it is very bitter, but it leaves you with the taste of coffee." She downed her little cupful without the sugar. "I like to take with me the flavor of coffee," she said before we went our separate ways.

Maybe baristas in Rome or Milan make works of art in the foam of a cappuccino, trailing dark espresso into the creamy milk to create paintings, but in Napoli? Neapolitans don't have the patience unless it is important to the flavor. A dusting of cocoa is about as fancy as it gets, though artistic drizzles of chocolate syrup are becoming popular: hearts, flowers, something simple. It all comes down to this question: Is it delicious?

Naples does have a tradition of extravagant, nearly baroque coffee drinks involving whipped cream, syrups, and chocolate; each *caffè* has its own version of a "house special." A little gaudy, a bit crazy, rich and excessive, perhaps involving hazelnut paste or chocolate syrup, and whipped cream? More restrained, sensible even, is *caffè affogato*, espresso poured over a scoop of ice cream: cool, warm, melty, it is dessert and coffee in one little cup.

On hot days a frozen *shakerato* is almost a necessity. Somewhere between an iced coffee and a granita, it is so invigorating: an icy glass of sweet and bitter with a little jolt of caffeine. I first sipped it in Benevento, so to me it tastes of Campania: the heat of a Naples afternoon, the barman's serious face and caring manner while serving this clearly necessary treat. When asked whether you would like whipped cream with it, you probably do.

Here are a few places to start your coffee exploration. A few descriptions, because there is an endless number and variety of *caffes* and *caffè* bars throughout the area, and you'll probably want to visit them all. Eventually.

Gran Caffè Gambrinus is the most famous of the historical literary *caffes* in Napoli. It is located next to the grand Piazza del Plebescito. Founded in 1860, Caffè Gambrinus immediately became the gathering place for the era's high society. On New Year's Day, it's traditional for the president of the Republic to go there for coffee.

Gambrinus's coffee respects the tradition of Neapolitan *caffè*: hot and dark and dense, and their pastries are sumptuous. I know this because when interviewing this generation's owner, he spread out an array of pastries and, seated in that elegant room under the painted ceilings, urged me to taste this, encouraged me to taste that. It felt beautiful and joyous rather than greedy (but who am I kidding?).

Among many others, Hemingway and Neruda were regulars at Gambrinus. I was once told that Oscar Wilde had worked as a waiter; I am not sure. Was his Italian good enough? (Maybe; he did spend time in Capri.) Or did he just hang out there, as so many in the *caffè*'s illustrious past have done?

Gambrinus is also the *caffè* where *caffè sospeso* originated.

Caffè Sospeso: Random Acts of Coffee

Despite its reputation as a rough, dangerous city, Naples has a huge heart. For instance, *caffè sospeso*. Born in Caffè Gambrinus during the war years (though some say postwar years), *caffè sospeso* was a way of expressing kindness.

No one could bear the idea of a fellow citizen unable to afford a cup of coffee. There was little to eat and people felt that at least coffee could warm you up, boost your spirits, energize you (and nourish you with a little sugar). And, being Neapolitan, how could a person go on without a coffee? It would be too cruel.

And so a practice came into being: One person pays for two coffees, drinks one, and the other is a *caffè sospeso* ("suspended coffee"). When someone else comes in without enough money for a coffee, whenever that may be, he or she asks the waiter, "Do you have a *sospeso* for me?" The waiter checks the list, and hopefully there's one left, and everyone is happy. (If you wish to do this yourself, when you order your coffee, ask for a second one to be put on the *sospeso* list.)

For a long time, the custom was dying out, but in recent years it has become popular again in many traditional coffee bars, especially in the old center. The tradition of *sospeso* has extended even to gelato, especially for children of poverty-stricken immigrants when the weather is hot. What Neapolitan could bear the thought of a child going without a summer gelato?

Down the street, not far from Gambrinus, is Il Vero Bar del Professore (across from a beautiful fountain where brides and grooms often go for wedding photos). It is one of Naples's legendary *caffes*: historical, full of life, and famous for its hazelnut coffee called *Nocciolato*, which combines dark espresso with sweetened whipped coffee and a hazelnut and chocolate paste. (There is a video of it on their Facebook page. I dare you to watch it and not long for one.)

La Caffettiera is the name of a coffee maker as well as this *caffè*, which has a charming collection of coffee makers. It specializes in coffee made in different types of *caffetieras*—Moka, machine espresso, filter, and *cuccuma*—and a choice of coffee blends. If you drink a *cuccuma* coffee there, you are given a small scroll celebrating the writer De Filippo's comments about coffee. It's a tribute to Neapolitan culture. La Caffettiera also offers good cocktails if you're all coffee-ed out, as well as sweet and savory nibbles. *Caffè sospeso* is alive and well there.

The name "Mexico" has long been a designated label for bars such as Bar Mexico, which use the renowned Neapolitan coffee brand Passalacqua, proudly keeping alive the Neapolitan coffee-roasting tradition. These days, many—maybe even most—*caffes* use Passalacqua, which is really okay because it's delicious.

Though all Bar Mexicos are different—some tiny, some large—I have a soft spot in my heart for the one across the street from Piazza Dante opposite the underground station. It has been serving excellent expresso since 1948 (or so the sign reads). Here, everything is traditional: coffee cups are kept in boiling water, coffee is served with sugar, and baristas are both serious and kind. *Caffè con panna* (hot coffee with whipped cream) is luxurious, and its icy *shakerato*, *caffè del nonno* (basically a *shakerato* with chocolate and hazelnut syrups, whipped cream, etc.), *caffè marocchino* (a mini cappuccino sprinkled with cocoa), and *macchiate* (espresso with foam on top or with a small amount of steamed milk) are all delicious.

Pay the cashier first and he or she will give you a colored paper ticket with your order to give to the bar. They also sell tins of coffee to take home, which I recommend. When I get to the end of the tin at home, I usually ask myself, "Why didn't I buy two?" At the register, a small coffee cup collects the "suspended" tickets for *caffè sospeso*.

Scaturchio is a landmark among Naples's historical coffeehouses and bakeries. Located amid the historical center facing the San Domenico church, the bakery is small and almost always crowded. (There is a handful of branches around the city.) Even if you are not having pastry, you must go inside and sniff the sweet air. Scaturchio is said to serve the best *sfogliatelle* in Naples, as well as babas (including a big one shaped like Vesuvio). You're sitting down for this one—across the way are a few tables set outside on the square.

Caffè Nilo, not far from Scaturchio, is named after an ancient statue near the *caffè* that represents the Nile River. It's easy to miss the entrance, so if you can't find it, look closer. The espresso at Caffè Nilo is *molto* Napoletano and *caffè sospeso* is there for partaking, but its true claim to fame is its Neapolitan obsession with football (soccer in the United States, *calcio* in Italian) and Argentinian Diego Armando Maradona. The bar is a de facto shrine to Maradona, its walls and surfaces covered with memorabilia, including a lock of hair said to be from his head.

Caffetteria Etoile is famous in the Pianura *quartiere* of Naples as a *caffè* as well as a *pasticceria* (bakery) and *rosticceria* (spit-roasted chicken and meats). It's a nice place to hang out over a juicy morsel or two of gossip. If you've had enough coffee, they have good cocktails/*aperitivi*.

Near the Central Station is the ordinary-looking Caffetteria Dolce Sosta, which offers that lovely sweet crema foam and an ever-so-pleasant staff. Just down the street is the pizzeria "Da Michele." After devouring that luscious Margherita, your espresso is just a short walk away.

Palazzo Venezia is an old palace on the edge of Spaccanapoli with a shady, secluded, lush green garden. Part museum, it is also part *caffè*, where one can mull the idiosyncrasies of life over coffee (or vino). Down the coast en route to Sorrento is Gran Caffè Napoli 1850 in Castellammare di Stabia. Recently reinvigorated, this elegant *caffè*/bar/restaurant offers a selection of the most beautiful, utterly irresistible pastries.

Wherever you are, wander the streets to find your own, new-old favorite.

Of Saints and Football

Of the more than fifty patron saints of Napoli, ex–soccer star Diego Maradona is among its most revered. Playing for Napoli in the late 1980s, this tough kid from the slums of Buenos Aires resonated in the hearts of Neapolitans. They treated him as their savior, and he did indeed lead Napoli to its shocking wins in the championships in 1987 and 1990. No team from the south of Italy had ever won a league title before. He upended the north's domination, an intensely emotional issue that is often played out on the soccer pitch. Maradona took the championship from the north and gave it to Napoli, and the people loved him.

Neapolitans took Maradona into their football-loving souls. He became their own, and when he left Napoli, they retired his number 10 soccer jersey. Throughout the city, streets are still scattered with painted murals and votive shrines dedicated to Maradona as if he were a saint. There, in Spaccanapoli, is a wall mural; there, on that motorcycle, a decal. He's still there, at least in image, everywhere. On his occasional visits, there is as much excitement as a visit from the pope.

PRESERVED FISH

Along the long, winding coastline of coves, beaches, and villages perched by the sea, fresh fish is a mainstay of the diet. Tiny boats come and go from the docks, and fish is fresh, maybe even affordable.

It is therefore surprising that preserved fish is so popular. Salt cod, smoked fish, tuna preserved in olive oil, dried, salted fish eggs pressed into a sausage (*bottarga*) and thinly sliced or grated over salad or pasta—these are all delicacies of Campania. The art of preserving fish originated at a time when there was no refrigeration and transportation was slow. The only way the inland areas of Campania could eat fish was if it was preserved. But preserved fish is so delicious! Necessity became tradition, and tradition became culinary love.

There are few places where preserving fish is not only an art but also the reason for a community's existence. Cetara, a beautiful, tiny town not much more than a village, is such a place. So intertwined throughout history with fishing, its name is said to have come from an ancient word for tuna. Tuna is still preserved there, but the main claim to fame these days is the anchovy sauce: *colatura di alici*. Evolving from the ancient Roman *garum*, it is made by layering anchovies and salt in a big vat, weighing them with a heavy object, and collecting the tasty *colatura* as it drains from a spout at the bottom. Nettuno is the only company still making *colatura di alici* in the center of Cetara.

Visiting the small *colatura* workshop is possibly the smelliest thing I can think of doing, and yet it is amazing. Little boats sail right up to the back of the shop and unload their haul of the silvery fish, flipping about and catching the sun's reflection. Then the real work gets under way, ending with the magnificent sauce.

When you taste *colatura*—only a tiny amount is needed—in a dish, it is delicate with a big umami hit from the amino acids. It's delicious on pasta, mozzarella, cucumber salad, and especially good added to anchovy sauces, such as *pesto alla Cetara*. You might not even know it's there, only that the dish tastes extraordinarily savory.

Salted anchovies are another delicacy of the area, and if you've ever eaten salted anchovies, I don't need to tell you what to do with them. Grab a hunk of bread, pour some olive oil, maybe slice a little bit of onion, and bite into a tomato. And, of course, mozzarella is a perfect partner for salty anchovies, in a pizza or on a plate.

Salt cod, known locally as *baccalà*, is a beloved Neapolitan food, dating from the time when salting was one of the only methods of preserving fish. These days, *stoccafisso* is very popular as well, though it is a different fish (stockfish), uses a different method of drying (not salted), and is fished for and prepared in northern Europe. Over the years *stoccafisso* has become as adored as *baccalà* is.

Even when fresh cod is available, salt cod is a treat: stewed in tomatoes, lightly battered and fried resting atop a bed of arugula, and, for many, Christmas Eve wouldn't be right without salt cod cooked with olives, capers, and tomatoes. It is the texture of salt cod that distinguishes it from fresh. Salt cod is milder but intensifies through the drying process. It is surprisingly un-fishy, and its texture is firmer than fresh. Salt cod must be soaked a long time to rehydrate—at least twenty-four hours for *baccalà*, perhaps forty-eight for *stoccafisso*—then it can be cooked as desired or eaten raw, much like sashimi.

OLIVES

The olive tree—*Olea Europaea*—is so ancient that no one really knows when it first sprouted, though some speculate that it likely originated in the area between the Pamirs, Armenian plateau, and Turkestan. It was first cultivated around 6000 BCE.

Greek mythology attributes its creation to the goddess of wisdom, Athena. Competing with the god Poseidon in an effort to become the patron deity of Athens, the goddess created an olive tree as a gift for the city.

In the days of the Egyptian pharaohs, Ramses III planted olive trees around the town of Heliopolis (now part of Cairo) to provide oil for the lamps in the temples of Ra. Cured olives were often left in the tombs of pharaohs as food for their afterlife; olive oil was at various times used to preserve mummies.

Both the Old Testament and the Koran mention that olive oil should anoint the heads of newborns. The Jewish festival of Chanukah commemorates the rededication of the war-torn, desecrated Temple of Jerusalem. There was enough oil to keep the eternal light burning for one day; it would be eight days before the new oil arrived. But the oil continued burning for eight days until more oil arrived and the Temple was reconsecrated. This miracle is commemorated each year on the twenty-fifth day of Kislev (according to the Jewish calendar).

It is generally believed that Phoenician traders spread olive trees throughout the Mediterranean. Others say no, it was the Greeks during Magna Grecia, or perhaps the Romans, who brought the olive tree to Campania. What is agreed, however, is that the Romans contributed to its cultivation in Campania by supporting and subsidizing its cultivation and pressing.

Don't think they did this out of benevolence, however, or because olives were a mainstay in the Roman diet. Olives were an important commodity for commerce, so Rome's prosperity depended on them. In museums you can view ancient ships, their shelves holding amphoras of oil to be shipped to the far reaches of the empire,

including England. Cured olives were exported as well as eaten locally as an antipasto; when the ruins of Pompeii were unearthed, archeologists found crocks of
preserved olives.

By the time Rome fell, the olive tree was firmly attached to the soil and the culture of Neapolitan lives (as with much of Italy). But like grapes (and their wine—
until fairly recently), olive oil was part of the culture but not of artisanal quality
and therefore underappreciated. For centuries, people ate the olive oil and drank the
wine without giving it much thought. "It grows, we press, it's part of our culture"
seemed to be the dominant ethos.

Then, after World War II, the popularity of olive oil declined. Now that people
were no longer starving and food was becoming more readily available, surely the
more scientific modern foods were better? The Neapolitan diet of vegetables, pasta,
pizza, fish, and eggs, all lavished with olive oil, was considered unhealthy—margarine and seed oils (extracted chemically) were recommended instead. And meat.

In the 1950s, the epidemiologist Ancel Keys discovered the nutritional value of
the Mediterranean diet in work he was conducting in the Cilento. Despite doubts
about Keys's methods, study after study continued to tout the health benefits of
cold-pressed, unrefined olive oil (the establishment of a food pyramid also de-
vilified pasta, bread, and pizza). By the 1970s, the nutrition world was buzzing with
a miraculous new way of eating that was rich with vegetables, cereals, and fish, all
glistening with beautiful, local olive oil—the Mediterranean diet.

It helps that olive oil tastes wonderful. Few flavors conjure up the Mediterranean
as does something—really, almost anything—lavished with olive oil.

Neapolitans eat cured olives, as they have since ancient times, as a savory snack
with wine or as an ingredient. What would pasta puttanesca or *insalata di rinforzo*
be without their olives? You may notice many cookbooks suggest using Gaeta
olives—no disrespect to Gaeta olives—they are internationally famous since ancient times, and they are divine. But there are so many wonderful olive varieties
in Naples. Go to Porta Nolana Market and get dizzy trying to choose, or go to one
of the little grocery shops, where there's always at least one crock each of green
and black. Buy some, taste, next time buy a different variety; olive eating is a great
adventure!

It's the oil pressed from the olive, however, that gives its unique taste to nearly
everything Neapolitans eat. It imparts health, pleasure, and sustenance and passes
along traditional countryside culture. For these reasons, the olive and its oil are
revered in an almost spiritual way. Mothers pour it over bread and tomatoes for an
afternoon *merendina* (snack), knowing they are doing the best for their bambini.

And, as with wine, olive oil tastes like the fruit from which it is pressed and
hugely reflects its own terroir. It is a seasonal fruit, and its oil varies season to

season—rain, heat, and other nuances of the weather all affect the olive. Like wine, few things have so much of "a taste of place" as does olive oil.

The best assurance that you have a good oil is the label: Does it announce its provenance? Is it from a small company with its location indicated? Stay away from large industrial olive oils.

Oils that are PDO and DOP as well as IGA always have a strong provenance and follow a strict regime of production from growing, cultivating, harvesting, and testing the olives to the pressing and bottling (and blending, if needed). One also needs to remember that every year is different for olives, as it is for grapes and everything that grows.

The variety of cultivars and cultivation methods is due to centuries-old farming wisdom: understanding the terroir, understanding which variety flourishes in which microclimate, and knowing the history of what has grown well in the area. Local olive oil at this point in time is a beautiful balance of technology and tradition.

No other oil—not seed, vegetable, corn, or others—is edible by simply pressing. Other oils need further extraction by chemical means or a higher heat extraction. It is often said that olive oil is basically fruit juice; it is that pure.

Handpicking helps keep the olives from bruising, which is important, since bruising encourages spoilage. Olives for extra virgin oil must be pressed within two days to prevent them from fermenting, developing rancid flavors, and oxidizing. Oxidization raises acid levels—for extra virgin oil, you want the lowest acid reading possible.

Traditionally, olives are pressed between large millstones; it is the touchstone of olive pressing. Contemporary pressing, utilizing science and technology, is based on this traditional method, yet streamlined for modern and greater production.

First, the olives are conveyed on a belt, washed, leaves discarded, then chopped into pulp. This pulp is then pressed (many still use traditional woven mats), separating the liquid from the residue (ground pits and skin). Modernized extraction washes the olives more times, crushes them using stainless steel blades, and places the pulp in a centrifuge where the oil is extracted, but the temperature remains cool enough so as to avoid damaging the oil.

The water is discarded, leaving the fresh-pressed oil, which is then filtered and bottled. (The ground pits, flesh, and skin are called pomace, which can be made into an inferior "pure olive oil" using chemical solvents.)

There are about seven hundred olive oil producers in Campania. Most are small family farms, many passed down from generation to generation. It is more than a job—it is their contribution to culture, culinary life, and their community.

Campania grows more than sixty native varieties of olives, which means it doesn't depend on only one type, lessening the risk of disease or blight. And though the cultivation of the olive itself and its terroir have much to do with the final olive (and oil), there are other considerations, such as when the olive is harvested.

Traditionally, olives were picked later and riper. Harvesting late gives some olives a stronger taste, but it also can produce high acidity levels in others (olive oils are judged by acidity level for "virginity"). Underripe fruit gives a fresher taste, though a smaller yield. Early picking also reduces overripe olives falling from the trees, lying on the ground, oxidized and ruined, possibly contaminating the whole harvest.

Olives are very small, difficult to grasp, and tedious to pick, so pickers loosen the fruits from the tree and let them fall to the ground onto a cloth cover rolled onto the ground beneath the trees. The olives form a pile, and any olives that sit for longer than a day or two in the pile can oxidize, so the olives are gathered for pressing as soon as possible. And, with a few unique exceptions in other lands, olive oil is always best at its freshest.

Oil-tasting vocabulary is similar to wine tasting; descriptions include "delicate," "fresh," "fruity," "strong," and "rustic." "Fruity" may refer to apple, banana, lychee, melon, or tomato; "vegetal" might mean avocado; "verdant" might describe leaves, herbs, grass, hay, violets, or eucalyptus; and "nutty" could refer to the scent of almond, brazil nut, or even chocolate. The taste of olive oil is complex and fascinating.

Reflecting their Greek heritage, oils from Campania are rich in flavor; yet, balancing their strength, they often have a delicate side. Their basic structure balances spicy and sweet.

Each olive oil farm I have visited in Campania has been enthusiastic about and devoted to their olives and olive oil culture. Even if you live in a city, who doesn't have a relative in the countryside who produces olive oil? Maybe it's time to get in touch with Uncle Giuseppe or Auntie Assunta. You need oil, and they might need help with the harvest. (If you would like to adopt an olive tree, www.pomora.com can hook you up with Antonio, a farmer in Avellino.)

Olive farmers usually also produce other things: fruit, vegetables, wine. If you are lucky enough to be invited for a meal at a farm, it is like traveling to the heart of *la cucina Napoletana*. Lentils ladled over rustic toast, beans and greens with potatoes, *freselle* with tomatoes—whatever is in season lavished with the fragrant oil. Unforgettably delicious.

Although most oils are a blend, some farms grow individual cultivars for specific tastes. "Individual olive types are popular, especially with local chefs. It inspires their creativity, each oil having its own distinct character," Anna Maria Mennella told me as we toured her and her husband Antonio's farm, Madonna dell'Olivo, in the Salerno countryside. Much of their farm is devoted to a wide variety of monocultivars. Working between high tech and ancient traditions, they nonetheless have a wide variety of oils, some pressed from olives that have already been pitted for a certain delicacy. (Like so many olive farmers, they sell online internationally.)

The most common types of olives in Campania are Ogliarola and Ravece nell'Avellinese in Avellino; Ortice, Ortolana, and Racioppella in Benevento; Sessana and Caiazzana in Caserta; and Pisciottana and Rotondella in Salerno.

Ravece olive oil is fruity and herb scented, with a hint of tangy green tomatoes balancing the bitter artichoke, and a slightly picante base. At harvest, the olives cover the color spectrum, ranging from green to wine red to dark purple. They have a lower yield than other olives.

The Sannio Colline oil from Benevento province is pressed from Ortice and Ortolana olives. The oil is yellow hued with shades of green and smells like ripe red tomatoes and sweet herbs, a tiny bit bitter and spicy to keep it interesting.

Caiazzana and Sessana (PDO Terre Aurunche), in the north of Caserta, are made of at least 70 percent Sessana olives with the remaining 30 percent Cornelian, Itrona, and Tonacella.

The Sorrento Peninsula DOP olive oil includes the Sorrento area, Lattari Mountains, and the island of Capri. Also pale yellow with a greenish tinge, it is delicate and herbal.

Colline Salernitane DOP includes olives grown in the area of Salerno, the Amalfi Coast, and about eighty-five smaller areas. Cilento DOP is produced mostly in the Valle di Diano, where ancient olive trees cover the landscape. DOP standards for this oil require at least 85 percent Pisciotta, Rotondella, Ogliarola, Frantoio, Leccino, and Solello olives. Slightly fruity with a hint of green apple, the scent of leaves and notes of nuts (almond especially) waft through. Again, whispers of bitter and picante keep it balanced.

Note: You will never be served oil in a saucer along with your bread for dipping. It is not done. What is done and rejoiced in is steeped in tradition: when you've finished eating and your plate is awash with sauce and oil from your meal, you make *la scarpetta* and wipe the bread across the plate, letting it soak up all the savory sauce. Then take a bite of the sauce-soaked bread. Who needs dessert?

FORMAGGI: THE CHEESES OF CAMPANIA

Mozzarella di Bufala: Buffalo Mozzarella from Campania

It is everywhere, the buffalo mozzarella of your dreams: big fat balls of milky curds, eaten fresh, so fresh that you judge its age in hours, not days or weeks. It is a unique cheese, starting with the beautiful buffalo milk. Stretching the curds gives an almost sponge-like, chewy consistency. The taste of each cheese balances a whole universe of flavor: sweet, slightly sour, rich, lean.

The first time I saw mozzarella presented in all its natural habitat was in a posh restaurant in Naples. Everyone was elegant: the waiters and diners equally. Waiters dashed about with plate after plate of antipasti, exquisite seafood, whole fish, al dente pasta. I felt a happy hum while watching the parade.

And then, what was that passing by on a plate? A big white cheese: no garnish, unsliced. Just a big ball of mozzarella. And another. And another, each being ferried to a different table filled with eager, elegant, waiting Neapolitans.

And oh, how the stylish citizens of Napoli raised their knives and forks—such gusto! No dainty little slices, no presentation of minimal slivers arranged like petals. Even the slender designer-dressed fashionistas who looked as if they couldn't manage more than a tiny morsel of food were devouring the plates of milky mozzarella and daintily wiping their perfectly lipsticked mouths.

I have been told that sitting down to a meal without mozzarella is sad for a Neapolitan—like sitting down to a meal without bread, pasta, or wine. Of course, there's no end to the ways mozzarella may be enjoyed, but a ball of truly fresh mozzarella needs nothing else: maybe a little olive oil, a few fronds of arugula. Eaten alone on a plate with knife and fork is properly Neapolitan. (Eaten out of hand like an apple is my little confession—don't tell anybody.)

And after having just finished exhorting you to serve the mozzarella on its own, a contemporary way to serve it is to surround it with tidbits of local tastes, varying in taste and texture: fried capers, salted anchovies, dried marinated tomato, shreds of basil, candied lemon. In this way one can taste, sense, and understand different aspects of the cheese compared with the varied tastes sampled with it.

A good mozzarella tastes fresh, has a stringy, almost chewy texture, is pure white in color with an extremely thin skin and delicate, milky taste. When cut, it oozes a white watery liquid, smelling of milk and fermenting enzymes. Apart from the typical round shape, buffalo mozzarella is also produced in small bite-sized shapes and large braids.

Italy and mozzarella are synonymous to much of the world, but *mozzarella di bufala* DOP, the *real* buffalo mozzarella, is made in only seven provinces throughout central and south Italy, mostly in Campania. Caserta produces the most (54 percent), followed by Salerno (38 percent), with the rest scattered among Benevento, Naples, Latina, Frosinone, and Foggia (Puglia). (Puglia also makes burrata, mozzarella stuffed with a nugget of cream. Next to a plate of olive oil–dressed bitter greens, it is perhaps the most defining dish of Puglia.) A map published by the Consorzio di Tutela della Mozzarella di Bufala Campana DOP/Denominazione d'Origine Protetta (www.mozzarelladop.it), the official certification consortium of mozzarella makers, details them all.

In ancient times, as now, buffalo were a familiar sight in the countryside, favored for plowing fields. They are strong, and due to the size and shape of their hooves, they do not sink too deeply into the moist earth during the rainy season. A native of India, the buffalo was introduced in Italy in the sixth and seventh centuries AD by the Longobards, according to Paul the Deacon, writing in his *Historia Longbardorum*. Another theory claims they were introduced by the Saracen and Turks to Sicily, later making their way along the coast to Campania and Latium. Whichever theory is correct, the beautiful beasts found a perfect habitat in the marshy mud of Paestum to the Gulf of Salerno and Caserta.

Homemade buffalo milk cheeses were made at this time; the Latin agronomist L. Giumio Moderato Columella (4–70 AD) noted a "hand-pressed" buffalo cheese. Mozzarella as we know it has been made since at least the twelfth century, perhaps earlier, according to the Consorzio di Tutela della Mozzarella di Bufala Campana DOP. Documents describe how buffalo were becoming a fixture on the coastal plains of the Volturno and the Sele Rivers. They also tell of a cheese called *mozza* or *provatura* (when smoked) that the monks of the San Lorenzo in Capua monastery offered to passing pilgrims accompanied by slices of bread. The term *mozza* appeared in a document of the Episcopal Archives of the Church of Capua, dated twelfth century, and the cheese was referred to from the 1400s on, though not by name.

Commercial mozzarella making is thought to have begun around the fourteenth century, with fresh buffalo cheeses destined for the prosperous Neapolitan and Salerno markets (smoking extended shelf life and added flavor). However, it wasn't until 1570 that the name *mozzarella*, diminutive for *mozza*, appeared for the first time in a famous text by Barolomeo Scappi, chef of the papal court. Scappi was famous as Il Platina, and his book, *Opera Culinaria*, was an important commentary on culinary times.

But it wasn't until the eighteenth century, when the Bourbons established a large buffalo farm and experimental dairy at Reggia di Carditello, the royal estate of the Spanish dynasty in the province of Caserta, that the cheese became widely eaten. I have heard that in the late 1800s, it became the rage in aristocratic homes to serve mozzarella as part of an all-white salad with thinly shredded white vegetables: fennel, celery, and so forth, dressed with olive oil.

With Italy's unification, a wholesale mozzarella and other buffalo cheese market (called Taverna) in Aversa, Campania, was established. The cheeses collected from farms were already weighed and wrapped in marsh rush or cranberry leaves and then carefully placed in wicker or chestnut crates to be transported to the market.

To make buffalo mozzarella, fresh milk is heated to 30° Celsius and rennet is added, which transforms it into curds and whey. The curds are cut, mixed to form a paste, and then left to sit in the warm whey for four hours.

The paste is drained, and the curd stretched and stretched, stretched, stretched, until it becomes elastic; then chunks are cut out of the big, warm curd mass (*mozzare* means to cut—hence the name). These chunks are formed into shapes, rolled into balls, or twisted into braids in a variety of sizes from small to medium to huge. Some shapes take two people working in tandem to form the big cheese; some are a one-person task; others are popped onto a conveyor belt gizmo that shapes the cheese mechanically. All shapes bathe first in cold water to firm them up, then a nice brine for salting.

Farming folklore claims that the taste of buffalo milk changes according to the influence of the moon and that the best mozzarella is made after the animals have grazed during the nights of a full moon.

In Campania, mozzarella is more than a food; it is a symbol of the goodness the people are surrounded by. Each family has its favorite brand, shop, farm, or restaurant that serves the mozzarella they prefer. Though all of the mozzarella I've eaten in Campania is better than what you'll find elsewhere, there is mozzarella, and then there is *mozzarella*. Some is better than others; sometimes it depends on your own taste and the quality of the cheese, of course.

To truly appreciate mozzarella and taste its lush milky splendor, you must visit Campania. Each area and even each farm gives its own particular perfume and texture to the cheese, often affected by atmospheric and weather conditions. Tasting one's way through a selection helps you discover the characteristics you prefer. Like wine tasting or learning about art, tasting mozzarella—*really* tasting mozzarella—brings joy and imparts expertise.

Tradition dictates that *mozzarella di bufala* is best the day it is made, before it ever sees the inside of a refrigerator (though if you're keeping it longer, it is best to refrigerate). Scientific preservation techniques are continually improving; mozzarella makers put a lot of attention into creating the best packaging to optimize the mozzarella-eating experience.

This fresh-pulled cheese owes its unique characteristics to the buffalo's milk produced in the place of origin. Every mozzarella maker I have ever spoken with has said something to the effect of "mozzarella's goodness comes from the animals."

Made from whole buffalo milk, it has a higher protein, fat, and mineral salt content than cow's milk. About four liters of milk are required to make one kilogram (about two and a quarter pounds) of mozzarella. In addition to the milk, mozzarella has only salt and rennet/fermentation.

To learn about good mozzarella, it's best to go to the experts: the water buffalo themselves. The start of a good cheese begins with the animals and the milk they give. In Caserta and Salerno, the buffalo roam, the cheese is made, and throughout the area, towns, and countryside are shops with signs advertising *mozzarella di bufala*.

Water buffalo are curious, affectionate creatures. The look on a mozzarella maker's face when you mention the animals usually turns into a warm, dreamy expression. It's hard not to fall in love with these adorable, long-lashed hulks. And it was no less true centuries ago. Reporting on peasant culture in the south of Italy—*contadini del Sud*—author and poet Rocco Scotellaro describes how the "bufalaro" (much like a shepherd or goatherd) knew each individual animal ("as if they were Christians") and gave them names such as Contessa (Countess), Amorosa (Beloved), Cambiale (Money Order), and Monacella (Little Monk).

If you are lucky enough to visit the buffalo, you will likely fall in love with them (as I have). The only thing to remember is that they are creatures who stampede at a moment's notice. A Neapolitan friend, Flavia Vitale, told me of a childhood trauma when she rode her bike onto a little road bordering an open field of buffalo. "*And I was wearing red!*" She made no sudden movements (good advice for those of us who find ourselves in the same situation) and lived to tell the tale.

Buffalo also have a strong animal smell (a polite way to say that they are a bit stinky). How they love the mud! (But not to worry; in between mud baths, the buffalo are kept pristinely clean, both animals and facilities undergoing frequent inspections.) From breeding to selling the finished cheese, great care is taken with DOP certified cheese.

During and after World War II, life was not kind: not to people or to buffalo. By 1950 the buffalo were in danger of extinction since those in the Caserta region had been decimated by the retreating Nazis. Salerno still had buffalo farms, but the marshy areas and large estates were now uncultivated and overgrown. But cheesemakers persisted, breeding and raising the animals, making the cheese, and returning the traditional cheese to its rightful place on the Neapolitan menu.

The animal population was just getting back on its feet when, in 1973, cholera broke out in Naples. Panic condemned fresh foods, especially those that were milk based, as unsafe (without scientific justification). The crisis was eventually overcome, but the buffalo and dairy industries realized that they needed to band together in order to face future disasters when they arose. In 1981, the consortium for protecting the buffalo was established, which twelve years later became the Consorzio di Tutela della Mozzarella di Bufala Campana DOP.

At a *caseificio* (cheesemaking factory) one can watch, often through a large glass window (for hygiene reasons), the production process: fresh buffalo milk is brought in (either from an outside dairy or from their own herd), curdled, and drained of whey. The curd is then cut into small pieces and chopped finely before being plunged into hot water, where it is stirred and stretched until it becomes rubbery. The cheesemaker kneads it by hand, like a baker making bread, until it becomes a smooth, shiny paste. Then a small chunk can be pinched off and formed into an individual cheese, which is put first into cold water and then into brine for a nice soak. In the brine, the cheese absorbs some of the salt, which flavors the cheese. The brine also affects the cheese's texture, which must be stretchy and springy, not soft and mushy. If it is poked, it should spring back.

Freshness is critical, but how can we know whether our cheese is fresh if we are not intimately familiar with its qualities, as Neapolitans are? First of all, the texture should be springy and elastic, its surface tight, smooth, and damp, neither too dry nor too wet, with a thin, filmy skin, whitish in color, with no yellow spots.

Slicing into it, droplets of milky whey should seep out. Inside, it should appear to have many layers, especially near the surface, and a slightly spongy texture somewhat like bread made with a sour *levito*. Tasting it, you can feel liquid almost spurting from the solid, the texture much like a milk-soaked sponge.

In the shop next to the cheesemaking factory (there is almost always a shop attached), you can buy mozzarella in a variety of shapes from the tiny *ciliegine* (cherries) or *bocconcini* (little bites, slightly less than two ounces each), *ovaline*, and *nodini* to a classic mozzarella that weighs somewhere between eight ounces and a pound. Then there's *la zizzona di Battipaglia*, the large, luscious buffalo mozzarella that ranges in size from about half a pound to slightly more than a pound, whose name refers to its shape, like a breast, complete with the "nipple" at its top. The braided *treccia* from Massa Lubrense near Sorrento is beautiful; my daughter and her husband cut one at their wedding instead of a cake. A braided mozzarella can weigh up to about one and three-quarters of a pound, but if it weighs more than this, it may not be called buffalo mozzarella of Campania and is simply referred to as buffalo cheese. Some say, however, that the larger the cheese, the better. Buffalo cheese can reach up to about seven pounds in weight.

A mozzarella might be smoked (*affumicata*), truffled, or wrapped in supple myrtle leaves, an ancient packing method that also produces a distinctive scent.

The mozzarella of Campania is made according to strict rules, fine-tuned by the Consorzio di Tutela della Mozzarella di Bufala Campana (Consortium for the Protection of Buffalo Mozzarella). Founded in 1981, it is the only institution recognized by the Italian Ministry of Agriculture and Forestry to protect, monitor, and promote *mozzarella di bufala* DOP from Campania. Thanks to the consortium, the buffalo mozzarella from Campania was the only one of its kind to obtain European DOP recognition.

The labels DOP (certified provenance EEC), PDO (DOP—Denominazione di Origine Protetta), trademarks, or DOC (certified origin brand) should be found on the packaging of the best mozzarella. It shows that the Association of Mozzarella makers, *il consorzio*, monitors the production and marketing of the buffalo mozzarella in compliance with the rules of production.

If not eaten right away, store the cheese in the refrigerator, leaving it in the water brine (called *aqua bianco*) in which it was packaged. Before you serve it, it's best to let it come to room temperature, as with most cheeses, though I like it a little bit cool.

If departing by air when you leave Napoli, there is good-quality mozzarella available at Naples International Airport (Capodichino) packaged in specially designed containers that work remarkably well.

Export technology and packaging enables mozzarella to be transported farther distances while maintaining high quality. The United Kingdom, Europe, the United States, Japan, and so many other places import *mozzarella di bufala*—soon China will be importing it as well (from experience, I can say that the Chinese are already in love with pizza).

Regardless of how well it is packaged and the care taken in its export, the truth is that buying mozzarella abroad is nowhere near as good as having it ladled out of a big jar or vat of brine. There is no better way of eating it than on the day it was made, with nothing else except perhaps a drizzle of olive oil. Close your eyes when you take your first bite; chew thoughtfully, feeling the pleasure as you do, your mouth filling with the stretched curds of tender, milky cheese. Eating it is knowing that you're in Napoli.

Visiting the Buffalo

Vannulo (Tenuta Vannulo), near Paestum, is the most legendary of the buffalo farms: first, because it is (as of this writing) the only mozzarella maker certified organic, and second, because of the lives those buffalo lead! Although buffalo adore the mud, at Vannulo they have lovely baths and showers, comfy rubber mattresses to loll about on, and massages consisting of rotating brushes (much like a carwash, but for the buffalo—heaven!).

Their tours, offered in different languages, cost a few euros and take you out to the buffalo, visiting the vast pens of buffalo girls of different ages and the few buffalo boys. For health reasons, tours can't go onto the cheesemaking floor, but there's a big window between visitor and the mozzarella, giving a great view of curd stretching, shape forming, and brining.

A small museum details the history of the farm, displays old tools and photos with one of the animals grazing amid the temples at nearby Paestum. The tour "encourages" visitors to spend time in their leather boutique (the male buffalo meet a fate far less pleasant than that of the females), but then there's the shop, which offers samples. Vannulo's mozzarella often sells out before noon, so take no chances and get there early. Next door is their *yogurteria* full of yogurts,

Visiting the Buffalo (*continued*)

gelato, and cakes, all made with buffalo milk. Some complain that Vannulo has become too touristy, but its products are of excellent quality, and its popularity brought jobs to the area.

Also near Paestum, Baronessa Cecilia Bellelli Baratta runs her family's atmospheric *agriturismo* buffalo farm, Seliano, breeding buffalo and Podolica cows and making cheese with raw milk, which features on its restaurant's menu. Food writer Arthur Schwartz has long brought groups there for food weeks in Campania; he still occasionally does. Seliano is a country farm hotel, a country restaurant, and a working farm; it also offers cooking classes (see chapter 7).

Since 1694 the Morese family has been raising buffalo and making cheese for nine generations in Pontecagnano, on the Sele plain, halfway between Salerno and Eboli, and selling it at their farm and shop, Taverna Penta Dairy. The Morese family is an old, French, aristocratic family. They currently have a herd of about six hundred animals. Besides the cheese making and shop, there's also a *yogurteria* featuring all sorts of puddings and desserts. The guided tour sounds great: visiting the animals, watching the cheesemaking, and tasting a wide variety of their offerings.

In Caserta, near the town of Capua, is *agriturismo* Masseria Giosole, run by Baronessa Francesca Pasca di Magliano and her family. It's a bed and breakfast vacation getaway that boasts a swimming pool, tennis courts, volleyball courts, and paths for bike riding. Fruit trees are interspersed throughout the property, and a garden produces grains and vegetables. The garden produce turns into elegant jams, pates, juices, pickled vegetables, and conserves using traditional family recipes, including pear preserves with basil, peach with almonds, and orange with rosemary, among others. I adored the pickled broccoli stems: bitter, tangy, and tender all at once. Eggplant pate, artichoke pate—the list went on and on—but it was the jarred cherry tomatoes smeared onto homemade pizza that burst into more flavor than you could imagine any little tomato doing.

There are no water buffalo on the farm, but one of Francesca's friends has a few of the shaggy animals and the baronessa will arrange an introduction.

Other Campania Cheeses

In addition to buffalo milk mozzarella and cheese, buffalo milk is often made into yogurt, ice cream, and butter.

Fior di latte (cow's milk mozzarella from Sorrento and Capri), *caciocavallo*, ricotta, provola, provolone, smoked provola, *scamorza Irpinia*, and more. Campania is rich with a variety of unique, distinctive cheeses. Soft and fresh or aged and pungent, they are often descended from ancient Roman and even Greek traditions.

Bocconcini del Cardinale are also known as *burrielli*. These are small mozzarellas preserved with cream or rich milk in clay pots.

When a mozzarella that otherwise would be DOP or DOC falls outside the regulations, whether for size (i.e., *huge*, which is pretty fabulous) or flavorings (such as oregano, paprika, or lemon leaves), it is not allowed to be called *mozzarella di bufala* but may be called *formaggio di bufala*.

Burrini di Sorrento are small provolone cheeses that are filled with a heart of butter, similar to the burrata of Puglia.

Made from the milk of the water buffalo, *scamorza di bufala* is firmer than mozzarella but softer than *caciocavallo*. After being made, it is soaked in salt water and set aside to dry for a few days. Sorrento produces a mini *scamorza* stuffed with hot chile and olives.

Caciocavallo is excellent eaten as is (say, for an antipasto), melted, or used in cooking. A symbol of the Italian south, *caciocavallo* is the cheese found hanging by string in the local grocers. It belongs to the family of stretched-curd cheeses typical of the south such as provolone, mozzarella, and *scamorza*, all firmish and slightly similar to Gruyere.

Its name (*cacio*: cheese; *cavallo*: horse) comes from the appearance of the cheese while drying. The cheeses, teardrop shaped with knobs on top, are tied together with a rope for hanging over a beam or pole for aging. The rope-tied cheeses appear much like a horse's saddlebags. Instead of the classic pear shape, sometimes it is formed into whimsical animals such as piglets.

The milk for *caciocavallo* comes from cows that are milked only once a day; cheese production must be completed within twenty-four hours. First, the milk is coagulated using both goat and calf rennet, with the resulting curd broken into grains the size of rice. Left in its whey on a tilted board, it drains slowly before being cut and beaten. After that, it is brined for a few hours and set aside to rest.

After resting, the cheesemaker, or *casara*, shapes the paste into individual cheeses according to the weight and size preferred. These are immersed in cold water, followed by brine, before they move into maturing, which usually takes about nine months. Some varieties of *caciocavallo* are matured in *tufo* caves. It is produced throughout the year but particularly from March to May.

Caciocavallo Podolico cheese is made only from the milk of the Podolica cow. Though its milk is rich in proteins and fat, its yield is low. The name "Podolica" reflects the belief that the cow originated in the Ukrainian region of Podolia. The southern Apennines, however, provided a perfect habitat; the cows—with their characteristic gray color and large horns—are now a cherished local breed.

They live a semi-wild life, not in barns, but in the open throughout the year. Following the ancient custom of transhumance, they are brought down to a lower altitude in the winter where the weather is milder; in the summer, they pasture high in the mountains, where it is cooler. With falling numbers in recent years, much attention is being given to safeguard and preserve this cherished animal.

When you see a *caciocavallo* named "Podolico," you know that it is exquisite: lush in taste, semi-hard, yet smooth in texture (though a bit grainy at times). Its aroma is of milk and straw. Each straw-colored cheese weighs between a little more than a pound to twenty pounds. It may be eaten fresh, but the cheese improves with long maturing, especially the larger ones. Five or six years is not unusual; twelve years is a rare treat. During aging, it develops complex aromas of pasture, seasons, and the herbs and Mediterranean scrub that the animals fed on: wild fennel, myrtle, licorice. When the cheese is slightly pink, it means that the cows have grazed on wild strawberries.

Wonderful in cooking, but if you have a particularly lovely one, serve it as its own course: before or after the meal, enjoyed at room temperature, served with a dab of local honey such as chestnut and accompanied by a typical southern red wine such as Aglianico.

Caciotta fresca is from the Sorrentine Peninsula. This cow's milk cheese is pale in color, aged for only a short time, and has a delicate taste.

At an artisanal food fair, I was watching raptly as a big fat cheese, *formaggio degli emigranti*, was cut open. Everyone around me knew what was coming and laughed as it opened. There, inside the cheese, was a whole salame!

Here is how it happened: When Italian immigrants to America started setting up restaurants, they needed "old country" salame and cheese to serve. They sent home for supplies only to find them confiscated by customs. Being unendingly resourceful, the Neapolitans did a little thinking. The result was *formaggio degli emigranti*: a big cheese with a salame stuffed inside. (Bear in mind there were no sniffer dogs or X-rays in those days.) Slice it open, and your cheese has a heart of salame. Locals are affectionate toward it and the spirit in which it was created. There are several brands available online. (In Sicily they have a similar cheese that's stuffed with lemon.)

The best fresh cow's milk mozzarella (*fior di latte*), fresh or smoked, is said to have originated in Agerola. Cow's milk mozzarella is not buffalo milk mozzarella; it is different—not worse or better—each has its own place to shine. *Fior di latte* is often used in cooking when a delicate buffalo mozzarella would be overwhelmed or release too much liquid when heated. If you're choosing gelato flavors and they have *fior di latte*, give it a try: milky, light, and wonderful.

Pecorino di Laticauda has a deeply milky aroma with a slightly spicy taste and a color that ranges from pale yellow to a deeper golden-beige, depending on its fat content. Its milk is particularly low in fat, as its metabolism distributes the fat from the rest of the animal's body right to the tail instead.

Pecorino di Laticauda is made from the milk of the Laticauda sheep that live in Benevento and Avellino. Though they are now considered a native Appennica sheep, they originated in North Africa, where they are prized for their fat tails (*latis*: big; *cauda*: tail). In North Africa the sheep's tails are often used in cooking with their rich, flavorful, plentiful fat.

Pecorino di Laticauda is typically prepared in a cylindrical form in sizes ranging from about eight ounces for fresh to up to fifteen pounds for the aged cheese. (Aging takes between four and twelve months depending on which characteristics you prefer, from a softer texture to a hard, grainy one that splinters into shards when cut.) The whey, when separated from the curds, is used to make *ricotta di Laticauda*, a much-prized cheese.

Provola affumicata is a cow's milk mozzarella that's lightly smoked over oak wood. It has a light brown, smoke-tinged exterior and is pale cream or yellow inside. Its scent of wood combined with its milky texture is fabulous indeed.

Provolone is similar to *caciocavallo* but aged differently and for different periods of time.

Provolone del Monaco is made from Mount Lattari cows of different breeds, including the rare Agerolese. Its name has nothing to do with the country of Monaco; rather, it is Italian for "monks," who were the first to make the cheese. It is smooth and beautiful, and if it matures longer than eighteen months, it's on the sharper side. A delicacy.

Soft and milky, ricotta is a low-fat cheese made using the whey leftover from the production of other cheeses. Whey left from buffalo mozzarella becomes *ricotta di bufala*, while ricotta made from leftover pecorino becomes *ricottine di pecora* (*pecora* means sheep). And so on for cow and goat—you can make ricotta from any kind of milk whey.

The word *ricotta* means "twice cooked," indicating that the milk is first heated to produce the curds and whey; after separation, the leftover whey is cooked with additional fresh milk, then strained to make a soft, fresh, ricotta.

After being lightly salted, it is spooned into small containers to drain and pressed gently by hand. The salting is the true sign of the expert cheese master. Not enough salt, and it is insipid; too much, and it is inedible. In Salerno, I once saw a cheesemaker layer ricotta with chopped arugula, and it tasted amazing, but when I've tried it myself, it hasn't worked out so well.

Ricotta fresca, fresh and milky, is eaten on its own with jam; added as an ingredient to pasta, along with either tomato sauce or Neapolitan ragù; used as a filling for ravioli; or layered in *lasagna di carnevale*. Ricotta cheese is often used as a filling in sweet pastries such as *sfogliatelle* or layered into cakes. A contemporary way to offer fresh beautiful ricotta is to surround it with a constellation of tastes and textures: local honey, preserved fruits, jam, spices, nuts; each bite different, depending on the ingredient with which it is combined.

Ricotta di fuscella is light, bright, and was originally sold in baskets; now the baskets tend to be plastic.

Ricotta affumicata has a subtle but real—no liquid smoke added—smoky taste and scent that overlays the milky ricotta: it is unique and outstanding, as the milky ricotta is so delicious and—milky—while the smoke is savory and strong. Really wonderful.

When fresh ricotta is salted and left to age, the result is *ricotta secca*, also known as ricotta salata. It is firm to hard, salty, and crumbly and should be very thinly sliced or grated into other dishes such as pasta. It is typical of Eastertime, since it is preserved from earlier cheesemaking. At the beginning of spring, the animals are having babies and not yet giving milk for cheese.

Scamorza is a small-sized *caciocavallo* that's available either plain or smoked. I recently purchased two that were tied together, *caciocavallo* style, on the same twine—one plain and one smoked.

Formaggio con Foglie di Limone (Cheese Melted between Two Lemon Leaves)

Serves 4

An unusual and wonderful dish from the land where lemons grow everywhere and mozzarella is smoked around each corner! Stick a slab of smoked mozzarella, *scamorza*, or smoked provala/provolone between two lemon leaves and heat in a hot frying pan until the cheese starts to melt. You can also cook the little cheese and leaf parcels over a barbecue if the leaves are big enough.

Whichever way you do it, the important thing is to eat them right away, as soon as the cheese melts: out of the pan and onto your plate!

Be sure to have a glass of wine along with them.

8–10 unsprayed lemon leaves, fairly large, and well washed	4–6 ounces smoked mozzarella or scamorza, sliced slightly smaller than the leaves

Take a leaf, shiny side down, and place a piece of cheese on top. Top with another leaf with the dull side facing the cheese and the shiny side on the outside.

Repeat until they are all finished. Heat a heavy nonstick frying pan until medium hot.

Place the leaf parcels into the pan, turning each one as soon as the cheese sizzles and melts. When the second side is done, plop them onto a plate.

Best eaten hot, fresh from the heat, when the cheese is tender and melty (though very hot—be careful) and the leaves are tender. If the leaves are tender enough, you can eat them, but it is traditional to peel the lemon leaves off and eat the melty cheese from it using your teeth.

Of Cheese and Long-Lost Relatives

I was once traveling in the countryside of Benevento with my friend, author and radio personality Marcy Smothers. Her grandfather and great uncle came from Benevento, and although tracking down long-lost relatives wasn't the mission for our trip—the mission was gastronomical—seeing the area her grandfather and uncle came from was her heartfelt desire. We didn't plan the side trip, so there we were driving down a little country road, nothing on the horizon except for trees and fields.

On the side of the road, a small food van had parked, selling hanging cheeses and salame; we stopped, of course. The weathered farmer/cheese and salame maker was standing in front of the van, cutting wedges of cheese to taste. We bought cheese, he sliced salame to sample, and we bought salame. In the course of our transaction, Marcy mentioned her grandfather and asked about the village. "That's *my* name," said our cheese and salame farmer. "The village is just over there, over that little hill." Marcy got excited, thinking she had found her whole family, which, as it turned out, she had. Kind of. "You will know you are in the right place because *everybody* has the same name."

Though this farmer was from the same village to which he pointed down the road, and though they were probably cousins, he didn't know anything about Marcy's family who had emigrated. We were still no closer to finding her relatives. We bought more salame and more cheese, and then we headed down the road, so near and still so far, but with a good supply of cheese and salame.

LA FELLATA: THE APPETIZER KNOWN AS SLICES OF CURED MEATS

To order a plate of sliced meats "of the house," just ask for *gli affettati* (a.k.a. "the slices"). Neapolitans don't eat a huge amount of cured meats, but, of course, they revel in those they do. They treat it with such huge affection that all they need to say is "the slices, please," and a plate of cured meats arrives.

Neapolitan cured meats are unique—usually pork, but sometimes other meats such as beef or veal, cured with salt or smoke and hung to dry. Sometimes Neapolitans (like neighboring regions) add a little hit of hot pepper to their salame, just enough to keep people happy with spiciness when they need it. Sometimes they borrow a little spicy *'nduja* from Calabria to the south and add it to pasta or pizza, just to shake things up a bit.

It's not unusual to make cured meats such as salame and dried sausage at home; often it is the Nonna or the Mamma who makes a batch each year. If a friend offers you a sausage her mother made, consider yourself blessed; she is a good friend.

Here is a short list of typical local cured meats.

Cervellatina is salame made from lean and fat pork spiced with a pinch of chile.

Pancetta and lardo of varying ages and seasonings are fabulous laid atop a pizza hot from the oven to gently soften.

Prosciutto di Montefalcone, smoked, is chili-laced ham from a mountain village in Alto Sannio. The same artisans who produce it also produce excellent capicola, soppressata, and salame.

Salame Napoli is smoked pork and veal salame flavored with orange zest and garlic steeped in wine. Sometimes it is preserved in olive oil or under ashes.

Salsiccia di polmone is sausage made from pork lungs.

Soppressata Napoletana is a spicy salame pressed under weights (hence its name) to acquire its flattened oval shape. Mugnana del Cardinale makes a particularly nice smoked version.

BREAD

Everyone knows: Go to Naples and eat pizza, *spaghetti alle vongole, mozzarella di bufala*, strong dark coffee, pizza, *sfoliatelle*, and babà. No one says, "Go to Napoli and eat bread." Except me. I'm telling you now: go to Naples and eat bread. Eat it at every meal, eat it plain, eat it with soup, with salad, seafood, and fish (but never with pasta). Bread, to a Neapolitan, is a constant of life. Without bread, how will you make *la scarpetta* (the wiping of your beautiful sauce's last remnants from your plate)? Fresh bread sits on the table with meals.

Neapolitan bread is fabulously good. The crust is crunchy, its inner crumb soft, tender, springy, and spongelike in texture from a natural fermentation. It has the flavor of wheat enhanced by the sour tang of natural *levito*. Neapolitan bread doesn't want a fancy spread—it just wants to be eaten.

The history of bread eating in Campania is long. Carbonized bread was found in the ruins of Pompeii, indicating how much a fixture of regional eating it already was.

The best bread is the *pane campagnolo*, country bread, which is crisp crusted and chewy tender within. In general, the more rustic the bread, the more delicious. *Il pane cafone* is, to this bread lover, irresistible (though its name is an unflattering term for those who live in the countryside—"bumpkin" but less affectionate; perhaps "hick" is more accurate). It has a thick crust, tender crumb, and sour taste of a good *levito*.

When cut into, the crumb of a *pane cafone* should be moist. It may be tight or airy with pockets of holes, depending on the *levito* (sourdough). Its color ranges from white to beige to a slightly nuttier brown. We know that *pane cafone* is almost the same sourdough bread described by Hesiod in the first century BCE. I have often thought that the famous San Francisco sourdough was a descendent of *pane cafone*, a bit of starter brought with the Italian immigrants as they followed the gold rush to the West Coast of America and ended up in San Francisco.

That magic is its sourdough: homemade *levito* that absorbs the microbes in the air and incorporates them into the flavor and aroma of the bread. Before you can even think of making a *pane cafone* at home—though it is perfectly doable—you must make the *levito* and feed it for at least two weeks. Then you make dough, let it rest a few days, and use it as a starter for another batch of dough. So far you haven't baked anything yet; you've just worked to create the most amazing *levito* possible. Keep the sourdough going, and when you bake with it, keep aside a portion of the starter for the next batch of dough. A trick for crisp crust is injecting a bit of steam (or simply placing a ceramic baking dish filled with boiling water in the bottom of the oven). The best *pane cafone* is made in a wood-burning oven, of course.

Il palatone is similar to *pane cafone*, but long, wide, and rounder at the ends. A pane Napoletano weighs between two and a half and five pounds. *Cocchia* is a similar sourdough bread but flatter, a bit more like ciabatta but not oily. *Pagnotta* is round, high, and huge. When you want to buy a hunk, you usually just gesture to the baker where you would like it cut.

There are also small breads and rolls studded with cheese, salame, greens, dotted with olives, rolled in sesame seeds, or kneaded with herbs.

And the bread at *ristorante pizzerie*! For years I admired the crusty, crunchy bread at pizzeria restaurants. I also knew that *pizzaioli* never use leftover dough for pizza. What they did with the leftover dough was a question that bothered me. How long did it take me to put two and two together? One day I was so happily chewing magnificent bread in a *ristorante pizzeria*, thinking, *It's so good; where do they get it?* The waiter, noticing my enthusiasm, told me, "I made this myself—we use the leftover dough and the pizza oven." When I asked around, I was met with incredulity: "You didn't know that?" Apparently everyone did but me. Still, it's good to know, both in terms of food waste and the knowledge that if a *ristorante pizzeria* has good pizza, the bread will be fabulous too.

Never throw stale bread away; it is considered a sin. The waste of people who have never known famine is upsetting to those who have. There's another reason not to throw away bread: It is a gastronomical treasure whether fresh or stale. Soaked and crumbled into Naples's famous meatballs, toasted for soups and lentil stews, made into all sort of crostini or the delicious and oh-so-simple crostini Napoletani (smallish, thinnish, rectangular slices of bread topped with mozzarella; anchovies or olives; tomato; oregano [dried], basil [fresh], or marjoram [fresh], and drizzled with olive oil and baked until sizzling).

Bread is sold not at a bakery—that is for sweet things (cookies, pastries, and confections). Bread you get at a *panificio* or in a small grocery store where it has been delivered from a *panificio*.

Once the bakers of Napoli were having a party in the shadow of Vesuvio, and I was invited!

So there we were, having been invited to a bakers' party, driving along country roads that snake back and forth through fields and orchards and farms, through a leafy suburb that lies in the shadow of Vesuvio, past a high school and its playing field, down a winding dirt road and into a parking lot. It seemed an odd place for a party.

When I stepped out of the car and sniffed the air, it was so charged with the aroma of bread and history, desire, culture, yeast, and wood smoke that the air itself felt nourishing. Also—and only the Neapolitans could manage this—sexiness. Yes, right there wafting in the scent of the bread was the sexual energy of a dozen bakers and several hundred years of lusty Neapolitans enjoying good bread and a good life. I could smell it all, and it smelled great!

A huge banner welcoming us on behalf of the bakers was strung across the entrance gate to the parking area and bakery. Along one wall of the building a mural

Il Cuzzetiello

A chunk of slightly hollowed-out bread, dunked (or drowned) into the ragù or whatever sauce is on the table. Spelled *cuzzetiello*, though pronounced "cuztiello," it can be stuffed with anything you like: ragù, sausage, and *friarielli* or oniony, beefy Genovese. (When filled with Genovese, it's called a "Maradona," in honor of the patron saint of Naples soccer.)

Cuzzetiello is part of a Neapolitan tradition of *marenne*, a snack that a Neapolitan Mamma might give her children after school, or instead of lunch or dinner, or simply anytime they are hungry. If you are Neapolitan, the flavor of your family's *cuzzetiello* tastes of home.

Cuzzetiello has inched its way into the street food lexicon as well: filled with zucchini, peppers, eggplant, mushrooms, and *friarielli*, in addition to ragù or another savory sauce. Octopus, mortadella, sausage, provola cheese, pizzaiola sauce and mozzarella, eggplant parmigiana, and cutlets of nearly anything can be stuffed into *cuzzetiello*. It can even be vegan, stuffed with olive oil–bathed beans.

The bread's crust holds it all together, and the sauce soaks into the bread from the inside. You should probably accept the fact that there is going to be a lot of dripping. Even if it gets all over your face and spurts onto your clothing, it's part of the joyful abandon of eating the messy and oh-so-satisfying *cuzzetiello*.

had been painted depicting great moments in the history of Vesuvio and bread. The bakery had a small shop in front and, in front of the shop, a big, long table piled high with breads and local bread specialties.

It was a cornucopia of carbs: massively huge loaves, long thin loaves, individual rolls and flat focaccia, fancy breads, and the everyday bread of Napoli. The loaves were all made from locally grown wheat and raised with natural *levito*.

Rolls cascaded from baskets: tender, round white ones, grainy lumpy whole wheat ones, ciabatta-like mini-breads stuffed with herbs or nuts or ham or hot peppers, and others studded with olives. There were trays of flaky rolls studded with cured meat that oozed cheese in each bite and a massive calzone stuffed with *friarielli*.

Gathered around the table were about a dozen bakers, nearly giddy with the pleasure of showing off their display. In their white coats and hats, they looked a bit like mad scientists as they led us into the bakery to see how it's all done. In the frenzy of excitement, white jackets were shed, exposing their undershirts. You know the ones—sleeveless with a dubious moniker in English—the kind of shirt that adorned the seething, handsome men in Italian movies, the type that Marlon Brando donned in *A Streetcar Named Desire*.

The bakers, though, had more important things to do than posing prettily. They were handing out samples: rolls and breads appeared, the bakers poured wine, urging us to eat between shuffling loaves into the ovens and retrieving them fresh and hot and insanely good. Caught up in the mania, I wondered whether there was an airborne gluten poisoning that was making me so giddy. But no, it was simply the collective and contagious joy of the bakers.

I was also keenly aware that every day they wake in the dark of early morning and are in front of their ovens so that the city of Napoli can enjoy fresh bread. It's a profession that demands devotion to their craft, to their bread. Our enthusiasm sent them scurrying into action, like a double portion of the seven dwarves on mega-caffeine.

Above the banner and mural, there was a huge sign over the whole fantastic thing, this party of bread and its bakers. The sign read, "*Pane: Poesia, Amore, Nobiltà, Eleganza*" (Bread: Poetry, Love, Nobility, Elegance). When was the last time you thought of bread like this? In Napoli, apparently, it is *normale*—completely normal.

When I got to the far end of the table, I discovered that the smallest and most enthusiastic of this group of *molto* excitable bakers was slicing tomatoes—small, thick-skinned, juicy fleshed, flavorful tomatoes—for eating on the bread, along dried herbs and olive oil. My first bite of tomato made me gasp, it was so delicious. When the little baker saw my joy, he took me by the hand and walked me to the end of the driveway, near the high school, then turned to face Vesuvius. "These are the tomatoes of Vesuvius," he cried with pride, for these incredible tomatoes and his place in the world, for sharing this spot with the tomatoes and with this fantastic and terrifying mountain. Pointing first to the dark volcanic soil, then to the intimidating and beautiful mountain itself, he continued, "I plant the seeds and grow them, but Vesuvio is why they taste so good!"

And that bread was so, so very good. If I could make such wonderful bread, I'd have a party, too.

Meanwhile, here's a little bruschetta snack from the bakers of Vesuvio: Cut slabs of the best crunchy sourdough bread you can get your hands on. If it's stale, that's even better; you can toast it if you like. Rub a little raw garlic over the slices of bread (optional, but I do love garlic, unlike many Neapolitans). Lay sliced ripe, juicy, utterly delicious tomatoes on top. Sprinkle with a little sea salt. You can add chopped celery, capers, thinly sliced onion, fresh basil—whatever you like. Then drizzle gorgeous, fresh, beautiful, rich, and flavorful olive oil over the top.

Eat on a plate with a fork and knife (unless you are like me and get your fingers involved). Permission granted to tip the plate, after you've eaten every morsel, to let the lovely juices run right into your mouth.

WINE: MAKING IT AND DRINKING IT

Archeological discoveries put the start of viticulture in Campania more than three thousand years ago, at least to the time of Greek and Etruscan settlement. The Greeks referred to what is now southern Italy as Enotria (Land of Wine). They were attracted by the local grapes and knew the difference between table grapes and those for wine—*vitis vinifera*. It was Greeks from Thessaly who were the first to settle in the area at the base of Vesuvio and who brought wine expertise to the fledgling grape growers.

In addition to wine making and appreciation, the Greeks knew how to export it, using double-handled terra cotta amphorae with pointed bottoms that fit into holes on ships' shelves. At first wine was sent to Athens; later, under Roman rule, wine (and olive oil) was shipped throughout the empire, including to Londinium (London) this way.

Horace mentions Campanian wines in his writing. Ischia is noted early on for its wine exporting. As Christianity spread, wine took on religious significance, representing the blood of Christ. Monasteries and convents grew grapes and preserved the tradition of wine making. Wrapped in sacraments and holiness, wine drinking veered away from pleasure of the pagans, Greeks, and Romans to a more serious realm.

During the Roman Empire, Campania Felix—what is now Caserta—created *the* wine of the era: Falernum. Most likely from Aglianico and Falanghina grapes, legend tells that the ancient Romans aged their Falernum for as long as one hundred years.

In the years that followed the Romans, each occupying force added its own wine-making traditions. During the Renaissance, Campania was famous for its wines; yet ensuing centuries saw wine quality stagnating, even declining. It was abundant, something to drink with food, but no more highly regarded than that.

In 1965, that began to change. A new set of laws dictating wine-making techniques, requirements, and structures of geographical production came into being. The acronyms DOC (*denominazione di origine controllata*) and DOCG (indicating a higher level—the G refers to *garantita*, or guarantee) were the result, which guarantees adherence to these rules. DOCG on a wine's label means that the wine should be something special, such as the Campanian Taurasi.

Winemakers focused on local varietals and techniques, realizing the potential for unique characteristics and aging possibilities. Foreign wine experts (especially journalists) noticed that the wines from Campania were becoming interesting and delicious. In response, local winemakers began improving their wines, erasing the old *vino da tavola* (table wine) way of thinking and working toward the prestigious DOC.

Pride in their own wines, constantly seeking to improve, plus a little healthy competition in tastings have worked together in coaxing the whole wine-drinking culture to increasing levels of quality and excellence. Modern technology enables the vintners to get the best from the grapes: plantings, readings, harvests, and pressings. Technology enables traditional winemakers to look forward while drawing on the heritage of the past, returning to the ancient vines, indigenous grapes, and varietals to produce wines with their own character and able to withstand the blandness of the globalized wine-making market.

The main grapes of Campania are Fiano (known to the Romans as Vitis Apiana for its sweet fragrance, which attracted bees), Falanghina, Aglianico, and Greco. The name *Greco* refers to Greece, meaning that the Greeks brought this ancient grape to Magna Grecia, as they did Aglianico, which means "Hellenic." Other varietals have since been imported for blending to support the character of the indigenous vines: Merlot, Primitivo, Piedirosso (named "red feet" by Pliny the Elder for their red stems), even Trebbiano Toscano.

Some, such as Falanghina, produce a DOC wine (Galluccio) but are also blended into others.

When Mount Vesuvius erupted in 79 AD, the ash that covered Pompeii and Herculaneum helped protect the area from phylloxera, sap-sucking insects that fed on the roots and leaves of grapevines, since the mites don't like ash. Indigenous grapes, called "vines of fire," grew from the ashes of these ancient vines. Lacryma Christi is perhaps the most famous; its name means "tears of Christ." Local legend claims that Christ wept when he saw the Bay of Naples, recognizing it as a limb from the sky torn off by Lucifer. Wherever Christ's tears flowed, Lacryma Christi grapevines sprung. Microscopic residue from the taps of the casks suggests that Lacryma Christi wine is the nearest equivalent to the wine drunk by the ancient Romans.

Some of the best wines of Campania are named for their geographical origins, others for their grapes of ancient lineage. Of the Campanian varietals, favorites include Aglianico for red, and Falanghina for white. They have the most character and taste of place.

The red Aglianico has deep, dark cherry flavors, savory spice, and leathery goodness. These wines can last decades but are also delicious younger, and they are reasonably priced.

And although the Falanghina is representative of local white wine grapes, an assortment of other character-driven white grapes is also indigenous to Campania. Greco di Tufo and Fiano (Fiano di Avellino) both have their own DOCGs. Other indigenous white wine grapes include Biancolella, Forastera Olivella (named for its shape), and Coda di Volpe (named for the way the grapes bunch to look like a fox's tail).

Aspirinio is the base for the local sparkling wine, Asprinio di Aversa. Many believe it is a precursor to France's Champagne.

Taurasi—Aglianico DOCG, and the primary DOC Aglianico del Taburno—is probably the red wine held in highest esteem: the aromatic Aglianico balanced by a hit of Merlot.

Near Pozzuoli, in the Campi Flegrei DOC area, there are wonderful wineries producing what I can refer to only as "heartfelt wines."

Capri and Ischia have good local red and white wines. The Amalfi Coast has its share of DOC wines: red Tramonti, dry white Ravello, and a dry rosé delicately scented of flowers and berries. In the Salerno area are red and rose DOC and also a sweet Moscato; down the coast in the Cilento, another DOC wine.

Two favorite whites are the Fiano d'Avellino—one of the few white wines that age well—which is also particularly good with raw shellfish, and Greco di Tufo, a wine of the Greco grape grown in the limestone soil known as *tufo*. Its almond and peach aftertaste are delightful; it is also made as a sparkling wine.

Gragnano produces a dark berry-colored red, and Sorrento scents the wine with violets from along Penisola Sorrentina. The naturally sparkling reds of Gragnano and Lettere are good with pizza and the sun-drenched local cuisine.

Many wineries are owned by families, linking the modern-day commerce of wine with the heritage of life in Campania. The Mastroberardino family has been making wine for three hundred years and is devoted to reviving the Pompeiian vineyards. Antonio Beradino revived the delicate white grape, Fiano, which had nearly disappeared. The lovely Villa Matilde is the vineyard responsible for much of the Falerno grape's return, its owners related to the exquisite Grand Hotel Parkers in Napoli. Mustilli grows Greco, Falanghina, Piedirosso, and Aglianico. The Alois family used to be in textiles; now they are winemakers and gastronomes.

The spectacular Feudi di San Gregorio wine estate was founded by a husband and wife and has earned a reputation as one of Campania's most exciting and dynamic wineries. It is located on some of the most ancient wine-producing land in all of Italy; records show wine being made in this part of the Irpinia region as early as 590 AD.

Spread over lush hillsides, the soil—volcanic, sandstone, and marly—imbues its grapes with aromas of cherry, cinnamon, and aniseed. The winery itself is stylishly designed and beautifully landscaped. Each vineyard is closely monitored with a meteorological station, and a state-of-the-art wine cellar ensures that each vintage is as close to perfection as possible.

LIQUEURS

Liqueurs are traditionally drunk as *aperitivi*, *digestivi*, medicinally, or simply for delicious relaxation.

Strega

When Strega was created in Benevento in 1860, the town was still a Papal State enclave. According to local legend, witches from all over the world gathered in Benevento once a year around a sacred walnut tree, creating a love potion that would unite forever all couples who drank it together. When the young Giuseppe Alberti was looking for a name for his company, he was attracted to this romantic tale and decided to name his liqueur in honor of the legend. (The word *strega* means witch.)

The recipe is said to have originated with local Benedictine monks; only two people are privy to the exact recipe. Warmly golden in color, Strega is made of seventy herbs and spices from all over the world, distilled in small batches and long aged in oak vats. It develops a kaleidoscope of taste and aroma: smooth, sweet, and slightly bitter with a beautiful balance of aromatics. Its ingredients include saffron, orange peel, star anise, mint, peppercorns, lavender, juniper, and cinnamon bark. Its box is as appealing as the drink: saffron in color with art deco illustrations. The company also makes other confections and since 1947 has sponsored a prestigious literary award.

Fruit and Nut Liqueurs

There are so many traditional liqueurs handed down generation to generation: anise, melon, strawberry, a local citrus related to the bergamot orange, *nocellino* (hazelnut), unripe walnut, the rare *nanniato* made from prickly pears with wild fennel.

I am especially fond of a creamy melon liqueur served very cold on a hot summer's day, and sour cherries distilled into the clear, alcoholic Maraschino is fabulous in local pastry, baked goods, or anything sweet.

Rosolio is an ancient liqueur that had been forgotten until recently. Named after the Latin *ros solis* (morning dew), it was originally made by nuns and served at baptisms and weddings. Both royalty and peasants (who made it at home) adored it, but in the late eighteenth century King Vittorio Amedeo III switched his *aperitivo* from rosolio to vermouth, and the people followed. Poor rosolio nearly disappeared. While its name doesn't refer specifically to rose petals, sometimes they are used for flavoring, though bergamot is more typical.

Concerto is one of the oldest liqueurs of the Amalfi Coast, a dark, dense, aromatic liquid, both sweet and bitter. Said to have first been prepared by the nuns in the Royal Conservatory of the Saints Giuseppe and Teresa in Pucara, Tramonti, it is made from herbs. The nuns gathered what they were able to find and added licorice, mint, dried fennel branches, and soaked barley and coffee at the end, as they do today. Like most herbal liqueurs, Concerto was an all-purpose medicine/ cure: coughs, chest colds, heart problems, whatever ails you. Many elders believe in its therapeutic ability.

It is still mostly made in homes, with a glass poured for guests as a gesture of hospitality. A loose recipe includes star anise, anise seed, cinnamon stick, cloves, coriander seeds, juniper berries, sandalwood, nutmeg, and lemon peel mixed with a strong, flavorless alcohol. Filtered, it's combined with boiled barley water, sugar, and coffee, then aged and bottled.

Limoncello (or lemoncello) is probably the most famous liqueur in Campania these days, maybe even in all of Italy. Until the last few decades, it was homemade, each family putting up as many bottles as they could during the long lemon season. A few decades ago, restaurants began making their own to pour for diners after a meal. Customers asked to buy a bottle to take home, and an industry was born. It is at its best very cold. Some serve it over ice but that dilutes the drink. I keep a bottle or two in the freezer; when it pours from the bottle, it is almost syrupy. *Mandarin-cello* (mandarin orange), *limecello* (lime), and *meloncello* are all divine, as are the ones brewed with milk—it's like drinking a gorgeous creamsicle.

BEER

A nice cool beer is refreshing, especially with pizza, even in Campania with its wine culture. Lately craft beers have developed a following among the young, locally made beers enjoyed in pubs with pub grub menus such as *stuzzichini*, meat-ball crostini, and other foods inspired by foreign beer-drinking cultures.

5

Pasta and Pizza

That a simple paste of wheat and water, transformed by Neapolitan culinary spirit, evolved into two categories of food recognized the world over is, to my mind, genius.

Wheat and water mixed well: craft it into morsels or long strings and boil, and you have pasta; stretch it flat and bake or fry for pizza. Each achieves its own unique character: pasta becomes supple, tender, and chewy; pizza is a cloud of bread-like dough, its bubbles filled with warm, yeasty, wheaty air. Millennia of attention to detail, care in preparation, and joy of eating have helped it evolve.

Dating to the most ancient of times and eaten in many places, Naples didn't invent either dish. However, it was Naples that made the dough its own, creating something—two somethings—that forged a vital link in its culinary culture from the past until today.

When durum wheat (flour) and water met the tomato, however, *that* is when the magic happened. Suddenly here was a bright red sauce (red, the Neapolitan color—the hue of fire, of red lips, of hot blood, red hearts, berries, cherries, beautiful flowers) that tasted zesty, so fresh, bursting with umami, good cooked or raw, the perfect adjunct to the blandness of dough.

That the tomato turned out to be full of vitamins *has* to be proof that nature loves Naples. That it can be preserved in jars and eaten on pasta or pizza for the year to come—that is pure miracle.

No one exemplifies Neapolitan pizza/pasta love more than Pulcinella. The seventeenth-century masked character from Commedia dell'Arte—a Neapolitan version of a Punch and Judy character—is close to the heart and soul of Neapolitans. His stories reflect the attitudes of being Napoletano (then, and even now).

One story tells of Pulcinella's love of pasta. When asked whether he likes *frittata di maccheroni* (the golden omelet made with leftover pasta), he wistfully whimpers, "I can never eat it." When asked why, he replies, "Because I never have any pasta left over to make the frittata with," admitting his gluttony: he always eats all the macaroni, no matter how much there is. He can't help himself; he loves it so.

In another tale, the always poor Pulcinella, by a crazy twist of fate, becomes the king of seventeenth-century Naples. At first he revels in his newfound status, giddy with its possibilities, wealth, and power: "I was born to be king!" But then he realizes that pasta and pizza belong to the tables of the commoners, not to royalty! He will no longer be allowed to eat pasta and pizza. And so he does what any sensible Neapolitan would. "I must de-king myself, immediately!" he exclaims. Because he would much rather eat pizza and pasta than rule the country—so understandable.

How did Naples transform from a class-focused diet to a cuisine for all? In large part, pizza and pasta helped. A couple of centuries ago, pasta and pizza were eaten in the streets by the hungry poor. The fancy people—nobility, aristocrats, even the wealthy merchant class—saw pasta and pizza as lower-class fare to be avoided. The fact that they ate with their hands was "filthy." And, as we know from Pulcinella, it wouldn't do for the rich and poor to eat the same type of food. But then as now, regardless of wealth or poverty, Neapolitans hold the pleasures of the table close to their hearts.

So there they were: the aristocrats and the wealthy, getting bored with stuffy French menus while the *lazzaroni*—poor, working-class Neapolitans—were eating pizza and pasta in the streets, with their hands, with gusto!

The wealthy began to get curious about what they were missing and instructed their chefs to cook pasta, adding it to the fancy French dishes to replace delicacies they couldn't find in Napoli. A whole tradition of *timballe* and complex pasta dishes originated during this time.

And pizza! The streets were filled with pizza eating. Aristocrats began "slumming" in order to taste the savory pies. When the kings and queens (including one particular Margherita) did the same and added pizza to the palace menu, everyone wanted it. Soon pizza was fashionable—who knew that "poor people's food" was so delicious?

And so, unintentionally, a huge thing happened: eating the same vibrant, tasty food was socially bonding, a force uniting all classes from the highest and richest to the lowliest laborer. Life in Napoli was never the same again.

That pizza and pasta combine with the seasonal scraps of the poverty kitchen is a testament to the brilliance of *la cucina Napoletana* and its beautiful frugality.

At the moment, pasta and pizza are enjoying a renaissance, the food of survival now the subject of culinary creativity. Pizza chefs are famous on television! Dolce & Gabbana fashion models eat spaghetti in advertisements. The world may love pizza and pasta (and it does) but Naples loves them even more.

How much does Naples love pasta and pizza? To a Neapolitan, pasta and pizza are more than food, they are identity. Eating them is an act of unity, of belonging, of paying homage. If you're visiting, it is an important part of appreciating local culture, as much as visiting an art gallery or musical concert. When one is born in Naples, eating pasta and pizza is your birthright.

PASTA

The film producer Federico Fellini once famously said, "Life is a combination of magic and pasta." I had never heard anything quite as poetic or profound. Thinking further, I realized that pasta sustains the body, while magic nourishes the soul. Together, they feed our wholeness.

Being Neapolitan means that you likely love pasta. I know Neapolitans who never travel abroad without a few packages of Gragnano pasta. After several days away from home, they crave a plate of spaghetti or linguine. And remember Sophia Loren's famous quote, "Everything you see I owe to spaghetti," as she motions up and down her body? Look into her eyes and her beautiful smile—you *know* this is true.

For a Neapolitan, pasta is both ordinary and emotional. A plate of pasta is a daily joy. Daily. Ordinary. How did we get so lucky? But it is also emotional: the aroma of braising onions or simmering tomatoes reminds you that Nonna is making Sunday or holiday pasta for the whole family. If she is no longer with you, it is her memory that feeds you.

If Italians eat between fifty and sixty pounds of pasta a year (depending on geography and other variables), I would suggest that Neapolitans eat far more than the national average. You can eat pasta for lunch, dinner, or midnight snack (*pasta della mezzanotte*). In the streets you might have a pasta croquette—*frittatine*—or a slab of frittata di pasta. If you have leftover pasta, you'll probably make your own frittata: Mix leftover pasta with grated cheese and eggs, adding anything you like or nothing at all, depending on the sauce. Fry it as a big, thick pancake in a small amount of olive oil like you would a Spanish tortilla or any other flat omelet. Invited on a picnic? Probably a frittata di pasta will be packed in the lunch basket. A barbecue on the beach? Be prepared to see a big pot of boiling water over the fire—someone will cook pasta. About the only time Neapolitans don't eat pasta is for breakfast (breakfast is sweet: cake or toast with jam or chocolate spread).

Gragnano (and originally Torre Annunziata, Torre del Greco, and Nola), about twenty minutes outside of Naples, is the epicenter of Neapolitan pasta making (many say for the entire world).

Most likely pasta began when nomadic life ceased. Instead of wandering, hunting, and foraging, tribes now stayed in one place, learned to plant seeds, and cultivated what grew. It provided a more predictable diet, allowing experimentation that enabled them to coax the best from what was growing.

One of these crops was wheat. Somewhere in the cradle of civilization about nine thousand years ago, cooks discovered that they could mash the grains with water, pat them into flat cakes, and cook them on hot stones. The resulting flatbreads were eaten in hot broth, evolving into something very pasta-like.

With overlap and influence between tribes, countries, and cultures, pastas of varying types seem to have popped up throughout the Mediterranean. Nomadic Arab tribes found that by drying, it could be a good, portable source of preserved food.

At this point, you might be thinking, "What about Marco Polo? Didn't he bring noodles from China? Isn't that how Italy got its pasta?" No. Just no. Pasta history predates Marco Polo's fateful trip by millennia.

In Gragnano itself, there is evidence that pasta has been made for at least two thousand years (a thousand years before Marco Polo's trip). According to Giuseppe Di Martino of Pastificio dei Campi and past president of the Consorzio di Tutela della Pasta di Gragnano, the making and drying of dried, hard wheat pasta is a local invention, created in 3 BCE as food for the Roman soldiers.

Gragnano, whose name loosely translates as "grains," grew wheat—the lovely hard wheat that still grows exceedingly well in the area today. These grains, high in protein and nutrients, were required to be given to Rome to nourish the Roman soldiers. Since it was easily infested by pests, the people of Gragnano decided to grind the wheat, killing the insects and their eggs.

In nearby Pompeii, Herculaneum, and Stabiae, the milled wheat was used to make bread. In Gragnano, however, it was discovered that the flour and water paste could be spread thinly to dry rather than using it for bread. The drying preserved the harvest for long periods of time. Then, when cooked in liquid, the dry, hard dough became softer, more digestible, and nutritious, building the strength of Rome's soldiers—and, as if this wasn't enough, it was delicious.

The environment offered a perfect balance of features. The spring waters that flow from the mountains above the city fed the wheat fields and helped the mills grind the hard wheat, ideal for both bread and pasta. The resulting semolina flour was made into pasta, placed on drying racks in the open air, and dried slowly and evenly by the breezes that wafted through Gragnano. A slow and even drying was (and still is) the key for the best dry pasta.

There's no consensus regarding the origin of the word *macaroni*. There are at least two possibilities from Greek times: the name *makaira* or *makairon*, which referred to a large-bladed knife possibly used for cutting pasta, or the word *macarius*, meaning "divine food."

Others maintain that the origin of the word *macaroni* comes from a character in traditional Comedia dell'Arte: Mascherone. He was a glutton; he *loved* to eat. It was, as we might say these days, his "superpower" (or his Achilles heel). Learning that a Neapolitan prince with a fine palate was fond of this fat pasta with a hole, Mascherone took notice. When he discovered, however, that it needed to be made by a specialist, a master pasta maker, and that he could not afford it, he exclaimed, "*Si buoni, ma caroni!*" (So good, but expensive!)

And then there's this: In *Il talismano della felicità*, author Ada Boni describes the legend of the word *macaroni*, telling of a Neapolitan cardinal whose chef offered him a plate of boiled dough in a rich tomato sauce. The cardinal looked at it and exclaimed happily, "*Ma cari! Ma caroni!*" which loosely translates as "Oh, those dear things! Those dear big things!"

Most likely the name came from *macare*, meaning, literally, "to make flat," as the wheat paste was spread into a thin layer. In Neapolitan, *maccheroni* is still the name for short cuts of pasta.

The large flat pasta sheet of ancient Greece, around the first century BCE, were known as *lagnanon*. The Latin *laganum* comes from this word, and these pasta strips traveled throughout the Greek world and later Roman Empire. As pasta adapted wherever it was adopted, it's likely that *lagnanon* equals *laganum* equals *lasagna*.

Apicious wrote about preparing pasta, though primarily for sustenance than for recipes to delight, as we would expect from a modern cookbook. A cookbook written by Ibran' al Mibrad in the ninth century described a dish popular with the Bedouin and Berber tribes, *rista* (macaroni) and lentils, still eaten today in Syria and Lebanon. In 1138, Al-Idrisi, the Arab court geographer to Roger II of Sicily, described the residents of Trabia, near Palermo, preparing and drying a dough formed into long strings called *itriya*, Arabic for string (like the Italian *spago* for string—that is, spaghetti). In 1244, a similar pasta was noted in Genoa, and we know that in Persia people were eating a type of noodle called *rishta*. This was before Marco Polo's travel chronicles. Perhaps noodles traveled along the Silk Road from Central Asia to the Middle East, where *rishta* was known, introduced to Italy by Arabs when they dominated Sicily.

At the Spaghetti Museum in Imperia, near Genoa, several documents from 1279 and 1284 refer to *maccheroni* and vermicelli; Polo didn't return until 1292. The myth of Marco Polo bringing back pasta is curious. Why did people link the two? It was that only two regions ate noodles as a staple—China and Italy—so people figured Marco Polo must be the link. But Polo didn't specifically mention noodles; he may have brought a sample of soft wheat, but maybe not. Anyhow, many of the noodles in China were made from soy, buckwheat, rice, bean, and pea, as well as soft wheat. These were nothing like the hard wheat noodles that would be the spaghetti of Italy.

Marco Polo didn't even pay much attention to China's noodles in his writings (to be fair, Polo's writings omit such a wide variety of observations that there has long been controversy as to whether he even got to China). Perhaps he was used to eating noodles from his home in Venice? Perhaps others, such as Rustichella of Pisa, worked with Polo, or Ranusio, his first editor, took a few liberties embellishing Polo's descriptions and discoveries? (It is thought that they did.)

We know that pasta was mentioned in the Anjou Court of Naples in 1295 and was referred to in Bocaccio's *Decameron*, and, unlike the soft wheat noodles of the north, the pasta of the south was hard wheat, grown near Gragnano.

Around this time, a major change in pasta preparation took place: instead of baking flatbreads first, and then adding them to broth, a new cooking method was discovered in which the shaped dough was cooked directly in boiling water and served with a sauce or condiment added afterward. (To experience how the early pasta must have tasted, toast a piece of pita until crisp, then break it into smallish pieces and add to a bowl of hot soup—chicken, vegetable, as you like. The pitas grow soft and slightly puffy, chewy, something like a fat noodle—and really good.)

Until the sixteenth century, pasta was always homemade. For the poor, it was a special occasion food (like meat); for the upper classes, they had only to command their chefs, though pasta was considered unacceptable except for intricate *timballi* or other elaborately constructed dishes. When they tried to eat it plain, they had a problem with those hot wet noodles: How to eat them? Eating with their hands was messy, not befitting their stations in life, and when it was hot, it burned the fingers.

But by the end of the century, family-run pasta shops began to appear. As the number of handmade pasta shops grew, people began to eat more of it. The artisanal craft of master pasta maker developed and was passed down from generation to generation.

Gragnano had been famous for its fine textiles, but in 1783 a blight destroyed the silkworms and the fabric industry collapsed. Needing to produce something else, the people of Gragnano quite naturally turned to pasta. They had the basic ingredients, skills, and love for the noodle.

Gragnano was one of the first cities in Italy to put pasta into production. New ways to make pasta were needed to keep up with demand. The only tools in use were a long-handled wooden knife called a *gramola* and a cylinder-shaped wooden press called a *torchio*, which forced the dough through the die to form a shape. And pasta did indeed rescue the area: tax records show that once the industry was established, the town's coffers were full again, to great local benefit.

This would usher in Gragnano's *Epoca d'Oro* (Golden Age). The excellent Garofalo pasta was founded during this time, in 1789, and is still a high-quality dried pasta today. In the homes of the wealthy, Russian service was adopted as a precise way to organize the courses of the meal. When they served a pasta course, it was usually in a rich broth of game or fowl or with a hearty ragù.

By around the 1830s, modern methods of machinery for making dried pasta from local durum wheat increased Gragnano's productivity. Large *pastifici* (pasta makers) sprang up along Via Roma and Piazza Trivione, becoming the very heart of town. Along these streets, the *pastifici* hung their pasta out to dry. Photos from this time show the streets lined with spaghetti-draped racks. Community-wide drying was part of Gragnano's landscape of life.

Unfortunately, the wealthy were still having trouble eating it. First, they used a pointed, wooden stick. It ended up making a mess, so they added another point. And then another. Three points was better, but the long slippery strands still ended up all over the place.

Even the king wasn't immune. So that his sovereign could enjoy pasta elegantly, Gennaro Spadaccini, chamberlain of court to the Bourbon King Ferdinand II, commissioned a designer. The result was a four-pronged fork, perfect to twist the pasta around and get it tidily into the mouth.

Next was the issue of production. When King Ferdinand II visited a pasta workshop in Torre Annunziata, he was horrified to see the dough being kneaded by hand (and even more horrified to see it kneaded by foot). And so, another invention: an engineer was commissioned to create a (more hygienic) machine. Though it worked well, it was never put to full use, as famine, drought, and epidemics wracked the area, disrupting life, and the factory fell into disrepair. The king's dream of machine-made pasta, however, opened the door to reality, eventually streamlining the whole pasta-making process.

This mini-industrialization put pasta on the tables of even the poorest people. Until then, only the rich could have pasta at will, prepared by their chefs. The masses ate pasta only on special occasions; every day they ate vegetables, usually as soup, with small bits of meat or fish for flavor. Pasta transformed the way the entire region ate. Not only did it help the poorest survive, thrive, and grow, but it also brought variety and pleasure to the daily lives of Gragnano's citizens. And because it was dry, it could be stored on the shelf for long periods of time without spoiling, ready to be cooked when desired.

Now no longer nicknamed *mangiafoglie* ("leaf eaters"—a slur), as they were when they scraped by on vegetable soup, they were known as *mangiamaccheroni* (macaroni eaters—also an unkind term), which had once referred to the pasta-eating Sicilians.

Whole streets were now dedicated to pasta: making, drying, and eating. Torre Annunziata's "La strada dei Maccheroni" (Macaroni Street) was redesigned—street width in balance with building height to allow just the right amount of sun and heat for perfect drying. It was the pasta manufacturers themselves, not the local sanitation department, who paid for local streets to be kept clean, so the pasta could dry in the open air hygienically.

The Kingdom of Two Sicilies (basically the entire south) joined the Kingdom of Italy in taking steps toward unification in 1861. This move opened new import markets throughout what is now Italy. By now, Gragnano's economy depended almost entirely on its one hundred *pastifici*, which made around 250,000 pounds of pasta a day! (Today, a pasta factory generally makes about 550,000 pounds an hour, with a machine producing 5,000 pounds of pasta an hour.)

And they celebrated their pasta-making identity. Picture postcards sent home from the European Grand Tour show crowds of people, hands raised above their heads, lowering fistfuls of spaghetti into their mouths.

Electricity also had a big impact on pasta production, as hand-operated machines were replaced by mechanized ones. Unlike other products, however, the pasta makers of Gragnano felt strongly (and still do) that human attention to detail keeps the quality high. Staying close to their artisanal roots is important for most local pasta makers.

New methods of transportation helped move the pasta to the rest of Italy. The railway line between Gragnano and Naples, opened on May 12, 1885, made a huge difference; the ports of Napoli and Salerno put the pasta on ships, where it was sent by sea to the rest of the world.

When Garibaldi liberated Naples in 1860, he is said to have proclaimed that pasta would be what held all of Italy together. Many of his men had never eaten pasta before—only polenta, rice, or dumplings. If they ate pasta, it was a different type: rich with eggs, tender, and made fresh by hand. After two months in Naples, the one thing they could agree on, the one thing that bound them together, was pasta. Spaghetti. *Maccheroni.* And like so many dishes and nations before them, they brought their love for this food home, which did help unite the collection of city-states into one nation.

When composer Rossini lived in Naples and wrote his opera *Othello*, he fell in love with pasta. After he left, he had it sent wherever he was working, not entrusting it to his chef but preparing it himself. He loved pasta.

Then there was the Marinetti Manifesto of Futurist Cuisine, which considered pasta food for weak people. But pasta is so delicious: it always triumphs in the end.

Gragnano's dominance of the Italian pasta market lasted until the mid-1930s, when Mussolini put an end to import and export. They could not import American or Ukrainian wheat (needed when they couldn't grow enough locally), nor could they export Gragnano pasta.

It was between the two world wars that pasta became *il primo*, the first course in an Italian menu. Then World War II came, and people were lucky to eat at all. By the end of World War II, many *pastifici* had closed, but thankfully postwar prosperity restored pasta as a thriving industry, though I hesitate to use the word "industry," because in Gragnano pasta is heritage, tradition, happiness—not just a matter of factory jobs.

Most of the world recognized spaghetti by the twentieth century; it starred in films such as *The Gold Rush* (1925), when Charlie Chaplin ate his shoelaces as if they were spaghetti. He didn't need words: the shoelaces were immediately recognized as his longed-for spaghetti. The vintage animated film *Lady and the Tramp* linked spaghetti with love when the two adorable dogs slurp up one long strand of spaghetti, ending in a sauce-coated kiss. And most of all, the scene of utmost *Napoletanità*: the great spaghetti scene from *Miseria e Nobiltà* (with two famous Neapolitans, Totò and Sophia Loren), eating with abandon, spaghetti everywhere, the whole group around the table digging in with their hands. Totò leaps onto the table, stuffing his pockets with spaghetti, his face radiating transcendental joy with each bite. They are not doing this with any other of the dishes on the table—only the spaghetti. To see this scene is to witness what pasta means to a Neapolitan. (You can find these scenes on YouTube.) A Naples restaurant, Tandem, specializing in ragù (known as *'o raù* in Neapolitan dialect), shows a never-ending video loop of famous pasta scenes in movies. Get a seat near the TV.

I might not be Neapolitan, but from the moment I forked up my first bite of Gragnano pasta, I become somewhat evangelical. Of course, I adore the tender, eggy hand-rolled pasta of the north and its delicate stuffed pastas, as well as the pastas from other regions of Italy—Genoa, Puglia, Sicily (who wouldn't?). But my heart belongs to Naples when I'm putting that pot of water on to boil.

In Naples pasta is a culture and a way of life. For me, it became a mission: at risk of being annoying or pushy, I simply don't want anyone missing the whole beautiful, chewy experience.

Manfredi con Ricotta e Piselli

Use any flat or tubular, wide pasta, so the ricotta and tomato sauce can cling: *paccheri, manfredine, fresine, fettuccelle, calamarata,* pappardelle.

2 cloves garlic, cut into a few flat slices or peeled and flattened slightly *or* ½ onion, finely chopped

2–3 tablespoons extra virgin olive oil

⅔–1 cup frozen peas (or fresh if it's springtime and they are young and tender)

2 cans (about 13 ounces each) or 1 large can of San Marzano tomatoes

Salt and black pepper to taste

12 ounces of flat pasta of choice (see above)

8–10 ounces ricotta cheese (whole milk—the best quality you can find, as the dish is very much about the ricotta)

Fresh basil leaves, as desired

Heat the garlic or onion in the olive oil until softened and starting to brown slightly; then add the peas, stirring them around, followed by the tomatoes. Raise the heat, cooking and stirring, until the tomato liquid cooks down; then season with salt and pepper and set aside.

Cook the pasta until less than al dente, and then drain, reserving a cup or so of the cooking liquid.

Over a medium-low heat, add the pasta to the sauce, and cook together a few minutes, adding a little of the cooking water as you go to keep it saucy and prevent drying or clagging. When the pasta is just al dente, stir in the ricotta, breaking it up, and serve right away, garnished with as many torn fresh basil leaves as you like.

Pasta di Gragnano

Gragnano has an Indicazione Geografica Protetta (IGP) from the European Union, a designation similar to that of a DOC wine appellation, a seal of certification that guarantees it is made according to precise regulations and is a traditional cultural product of the area. To be called Pasta di Gragnano, it must be produced in a legally defined area, mixing durum wheat with the low-calcium water of Monti Lattari. It must have at least 13 percent protein. It is naturally high in protein, which means that gluten-free pasta cannot be made Gragnano IGP.

The Consorzio—the Consortium for the Protection of Pasta di Gragnano IGP—is a group of traditional pasta makers (numbering fourteen at the moment) that issues guidelines for the making of Gragnano pasta: The water must be a certain temperature, semolina grain mature at harvest and milled precisely. Only bronze dies are allowed; then it must be slow dried at low temperatures. The Consorzio also sponsors events such as "Pasta on the Beach" or the Festa della Pasta, Gragnano's joyous street festival honoring everything to do with pasta, with dancing and music and carrying on in between plates of pasta dishes.

After harvesting and milling the grain, and mixing the dough, comes extruding it into shapes.

At least three hundred shapes of pasta exist today, each one with the choice of size and surface: *lisci* (smooth) or *rigati* (ridged). The assembly lines make different shapes each day. Some *pastifici* will, upon request, create a special shape for you. Though we take pasta names for granted, each shape has a specific meaning, usually deriving from the name of an ordinary object. Each shape gives the dough a different texture, which provides endless variation of taste and feel in the mouth.

The short cuts of pasta include macaroni, ditalini (little fingers), *lumaconi* (shells), ziti (bridegrooms), farfalle (butterflies), and so forth. At the beginning of pasta's industrialization there were only long pastas—thin (spaghetti), flat (linguine), or fat and hollow (*candele*, bucatini); the short pastas hadn't been industrialized yet. The first written mention of dried pasta was in 1846, and by 1861 spaghetti was listed in the Bellini Dictionary. Another ancient shape is the *rosmarino*, a pastina (tiny shape) the size and shape of rosemary sprigs and traditionally served in light soups and broths.

For what we would call macaroni today, customers purchased *candele* (long, hollow wide pastas, like a candle), then broke them up into the length desired. The breaking of the pasta also offers a complex sensation, its uneven shapes and broken edges giving a variety of textures, with starch and wheaty perfume enriching the finished dish. In a family, the lengths would differ depending on who was doing the breaking—if a tiny child was given the job, the pasta shapes usually turned out small because a child's hands were small.

Then come the tubular ones, especially the very Neapolitan *paccheri*. The name means "slap," for the way it collapses when cooked, slapping onto the plate as it's served. *Calamarata* are a variation, cooking up much like squid (calamari) rings. Twisted fusilli, strands of pasta wrapped around knitting needles, was one of the first shapes created in Campania and sometimes is still made by hand.

Bucatini are halfway between the long strands and tubes: a pin-sized hole runs through the length of its middle (*buca* means "hole"). The hole helps the pasta cook evenly, as the hot water flows in and out; when sauced, it is the sauce that fills the holes.

Pasta *mista* is a mixture of many different types of pasta, each a similar size for even cooking. When there was only a small amount of a certain shape of pasta left, not enough for a whole serving, it was put in a jar, repeating each time there was a small amount of leftover dried pasta. By the time the jar was full, it contained a whimsical collection that was fun to chew because of the variety of shapes and textures in the mouth. Ironically, for Italian Americans (often Neapolitans who had migrated to America), there was a sense of shame attached to these mixtures. Many felt it was an announcement to the world outside their home that they were poor.

To extrude dough for any shape, bronze dies (*trafile al bronzo*) were invented in the late nineteenth century. The die is affixed to the machine and the dough pushed out through its holes, the same way it is today. The twentieth century gave us Teflon, which is inexpensive and long lasting, though it provides a lesser result than bronze. Many *pastifici* do use it, but not in Gragnano, and not in *pastifici* that care about quality. The choice of die is a crucial part of pasta making. Bronze dies might cost more (they do) and need to be replaced more often (they do), but pasta made with bronze dies has a surface that is just slightly rough, perhaps not even noticeable to the eye, but it makes a pasta to which sauce clings fervently. With Teflon, the surface is too smooth, and the sauce slips off the pasta onto your plate.

Watching the dough being extruded is mesmerizing: it squishes through the holes, twists and turns, changing shapes depending on the die chosen. The number of grooves, curve, length of cut all come together with the speed of the machine to create the shapes desired. To dry, they are scattered on a flat drying screen.

The long strands—the spaghetti, linguine, and *fettuccelle*—are draped over rods, starting their initial drying waving back and forth, looking like a massive length of golden hula skirts in mid-dance.

Small shapes eliminated the need to break up long tubes of pasta, but today breaking up the long pasta such as *candele* is still a Sunday lunch tradition for many. Even if the pasta is uncooked, its wheaty perfume fills the air. Breaking the pasta into pieces while waiting for the ragù becomes an evocative memory of sharing good pasta with those you love.

Drying Pasta

You would think that the most important part of pasta would be making the dough and shapes. It is important, but drying the pasta correctly is the secret of pasta excellence. Fast drying does not bring out the best in the wheat, though it saves money. The longer it takes for slow drying, the more it costs the producers; yet slow drying is one of the special characteristics of pasta Gragnano.

Slow drying requires a higher protein wheat, which you can't see in raw pasta but you can taste when it's cooked. Higher protein gives a chewier texture with a nuttier flavor and aroma and less starchy stodge. Gragnano pasta has a protein level of at least 13 percent, while Pasta Di Martino has at least 14 percent protein, and in some years the harvest boasts 15 percent; the protein is where the gluten is—and the gluten particles are what holds it all together. Soft wheat is good for stretching; hard wheat not so much, as having a memory of shape makes it difficult to knead with the hands but perfect to work with the traditional Italian machines.

Slow drying contributes to a lighter, more easily digested pasta, allowing for more water absorption, satisfying but not heavy. Slow drying helps keep its wheaty fragrance and gives the pasta a pale yellow color (too dark a pasta indicates drying that was too fast over too high a temperature; in a sense, it cooked the grain).

Surprising to many of us, pasta is a fermented product (no yeast is added, but there is some present on the wheat itself and in the air), which begins within minutes after ground wheat is combined with water. Drying slowly allows control over the fermentation; this develops better flavor. Cheaper products cut corners, risking an overfermented product with an acidic or musty taste. In the past hand-made era, fermentation was a consideration and needed to be monitored; now fermentation is not even part of the picture, as the pasta-making process is so well developed scientifically.

Until 1950 pasta was dried outside in the streets; old photos show endless lines of rods and poles (called *le canne*), with fringelike lengths of pasta hanging over them. Specialized skilled workers, the *spannatori*, cut the pasta and hung it on the poles, carefully carrying the pasta by hand without allowing it to stick together.

There are basically three stages to the drying. The first is *incarto*, when a natural crust forms on the outside of the soft pasta dough. In the old days, this was done by putting racks of fresh pasta in direct sunlight on the street. The second stage, *rinvenimento*, leaves the pasta to "recover" in cooler, damp rooms, which softens the crust. The last stage is *essiccazione*, slowly drying all the way through, traditionally in shady areas such as courtyards or attics.

Long hanging pasta strands were the most delicate. Since pasta breaks easily, they were difficult to move between warmer and cooler temperatures to get the drying just right.

Today, drying is done indoors, by machine, at a temperature of about 90°F. Commercial producers dry long pasta strands such as spaghetti in about seven hours; artisanal pasta makers about two days. For commercial short pasta shapes, three or four hours is usually allowed; for the artisanal pasta company, a day and a half is about right. The long pasta is cut and hung on rods by expert "cutters." Short pasta is scattered onto wooden frames by speaders, then moved to special areas for slow drying.

The work is not finished once the pasta is dried. Packing by machine could ruin it. The packaging should therefore be done according to tradition, by hand, and sold in boxes and bags that best preserve the integrity of each shape. Some brands of excellence are Pastificio Di Martino, Gentile, Faella, Garofalo, and Setaro (its third-generation pasta makers are located in Torre Annunziata).

Cooking: Al Dente and Beyond

With pasta made from good wheat—carefully crafted and slowly dried—it is of the highest importance not to overcook it! Overcooked pasta is flabby. The meaning of *al dente* is "to the teeth"—your teeth should feel a bit of resistance when you bite in. You don't want it to crunch, but you want a good chewy sensation.

Neapolitans—and traditionally all southern Italians—take al dente one step further and cook their pasta *fujennì*, which is just this side of al dente. At first you might wonder whether it is cooked enough, but after the first bite or two, the lovely wheaty taste emerges, and it feels less stodgy, less heavy, less carby. Once used to this way of cooking, you may find even al dente a little bit too soft for you.

Commercial industrially produced pasta doesn't cook properly al dente. It is made with lower protein grain and less attentive industrial methods. When added to boiling water, it loses much of its starch, blurring its shape and losing its integrity. A good way to assess the quality of the pasta is to cook some and then let it cool. Lower-quality pasta tastes like gummy flour paste. Well-crafted pasta tastes of wheat and the harvest (and, to me, of happiness).

Every so often miracle discoveries are announced about cooking pasta. I try them all and keep coming back to the traditional Neapolitan way: water (lots of it!) rapidly boiling, salted well (*after* boiling—some say as salty as the sea, others say as salty as tears). After the pasta has cooked in it, you have a liquid that can be added, a ladleful or two at a time, as you toss the drained pasta in the pan with the sauce. It makes the dish—pasta and sauce—come together as one.

Don't listen to anyone who says to add oil to the cooking water. It weighs down the pasta when it's drained and keeps the pasta from melding with the sauce—a big no-no.

Serve pasta in a shallow, warmed bowl, sort of huddling together to keep warm. If serving long strands such as spaghetti, vermicelli, and so on, twist it around a fork into a nest that looks so fetching that it could have been done for presentation. But no, it's cleverly practical: the shape retains the heat longer so it doesn't cool as quickly.

There are other ways to eat pasta than fresh from the pan, hot into your bowl, in Campania. For example, frittata di pasta (mentioned earlier). Then there's the *timpano*, the big-deal pasta pie inherited from the kitchens of the Monzù. Line a deep, oiled baking pan with sheets of fresh pasta, fill it with layers of pasta in a creamy, cheesy sauce (cooled—I've used leftovers), along with layers of spinach or peas, layers of cured meats, and cheese, and then close up the top with a few sheets of buttered fresh pasta. Bake, invert, and serve with tomato sauce.

What Shape with Which Sauce?

Like so many things, it's complicated. Throughout Italy, rules govern pasta saucing. Campania also has rules—some Italian, some its own. You can find rules in cookbooks, as well as charts of which pasta goes with which sauce online, and almost any chef or Nonna will tell you the definitive answer—though it might contradict all the others.

Some things a Napoletano is born knowing: for instance, never ragù with spaghetti! Ragù is too strong for the thin pasta. It will weigh it down and slide right off. Thin strands are great for light, clinging sauces: *aglio e olio*, puttanesca, tomatoes, lemon. A light, delicate sauce with sturdy, chunky pasta will make you sad when you taste how bland and heavy it is.

Yet sometimes even experienced pasta chefs make mistakes, as I did recently. I had last-minute guests, so thought I'd whip up a puttanesca sauce. Olives, anchovies, garlic—it was utterly delicious. Opening the cupboard, though, I realized that I had no spaghetti—only a flat, fairly thick *fettuccelle* or pappardelle-like pasta. It was too late to turn back; guests were already sitting at the table. What could I do? I cooked it, tossed it with the sauce, which I have already noted was perfection. The thick, chewy pasta was terrible with the sauce: the whole plate heavy and sodden. Don't make this mistake.

Penne, ditalini, *conchiglie*, gemelli, and the very Neapolitan ziti are superb with vegetables, and a mixed selection is wonderful in a sauce of tomato, cheese, beans, cream, and vegetables such as potatoes. Use in pasta e fagioli, with seafood (or seafood and beans) and sausage—abundant flavors that can stand up to the chunky little shapes. Long, fat, flat pastas such as *fettuccelle* are good with the heftier sauces, too. *Paccheri*—big, fat, round pasta tubes about four or five inches long—is specific to Campania and, together with fish or simply a delicious simple tomato sauce, is typical of Naples, perfect with the savory sauces popular there. Its name means "slap," as in the slapping noise the pasta makes when it hits the plate.

The basic rule of Neapolitan-style pasta saucing is to first cook the pasta until almost but not quite al dente, still with a little edge of almost-crunch; then drain, reserving a cup or so of the cooking water. Finish cooking in the pan, with the sauce, adding a little cooking water as you do so. Having absorbed starch and wheaty taste from the pasta and seasoned by the salt, pasta cooking water is your secret power: it brings the dish together and lets you taste the pasta, not just the sauce.

Two basic sauces can give you a palette of pasta.

To make *aglio e olio*, warm lots of sliced garlic in olive oil until golden; add hot pepper flakes if you like. Add a ladle of the pasta cooking water, your drained pasta, and cook a few minutes, tossing, until it comes together. *Aglio e olio* is best for long, thin, or narrow pasta like spaghetti or linguine. Now, make it your own. Add thinly sliced winter squash to sauté in the olive oil and garlic, or do as they do in Cetara and toss in some chopped parsley and a few shakes of *colatura di alici*. You could add chopped anchovies instead, or finely chopped fish (snapper, tuna, or whatever is available), into the olive oil, garlic, and chopped parsley, finishing with a squeeze of lemon.

Pummarola/pomodoro is a tomato sauce. Eat it with almost any shape or size of pasta. Make it your own by adding peas, pancetta, fried eggplant, chunks of fish (fresh or rehydrated salt cod), clams or mussels, whole shrimp in their shells, roasted peppers, sausage chunks, capers, or olives.

Fettuccelle con Broccoli (Fat, Wide Pasta with Broccoli, Garlic, and Anchovies)

Serves 4

I can tell you that *fettuccelle* is great with broccoli, as is linguine, any flat ribbon pasta, and spaghetti. How can something so simple with such ordinary ingredients be so wonderful?

You can make the dish with orecchiette, the ear-shaped pasta, though that's more typical of Puglia, or you can use seashell pasta, ziti, or rigatoni—any pasta that has enough heft to withstand the long-cooked broccoli, garlic, and anchovies.

This dish is the kind of wonderful that makes you want to purr like a kitten drinking milk; the kind of wonderful that makes you say, "Of course!" when asked whether you'd like seconds; the kind of wonderful that makes you want to stand up and applaud the culinary sensibility of Naples and Campania and all of Italy's south! And if any dish makes you always keep a tin of anchovies on your shelf, it will be this one.

Note: Sprinkling crisp, crunchy breadcrumbs on pasta instead of cheese is a very southern Italian thing to do. The crumbs not only provide crunch but also soak up excess liquid in the sauce as they soften. Breadcrumbs are simple: crumble up stale bread, and sauté them in a little olive oil. Another very southern way is to crush taralli into crumbs, toast in a pan, and sprinkle them over the pasta.

Fettuccelle con Broccoli (Fat, Wide Pasta with Broccoli, Garlic, and Anchovies) (*continued*)

Salt as needed

1 large or 2 smallish heads of broccoli, cut into florets, the stems into bite-sized pieces

1 small tin anchovies, including the oil (if desired), or a tin of salted anchovies, rinsed

6 cloves garlic, chopped

2–3 tablespoons extra virgin olive oil, or more, as needed

Pinch hot pepper flakes (optional)

1 pound *fettuccelle* pasta, or any wide, flat pasta such as fettuccine (alternatively, you can use either spaghetti or linguine)

Black pepper to taste

About 2 tablespoons toasted bread-crumbs, optional

Put on a large pot of water to boil; then salt the water and blanch the broccoli until bright green and just tender. Remove from pot with a slotted spoon and set aside while you prepare the rest.

Chop the anchovies, and, in a heavy, large frying pan, warm them until they begin to melt and sizzle; then add the garlic, a little olive oil, and some pepper flakes, if using. (If desired, you can divide the garlic, using half here and half once the pasta is in the pan with the broccoli.) Cook a few minutes, and then add the broccoli to the pan. Toss a bit in the fragrant oil; then remove from heat and set aside while you cook the pasta.

In the same water you blanched the broccoli, cook the pasta until not quite al dente. Drain and reserve about a cup of the cooking liquid.

Return the broccoli and fragrant oil to the heat, toss and cook for a few minutes, and then add the drained pasta, toss through, then a little bit of the reserved water, about ¼ cup. Toss and cook, and then add some more of the water and more olive oil, if needed. Keep tossing, adding water, until the pasta is al dente and the water has become a small amount of sauce.

Serve right away, sprinkled with a little salt or black pepper, if needed, and the breadcrumbs.

Fresh Pasta of the South

Though Campania is justifiably famous for its excellent dried pasta, a smaller and more regional tradition exists of making fresh pasta. Unlike the eggy, almost crepe-like pasta of the north, fewer eggs are added, and often no egg at all. The dough can be rolled into long strands, shaped into fat chunks, or twisted around a wire to create a hole in the middle.

Most of the fresh pastas are traditional and ancient, with a delicious exception called *scialatelli* (also known as *sciliatielli* and *scivatieddi*—variations of a word that come from the description of "ruffled"). The thick, short, fat noodle was created by chef Enrico Cosentino in the late 1960s, made from flour, eggs, milk, cheese, and parsley or basil. At the time he worked as a chef in his native Amalfi and entered the international culinary competition, taking the Entremetier Prize in 1978. The pasta's fame spread throughout Campania, especially inland, since its texture goes so well with the heartier smoked cheese, cured meats, and wild game inland, as well as with the lighter seafood and tomatoes of the coastline.

Stuffed fresh pasta is usually made either at home or in a restaurant. Cheese-filled ravioli alla Caprese is the most famous. Sorrento has a lovely fish-filled pasta, and the big fat pasta roll of Sarno is exceptional.

The Raccolto: Wheat Harvest

When the grain has ripened, it's time to harvest.

Giuseppe Di Martino, past president of the Consorzio di Tutela della Pasta di Gragnano IGP and owner of his family's pasta company, Pastificio Di Martino, explains, "It all starts from the durum wheat. For Pasta dei Campi, the part of our company where we make pasta using only local wheat, we use Italian grain taken from about one hundred miles around Gragnano. For the *pastaio* [pasta maker], it is very important that the grain has been cultivated in a place with historical tradition.

"The durum wheat of this area has a protein content of around 14 percent, compared to about 10.5 percent found in ordinary durum wheat. This amount of protein gives the characteristic consistency, taste, and fragrance to the pasta." Worldwide, hard wheat makes up only 10 percent of the harvest, and soft wheat 80 percent; the remaining 10 percent varies.

Soon after picking, the wheat is milled. This must be done with a low-power machine that lets the pasta maintain its fragrance and not heat-blast away its wheaty perfume. It takes about 350 pounds of grain to yield 225 pounds of high-quality durum wheat.

In ancient times, a *festa* known as Capocanale was held at the end of each harvest. Inspired by this, the growers, millers, and *pastificio* Di Martino revived the festival. On the day in late spring or early summer when the growing wheat in Casalnuovo Monterotaro is declared ready, the party gathers in the fields.

The celebration pays tribute to the collaboration between pasta maker and grower/miller. Guests, families, and workers wander the fields and the nearby mill, Molino De Vita, ready to help with the harvest while admiring the wheat for its timeless beauty, tradition, and potential. Afterward, all gather around the festive table prepared by the family De Vita.

The Raccolto: Wheat Harvest (*continued*)

In fact, the traditional rules of the Capocanale stipulate that it must be the owner of the company who prepares the food for the guests. It is meant to thank the workers for their hard work and devotion—and with it local music, dancing, giddiness, gratitude for life's blessings, satisfaction with their work, and a special menu honoring wheat.

The menu from Il Raccolto 2015, of Pastificio dei Campi and Molino De Vita:

A salad of cooked whole wheat kernels dressed with olive oil
Mozzarella di bufala (buffalo mozzarella) and *fior di latte* (cow's milk mozzarella)
Fresh local ricotta
Formaggio frumentino (slightly aged buffalo cheese coated with coarsely ground wheat)
Caciocavallo Podolico
Torcinelli (intestines wound around a spit and roasted)
Sausages
Affettati di Nonna Pina (a plate of mixed cured meats made by Grandma Pina)
Grano di mosto cotto (cooked grains tossed with a sweet, cooked wine, much like a syrup or a sweetened balsamic vinegar)
Pastiera di grano (the classic regional pie filled with ricotta custard, candied fruit, cooked wheat grains, and scented with orange flower water)

And then, at some point, fresh pasta from the new crop of wheat was made.

PIZZA

Wherever you are, if you're eating pizza, you probably feel that it is part of your own life. Like Neapolitans, pizza is outgoing; it wants to please. That the whole world has fallen in love with it is a perfect example. For instance, recently I saw pizza on a buffet in Yantai, China, and was told about the local (thriving) pizza culture. Japan has at least one master *pizzaiolo*, and in India, instead of a sausage topping, you'll find kofta kebab. Worldwide, some pizzas are not good, but some are wonderful. I know of an awful one near me, but a great one in Moldova!

One can forget exactly how much of a traditional inheritance pizza is. It's not just a food.

A Story of Neapolitan Pizza

Eating pizza in Napoli is a rite that celebrates tradition. Can you imagine life in Naples without pizza? The soundtrack to life there includes the slapping noises of a *pizzaiolo*'s hands patting the dough and the chatting, in dialect, of *pizzaioli* with customers. There is a "smell track," too: when you walk past a pizzeria and the fragrance of hot, baked dough hits your nose, and then the thrill as your order is whisked to you. Before you even eat the pizza, you are gathered into the drama of Neapolitan life. Regardless of its origins, this is where pizza came from.

In one of its many guises, pizza has been a Mediterranean food since the Stone Age. It could have been invented by anyone who figured out that mixing flour and water made dough, that flattening it and baking on a hot stone made it crisp and tender, and that topping it with seasonings and oil made it delicious.

The name *pizza* may come from the Italian word *pizziare*, which means "to pinch" or "to pluck," referring to pinching a ball of dough from the big mass of dough. Its name could be related to pita, *pide*, or *pitta*, which is likely, since these words refer to the flatbreads and savory pies of the Mediterranean and Middle East, to which pizza is likely related.

In the days of the Persian Empire, soldiers of Darius the Great (521–486 BCE) baked a similar flatbread using their shields as a baking sheet or pan, heated on a fire. This they covered with cheese and dates. Perhaps it was this flatbread that came with the soldiers when the Persians attacked Athens, and so from Greece to Magna Grecia, then Neapolis (Naples), and later Rome?

Marcus Porcius Cato (Cato the Elder) wrote in the first history of Rome about a "flat round of dough dressed with olive oil, herbs, and honey baked on stones." Virgil (70–19 BC) describes in *The Aeneid* flatbreads used as plates, eaten "under the shade of a tree."

Some say that Roman soldiers, stationed in the Middle East, developed a taste for the unleavened flatbreads eaten by Jews there. Called *maza*, it sounds very much like the ritual flatbreads matzo or matzot. The soldiers may have added cheese and olive oil to the matzo, returning home with a love for this flatbread.

The main sources of ancient Roman cooking come from the great cookery book, *De Re Coquinaria* by Marcus Gavius Apicius, as well as the excavations at Pompeii. Apicius's love of food was so sincere and intense that he poisoned himself when his finances failed, so terrified was he of dying of hunger. One of the dishes in his culinary opus magnus is a recipe for flatbread with chicken, pine nuts, cheese, garlic, mint, and olive oil. It sounds like pizza. Sort of.

The destruction of Pompeii also preserved pizza in situ. We can see how everyday life was lived, what the people did, what they ate. Along with flattish breads, there are what appears to be shops with the tools of the pizza trade: ovens, baking utensils, even a statue called *i pizzaioli* (in Neapolitan dialect *pizzaiuoli*), now on exhibit at the Museo Nazionale.

The actual term *pizza* is first found in 997 AD in a rental contract for a mill in Gaeta; twelve *pizze* (probably more like a focaccia) were to be paid every Christmas and Easter.

In 1570, Bartolomeo Scappi, personal cook to Pope Pius V, described a dough that could be dressed with whatever the diner desired, such as a local cheese made from water buffalo milk.

Pellegrino Artusi published three pizza recipes—all sweet, interestingly. So it would seem that a pizza could go either way, like other pies: sweet or savory.

It was, however, the marriage of the baked dough to the newly discovered tomato (and often cheese) that created the pizza as we know and love it today.

Neapolitans were the first Europeans to eat (and fall in love with) tomatoes. Because of their high solanine content and membership in the nightshade family, "the deadly fruit" terrified most of Northern Europe. Since the Neapolitans showed no harmful effects, the tomato's popularity spread. It was discovered to be full of vitamins, as well as tasty; it transformed anything it was eaten with.

Until this time, pizza was eaten only in the streets—the dirty, uncouth, rough, lower-class streets of Old Napoli. Vendors carried—or wore on their heads, perfectly balanced—box-like contraptions made of metal (sometimes with a layer of coals), insulated to keep the pizza nice and warm on the shelves. The first pizza was nice and hot, but by the last one, not so much. The first slice was expensive, the last cold one discounted. This was the traditional way pizza was sold in Naples.

As pizza grew in popularity, workshops were set up in the street where customers could buy directly from the *pizzaiolo*, fresh and hot from the oven, instead of from a wandering vendor. Since the *pizzaioli* were making the pizzas right there, customers could request toppings, and pizza makers grew more creative.

This new type of pizza-eating place was called a pizzeria. The first pizzeria, Antica Pizzeria Port'Alba, opened in 1830, and it is still open and still serving good traditional pizza. As pizzerias proliferated, many set out benches for customers to sit on and chat with the other pizza eaters as they ate. Small tables and chairs appeared, even knives and forks.

By then, Naples was a thriving waterfront city with a huge number of working poor called *lazzaroni*. They lived in a densely populated area—sometimes whole families in a small room. For many, life was lived in the urban outdoors—there was no space inside, and outside was where your friends were, where amusement, theater, and often food was to be found.

And pizza was cheap. Wait, let me start again: People were poor, hungry, and yearning for something delicious. Pizza was cheap, delicious, and nourishing, and eating it on the street was socially engaging. The combination was irresistible to Neapolitans.

Even royalty was smitten. Queen Maria Carolina d'Asburgo Lorena, wife of the king of Naples, Ferdinando IV (1751–1821), had a special oven built in their summer palace of Capodimonte. One of the first references to a pizza that included both cheese and tomato was in 1835, by the celebrated writer, Alexandre Dumas, author of *The Three Musketeers* and *The Count of Monte Cristo*, during a visit to Naples.

When Naples was still under the control of the Spanish viceroy, the soldiers stationed there loved hanging out in the streets and taverns, lustily enjoying pizza and strong drink. Spanish dominion ended when "the Thousand," led by Giuseppe Garibaldi, marched into town and united Naples with the Kingdom of Italy. It was proclaimed in 1861 by Vittorio Emanuele II, whose son, Umberto I, would inherit the throne. Naples was now part of Italy.

Though today the pizza Margherita is a symbol of Italy, its colors representing the nation's flag, it came to exist by accident. Vincenzo Pagnani can tell the story. He is the current owner of Pizzeria Brandi, where the story of the Margherita began. He is so passionate about his pizzeria's part in pizza history that if you show interest, he may sit you down, feed you pizza, and tell you the story (as he did with me).

In 1889, *pizzaiolo* Raffaele Esposito (and, some say, his wife), from the pizzeria Pietro e Basta Così (founded in 1780, now known as Pizzeria Brandi), was summoned to Naples's Capodimonte Palace to prepare pizza for King Umberto I and his wife, Margherita of Savoy. They were bored with French cuisine and the queen especially wanted to try the local dish people were talking about.

Esposito is said to have prepared three different *pizze*: one with pork fat (pancetta or lardo), cheese, and basil; one with garlic, olive oil, and tomatoes; and the last one, inspired by the colors of the Italian flag, white mozzarella, green basil, and red tomato. The queen loved the tomato, basil, and mozzarella pizza the best and asked what it was called. Thinking quickly, Esposito answered, "Margherita, in your honor, your Majesty."

No doubt the combination of toppings already existed—Neapolitan author Emanuele Rocco mentions mozzarella, tomato, and basil in an article published in 1866. But it was Esposito's talent for quick thinking (and flattery), that particularly Neapolitan genius, that transformed a simple street food into worldwide legend.

A marble plaque commemorating the event appears on the wall of Pizzeria Brandi, marking the hundredth anniversary of the event: "Qui 100 anni fa nacque la pizza Margherita 1889–1989 Brandi." (The creation of the pizza Margherita and the establishment of Raffaele Esposito as king of pizza was subscribed in a letter from the royal household stating, "I confirm that the three styles of pizza created by you for her Majesty the Queen were found delicious." Dated June 11, 1889.)

Once the king and queen approved, aristocracy and the wealthy aspirationals who had once looked down their noses at this crude peasant food flocked to streets. Visitors came from other areas of Naples, venturing daringly to taste this intriguing dish. For foreigners, it became the thing to do.

When the British traveling through Naples on their Grand Tour saw what was going on in the streets of Naples, they were shocked. The highest duke and lowest servant could be found sharing the sacred act of the Neapolitan: eating pizza. The travelers found the places "filthy," the mixing of classes scandalous, but, oh, the pizza was marvelous.

And even if cavorting with commoners in the rougher parts of town was challenging, pizza was climbing the social ladder. It became acceptable to share in pizza eating, and it was communally and culturally beneficial for all of the social classes to eat together. It loosened the class-ridden societal strictures. The former food of the poor was no longer bonded with one's status. Eating pizza became a bridge to unite all classes, which has since been a characteristic of life in Naples.

Pizza is so embedded in Napoli's culture is that the Christmas nativity scenes, the *presepe*, always include a pizzeria. Right there in Bethlehem, tiny legs of prosciutto hanging from rafters, wreaths of garlic in doorways, pots of sauce simmering on a fire. Among the shepherds, wise men, and camels are *pizzaioli* tossing dough. This is Napoli's view of Christianity's holiest night.

One of the most important things to know about eating pizza in the street (*pizza a libretto*, "pizza to go") is the pizza *a portafoglio*. Meaning literally a wallet, it refers to the way a round pizza is folded into four quarters, its juicy insides all tucked into the saucy, hot baked dough, wrapped into paper so that the fillings don't leak out. The paper wrapping lets you eat the pizza by hand, instead of with a knife and fork, as one would in a more formal pizzeria.

When you stand at that window or counter and receive your pizza, you know it is something you are entitled to. It is, in many ways, your birthright. Each ingredient belongs to your city, as the pizza ritual belongs to you: eaten standing up, on the street, surrounded by other happy, grateful souls.

The true sit-down pizzeria restaurants with formal dining areas have been around only since the 1950s. Pizza at a sit-down ristorante pizzeria is slightly different: bigger, juicier, and saucier and flat on the plate rather than folded. *Pizze a portafoglio* are usually only two basic kinds: marinara (without cheese, but with tomatoes, garlic, and oregano) and Margherita, with its smidge of mozzarella and leaf or two of basil.

Pizza in a sit-down pizzeria, however, can be topped with so many things that the menu may run to pages: porcini mushrooms, artichokes, different cheeses such as provola, *fior di latte*, or *mozzarella di bufala*, golden tomatoes, cherry tomatoes, potatoes and rosemary, basil pesto, artichokes, seafood (fresh and dried/smoked, especially anchovies), sausage, *friarielli*, pancetta, prosciutto, peppers, olives—the list can go on endlessly. But there's a reason that Margherita has the heart of so many: its taste and texture is a perfect balance, nothing extra; each taste and texture, from the tomato to the melty cheese to the fragrant basil, is quintessential Napoli.

Neapolitan pizzas aren't cut into slices (unless they are *a taglio*, by the slice, and then they are a completely different kind of pizza). If the *pizzaiolo* cut the pizza before sending it out to your table, its soupy toppings would leak and turn the bottom soggy.

You have a knife and fork with which to dig in when your pizza reaches you. Eating a pizza is all about diving into its texture, biting through its layers of dough and sauce (and any toppings): how it feels on your teeth, on your tongue, your lips; the softness of dough, the crispness of dough; the meltiness of cheese; the pure essence of tomato—no two bites exactly the same—and a waft of sweet basil that settles over the whole thing and wraps you in its pleasurable sensations.

Some people actually leave behind the *cornicione* (how can they not eat that luscious, crunchy, crisp bread?) and eat only the soupy inner part of the pizza. I know, I know, the baked dough is the most filling part, but with so much flavor, I often risk being overly full.

Even in the "old days," some people did not necessarily eat their *cornicione*. During days of hardship in the late nineteenth century, many *pizzerie* kept the uneaten *cornicione* each evening for families who could not feed their children.

The one true taboo regarding pizza in Naples is eating it cold. Woe to the person who wants to take home their Margherita leftovers. I swear I once saw tears in the eyes of a pizzeria owner when I asked. He was horrified, explaining that the cheese undergoes a chemical change: "It's dangerous!" I didn't have the heart to tell him that in America, leftover pizza is considered breakfast food (though the cheese is different—perhaps he is right?).

But, you know, the old ways are still observed, especially in the historical, traditional *pizzerie*. Veteran eighty-something *pizzaiolo* Michele Triumfo, a *pizzaiolo* since he was twelve years old, remembers the last Vesuvio eruption and the pizza-eating American GIs. His advice regarding his art: The dough needs to be adjusted to the day's humidity. When properly mixed, it should be soft like the proverbial baby's bottom. And—about this he is adamant—"Don't sweat into your dough."

The new *pizzaioli* are often chefs, using their passion and artistry to reinvent the genre, each experimenting in different ways. One uses seawater for the dough, another chooses the grains and has them both specially grown and milled. They feel that they need to make their mark for a new generation of pizza lovers.

I grew up eating suburban American pizza (my mother made little ones, on bagels, which I *loved*). But my first bite of pizza on my first trip to Naples on my first visit to Europe made me gasp. Then laugh. I wanted to dance naked (to be truthful), but instead I just reached for another bite. It was *nothing* like the pizza I had grown up eating. Of course not—I hadn't grown up in Naples.

I hadn't gone there looking for pizza. But when I got to Naples, pizza found me. The charming, slightly intimidating streets of *il centro storico* were like a scene from a film. I passed a few tables set outside a restaurant and something smelled so good I didn't know what to do. It was almost as if I had no choice; a mysterious force overtook me. There was a table, so I sat.

I didn't even know what was on the menu, so I smiled. I gestured, then smiled again. I was very young, blonde, kind of cute, and pretty stupid. I was also extremely lucky, because, before I knew it, a pizza was plopped down in front of me. A whole pizza, not a wedge, meant for me and me alone. Then I thought disappointedly, *So little sauce on top and only one basil leaf?* I took a tentative bite of the blistered dough and its thin layer of tomato essence.

That full-mouthed moment was the dividing line between pizza *before* and pizza *after*. My pizza life realigned in those moments when I realized that it was all about the dough, tender and airy, slightly crisp at the bottom, with a slight fragrance of char. The outside rim was puffy and chewy, there were a few big bubbles inside the thin dough, and the tomato tasted like a whole field of tomatoes condensed into a spoonful or two. It was so pure and tender.

Everything about Naples changed afterward. I became aware of pizza eaters walking in the street, sitting at tables, standing in front of the shop or at a bar. Everywhere pizza was being eaten with unabashed joy.

And suddenly eating pizza was not *just* about eating. It was like nothing I had ever done before, an act of culinary solidarity and appreciation.

UNESCO

In 2011, a request was submitted to UNESCO nominating pizza as part of the "intangible patrimony of Naples." For too long, *pizzaioli* have led somewhat marginal lives: long hours, hard work, low pay, and lack of respect for their contribution to the quality of Neapolitan life. And not only the pizza makers but also pizza itself; after all, what would Napoli be without it?

Naples and Neapolitan *pizzaioli* campaigned for it, and Italian gastronomes and journalists supported it. Still, a year came and went, then another.

Then, finally, out of the blue, on December 17, 2017, the list from UNESCO's Committee for the Safeguarding of the Intangible Cultural Heritage was published. On it were the pizza makers of Napoli (about three thousand) as "Representative Intangible Cultural Heritage of Humanity." Finally, they and their skills were honored as a cultural treasure of Naples!

The city went wild. Pizzas were made with the letters spelling out UNESCO in mozzarella, there was tarantella dancing in the streets, the whole of Naples was giddy with partying and pizza eating.

Gino Sorbillo, legendary Neapolitan *pizzaiolo* and pizzeria owner (with a branch in New York City) and Italian television personality, handed out free *pizze a portafoglio* to the crowd. People gathered and sang and chomped on pizza in celebration. Via dei Tribunali, one of Naples's traditional pizza streets, was filled with throngs of eating, singing, happy people clamoring for pizza! Pizza! A pizza maker sang in Neapolitan dialect a love song to the people who eat the pizza; to the tomatoes, mozzarella, and dough; and to the city that suffers, and triumphs, and its unsung heroes, the *pizzaioli*. It was a red-letter day in Neapolitan pizza history.

Weeks later, excitement still pulsated and social media was filled with pictures of pizza in front of iconic Neapolitan landmarks. I am sure that the other thirty-two nominated crafts of intangible gifts to humanity awarded by UNESCO were thrilled. I have no doubt that the storytellers, musicians, artists, and martial arts practitioners in the High Atlas were pleased—excited even. But in Naples, crowds still surged through the streets in a heady, tomato-sauced, happy insanity long afterward.

Traditional Pizza: Associazione Verace Pizza Napoletana

In 2010, the Neapolitan pizza (or pizza *verace Napoletana*) was granted the EU qualification STG (*specialità tradizionale garantita*, "guaranteed traditional specialty"). The Associazione Verace Pizza Napoletana acts as a certification organization (to pizzerias all over the world, not just to Naples), its role of guardian of what makes a true Neapolitan pizza.

Its directives and rules run to eleven pages, detailing each element of Neapolitan pizza—ingredients, methods, size, and so forth—and emphasizing that a classic Neapolitan is characterized by its crust: airy lightness, crisp edged, slightly charred (which adds a complexity of flavor to the simple dough).

The water temperature, speed of mixing with the flour (slowly for ten minutes), yeast, and salt are included in the directions, as is total mixing time: twenty minutes precisely. No fat of any kind may be used in the dough, and when stretching the dough and forming the pizza, only the hands may be used—no rolling pins or other mechanical means. (Some say that the secret of Neapolitan pizza is the water of the Serino Aquaduct, but this is more of a folkloric belief, usually expounded after a few glasses of wine.)

Baking yeast is allowed, but most *pizzaioli* prefer *levito naturale*. Vincenzo Pagnani, owner of the legendary Brandi Pizzeria (and pizza maker since he was fourteen years old), uses the previous day's dough as today's *levito naturale*.

The length of time the dough should rise is not stipulated, depending as it does on the temperature, humidity, and other vagaries of weather, as well as the design of the kitchen. The feel and judgment of the *pizzaiolo* is factored in. Rising usually takes between twelve and twenty-four hours.

The pizza can be no larger than fourteen inches, with a thick, high, yet soft border of dough. Known as the *cornicione*, it is crunchy on the outside, bubbly and airy within, and not covered with sauce. This structure gives pizza its form: if the dough was an even thickness and topped with sauce to the edge, the laws of physics would not be able to work their wonders to give that balance of textures.

The traditional domed, wood-fueled pizzeria, unchanged for hundreds of years, is the only pizza oven allowed by the Associazione Verace Pizza Napoletana's guidelines. No other can reach the 800°F air temperature and 905°F floor temperature that makes a true Neapolitan pizza.

When the dough leaves the *pizzaiolo*'s peel and hits the oven floor, the moist, soft dough should start to puff immediately. The smoke from the woodfire begins to perfume the dough with its slight whiff of bitterness. This all helps create that beautiful complexity of taste that's specific to true Neapolitan pizza.

If using mozzarella, it must be certified *mozzarella di bufala* Campana DOP or mozzarella STG. Any tomatoes used must be one of the following: *S. Marzano dell'Agro Sarnese-nocerino* DOP, *pomodorini di Corbara* (Corbarino), or *pomodorino del piennolo del Vesuvio* DOP. Paolo Ruggiero of Gustarosso San Marzano and Dani Coop described to me a San Marzano on a pizza: "Its perfume so intriguing, a perfect balance of sweet and acid, its firm texture . . ." he trailed off, adding, "It is the most coveted tomato among pizza masters."

Because tomatoes are 94 percent water, most pizza makers drain the tomatoes before using them so that the crust doesn't get soft and soggy. It's not a *verace pizza Napoletana* rule, but one of those *pizzaiolo* things: they know to drain, puree, and cook the tomatoes for about ten minutes to concentrate the flavors. It makes a difference between a soupy crust and a soggy one—a soupy pizza is a fresh tomatoey sauciness; soggy is heavy and doughy.

Only three versions of pizza are permitted to be called *verace pizza Napoletana*. Two have cheese: the Margherita with basil, tomatoes, and cheese from the southern Apennine Mountains, and the "extra Margherita," which must include buffalo mozzarella from the Campania region. The guidelines include how many basil leaves must be used and where they are placed so that they can perfume the entire pizza as they cook. Raw basil on a classic pizza is considered too "urgent" a taste—it calls attention to itself and diminishes the other ingredients.

The third variety is the marinara pizza. No cheese—it combines tomato sauce, oregano, oil, and garlic. It doesn't have seafood, so why is it called marinara? Its name came from the Neapolitan fishermen who, after a long day fishing, climbed off their boats and headed into the city streets. Some were in a hurry to get home but hungry and in need of a snack to help them along the way. Others wanted a cheeseless pizza to go with the seafood they had caught. Either way, the savory, garlicky pizza without cheese was a big hit with the fishermen, taking its name from them.

A good pizza is not its toppings. The best pizza may be topped lavishly with excellent, local products, or it can have almost no toppings, just a thin smear of rich tomato conserve and perhaps a leaf of basil, a little crushed garlic, and a sprinkling of oregano—the marinara of my dreams.

Though the regulations about tomatoes and cheese are strict, the rest of the toppings may be as creative as desired. The only caveat is that the toppings be Neapolitan in spirit and culinary tradition and, of course, that they follow the directive "don't offend the rules of good taste and gastronomy." A Neapolitan pizza is all about the symphony of balance: dough, fire, smoke, sauce, and oil uniting as one.

While the association specifies how much oil with which to anoint the pizza and the shape of the stream of oil (the number six), surprisingly, it doesn't demand olive oil (though most insist it gives the right flavor to their pizza). As for the amount, too little will make it tough and dry; too much, and it will be greasy.

After its sixty- to ninety-second bake, the *pizzaiolo* removes the pizza from the oven with a metal pizza peel and places it on a flat, dry work surface. Longer than 90 seconds in the oven breaks down the structure of the oil—especially olive oil—whose fatty acids can alter and spoil both taste and digestibility.

Emerging from the oven, the pizza should look and smell irresistible: the tomato should be dense, not watery; the mozzarella melted softly; the basil, garlic, and oregano intensely aromatic, the whole thing fragrant with a slight whiff of oven char.

To be a *verace pizza Napoletana*, it must be eaten immediately, straight from the oven. It cannot be frozen for sale at a later time. To judge a good pizza Napoletana, one must consider the olfactory sense—its aroma, the pleasurable sensation it gives—and, of course, the taste must be assessed. But the most important consideration is joy. It is the most important aspect of eating any pizza.

Pizza Styles

There are two styles of true Neapolitan pizza: on the dryer side (that is, with a typical melty topping) or on the soupy side (in which the pizza, in the middle of its puffed, slightly charred *cornicione*, is liquidy). The edge keeps the melty tomato and cheese intact.

The real difference between Neapolitan pizza and other pizza is texture. Neapolitan should be soft, uneven, with a little bit of char, a hint of crisp to keep the dough together, and big air bubbles here and there.

And it's *light*. Oh, so light. A Neapolitan pizza should be so light that after eating one you *feel* light: sustained but light. In a recent terrible heatwave, I found that the only thing I really felt like eating was a marinara pizza: somehow it was so light that I felt refreshed rather than weighed down.

I recently had a discussion with a waiter who advised me against having salad with the pizza. "Salad is heavy," he said. "Too much food! Pizza is light. Better take the pizza, it's lighter." Of course, I took his advice, and the pizza was oh so light and oh so good.

In fact, the digestibility, the lightness of a pizza's being, is one of the most important qualities of a modern Neapolitan pizza. *Pizzaioli* explain that it is their gift to the pizza eater: the gift of health and well-being.

The drier pizzas are more familiar to anyone who isn't Neapolitan. And sometimes they are even baked untopped. After emerging from the oven, toppings are added so that they melt slightly without cooking from the heat of what is essentially a hot flatbread.

Then there is the soupy pizza: irresistible, swoonworthy. But the eater should be forewarned: inside the border of *cornicione*, the cheese and tomato melt into, and almost become one with, the dough.

You may prefer a drier pizza, but, like many acquired tastes, it's worth trying soupy pizzas several times to see whether you fall in love. You don't need to eat it that way always, but there is so much pleasure that awaits you in Naples once you have developed the taste that you shouldn't deny yourself the possibility of pleasure.

Calzone

A calzone is a closed pizza. The dough, filled with delicacies such as ricotta, spinach, cheeses, and an olive or two, is folded over like a big, fat turnover and baked quickly in the pizza oven. Sometimes there's a bit of tomato sauce on top either before or after baking.

Famously, calzone translates as "loose trousers." I don't understand the meaning, but it doesn't bother me because a calzone is wonderful: a different way to enjoy the pizza experience.

At the moment, restaurants are serving a dish that's part calzone and part pizza. From an authenticity standpoint, I feel horrified, but the pleasure-seeking part of me is kind of in love. I like variety.

Pizza Fritta: Fried Pizza

Fried pizza is as Neapolitan as baked pizza. I'm told that at one time pots of oil, an endless stream of frying pizzas, and eager customers were a common sight on Naples's streets.

Traditionally, baking and frying was divided by gender: men baked, women fried. But these days, some men are frying, their fluffy, crisp-edged *pizze* objects of delicious wonderment. The great Enzo Coccia recently wrote a book devoted to *pizza fritta*.

The classic fried pizza is a round of dough stuffed with ricotta, ham, sausage, tomato, mushrooms, or your desire placed atop of the dough, which is then folded over into a half circle and its edges sealed. It is lowered carefully into the hot oil, with the pizza maker still holding its tip until the pizza begins to fry and hold together. By then it has stretched to nearly a crescent shape. When done, it is golden, crisp, huge—and magical, because it takes a lot of skill to keep the filling from leaking out. After frying, sometimes a spoonful of sauce is spread on top.

There's a hybrid, the Montanara, for which Pizzeria Starita is famous. The fried disk of dough is topped with sauce and cheese, and then baked. You might think it would be greasy, but no: it's as light and delicate as an edible cloud—a cloud topped with tomato sauce and mozzarella.

Pizza al Taglio

Pizza by the slice is sold everywhere in Italy, often (but not always) thicker than Neapolitan pizza, cooked on a sheet pan much like a focaccia, sold on the street or in bakeries and shops throughout Italy. They like it in Campania, too; it's not exactly Neapolitan pizza, but it's delicious. In Vico Equense, the restaurant Pizza a Metro, or pizza by the meter, has been famous for it since opening in the 1960s. It is usually offered with a variety of toppings so that each diner can sample sauces, toppings, and textures.

Pizza al taglio has a different consistency than pizza Napoletana, as it usually has lard in the crust, a big no-no for Neapolitan pizza.

The huge, flat trays of pizza may not be the local tradition, but, oh, they too can be wonderful. Until recently, I was a bit snobby about them. But at a dinner in the Sarno countryside, a parade of pizza slices was cut from a huge slab on a cart. Every so often it rolled from diner to diner, almost like dim sum, with a new type of pizza each round. We ate our way through the local pizza lexicon: prosciutto, fresh tomatoes and buffalo mozzarella, roasted peppers and olives, pesto with melted provola (which was absolutely luscious), marinara, preserved artichoke hearts. It was exciting. Everyone agreed that it was not traditional Neapolitan pizza, but it was so good. You'd think that one might feel over-full after such a marathon, but this is Napoli. Pizza is *light*!

Pizzerias in Naples

According to the website Napoli da Vivere (https://napolidavivere.it), there are 8,200 pizzerias in Naples. Other sources give a different tally. For accuracy, it's best to simply say that there are a lot of *pizzerie* in Naples. Whatever the exact count, you'll have a hard time making the rounds. You could visit a different pizzeria each day for more than twenty years without taking a day off to enjoy a different menu!

For this reason, it's good to get recommendations. Life is too short for disappointing pizza. In any event, asking around is fun. Everyone has his or her favorites and is glad to share. Ask a cab driver, teacher, doctor, or dentist, market vendors, ship captains, yacht owners, and hotel clerks: everyone has an opinion and a suggestion (or two or three).

These days, you can choose from traditional, classic *pizzerie* or innovative *pizzerie* that are breaking the mold about what a pizza restaurant—and pizza—should be. Of course, the very *best* pizzeria in Naples is the one that you love more than the others.

It's always good to have a list of *pizzerie* to try. The website Top Fifty Pizzerias in the World (www.50toppizza.com) launched its annual awards on July 21, 2017, in the grandeur of the Castel dell'Ovo on the Naples seafront. It is an updated, online pizzeria guide, judged by exacting pizza gastronomes.

Unsurprisingly, many of the awards went to *pizzerie* in Naples and its vicinity. Unsurprisingly not only because the awards were held there, because Naples is the home of pizza, and because many of the judges are Neapolitans, but also because so many brilliant *pizzerie* are in Napoli. It is the home of pizza.

Despite pizza's fashionability at the moment—Rome! London! Paris! New York! The rest of Italy!—it is Naples's heritage. Much like a cassoulet of Toulouse, excellent tacos of Mexico, and duck in Beijing, the terroir aspect makes a huge difference. It can be good elsewhere, but it's always better on its own home ground, where there is much competition and the best is truly excellent.

Being judged among the top fifty *pizzerie* is amazing. To be number one is to be a pizza star. This award, for best pizza in the world, went to Pepe in Grani, the Caiazzo pizzeria where Franco Pepe holds forth, redefining what is the absolute best about pizza and creating delicacies in this form. His Margherita *sbagliata* is a Margherita pizza turned inside out: the layer next to the dough is a sea of molten cheese, atop a precisely drawn tomato and basil sauce topping. The list of excellence includes traditional choices as well as newcomers, and each year a new list will be unveiled.

Daniel Young, food writer, author, and creator of the blog *Young and Foodish*, followed his love of pizza to Napoli, where he fell in love so hard that he reinvented himself as a pied piper of pizza. His book *Where to Eat Pizza* propelled him into the pizza stratosphere, hobnobbing with pizza celebs. On his website he has a wonderful array of pizza-related videos, and each year he hosts London's Pizzafest at Borough Market.

Several times a year Dan leads a pizza tour of Naples called "Journey to the Center of the Pizza Universe." Pizza tastings are punctuated with a class or two and a visit to a mozzarella maker (www.youngandfoodish.com/pizzatours).

Classic Pizzerias

I'm not going to kid you: Although Neapolitan pizza can be fabulous, it can also be indifferent. You want to always minimize your chances of eating a mediocre pizza. So if you head out to one place for a pizza and find it crowded, you need a backup that isn't too far away. That's why Via dei Tribunali is a great street for pizza eating: many of the old pizzerias are found there, and it's a great street for walking.

Restaurants that serve pizza usually prepare it in the evening only. Traditionally, pizza is considered an evening food. Midday is for a proper meal. In Naples, you need to know that *pizzerie* sell not only pizzas but also an array of fried things, especially the *frittatina* (a chunk of pasta mixed with cheese, vegetables, béchamel, and ham, coated in batter/crumbs, and fried). It is not to be missed—even if it takes a day or two to digest. It's worth it!

Antica Pizzeria e Friggitoria Di Matteo

When President Bill Clinton came to Napoli for the 1994 G7 summit, he went to Di Matteo. His picture is on the wall. The *pizzaiolo*'s brother served Clinton his pizza;

then he opened his own pizzeria, naming it in honor of Clinton's visit, calling it Il Pizzaiolo del Presidente. Both make great pizzas.

Antica Pizzeria Port'Alba

Founded in 1738, Antica Pizzeria Port'Alba is Napoli's most historical pizzeria. Because it is the first in Napoli, it is therefore the first in the world. Antica Pizzeria Port'Alba still makes great pizza, from its *portafoglio* of marinara and Margherita to its wide range of local toppings. There is the Altamura: mozzarella, provola, ricotta, salame, yellow tomatoes, sweet basil, olive oil, and *fiori di zucca* (squash blossoms). The Amalfi pizza combines two of the flavors from the peninsula: the lemon and *provolone del Monaco* cheese.

Gino Sorbillo Artista Pizzeria Napoletana

The Sorbillo family fired up their wood-burning ovens in 1935 and haven't stopped since. They now own a number of pizzerias: popular, crowded, and delicious. I am a fan, especially of their *funghi* pizza, and I worship at the altar of the marinara: Gino Sorbillo understands tomatoes, oregano, and garlic.

Once, wanting to bring a beautiful pizza home to the pizza-impoverished English countryside, I organized a do-it-yourself takeout pizza run, stopping by Sorbillo for a marinara on my way to Naples Airport. I wrapped the flat box with a towel or two as insulation and zipped it into my suitcase. (Knowing how disapproving most *pizzaioli* are about eating leftover pizza, I'm asking you not to tell Gino.) On arriving home, I cranked up my oven super-stratospherically hot and stuck the pizza in for a short time. When it came out, it was good—maybe even close to Naples good.

Lately, Gino has been introducing a tasting menu of haute cuisine dishes including pork jowl pizza puffs, artichoke sandwiches, fried amberjack calzones, and marinara slices that combine local products with sophisticated taste and technique.

Da Attilio

Da Attilio is an old-school pizzeria run by three successive generations. The crusts are airy and light, quite thin, and the pizza Cosacca—a mashup Margherita and marinara scattered with grated Parmagiano and Pecorino Romano—is wonderful.

Trianon

Trianon is a sprawling, three-floor pizzeria with a huge array of toppings and variations. They are busy and they don't smile, but the pizza is good, on the drier side rather than saucy and soupy.

Gorizia

Pretty, old-fashioned Gorizia is one of Naples's historical pizzerias with a devoted local (Vomero) clientele; it's usually crowded but manageable. Opened in 1916, it was named after the battle of Gorizia, which ended a few days before the pizzeria opened. All of the traditional pizzeria dishes are there: the fried things (if it's zucchini flower season, you must try them), pastas, and a wide array of pizzas.

Pizzeria Da Michele

This is the pizzeria that Elizabeth Gilbert wrote about in her best seller *Eat, Pray, Love* (it is also where Julia Roberts ate in the film). You could say that it is the *eat* part of the title. For a while, everyone who had seen the movie or read the book wanted to go there, and it was crowded. The crowds have since thinned, and Da Michele has pizza making down to a science: two *pizzaioli* working together, one lowering a pie onto the oven floor just as the other removes one. At sixty to ninety seconds a pizza, no sooner have you ordered than it's in front of you, hot, wrapped in paper, and ready to go—the line moves fast.

It was in 1870 that Salvatore Condurro began to make pizza and 1906 when his son Michele opened the family's first pizzeria. They serve two classic pizzas, the marinara and the Margherita. Both are fabulous. Of the soft, soupy type, they have long been venerated. (Da Michele also offers a secret menu: ombra, a thick layer of *fior di latte* cheese, or the cosseca, a plain tomato sauce pizza topped with both grated Parmigiano and pecorino cheeses.) Da Michele opened two always crowded branches in London. My own quibble is that the oil flourish on top of the pizza is sunflower oil rather than olive. A sign on the wall explains that this is "to let the tomatoes and cheese stand out."

Pizzeria Starita

In the classic 1954 film *L'Oro di Napoli* (The Gold of Napoli), it is in Pizzeria Starita that Sophia Loren sells pizza, portraying the intrinsic role of pizza in Naples.

It is most famous for its Montanara, an unstuffed fried pizza topped with sauce and smoked mozzarella and finished in the oven until crisp edged and super puffed. Though logic dictates that it should be greasy, it isn't.

Its classic Margherita is less soupy than many other *pizzerie*. If you like a crisper top and a less liquidy center, this might be the pizza for you. Again, don't forget to place your order if the zucchini blossoms are in season. They are stuffed with ricotta before frying. Delectable.

Starita has had a big influence on New York City pizza with its restaurant Don Antonio di Starita, opened by Roberto Caporuscio, a protege of Antonio Starita. Caporuscio went on to create Keste and set off a tidal wave of Neapolitan pizza love throughout the city and beyond. I am one of Roberto's—and Don Antonio's—huge fans.

L'Arte della Pizza

Several years ago I was at a Christmas gathering (and *presepe* exhibition) with the theme "*Pane, Amore, e Fantasia*" (Bread, Love, and Imagination) in Naples's city hall. There were massive tables filled with local specialties, and awards honoring those who put together the bread, love, and imagination of Naples. Gaetano Esposito won for his book *Pizza*. When he went up to claim his award, I was struck by his sincerity, his humble devotion to his art and métier, pizza.

"It is a calling—after a *pizzaiolo* has worked in Napoli for a while, it becomes time to go out into the world to share the real pizza Napoletana." Gaetano went on to describe a real *pizzaiolo* as "*un vero artista*," or a real artist. The craft is often handed down from generation to generation, and he said that his father had been a *pizzaiolo*, as is his son. "It's not unusual this way."

I suddenly realized that it was not the first time I had seen Gaetano. The first time had been at a film festival party in Capri. A small, wiry artist of a pizza maker with a red bandana around his neck had performed onstage to music, creating a pizza in the shape of the island of Capri. How could I forget such a thing?

Since Gaetano and I apparently went "way back," I decided to visit his pizzeria, L'Arte della Pizza in the Vomero neighborhood. Wearing a blue baseball cap and signature red bandana around his neck, he popped out from behind the counter to say hi before making me a pizza. Being a *pizzaiolo* is really "*una vera passione*" (a true passion), he said as he tossed a supple disk of dough.

As I wandered around the restaurant awaiting my pizza, I checked out the walls of celebrity photos, all joined by the love of pizza. "*Presidenti, papi, e re, tutti mangiano la pizza da me*" (presidents, popes, and kings all eat my pizza), he called out to me.

I glanced from framed photo to framed photo and came to a familiar face. Was I really framed on a Naples's pizzeria wall, where photos of celebrities who have eaten the pizza are proudly displayed? The photo taken the night of film festival in Capri was hanging on the wall: me, along with Gaetano and his creation of a pizza shaped like Capri, as well as an entire pizza *presepe* (nativity scene).

I ate pureed eggplant pizza topped with provola, tomato, prosciutto, and buffalo mozzarella. My lunch companion ate Gaetano's spaghetti *aglio e olio* with porcini.

Pictures of Gaetano's specialties are on his website and various social media accounts. You can see pureed broccoli with provola and pancetta, sliced eggplant with Parmesan shreds, and of course, like all good *pizzaioli*, fried pizzas. The only thing I can't guarantee is your picture on the wall.

50 Kalo

Glamorous, sophisticated, 50 Kalo reflects pizza's new stylish status. As you enter 50 Kalo, there is Ciro Salvo, devotedly stretching the dough. He'll pose for a photo if you are lucky, but get it before you eat, because the transcendent experience of biting into it might obliterate the idea of focusing and clicking. You'll want to keep eating without pause.

Salvo's toppings are well chosen, but it is his crust that he is famous for: so light, airy, and beautiful. He prefers the Margherita or marinara in order to more fully appreciate the crust, which is the heart of the pizza experience.

Pizzeria Vesi

Sit outside under a canopy, drink chilled water or beer, and lift your knife and fork. This was me on one of 2017's hottest Lucifero days. Waiting for my pizza, cooling in the shade while all sorts of pizza flew by: porcini, prosciutto, cheese. Then the waiter stopped by me and handed over my Margherita *bufalina*—a Margherita with buffalo mozzarella melting on top. It was delightful.

The Creatives

If La Verace Pizza Napoletana is the arbiter of tradition, then Enzo Coccia of Pizzeria La Notizia, Franco Pepe of Pepe in Grani, and i Fratelli Salvo at Pizzeria Salvo are among the new wave of creatives. These *pizzaioli* are artistic chefs, working with the form of pizza as one would work as an artist with watercolors. Their dishes are no less serious than those at fine dining establishments.

Their pizzas—and the philosophy behind them—are all different, innovative, personal, and, of course, delicious. They take the traditional pizza and reinterpret it in a way that encompasses modern Naples. In a way, the fresh, new attitude enhances the timelessness of pizza. And while they stray from our image of tradition, their tastes and textures somehow manage to become the absolute definition of tradition: innovation that works so well that others keep doing it, and it gets passed down from generation to generation.

Pizzeria La Notizia

Legendary *pizzaiolo* Enzo Coccia honed his pizza-making skills in various *pizzerie*. His face still reflects the excitement and joy of a little boy biting into a paper-wrapped pizza, skipping down a cobbled street.

He comes from a pizza-making family whose pizzeria in Sorrento, La Pizzeria Fortuna alla Duchesca, is still great. Enzo runs La Notizia while his two brothers run the Sorrento restaurant.

At La Notizia, he does both classic and inventive toppings. Even the inventive toppings are steeped in tradition and terroir—Ventresca pancetta, *piennolo* yellow cherry tomatoes, and *ricotta di bufala*. His *pizze* reflect the seasons: summer has light, vivacious toppings; winter, more hearty, rustic ones. He believes that too much quantity and variety of toppings takes away from the pleasure of the pizza-eating experience. Only the right amount of the high-quality toppings can combine thoughtfully and stimulate the palate, connecting with the brain to give a joyful experience.

Coccia also consults and runs a pizza-making class for professionals.

Pepe in Grani

A third-generation *pizzaiolo*, Franco Pepe has the feeling of making pizza in his hands, its spirit in his heart. So of course he decided to open a pizzeria. Instead of heading down to Napoli, thirty miles to the south, where the big-time pizza players strut their stuff, he decided to stay in the town he is from, where his father and grandfather started.

His pizzeria captivated local and Neapolitan fans. He was named one of the ten best *pizzerie* of the world by Corriere della Sera, best pizza in the world by *Food and Wine Magazine*, and his Margherita *sbagliata* was named best dish of the year for 2016. Its name, which translates as "a badly put together Margherita," also means deconstructed, or put together differently. The bottom of this pizza is a sea of melty cheese topped with a few graphic lines of pureed tomato, the opposite of the classic tomato on the bottom. Franco also took best of the year in 50 Best Pizzerie's competition and on its website.

Franco's Sfizio ai Pomodori combines sundried and fresh cherry tomatoes, sweet and tangy tomato on top of the crisp dough. The Scarpetta is topped with creamy, melted twelve-month-old Grana cheese and shavings of a twenty-four-month one. For a charming verbal listing of the pizza available on special by the waiter, see Dan Young's video (www.youngandfoodish.com/three-franco-pepe-pizzas).

Franco Pepe has been feted in New York, Los Angeles, and San Francisco by the international Italian food literati, but what exactly makes the pizza so special?

According to Franco Pepe himself, it is his vision. When he considered opening a pizzeria, instead of simply following the traditional ways, he thought deeply about what qualities make the best pizza. When developing his dough, he chose a wheat that hadn't been grown in fifty years. He felt it was the best for his pizza (it is), and he brought this wheat back from extinction.

Making the dough, he relies on touch and feeling rather than a static recipe and the clock. Each day he changes the basic mix—this much water, that much flour, this much rising, less today, more tomorrow—to suit the weather and humidity.

His toppings are locally sourced, often named for the village or province they are from. The onions are grown for him, the cheese is made for him, the beer is produced for him. Eating these local things gives the diner a very personal experience.

Pizzeria Salvo

The brothers Francesco and Salvatore Salvo run a namesake pizzeria both traditional and innovative. They consider themselves "a *pizzeria moderna*."

Their dough is beautiful, the pizzas are topped creatively, and the brothers are enthusiastic. Not located in center of Naples, Pizza Salvo is outside the city a bit in San Giorgio a Cremano.

Their menu is classic pizzeria: pizza, antipasti, and fried things (including pizza). When they get creative, they become enthusiastic. I follow the daily specials on social media to see what's new each day. "*Oggi 3 pizze nuove!*" (three new pizzas today!) was the headline one day. Another day, a photo appeared with multihued handmade potato chips, captioned, "I am inspired by these colors and tastes." The next, they posted a *pizza oceano* topped with buffalo ricotta, smoked amberjack fish, seaweed, lemon zest, and pink peppercorns that reminded me of California. That smoked fish and creamy cheese on a pizza is perfect in the same way that smoked salmon and cream cheese on a bagel is. And this description accompanies photos of their Margherita and a fried pizza: "Two little masterpieces, one fried, one baked."

Carmella

Carmella is a pizzeria in the neighborhood where the Elena Ferrante Naples Quartet is said to be set. Its owner, Vincenzo Esposito, invented a pizza to celebrate the world's current favorite Neapolitan author and the world she portrays. Esposito has created a pizza honoring the fictional Lenu, topped with all the ingredients of a traditional Neapolitan Sunday lunch: ragù, ricotta, *fior di latte*, Parmagiano, and basil.

Street Pizza: Pizza *a Portafoglio* or *a'Libretto*—Pizza to Go

The streets of Napoli are, to borrow and adapt a phrase, paved with pizza. Wherever you look, wherever you sniff the air, everywhere are street *pizzerie* ready to feed and revive you. All of the usual characters are there, as well as every age and class. Eating pizza *a portafoglio*, you'll rub elbows with them all.

My favorite *portafoglio* at the moment is Pizza a Portafoglio di Gennaro Salvo on Via Toledo. I found it by accident. Suddenly starving, without a recommendation or knowing where to eat, I looked up and saw its sign.

I ordered a marinara, found a place at the nearest standup table, and opened my paper-wrapped pizza just enough to inhale its oh-so-enticing steam. I won't elaborate, as we all know the beauty of tomatoes, garlic, oregano, and olive oil, but even with my long history of eating these ingredients, suddenly I became very alert. I had to toss it around in my hands a few times until it was cool enough to eat, but—oh!—the dough, so tender; the sauce, intensely tomato; a whiff of oregano; and so garlicky—hello lovely big chunk of garlic!

I should have known when I saw the name Gennaro Salvo. He is, shall we say, legendary even among legendary *pizzaioli*. Part of the Grasso family of pizzeria Gorizia, he has moved around, pizzeria to pizzeria, owned his own, worked for others, taught classes. Pizza Portofogio di Gennaro Salvo is one of the go-to *pizzerie* of the Gino Sorbillo empire, which extends throughout parts of Italy. At its heart is the most delicate, chewy, tasty, digestible crust made from the dough guided and nurtured by pizza legend Gennaro Salvo. This wonderful quality of crust won the heart of even Italy's north. That dough—that incredibly tender, flavorful dough—is a result of Salvo's mastery with the *levito naturale*.

They offer only marinara and Margherita; sometimes they have pizza stuffed with greens. There is also fried pizza in the front case next to the array of beautiful fried delicacies: the arancini, potato fritters, and *frittatine*.

"When it's Saturday night," a friend told me, "like any good Neapolitan, it's time for pizza with the family. It's what we *do!*" Later in the evening, especially on a warm summer evening, it is the young people hanging out, crowding the pizza-to-go counters, jostling to catch the eye of the *pizzaioli*. The streets of Napoli at times are like a big pizza party.

Pizza Women

The profession of *pizzaiolo* has a long tradition of being handed down from father to son to grandson. But, in fact, pizza making has been a preserve of both men and women, though divided by gender. Men work the fiery ovens, hefting the big shovel-like peel with its disk of dough, then pulling it out a minute or so later, all in one hot and tasty piece. It's hard, hot work that demands brute strength.

Women traditionally made *pizza fritta*, or fried pizza. In Vittorio De Sica's *L'Oro di Napoli*, Sophia Loren does the frying while her husband mans the ovens.

Though definitely still in the minority, a handful of pizza women are vying for their share of the (pizza) pie, challenging the male-dominated pizzeria and adding the oven to their expertise in frying.

The three most well-known pizza women currently are Isabella de Cham, Teresa Iorio, and Maria Cacialli. Isabella de Cham of 1947 Pizza Fritta is, at the young age of twenty-four, considered one of Naples's best pizza makers. In 2017, she was awarded the title of pizza champion at the Campionato Nazionale Pizza DOC in Nocera for her Sorrento pizza of *caciocavallo*, arugula, and lemon zest. She explained that fried pizza became a women's skill because their hands are smaller, better for kneading small pizzas and slipping them gently into the pan of hot oil.

Teresa Iorio is the first woman to win the Trofeo Caputo pizza championship, earning her the title of worldwide champion *pizzaiola* 2015. Photos hang on the walls of her pizzeria, Le Figlie di Iorio, which she opened in 2006. In fact, she is twice a world champion as of this writing. I would be remiss if I didn't mention her adorable style: big smile, shiny blonde hair, *contadina* dress with the low-cut neck, full skirt, and red bandana-like head wrap. She is usually holding a pizza, especially for photos. She isn't shy in front of television cameras, either. (But is any Neapolitan?)

Iorio inherited her love of pizza making from her father and, from her mother, her love for fried pizza. There were twenty children in the family, and she is next to the youngest. At age twelve she started work in the family pizzeria. Now she employs two of her sisters and a niece in her own family business, which translates to "The Daughters of Iorio." She is also active in creating opportunities for other women and keen on passing along the art of being a *pizzaiola*.

Another Neapolitan *pizzaiola*, Maria Cacialli, feels it was her calling to make pizza even before she was born: her parents met in a pizzeria. She works alongside her husband and her son at her pizzeria, La Figlia del Presidente (The Daughter of the President). It is named for her father, Ernesto Cacialli, who became famous in 1994 as "the president's *pizzaiolo*" for making a pizza for former U.S. president Bill Clinton.

And I would be remiss if I didn't include a fourth Neapolitan pizza woman: Giorgia Caporuscio, daughter of Roberto Caporuscio, owner of Kestes mini empire in New York City. Georgia may live in New York, but she has not left her Neapolitan heart behind: inspiring to watch, she is a dedicated *pizzaiola*.

6

Festivals, Celebrations, and Their Specialties

The Neapolitan year flutters from holiday to holiday, festivity to observance, each a reason to feast and to eat with deeper feelings and connections that differentiate it from everyday food. And you're never far from the next feast: whatever the day, whichever season. Religious holy days, secular holidays, or family celebrations, the goodie-laden table awaits. For a heartwarming Italian American take on the holidays, Peter Francis Battaglia writes (in his blog, *A Food Obsession*) about his Campanian grandparents and relatives and the dishes and celebrations they brought with them.

In Naples, the one necessity is that on big-deal holidays, specific dishes *must* be eaten. Christmas without *struffoli*? I don't think so. Carnevale without lasagna? What are you thinking? And don't even consider Easter without *pastiera*.

On secular holidays the menu is less organized, but there's always, always much eating and drinking. And as one navigates the passages of life—its joyous celebrations or solemn mourning—all is shared at the table.

Then there are the festivals devoted to food. In villages, towns, and countrysides, most places hold a *sagra* (food fair) to celebrate whatever delicious specialty they are known for. Filled with atmosphere, laden with good things to eat, a *sagra* is often an opportunity to experience folkloric music and dancing, too.

In Naples, the year begins on January 1, as it does throughout the Gregorian/ Western calendar, but at this time Naples is still in the throes of Christmas celebrations. In Naples, like the whole of Italy, Christmas is not a one-day blowout as it is in America. Instead, Christmas is part of a string of holidays, each with its own traditions, and New Year's Day is near the end of the many weeks of festivities.

CHRISTMAS FROM START TO FINISH

Getting ready for Christmas and the New Year holidays begins early in December. Though it is not marked on a calendar as the "start of Christmas," most agree that December 8, the Immaculate Conception, is when the holiday season begins. Throughout Campania, lights are strung over streets, special events are planned, shop windows are decorated. The atmosphere fizzes with excitement.

Everyone has his or her own way of starting the festivities. For instance, a friend once invited me to San Bartolomeo in Benevento for the Immaculate Conception. When I looked a little puzzled, she continued, "They're holding a *sagra* to start Christmas by eating lots of polenta and sausages." Who could argue?

This is when Christmas markets begin in each city, town, and village. Naples holds one in its magnificent indoor Galleria Umberto, filled with traditional foods and specialties.

And the *presepi* begin to appear. Naples has a very special *presepe* (nativity scene) culture. The miniature tableaus do not limit themselves to the manger, to the Madonna and baby. There is also a restaurant, pizzeria, perhaps a table for eating. The three wise men might be joined by a *pizzaiolo*. And perhaps Barack Obama, Diego Maradona, or whoever is famous and beloved at the moment. If the nativity scene camel is hungry, there are tomatoes, a prosciutto, and pasta hanging to dry. But what, you might ask, does the nativity scene have to do with food? Ah. Remember, we are in Napoli.

The Tradition of the *Presepi*

In the thirteenth century, in a cave near the small town of Greccio, St. Francis of Assisi created the first nativity scene and there celebrated mass. The tradition spread throughout Italy, throughout the world, but the Neapolitans took to it with great passion.

A *presepe* can be small and simple or massive, rambling, and sculptural. Every church has a *presepe*, as do most families, businesses, and offices. Each year the old figurines are taken out of their storage wrapping in the same way that others might unpack their Christmas tree ornaments. Each year most families buy a new figurine to add to their *presepe*.

To understand how much of an expression of the local folkloric art they are, try to see as many as you can—exhibits are usually publicized. The Stock Exchange building has shown amazing scenes in its glass display cases. The Museo Nazionale di San Martino, a former monastery, exhibits a magnificent Presepe Cuciniello with more than one hundred and sixty characters, eighty animals, twenty-eight angels, and more than four hundred miniature objects.

The Tradition of the *Presepi* (*continued*)

The historic area of San Gregorio Armeno is filled with ateliers. Walk its crowded streets; peer into the shops. Watching artists carve the wooden figurines reminds me of Geppetto creating his beloved Pinocchio.

Everything you might need for your *presepe* is sold in the shops there, including special kits ranging from elaborate—such as moss-covered houses and wells that run real water—to simple. For the most personal (and often artistic) *presepe*, however, you do not need to shop: create your own from found objects.

The *presepi* usually stay up for a month until after Epiphany. (For a wonderful behind-the-scenes glimpse of both a creator and a collector, see Marjorie Shaw's blog, *Insider's Italy*, at www.insidersitaly.com.)

To me, the start of the season is the appearance of *insalata di rinforzo*. No Neapolitan home could celebrate Christmas without it. Put it together at the start of the holiday and keep adding different ingredients as the season progresses; it all pickles together deliciously. Literally meaning "reinforced salad," it acts a refreshing balance to the rich wintery foods. When the bowl gets low, more ingredients are added, "reinforcing" the mixture that is already there. You pull the bowl out, eating and adding and eating your way through olives and pickled vegetables until La Befana comes.

Having a salad available at all times "reinforces" whatever else you have on hand, so that people can stop by on the spur of the moment, and there is always something ready to eat.

Insalata di Rinforzo: Christmas Salad of Marinated Cauliflower and Pickled Vegetables

You can purchase it in a shop or prepare it yourself starting early in the Christmas season. I discovered the salad during my first visit to Napoli. I was young, on my own in a foreign land surrounded by amazing though strange-to-me foods, and yet there it was: a big bowl of cauliflower, olives, pickled peppers, capers, and more. It was like seeing a beloved friend. I felt immediately welcome.

1 medium-large cauliflower, about 1¼ pounds, trimmed of stalk, stem, and outer leaves, then broken into large florets or chunks

1 carrot, sliced
1 stalk celery, sliced
1 fresh but not too hot/spicy red pepper, stem and seeds removed and finely chopped

Insalata di Rinforzo: Christmas Salad of Marinated Cauliflower and Pickled Vegetables (*continued*)

20 or so pepperoncini, the green spicy peppers in a jar, with a little of their brine

2 tablespoons capers, either salt cured or brined

2 red, roasted (and/or pickled) peppers from a jar, cut into bite-sized pieces

10–15 big fleshy green olives, with the pits/stones in them

10–15 black olives as desired, with the pits/stones in them

White wine vinegar, to taste

Brine from capers, olives, or any of the pickling juices

Extra virgin olive oil, as desired

Salt to taste

For garnish: four fillets salted anchovies, optional

Add enough water in a saucepan to cover the cauliflower, carrot, and celery. When the water boils, add the vegetables and cook about five minutes or so, only until they are crunchy al dente. Drain and place in a bowl with ice water. Leave to cool.

Into a large bowl or crock, place the hot pepper, pepperoncini, the capers, the roasted or pickled peppers, and both green and black olives. When the vegetables are cool enough to handle, add them to the bowl with the pickled ingredients.

Season with vinegar, shaking it on to taste. I usually do this gradually, adding a little at a time, tasting it, adding other vegetables, and then going back to the vinegar. Add a little of whichever brine or juices you wish, plus a little salt to taste, then add the olive oil, and toss together.

Taste for vinegar, sprinkle a bit of salt, and let marinate for a few hours before serving. Garnish with the anchovy fillets.

When you have eaten all the cauliflower, celery, and carrots, cook and add more to replace them, as well as more vinegar, brine, and so on, to bathe in the marinade. At any time throughout the *insalata*'s life, I might add twenty or so small pickled onions, caper berries, marinated artichoke hearts, different types of olives, a jar of Giardiniera (mixed pickled vegetables), a jar of Italian green pickled peppers (slightly spicy is good), and small, fat, red pickled peppers. It lasts about two weeks, as you keep adding and eating.

December 13, shortly after the Immaculate Conception, commemorates Santa Lucia's martyrdom in Syracuse, Sicily. The event itself took place around 310 AD and has been observed throughout Europe since about 1337. As many winter holidays are, it is a commemoration of light, poetically linking with the blind Santa Lucia.

Though candlelit processions often mark Santa Lucia, in Napoli it was the first light of dawn that announced Santa Lucia to me. I was asleep, staying in (appropriately) the Santa Lucia quarter of Naples, and suddenly heard a loud, explosive noise. The sky was pale gray before the sunrise, and the noise felt hugely alarming. Was it a bomb—could it be terrorists? Mount Vesuvio? Criminals? Peering out my window down to the street, hiding from view in case of danger, I saw people moving, slowly and slightly aimlessly, with a great aura of seriousness. It looked ominous.

I dressed fast, ran downstairs and found a milling crowd in front of the Santa Lucia church. The life-sized statue of Santa Lucia was carried aloft on their shoulders, the group headed down the street. I needed coffee.

When I returned it was daylight, and I could see Santa Lucia rounding another corner, headed back. In the church, believers had brought flowers with which to surround her. It was eerie and beautiful and touching.

Since Sicily and many northern European countries have special foods for Santa Lucia, I asked about Napoli. Ironically, for a city that so loves to eat, I was told that there are no special Neapolitan dishes for Santa Lucia. In fact, in Naples some people like to fast that day.

But you won't go hungry long. December 16 is one of three days throughout the year devoted to Naples's patron saint, San Gennaro (the other two are the first Saturday in May and September 19). On this day the dried blood of the martyr, San Gennaro, is believed to liquify in its tiny vial. This miracle shows that San Gennaro protects Naples.

Starting early in the morning, huge crowds gather at the Duomo to witness *il miracolo*. Radio, social media, and television reports keep the public updated. It could happen in the morning or later in the day, but once the blood turns liquid, a big sigh of relief echoes through the area: Life can go on. Naples is safe. Time to celebrate and eat something delicious.

And, as sometimes happens, if the blood does *not* liquify, it could augur a catastrophe such as a Vesuvio eruption. This, too, is reason to eat something delicious as a consolation and fortification for whatever happens.

There are lots of sweet treats to choose from: the usual characters of babà and *sfogliatelle*, of course, and also Christmas confections such as round, nutty *rococco*, toffee-coated *struffoli*, chocolate-dipped *mustaccioli*, and S-shaped *susamielli*. Though a northern specialty, many families buy a panettone for Christmas. So good with butter and honey, stuffed with sweetened ricotta, or dunked into hot chocolate.

In rural Campania, live nativity scenes (*presepi viventi*) pop up in town squares or near churches, with farm animals playing cameo roles in the life-sized creches.

One of the most evocative sounds of the season throughout the entire region is the music of the bagpipe played by bands of shepherds called *gli Zampognari*. They come down from the mountains of Abruzzo dressed in traditional sheepskin vests, leather trousers, and dark woolen overcloaks, with bagpipes made of animal skins. Along the way, they stop at every nativity scene to pray to the Madonna and play their special music. Outside churches, in city squares, and sometimes door to door, people give them a little money for the pleasure of their musical visit; at restaurants they are happily fed. I didn't know about the *Zampognari* the first time I encountered them, but when they played their ancient music, it felt like magic.

Christmas Eve

Because families will be getting together that night and the menu of the *festa* is fish, special markets open early to sell fresh fish (and to celebrate as well). In Ischia Porto, the early morning Christmas Eve market is as much a *sagra* dedicated to *pizza di scarola*, as it is a market with lots of specialties to taste. Often, a marching band performs.

The focaccia-like pie of bitter greens is served with a few drops of *vino cotto*. Meaning cooked wine, *vino cotto* is a boiled-down, intensified condiment much like balsamic vinegar (which explains why there is so much balsamic vinegar in Campania—people already have a taste for *vino cotto*).

Christmas Eve dinner, *La Vigilia*, is eaten with family and is traditionally meatless. When I say meatless, what I mean is fish, fish, fish. Throughout Campania, urban or rural, you might be served *baccalà* (salted dried cod fish), *capitone* (eel), calamari (squid), *scungilli* (conch meat), and *vongole* (clams). Some have a tradition of seven types of fish (representing the sacraments), but it is not the Feast of the Seven Fishes, as in America. In fact, some in Campania consider thirteen traditional.

Then everyone goes to midnight mass—usually when the "baby" is placed in the cradle. In Ischia, while midnight crowds gather at nativity scenes to welcome "Baby Jesus," free hot chocolate and panettone are handed out to warm those gathered during the cold winter night.

Christmas Eve is fishy; Christmas Day is meaty. Tradition calls for a *minestra maritata*, which translates to "wedding soup" but it is nothing like other wedding soups of delicacy. Instead, it is filled with chunks of pork or beef, fresh sausage, a little salame or cured pork for extra kick, and maybe a little wine; then it's simmered (including bones) until a rich broth forms. The "wedding" in the name has nothing to do with matrimony; rather, it refers to how the meat and greens marry as they cook together, the meat flavoring the greens and the greens enriched by the meaty broth. Seven—again, the sacraments—types of winter greens are suggested (more if you can find them).

December 26 is Santo Stefano. Like Britain's Boxing Day, it makes a one-day celebration into two, adding get-togethers with more family, more friends. On Christmas Day, families stay close to home in somewhat somber observance. On Santo Stefano, people are out and about, socializing and visiting restaurants.

Many restaurants have a special *pranzo* (lunch) menu. I loved this one from 2014 Santo Stefano at Tenuta Antica Braceria in Cava de Terreni, SA (between the Amalfi Coast and Salerno). Located on a country road, it serves rustic local foods. When you step inside, it smells beautiful. Tables are filled with locals: Campanians love good food.

Pranzo Santo Stefano
Salumi e Formaggi—a platter of gorgeous locally cured meats and cheeses
Gnocchi di Patate (potato gnocchi) stuffed with local, revered *provolone del Monaco* cheese, in *ragù di pezzentella* (a lamb ragù)
Maiale con Pappacelle (pork roasted with the unique Neapolitan green pepper)

There was dessert, but by then I had drifted away in a food and wine daze.

Now you have an entire week to regain your appetite before *Capodanno* (New Year's Eve).

New Year's Eve

New Year's Eve in Naples sees fireworks over the Castel dell'Ovo and an all-night musical concert in Piazza del Plebiscito: classical, traditional, and rock. Of course, earlier you will have eaten a big New Year's Eve dinner. *Cenone di Capodanno* is basically a repeat of Christmas Eve's fish-based dinner, though while Christmas Eve is solemn, dignified, and less lavish, on New Year's Eve (a.k.a. San Silvestro) one can be as celebratory and lively as desired. As it is said in Naples, "Everything is permitted"—both foods and attitudes!

A sample menu might read:

Antipasto: Frutti di mare crudi is the Neapolitan version of sashimi—raw fish, raw shellfish, perhaps oysters, sea dates, raw salmon—refined, refreshing, invigorating.

Primo piatto: Spaghetti con l'astice—lobster spaghetti (or linguine). Or vermicelli with clams or prawns, spaghetti with *fruitti di mare*, or *lasagna di pesce spada* (wide noodles with swordfish sauce) are also perfect. But lobster linguine? Could you welcome *Capodanno* more enthusiastically with anything else?

Secondo piatto: Here comes more fish! *Capitone marinato* (marinated eel), *frittura di paranza Napoletana* (little fried fish), chunks of *baccalà* simmered with tomatoes and olives, or a whole sea bream roasted with potatoes.

Contorno: Traditional side dishes are *insalata di rinforzo* and broccoli served with lemon.

Dolci: There have been enough cakes and sweets this season. For dessert, continue sipping your wine, nibble on dried fruit, and crack fresh nuts in their shells.

New Year's Day

Capodanno—New Year's Day—means (as it does for the rest of Italy) lentils, usually cooked with a big, juicy *cotechino* sausage. It's believed to bring prosperity in the coming year. Eating lentils on New Year's is a wish, a hope, a prayer, that the multitude of lentils will transform themselves into an abundance of riches. Eat up!

Epiphany

January 6 is Epiphany, when La Befana takes to the skies. Although Babbo Natale (Father Christmas, a.k.a. Santa Claus) is becoming more common, traditionally it is La Befana who brings the children presents. The name *La Befana* is believed to be a mispronunciation of the Italian word *epifania*, meaning Epiphany.

In a uniquely Italian twist to the story of the three kings, with a pinch of Santa Claus thrown in, La Befana flies from house to house on her broomstick bringing treats for good children (leaving coal for naughty ones). In Naples, La Befana arrives at Piazza Plebescito for a huge celebration for La Befana (and holiday marketplace as well). Did I mention that it is crowded?

Epiphany is considered the last day of the Christmas holidays.

La Befana

According to legend, La Befana was an old woman who lived in a small village in Italy—many say Naples or the Campania area (the witches of Benevento). La Befana was known to all for her wonderful baking and for the cleanliness of her home. When not baking, she was cleaning, often while muttering, "No time to do anything else, so much to do!"

One wintery day, as she was sweeping her walkway, three travelers stopped and requested a drink. As she filled their glasses, they told her they were three kings following a star to the birthplace of the holy child. La Befana gave them

La Befana (*continued*)

water and shared her meal with them, but when they invited her along, she demurred: "No, I have too much work to do."

Back to tidying and baking, she was in the middle of making a cake when next interrupted by a shepherd who stopped and invited her along with him. Again, La Befana said, "No, I have baking and cleaning, far too much to do"; then she went back to her cake. Later, however, the sky lit up with a bright light, and she suddenly thought, *What if I've made a mistake? Perhaps I should have gone!*

She put the cake into a basket, gathered up toys from her own child who had died, draped herself with a warm shawl, and went running to the door. At the last moment, she grabbed her broom, thinking you just never know when you might need to tidy something.

She ran to catch up with the kings and the shepherd to no avail. She ran as fast as she could, all night, then even out of breath, she ran some more. She ran so fast that her broom lifted into the air, like an airplane, and once airborne, she flew and flew and flew, searching for the newborn baby. Alas, she found no signs of kings, the shepherd, or a baby.

Ever since that night, La Befana is believed to fly through the night sky on her broom (though some stories have her scurrying across rooftops with her broom in hand) on Epiphany Eve, January 5, sliding down the chimney with her bag of presents, hoping that one of them will be the child she missed that fateful night.

In the house, stockings are hung, a plate of goodies set out for her arrival (forget milk—La Befana prefers a nice glass of wine). She fills the stockings and moves onward to the next house. Some legends have her sweeping the floor on her way out, for the family to start the year with a clean slate.

In La Befana's honor, some pastry shops make a confection like a honey-comb crunch, coloring it with cocoa to look like the charcoal that is given to the naughty children instead of toys and treats.

OTHER HOLIDAYS AND TRADITIONS

There are a few traditions, such as Cippo di Sant'Antonio on January 17, when Neapolitans clear out their unwanted belongings, pile them up in the street, and then set them on fire (*a cippo* means bonfire).

And there is the countryside tradition of pig butchering in January. The whole village gathers to help dispatch the pig raised throughout the previous year, transforming it into salame, prosciutto, and more. Each part of the pig is preserved, cooked, and utilized. (Often it takes place on an *agriturismo* farm—it's always worth trying to wangle an invitation.)

January 31 marks San Ciro e Giovanni all over the south, especially Sicily and towns such as Vico Equense, which count Ciro and Giovanni among their patron saints. Statues of the saints are paraded through the streets and special services are held during the course of the celebrations, ending with the Veglia di San Ciro, a family feast.

By now, La Befana was a while ago, and life is feeling a little gray and bereft of festivities as Neapolitans await Carnevale. If you're ready for another celebration and feeling the winter blahs, you understand this Old Neapolitan joke: *"A Pasca Epifania 'tutt'e ffeste vanno via.' Risponne 'a Cannelora, 'No, ce stongo io ancora!'"* (Easter said to Epiphany, "Now all the holidays are gone until me," and Candelora spoke up and said, "I'm still here!")

February 2 marks La Buona Festa della Candelora, commemorating forty days since the birth of Jesus and his presentation at the temple. Its name comes from the medieval English Candlemas. France celebrates Chandeleur (with rich buttery crepes), and Spanish-speaking lands, La Fiesta de Candeloria. In Campania it is all about *'O Migliaccio*, the tender, citrus-scented, candied fruit–studded delicacy whose golden color recalls the light of candlelit processions that once took place.

Originally in the Sorrento Peninsula, the batter was like any other cake—flour, eggs, sugar—but when ricotta filling (for *sfogliatella*) became fashionable, *migliaccio* makers added ricotta to their batter. Suddenly it was less like cake and more like a crustless cheesecake. And while it is so beloved for Candelora, many continue enjoying it until the end of Carnevale.

Spring is on its way, and Neapolitans have a saying for the change of the seasons vis-à-vis the holidays: *"Cannelora, 'state dinto, vierno fora"* (On Candlemas, summer comes in and winter goes out).

Il Migliaccio

A typical sweet from San Giorgio a Cremano, which is celebrated every February 2, when the festivities of Candelora and the festival of light signal the start of Carnevale.

Some say that the *migliaccio* has been made since 1600, when the sisters at a monastery on the Amalfi Coast decided to cook *semolino* with milk, sugar, dried fruit, and lemon liqueur, baking it until golden, for the festival Candelora. It has been a tradition ever since.

Others say that it is far older, an ancient recipe that once was made with pig's blood (which, since 700 AD, has been replaced by sugar). At some point, ricotta was added, making it somewhat like the filling of *sfogliatelle*, the crisp pastries of Campania.

Il Migliaccio (continued)

It is a *dolce* typical of what is served between Carnevale and *Martedi Grasso*, or Fat Tuesday. When the ricotta was added to the recipe, it became much like a *sfogliatelle* filling.

Traditionally, candied fruit such as orange and lemon are used in the *migliaccio*, but I find that diced, dried apricot makes for a lighter, more rounded taste, and it is a good way to use the exceptional apricots that grow in the rich soil of Vesuvio (though I use them dried).

2 cups milk
2 tablespoons butter
Pinch of salt
Zest of 1 lemon, grated, cut with a zester, or peeled with a sharp paring knife, then chopped (more traditional is to leave it in one long strand and then remove after cooking, but I like the lemon in the mix)
1 cup sugar (I prefer organic cane sugar, unrefined and lightly golden for a richer taste, not just sweetness)

½–⅔ cup semolina (Cream of Wheat)
1 container, about 15 ounces, whole milk ricotta
4 eggs
3 tablespoons finely chopped dried apricots (traditionally, candied lemon rind and/or other fruit is used; golden raisins, though not traditional, are good, too)
2 teaspoons vanilla extract
2–3 tablespoons whiskey (or, more traditionally, limoncello or Strega)
Juice of 1 fat, sweet lemon

Combine the milk, butter, salt, lemon zest, and sugar until it boils; then reduce heat to medium low, and slowly sprinkle in the semolina, a small amount at a time, stirring to incorporate.

Stir well with a wooden spoon to keep mixture from lumping up. Cook for about six to eight minutes or until thickened and creamy. Remove from heat and beat with the wooden spoon, stirring every so often as it cools (the stirring and beating helps it cool).

While it cools, place the ricotta in a bowl and stir well to loosen it. Add the eggs, the candied or dried fruit, and finally the vanilla, whiskey, and lemon juice.

When the milk and semolina mixture is lukewarm, beat a little bit of the ricotta and egg mixture into it, stirring well until combined. Continue adding more, a little at a time, until all the ricotta mixture is gone.

Prepare a ten- to twelve-inch diameter, three- to four-inch-deep baking pan by buttering it and sprinkling it with sugar (be relatively generous, as the butter and sugar form a sticky sweet coating); then pour in the cake batter.

Bake in a 350°F oven for thirty to forty minutes or until it feels firm and is brown around the edges.

Remove, sprinkle with powdered sugar, and chill until ready to eat.

Hot on the heels of Candelora, Ash Wednesday ushers in the forty-day meditative fasting period of Lent. Before one gives up the goodies, however, there's one last blowout—Carnevale. Eat, drink, and be merry, because, yes, Lent is coming.

Literally translated as "the meat goes away," Carnevale is a last flash of indulgence before the somber abstinence of Lent. Besides overdoing rich foods, it's okay to act a little wild. (Throughout the Catholic world, it is a time to dance, parade in costume, and let loose with merriment.)

Another Neapolitan saying, "*a Carnevale ogni scherzo vale*," advises that any trick is allowed during Carnevale. Usually, though, such tricks include children spraying foam, throwing eggs, dressing up, and parading through the streets, unlike the dangerous, violent happenings in other Carnevale destinations.

Pulcinella, Napoli's beloved puppet, rules with his mischievous antics. Today the fest is a mere shadow of its formerly wild and out-of-control self. Predating Christianity, the holiday evolved from the pagan Saturnalia dedicated to Saturn, father of Jupiter. At Saturnalia, people wore masks to frighten away evil spirits, made sacrifices, and had sexual orgies, their identities concealed behind the masks. (The sexual element remains in two rural celebrations: the Carnevale Tarantella of Montemarano, in which couples parade while dancing the tarantella, and the Sirignano, in which couples dance around a maypole, that phallic symbol.)

People enjoyed upending social roles—landowners become slaves, rich become poor, and poor become rich—for the duration of the festival. It was wild.

With the spread of Christianity, pagan elements gave way to more socially acceptable indulgences (such as eating to excess). Partying and going a little bit crazy was now done in a more respectable way, with masked balls and elaborate costumes. The link between celebrations and the church forged a bond, from a food standpoint, such as the sweet fried pastries handed out in the churches and streets. They were easy to make ahead of time, one could distribute a huge amount so no one was overlooked, and the crowd clamored for them.

Since many lived in abject poverty, sweets were a rare treat, and Carnevale was often the only time of the year that they ate meat. So, of course, *lasagna di carnevale* is not just a luscious pasta dish but also a meaty celebration of joy: wide pasta, Neapolitan ragù, tiny meatballs, ricotta, salame—whatever beautiful thing you want to stuff in!

And perhaps you'll have just one last bite of *migliaccio* before Lent? A few *chiacchiere*, deep-fried pasta dough cookies, served with a *sanguinaccio* (a chocolate dip originally made with pig's blood). *Chiacchiere* curiously translates to "gossip," possibly for the sound made when bitten into and crunched on—a bit like the nattering of gossip?

With so many good things to eat at Carnevale, you understand the Neapolitan saying, "*a Carnevale, la dieta non vale*." (There is no sense in dieting during Carnevale; it just doesn't work.)

Lasagna Napoletana o *"Carnevalesca"* (The Fabulous Neapolitan Lasagna)

Serves 4–6 hungry souls or 8 more moderate ones

If you have a Neapolitan grandmother, or Nonna, you no doubt have memories of her making this dish. Maybe you even rolled the meatballs at her side or peeked into the pot of bubbling sauce when she did. If you didn't have a Neapolitan Nonna, have a look through YouTube for instructional videos (and nonnas just waiting to be yours).

Though lasagna is eaten all over Italy, the only constant is the wide noodle—everything else is regional: bechamel or ricotta, ragù or pomodoro, *bianco* with sausage or red with tomato. And lasagna is eaten for all sorts of occasions—including for no reason at all—thoughout the rest of Italy, often in chic and elegant little squares. A Neapolitan lasagna? It's is a big, fat celebratory thing! Wide noodles, thick layers of ricotta, mozzarella, tiny meatballs, and a ragù in which sausage and salame have simmered.

There are many steps, but none difficult: do them ahead as much as a day. (Note: If you are an Italian Nonna, you'll make your own fresh pasta and lightly parboil it. For the rest of us, purchased fresh or dried lasagna noodles are still pretty wonderful.)

For the Meatballs

1 large slice sourdough or other rustic bread, such as *pain levain* or *pane cafone*

Combination of half milk and half water to just cover the bread

12 ounces ground beef or a combination beef and pork or beef and veal

4 heaping tablespoons grated Parmesan or pecorino

2 tablespoons chopped flat leaf parsley

Pinch or two dried oregano leaves, crushed

Salt and pepper to taste

1 egg

½ onion, finely chopped

Flour for dredging

Olive oil for frying

Place the bread in a bowl and cover with the milk and water. Let sit a minute or two until it is soft; then drain and squeeze out the excess liquid. Break up the bread into small morsels.

Add the meat, Parmesan or pecorino, parsley, oregano, salt, pepper, egg, and onion. Mix well.

Place a little flour on a plate.

Wetting your hands with water, roll tiny meatballs about the size of half a walnut. Place each rolled meatball onto the plate with the flour. When all the meatballs have been rolled, dust them on all sides with the flour.

Heat a small amount of oil in a large, heavy, preferably nonstick frying pan, then gently add the meatballs one or two at a time, shaking off the excess flour

Lasagna Napoletana o "Carnevalesca" (The Fabulous Neapolitan Lasagna) (*continued*)

before adding them to the pan. Brown them lightly on all sides but do not cook them completely through. They will finish cooking in the sauce.

When all the meatballs are fried, set them aside while you make the sauce.

For the Sauce
The secret to this sauce is the sausage and salame you cook in it—and the meatballs, of course.

1 onion, chopped

2 Italian sausages, whole, uncooked, preferably mild

Pinch of red pepper flakes, optional

1 cup beef broth (or water plus half a bouillon cube)

1 large can San Marzano tomatoes, broken up (have another small can ready in case your sauce cooks down too much and you need more perky tomatoes in it or more sauce)

Chunk of air-dried zesty salame (cook whole in the sauce, chop up afterward to layer into the lasagna)

1–2 bay leaves or 1 sprig fresh rosemary

Salt and pepper

In a large pan, lightly sauté the onion and sausage together until it browns slightly. Add the red pepper flakes (if using) and the broth. Cook together a few minutes, and then add the tomatoes. Bring to the boil; then reduce heat to a low simmer and add the reserved meatballs and the salame. Cover and cook over low heat, taking care that the sauce doesn't burn (tomatoes being high in sugars). Move around the meatballs with a wooden spoon occasionally to keep from sticking to the bottom but take care not to break them up. (Note: Some of them inevitably break up a bit; that contributes to the flavor of the sauce.)

Cook for about twenty minutes covered; then remove cover and cook another twenty minutes. If sauce seems too thick, add a cup of water to it and/or return cover to the pot as it cooks.

Remove from heat and allow to cool. When cool enough to handle, remove the sausage, meatballs, and salame from the pot. Cut up the sausage and dice the salame. Set aside.

To assemble the lasagna:

1 pound dried lasagna noodles or 1½ pounds fresh lasagna noodles

Salt

Extra virgin olive oil

Reserved sauce

Pinch or two of fennel seeds (optional)

Small handful basil leaves, torn or thinly sliced (optional)

Reserved meatballs

Reserved sausage

Lasagna Napoletana o "Carnevalesca" (The Fabulous Neapolitan Lasagna) (continued)

Reserved salame
8–12 ounces whole milk ricotta
1 pound fresh *fior di latte* (cow's milk mozzarella) or about 8 ounces mozzarella, shredded or torn apart

¾ cup freshly grated Parmesan or pecorino
2–3 ounces *caciocavallo*, or other full-flavored meltable cheese, diced

Cook the lasagna noodles in salted, boiling water for a few minutes, or about halfway done—they should still be uncooked in the center. Cook three or four lasagna noodles at a time to keep them from sticking. Remove with a slotted spoon, place in a pan of cold water to stop the cooking, and then add more lasagna noodles to the pot. After the lasagna noodles have cooled a minute or so, remove from the cold water to a plate and drizzle them with olive oil. (If using fresh noodles, there is no need to precook, but add a little extra liquid to the pan before baking.)

When all the lasagna noodles are cooked and cooled, add the fennel seeds and basil (if using) to the reserved sauce.

Turn oven on to 375°F.

Start assembling the lasagna. You are going to have about three layers of noodles, two layers of cheese, sauce, and meats, and a topping of sauce and Parmesan and mozzarella on top.

In a large rectangular baking pan or casserole, drizzle a little olive oil on the bottom; then smear on a spoonful or two of the sauce. Cover the bottom with a layer of the cooked lasagna, fitting them tightly together so there are no spaces between them; overlap if you like.

On top of the first lasagna noodles, scatter about half of the meatballs, half of the sausage pieces and diced salame, about a third of the sauce, about half the ricotta in dollops, a third of the mozzarella and other cheese (if using); then top with another layer of lasagna noodles. Repeat with the meatballs, salame, sausage, ricotta, mozzarella, and sauce. Top with remaining lasagna noodles. Pour or spoon the remaining sauce over the top, sprinkle generously with the Parmesan or pecorino, and drizzle with olive oil. (If the sauce seems too concentrated or if there isn't enough to cover the top generously, add another can of San Marzano tomatoes, broken up or chopped.)

Cover the pan with foil and bake for half an hour. Remove foil and bake uncovered for another fifteen minutes. Remove from oven and loosely cover with the foil for another fifteen minutes or so, or until the dish absorbs some of the liquid on the bottom.

Cut into squares and serve.

San Giuseppe Day

So now we eat in a fasting way until Easter, right? Wrong. You didn't think we were going to leave you lost in Lent without at least a day to eat something rich and sweet and happy? Of course not. San Giuseppe (a.k.a. Saint Joseph) Day falls on March 19, and since San Giuseppe is the protector of families, it has become Italy's Father's Day. It's also the name day for all Giuseppes (or Peppe, as known in Napoli).

San Giuseppe Day is the holiday of cream puffs—zeppole—filled with lemon custard, sweetened ricotta, whipped cream and lemon marmalade, and even ice cream. It is said that these cream-filled puffs were invented in 1840 by Don Pasquale Pintauro of the *pasticceria* of the same name, which is still in business today. He is also credited with selling the first *sfogliatelle*.

The cream puffs of San Giuseppe give one the strength to make it through Lent to Holy Week (*Settimana Santa*). During Holy Week, the streets are filled with costumed processions, floats held aloft in the hands of strong young men, and the strains of ancient-sounding street music—sometimes pleasing, at other times a cacophony. You don't really know when and where an Easter parade will pop up.

Palm Sunday

La Domenica della Palma—Palm Sunday—begins a week filled with religious devotion among believers. For everyone else, it's a communal wonderment of spring. Blossoms turn the trees into pink and white clouds of fluff, the air smells sweet, flowers bloom in all directions.

In a touching tradition called Lavurjelle, also known as *il grano germogliato* (the grain sprouts), a handful of seeds is allowed to sprout in the dark. During Holy Week, people take these to church as an offering, a symbol of rebirth.

In the city, this is a week to dress up, wander about, enjoy the first whiffs of impending spring. Many take part in a church to church walk known as *Lo Struscio*. With five hundred ancient churches in the city, there's always a new church to discover, streets to walk down, and friends to greet along the way.

There is a great tradition of elegant chocolate eggs. Windows are filled with beautiful artisanal creations from traditional local chocolatiers such as Gay-Odin. The exquisite eggs make a perfect Easter gift; happily, no law exists to prevent you from giving one to yourself.

On Thursday the church bells—which ring regularly, dependably, throughout the year—stop. Their silence is a mournful acknowledgment of Jesus's death. The bells are quiet on Good Friday (Venerdi Santo) and do not ring on Saturday. It isn't until the stroke of midnight, which announces Pasqua, Easter Sunday, that they peal joyously to welcome his rising.

Easter

Most Neapolitan families gather on Easter for a big meal—is there any holiday in which they don't? It might be eaten at home, but it could be eaten at a restaurant. It is the usual celebration meal—antipasti, pasta, roast meat, seasonal vegetable specialties—and always includes *pastiera*.

The pastry for Easter, *pastiera* combines ricotta and whole, cooked grains in an orange-flower and cinnamon-scented custard, which is baked in a pie. It might be eaten throughout the year, bakeries sell them these days, but as yet another Neapolitan saying goes, "*Non puo mancare sulla tavola di Pasqua*" (*Pastiera* can't be missing on the Easter table). And if you're at Nonna's, you'll break her heart if you don't eat it!

Often there is a soup—*minestra di Pasqua*—a pot of meat and vegetables that should express springtime. In fact, expressing spring seems to be its only requirement. The broth is usually made from a chicken, such as the elegant consommé of boneless, stuffed chicken I ate once: cut into mosaic-like slices that rested atop of spring herbs, rich broth ladled around. Or diced spring vegetables cooked in chicken broth with ricotta dumplings. There is a lot of leeway allowed in this soup's interpretation.

The main course is usually lamb or kid, symbols of springtime, cooked simply with vegetables of the season: peas, artichokes, spring onions. And *casatiello*, a cheese- and ham-filled yeasted, lard-enriched bread topped with raw eggs in their shells, which hard boil as the bread bakes. The *Tortano* is basically the same yeasted dough, stuffed with diced salame and cheese, but instead of whole raw eggs in their shells pressed into the top, it has diced hard-cooked eggs mixed into its filling.

In the villages around Avellino, Easter is a time of ricotta pies known as *pizze*. There is a *pizza dolce*, filled with sweet ricotta and candied fruit, a savory *pizza di Pasqua*, and *pizza chiena*—filled ricotta, salame, cheese, and egg. Writer Lisa DePaulo tells of how her Avellino family makes it with savory filling but sweet crust, a very ancient recipe.

And even though it is from the north, Neapolitans love *colomba di Pasqua*, the dove-shaped, fruit-studded, sugar- and nut-topped sweet yeasted bread. It is so delightful to bite through the crunchy topping into the light and not-too-sweet bread. It is good with coffee or wine, or hollow it out, sprinkle with a little rum or brandy, and fill with sweetened ricotta. Even better.

La Pasquetta, Easter Monday follows Eastern Sunday, a lighthearted day for friends, family, picnics; soccer in the sand on the shore, visiting Nonna; sailing to a hidden cove with a big hamper of goodies; or cooking pasta on the beach. If the weather is warm enough, have a swim in the springtime sea.

The Feast of the Assumption

The Feast of the Assumption—Ferragosto—is both an Italian national holiday and a religious holy day. The modern religious Ferragosto dates from 18 BCE and commemorates "The Feast of the Assumption of the Blessed Virgin Mary," the day that Mary, mother of Jesus, died and her body ascended to heaven; it is also the "name day" for anyone named Assunta. Like many religious holidays, it coincides with a previously existing pagan holiday celebrated before even the founding of ancient Rome. A tradition dating back to Augustus's time is adorning horses with flowers and giving working animals the day off from agricultural duties.

Celebrated on August 15, it is also the start of the nationwide annual vacation, in which most things—restaurants, shops—close (except in vacation areas). For the next several weeks, even the most chaotic and loud places seem quiet. It feels as if the whole country breathes a collective sigh: the year was hard, we worked, and worked, and worked; now, let's relax and have a good time! Many say that it's not Ferragosto without a nice baked pasta, made the night before and carried to the beach or wherever you are picnicking.

During the era of fascism, the Mussolini regime used Ferragosto as a populist holiday, with special travel offers to woo the working classes. If Ferragosto falls near a weekend, Napoletani, like all Italians, *fare il ponte*—they make a bridge of the weekend by taking off an extra day or two between the holiday and their vacation time.

Naples Festival of San Gennaro

On September 19 Naples once again awaits the miracle of San Gennaro—of the three days of blood liquefaction miracles, this one is the biggest. It is nothing like New York's Little Italy, where it is also celebrated (and has become like any other New York City neighborhood fair); in Napoli, it is a very important (and serious) day.

Regularly recorded since 1389, the liquefaction occurs several times a year. San Gennaro was bishop of Naples in the third century and was beheaded in the persecution of early Christians (about thirty-five hundred died) by Roman Emperor Diocletian. Saint Januarius, or San Gennaro, is Naples's patron saint. His blood was gathered by a disciple in vials and stored. Over the years, it dried. It now is presented thrice yearly to liquify as a miracle to the people, a sign that Naples is protected by San Gennaro, its patron saint.

Throughout the day, radio and television keep the city updated on the situation from the city's thirteenth-century Duomo. In the course of the day, you ask random people, "Has it happened yet?" When the miracle occurs, all of Napoli breathes a sigh of relief. It's a nervous wait, because if the blood does not

Naples Festival of San Gennaro (*continued*)

liquefy, it is thought that something terrible may happen. Vesuvio? An earthquake? When the blood does not liquify, Napoli holds its breath.

In 1939, the blood failed to liquify (the year World War II started); in 1980, it again failed, and Irpinia suffered a terrible earthquake. In December 2016, the blood once again failed to liquify. Urging Neapolitans not to pay too much attention to this, Monsignor Vincenzo De Gregorio, abbot of the chapel, was quoted in *La Stampa* as saying, "We must not think about disasters and calamities. We are men of faith, and we must continue to pray." Since a huge Neapolitan catastrophe didn't materialize—that we know of—perhaps all will be well after all.

Festival of San Gennaro

Every September 19 is Festa San Gennaro, one of three days of the year (also December 16 and first Sunday in May) when the blood of San Gennaro liquifies.

San Gennaro is the patron saint and protector of Napoli. According to legend, he was born into a rich patrician family in the third century. At age fifteen, he became a priest.

When Emperor Diocletian led a campaign of persecution against Christians, San Gennaro was beheaded in Pozzuoli in 305 AD, a scene painted by baroque artist Artemisia Gentileschi. Just after his death, a woman named Eusebia saved his bones and blood, putting the blood into a vial.

In the fifth century, his remains were interred in what is known today as the Catacombs of San Gennaro. You can still see his tomb and the oldest known portrait of him there today. His remains were moved again in the tenth, twelfth, and fifteenth centuries, finally finding a home in a special crypt beneath the altar at the Duomo. In a side niche of the church, the vial of San Gennaro's dried blood is stored in two hermetically sealed ampoules and adorned in a silver reliquary. Three times a year these vials are removed, and a procession takes the bust of San Gennaro and the vials of blood to the high altar of the cathedral.

The blood doesn't always liquify on command, sometimes taking several hours, liquifying several days before the celebration, or—most ominously—not liquifying at all. Many people note that when San Gennaro's blood has not liquified, terrible events have happened to the city. Others claim that when they witness the liquefaction, miracles such as healing from an illness occurs.

Scientists want to study the phenomenon, but church leaders will not allow it, fearful of damaging the blood. Therefore science still does not have an adequate explanation for the phenomenon.

On the designated days of the miracle, things are a little tense. All of Naples is on edge. Devotees crowd into the Duomo to witness the miracle. Shrouded in myth and superstition, the liquefaction is a religious ceremony that dates to the late 1300s. The church is usually packed. The cardinal himself holds the mass, and after the blood liquifies, he walks down the middle aisle of the church with the blood, for all to see. He continues the outside the church and announces to the city that the liquefaction has occurred; then he returns the blood to the altar, where it is kept for eight days to show the people of Naples that San Gennaro has yet again blessed the city.

After the miracle comes the celebration: the streets are closed off, religious processions snake through the cobbled streets, candies, street food, and children's toys are sold by street vendors, and a festive air fills the city.

All Souls' Day

Ognissanti, All Saints' Day, is November 1, and All Souls' Day is the following day, November 2, so they tend to be celebrated as one, sometimes including a little bit of that American import, Halloween (October 31). Neapolitans may go to mass, enjoy a big family lunch, visit the graves of deceased family and friends, and share a special confection: *torrone dei morti*, made not with honey and almonds but with cocoa, hazelnuts, preserved fruits, and often coffee.

THE CYCLES OF LIFE

As the communal year forms our lives with religious observances, national holidays, and secular festivals, so the personal year is marked by family celebrations of life's passages.

Everything, of course, involves food, even when no specific food is associated with the event. Feeding each other celebrates (and at times, helps ease) our way through life. Eating together, sharing our sustenance, gives us a sense of belonging.

It starts at birth, the most joyful of occasions. Throughout Italy it is traditional to hang a bow—blue for boys, pink for girls—on the doors of new families—all are then invited to visit. In the south, superstition dictated that a child should be kept indoors for the first forty days to protect against *malocchio* (evil eye). Friends, family, and neighbors come to ooh and aah over baby, bringing the family something good to eat.

Holy Communion at the church occurs when a child is nine or ten years old. The ceremony is followed by a big party for family and friends, lots and lots of food, and a celebration. It can be held at home or in a local venue, such as a hotel. It reminds me of the bar/bat mitzvah parties of my own Jewish culture. There is music, dancing, wine drinking, and merriment for the adults as well as for the kids. Everyone is dressed up and in the happiest of moods, and even the frosted celebration cake looks like a bar/bat mitzvah cake!

The host makes sure everyone has *bomboniere* (multicolored candies similar to Jordan almonds but more brightly colored and tastier), usually presented in a sort of gift bag. The tables are laden with all the good things—mozzarella, salame, lasagna, meatballs, *la parmigiana di melanzane*, there are no rules. Just abundance and joy! *Mangia! Tutti a tavola!*

At age eighteen, most families throw a big coming of age party in a rented venue with music, lots of drinks, and food.

Then there is the celebration of marriage. The whole area, especially the coastline, is an exquisite place to get married. On beautiful weekends, it seems as if the whole world consists of brides and grooms. You see them posing for wedding portraits by fountains, along the seafront, on quaint cobbled streets. The brides are beautiful, the grooms are beautiful, the setting is beautiful, and the wedding feast—that is beautiful, too!

A wedding in Campania is like a wedding nowhere else, at least the feast part of it. Everyone looks lovely, dressed glamorously, socializing happily with each other between visits to the antipasto table.

The antipasto table is laden with cured meats, exceptional cheese, all local treasures. (Here is where I confess to having crashed a wedding antipasto table in the garden of a hotel where I was staying. Just a tiny bit of salame, I swear. Well, and a little bit of cheese.)

Pastas—maybe one, maybe three, maybe a parade of them—and meats, vegetable specialties, fish, and seafood: all the good things are there. It is a meal of happiness and abundance. Sometimes the abundance is too abundant—especially in the country villages. There they have a tradition (like so many, sadly disappearing) in which there is so much to eat that a special box for leftovers is given to guests who can't keep up. It's like a doggy bag, but also a special remembrance of the happy occasion to enjoy over the next few days as you fork your way through.

At the end of life, the dead may no longer eat, but those who survive must be sustained. It is a very somber time (some widows still dress in black for the year afterward). Friends bring dishes to feed the family—soup, meat, nourishing foods. Neapolitans know that eating, and eating well, is most crucial—*ti fa bene* (it does you good). A good appetite is a sign of being alive.

CULTURAL EVENTS AND FESTIVALS

As the big religious festivals of the year recede, Campania gives itself over to cultural events. (I mention the Naples Marathon in April, not because I'm a runner [sadly] but because where better than Naples to carbo-load?)

Whether food focused or not, it is at the cultural festivals that you're likely to experience the exuberance of Neapolitan life, which can get overlooked in the ordinary business of life. Traditional costumes, parades, dances, music, sometimes fireworks; it's all there in between eating. No matter what, there will be many local dishes to try and treats to indulge in.

Most summer activities consist of some variant of sitting outdoors in the cool of the evening, enjoying concerts, eating and drinking, watching the star-filled sky, perhaps fireworks—who knows when the sky will light up? And food festivals basically involve walking and tasting many, many local delicacies.

Ravello holds a unique classical concert each summer, the *concerti all'alba*. Beginning at 4:00 am, the orchestra plays to welcome the sunrise. It is an uplifting celebration of life as darkness turns to light, night to day. When the sun is fully risen, the concert is over. Then it's time for coffee.

In rural areas, late spring means the transhumance, the movement of sheep from the pastures to the cooler mountains for the summer. Sometimes there are festivals along the way.

The Festa della Republica, the national holiday commemorating Italy's statehood, is held June 2. It's a national holiday: let's eat!

If you love to dance, Capri hosts a tango festival: feel the music stirring you, dance until you are physically and emotionally spent, and then sit under a lemon tree and eat a plate of beautiful spaghetti.

Napoli Pizza Village

A big pizza party used to be held in September, going by the name Pizzafest. In recent years, it has morphed into the International Pizza Village, held in June.

A number of years ago, before its current incarnation, I had a newspaper assignment to report on the pizza festival. So excited, I rang the organizer for details, and he broke some sad news: the festival was cancelled. I was bitter—not only was there no Pizzafest, but now there was also no assignment, no opportunity to be in Naples. Hearing the distress in my voice over the phone, the organizer comforted me: "You don't need a special festival to enjoy Napoli's

Napoli Pizza Village (*continued*)

wonderful pizza! No! In Napoli, *every* day is a pizza festival!" And it did cheer me up. He was so right.

Now the festival is back and better than ever. Held along the Lungomare Caracciolo waterfront overlooking the island of Capri, admission is free and tickets for pizza tastings are inexpensive. Wander from booth to booth, sampling a wide array of pizzas, comparing tastes, reveling in the joyful experience of eating pizza. You should go, though it won't be easy. The weather is usually hot, crowds push all around you, though oh-so-good-naturedly, and you may well end up in conversation laughing even if you don't know what you're laughing about.

Cultural activities, demos, an international *pizzaioli* competition, children's activities, pizza-making tutorials, musical and theatrical presentations. In 2017, fifty historical *pizzerie* participated. I don't know what the plans for the future are, but I have no doubt it will be delightfully excessive.

A *sagra* is an Italian festival devoted to local foods and crops. *Sagre* (plural) tend to pop up—often at short notice—here, there, wherever locals want to celebrate whatever delicious thing they grow or produce. Keep your eyes open for posters and fliers splashed across roads, walls, and telephone poles. When you see a sign, follow it! (Warning: If looking online, be aware that Naples can be unpredictable—events come and go and dates change, so check before you make plans. But don't worry; if you miss one *sagra*, you might find a different one down the road that's even better.)

If you love artichokes, during the season there are festivals all around, as it's such a major crop. Paestum holds its *festa del carciofo*, where it is used in everything: pasta, pizza, parmigiana, frittatas, salads. Pertosa holds a festival honoring their own, the *carciofo biano di Pertosa*. It is far less bitter than other varieties and delicious thinly sliced in salads or even pasta. Of course, the island of Procida is devoted to artichokes as soon as the season arrives.

To taste *ciccimmaretati*, a soup of grains and beans meant to bring good luck for the new season of growing, go to the Cilento on May 1. Casatiello has its *sagra* in Sant'Arpino in June (you'll need a glass of wine to help you digest). A snail festival is held in Letino, honoring the slow but delicious little critters, while in Forchia, Benevento, it's all about cherries.

If you love mozzarella, don't miss any mozzarella festival. No opportunity for a comparative tasting should be passed by. It's educational and can help you discover

your favorites. A *sagra della mozzarella nella mortella* is held in the Cilento village of Novi Velia. This celebration is for a unique mozzarella wrapped in myrtle
branches.

In Campania life *is* one big lemon festival. And there are other festivals, such as
the *sagra dell'albicocca* in Sant' Anastasia devoted to local apricots, and the truffle
fair in Irpinia—*mostra mercato del tartufo estivo*. Porcini have their own fair in
Montoro Superiore.

The little town of Tovere, up the hill from Amalfi, holds a *festa della patata*,
with lively Neapolitan songs setting the mood for the star of the evening: the potato. Gnocchi with tomato sauce, sweet doughnut-like zeppole or krapfen, *pasta
con patate*, crunchy croquettes, and *patatine* (French fries)—could it be a potato
festival without them?

The Cilento village of Felitto holds a fusilli fest. Handmade, wrapped around
a thin stick to form a corkscrew-like pasta, fusilli is perhaps Campania's original
pasta shape.

The *sagra dei piatti poveri*, dedicated to *cucina povera* (the "poverty kitchen"),
is a Cilentro tradition. *Foglie e patane cu lu vicci* (beet greens and potatoes with
garlic, oil, and *peperoncino*) and *mulegname mbuttunate* (stuffed eggplant) are two
of the specialties.

Cetara hosts a week-long *sagra* to celebrate the homecoming of the fleet, in
which the boats return home to Cetara and their haul is transformed into preserved
fish–filled bottles and tins.

Each year around June, the Consorzio of Gragnano pasta makers holds a celebration, Pasta in Spiaggia (pasta on the beach), at a different location on the Sorrento
or Amalfi Coast.

If you would like to celebrate eggplant (who wouldn't?), Santa Maria la Carità
holds a *sagra delle melanzane* and il Convento Santa Rosa holds a *sagra* for
sfogliatelle. Of course, you should never pass up any tomato *sagra*. It goes without
saying that Striano, home to delicious tomatoes, holds one annually.

At Padula, near Paestum and Valle di Diano, August 10 marks the anniversary of
the thousand-egg omelet that the monks of il monestario la Certosa di San Lorenzo
made for Charles V in 1534. Each year they reenact the event, though I'm not sure
about the omelet.

The lovely town of Campagna hosts a yearly festival called Portoni Ghiottoni
(doorways to gourmandise). For three days, the doors and gates of its palaces and
convents—usually closed to the public—are opened to all. In each courtyard local cooks prepare a different specialty such as pasta e fagioli (*matass'e fasule*)
and *percuoco'cu vino* (cookies made with wine). People wander the streets, from

palazzo to palazzo, convent to convent, stopping along the way to sample one deli-cious dish after another, accompanied by live music and happy socializing.

When autumn arrives, wine fairs are held throughout the grape-growing regions of Campania. The largest is Solopaca Wine Fest. Each year the mayor leads the parade of handcrafted floats made from grapes, the streets lined with cheering townspeople. There are even a few beer festivals: one in Ischia and one at a villa in Castel San Giorgio.

Irpinia celebrates chestnuts and truffles in its *sagra*. A brass band plays as you gaily lick your chestnut gelato and consider which truffle delicacy you will sample next.

Around the end of November, the village of Controne holds a *sagra* for its indig-enous bean, *il fagiolo di Controne*. Medium sized with a creamy texture and thin skin, it is traditionally dried in the sun. Unfortunately, many other beans *look* like the authentic Controne bean but are not. Going to the bean *sagra* is a good way to learn about them by tasting and by speaking with the farmers.

But first, Gragnano has a pasta party, a great big pasta party with music and dancing and star chefs, lashings of pasta, and a lot of fun. The Festa della Pasta di Gragnano is like living in an Italian movie, with the sounds of "Mambo Italiano" ringing in your ears and twinkling fairy lights turning the streets into a pasta-fueled wonderland. With stalls set up throughout Via Roma, chefs preparing their restau-rant specialty, crowds gathering for a plate of this, a plate of that, the street is like one big party!

And, oh, the dancing! The festival of 2017 featured Sven Otten, a hip-hop dance sensation with the grace of Fred Astaire who not only danced his way through Na-ples but also took with him the citizens of Gragnano, leading impromptu rehearsals and dancing sessions throughout days of the fest.

In a post on Facebook, then president of the Pasta della Gragnano Conzortium, Giuseppe Di Martino, on the eve of the September 7, 2017, Festa della Pasta, wrote:

Gragnano, Naples, Italy

I come to Via Roma very late the night before we put together the festival, two nights before the big party, and imagine the pasta hanging from the drying racks, the wind that moves it like the strings of a single harp, wonderful, fragrant, golden pasta as in ancient days.

Palace-like buildings filled with pasta makers once lined the street. This road was designed especially to dry pasta. For at least five centuries, maybe more, they dried the pasta like this, on reeds balanced on the benches. The slow drying was unique, and so, too, was the excellence of dough made from the local high-protein wheat and the excellent water. My ancestors, 105 years ago, began making pasta here in Gragnano.

Then I return to the present and think about the Gragnano Pasta Festival. It has been five years since the last one, but now we are back! I imagine how it will be at night, with thousands of guests, the noise of the party, children having fun, mothers feeding them with a spoonful of pasta, a happy electricity of moments to which I daydream and look forward.

Of course, I try to anticipate any of a thousand things that could go wrong. A hundred thousand details, a thousand authorizations, some of the famous Italian red tape, prayers for weather, juggling all of the ingredients that will come together to welcome the public to our party. My buddy Maurizio Cortese [director of the Consorzio di Tutela della Pasta di Gragnano] and I have worked together. He'll call me hundreds of times during these last days of planning.

Tomorrow this road, Via Roma, will be draped with rows of colored lights, stands of exquisite foods, tomato producers, kitchens, and local chefs (twelve!). The chefs will repeat the magic they produce in their restaurants: one will be serving our beloved pasta with tomatoes, another the garlic and olive oil spaghetti that comforts us all, and another will serve a spicy pasta, with the spicy soft sausage from neighboring Calabria, *'nduja*.

There will be an orchestra, singers, dancing, including this year a hip-hop dancer extraordinaire. I love every moment and every detail of the pasta festival, as chairman of the Gragnano consortium I take responsibility and commitment before any honors. It's a gift to my land.

Tomorrow the festivities will start. Meanwhile, what a beautiful moon tonight! What a beautiful street Via Roma!

Giuseppe Di Martino

7

Sharing Culinary Culture

Chefs, Cookbooks, Teachers, and Iconic Dishes

Even with culinary traditions closely passed from generation to generation, when one learns to cook by watching Nonna or Mamma, there is still a place for learning from the professionals: books, chefs, and teachers. Not all of us grow up in Nonna's kitchen, and even for those who do, there is joy in the printed word, in the chef's creativity, and in learning from teachers what even Nonna doesn't know (don't tell her I said this).

There are always chefs who cut corners or who make outrageous foods for media attention or who dismiss making good food in an effort to make their own fortune without regard for culinary sincerity. But even though there are fast and processed foods, plus websites devoted to outlandish trendy foods (even Italy has the Food Network), so far *la cucina Napoletana* remains mostly safe. I have high hopes that the culinary life of Napoli will continue to evolve. Authenticity still exists, cooking from the heart is still important, and the cuisine is always evolving. That's why it's so good to have the books and cookbooks, the chefs and teachers, to see where we have been and therefore where we are headed culinarily.

THE BOOKS

Before cookbooks even came into being, we have scraps of observations here and there. Pliny, for instance, was very keen on the natural/scientific world, including food. From him we know that Augustus kept moray eels to serve at banquets.

Gaius Matius (first century BC) was a citizen of ancient Rome and a friend of Cicero and Julius Caesar who wrote three volumes on gastronomy. He was said by Pliny the Elder to have invented the art of topiary, as he grew trees as a hobby, including a fragrant golden apple tree. Latin for apple is not *mala* but *matiana*, perhaps referring to Matius. *De Re Coquinaria* ("About Cooking") is the book usually referred to simply as Apicius, whose name has become synonymous with a love and knowledge of fine eating. The book is attributed to Caelius Apicius, as several of the recipes were credited to him, but the name "Apicius" also referred to the luxury eating habits of Marcus Gavius Apicius, a Roman gourmet. He lived sometime in the first century AD during the reign of Tiberius and is believed to be the inspiration of the book (though some mistakenly refer to him as the author). The book is said to have been compiled in the late fourth or fifth century, written in an early form of Latin.

It gives a glimpse into how the ancient Mediterranean world ate, both opulently and more down to earth: a dish of flamingo is there, as is braised lamb or goat (with more spices than would be used today—onion, coriander, pepper, lovage, cumin, garum, oil, and wine).

Centuries later, probably 900 AD, more recipes were added. It was written in classical Latin and organized in a surprisingly modern way: divided into chapters that cover housekeeping, ground beef, vegetables, beans, poultry, dishes with many ingredients, meat, seafood, and luxury dishes. In 1541, it was relevant enough that a new edition was published in Lyon by Sebastianus Gryphium.

Neapolitan cookery books of the fourteenth century included dishes from the rest of Italy, and sometimes Neapolitan interpretations of "foreign" dishes. The provenance of dishes was important to distinguish between Neapolitan and foreign food styles. It was not unusual to find *cotoletta alla Milanese* or *sugo alla Bolognese*.

Written sometime between the thirteenth and fourteenth centuries, *Liber de Coquina* ("The Book of Cooking") is one of the oldest medieval cookbooks. The book consists of two independent parts: the *Tractatus* (part 1) and *Liber de Coquina* (part 2). It is believed that *Tractatus* had a French author and *Liber de Coquina* a Neapolitan author. Two codices survive, preserved at the Bibliothèque Nationale in Paris, France.

Tractatus addresses wine, poultry, meat, fish—"dishes for the rich"—legumes, eggs, leeks, and gravy, whereas *Liber de Coquina* includes vegetables, (more) poultry, pastry, (more) fish, and dishes of varied ingredients. Many of the dishes are similar to what Neapolitans eat today: braised cabbage, stewed beans, and the most popular dish of the day—a big, fat, melted cheese pie.

Written in the second half of the fifteenth century, *Cuoco Napoletano* (The Neapolitan Recipe Collection) reflected the era of the Aragonese Court of Naples. Far more spices were used than now; yet onions came with a warning by the author, Martino: "Only use onions if the master so wishes." His recipes were later published by Il Platina (see below). It had no table of contents or index, which made it difficult to use. The English translation and critical appraisal is written in modern times by Terence Scully and published by University of Michigan Press. The original manuscript is at the Pierpoint Morgan Library.

Chef Maestro Martino, author of *Cuoco Napoletano*, inspired and urged his close friend, the Renaissance humanist writer and gastronome Bartolomeo Sacchi, to write his book on gastronomy, *De Honesta, Voluptate et Valetudine* (On Honourable Pleasure and Health). It is considered the first printed cookbook. Bartolomeno Platina (1421–1481), known as "il Platina" (after his birthplace, Piatena), began his career as a papal writer in Rome to the humanist Pope Pius II.

A collection of seasonal Neapolitan menus, *Lucerna de Corteggioni* was published in 1643 and written by Giovan Battista Crisci. Along with menus, it included local products and flavors redolent of the south, providing a portrait of Neapolitan culinary life at the time.

The first cookbook with tomato recipes, *Lo Scalco Alla Moderna*, by Antonio Latini, was published in Naples in 1692. (Tell me, would you have expected otherwise?) After that, written between 1692 and 1694, Latini published *The Modern Steward*, dedicated to organizing banquets—a very Monzù theme.

Francesco Leonardi published *Apicio Moderno* in 1790. It consisted of endless food observations gleaned from his kitchen service in an array of aristocratic grand houses. A regional highlight is his attention to the French way of preparing pork in the areas stretching from Lazio to Naples.

Vincent Corrado was one of the most famous philosopher chefs from the nobles' courts in Naples. He began as a page in the court of Don Michele Imperiali, and then he studied for the priesthood: math, astronomy, and philosophy. When he stepped into the kitchen, however, he found his calling.

He worked as chef for the prince of Francavilla (his "master")—of whom he was very fond—at the Palazzo Cellamare overlooking the Bay of Naples. Prince Francavilla entertained guests every day, often hundreds. Corrado was given the title "Capo dei Servizi di Bocca," which loosely translates as "boss of services to the mouth"—in other words, the royal arbiter of deliciousness.

Corrado's book, *Il Cuoco Galante* ("The Gallant Cook"), first published in the Neapolitan language in 1733, was perhaps the first Neapolitan cooking manual taken to heart by the members of the public who could read. It became cooking counsel for cooks of all levels of life, not just aristocrats.

His master adored Corrado's vibrant creations and encouraged Corrado to share them with the public. Though it would be centuries before the healthfulness of the Mediterranean diet was scientifically recognized, his dishes resonated—eating them "felt good." From 1773 to 1806, the book was republished six times. His simple, excellent foods were almost modern: prawns and prosciutto with olive oil; squid stuffed with eel, anchovies, parsley, and truffles; creamy pine nut–truffle pesto. There's even a grilled cheese sandwich, contemporary except for the sweet flourish of sugar and cinnamon.

After *Il Cuoco Gallante*, Corrado wrote *Pranzi Giornalieri Variati Ed Imbanditi in 672 Vivande Secondo i Prodotti della Stagione* ("Cucina Napoletana: 672 Seasonal, Varied, Daily Lunches"), a cookbook focusing on everyday meals and local, seasonal foods. Published in the Neapolitan language in 1832, it also proved popular with the cooks of Campania. His volume *Del Cibo Pitagorico* ("Herbacious Food for the Nobiles and Literati") was the first vegetarian cookbook in Italy, based on Pythagorus's diet of vegetables for health, and included both tomatoes and potatoes. His *Il Credenziere di Buon Gusto* ("A Collection of Good Taste"), published in 1778, was devoted to cakes and confections.

Corrado lived to be one hundred. One of his most important contributions to Neapolitan cuisine was taking the tomato seriously. In *Il Cuoco Galante*, he hollowed out tomatoes and stuffed them, but by 1828 he published the first printed recipe for a tomato and meat ragù—a dish now at the heart of the Neapolitan family table. Strangely, just prior to this, the first recipe for pasta with tomato sauce was published not in Naples but in Bassano, Le Marche, a region of Italy. Antonio Nebbia's recipe book *Cuoco Maceratese* was published in 1820 by Remondini.

In 1837 or 1839, a new book captured the public's imagination. Ippolito Cavalcanti, author of *Cucina Casareccia* (Neapolitan language), overtook Corrado in popularity. His next book, *Cucina Teorico-Pratica*, published in 1852, kept Neapolitan cooks in thrall. His pedigree, Duke di Buonvicino as well as Knight of the Gerosolinitan Order, increased the public's fascination. He offered a recipe for vermicelli with tomato.

Corrado and Cavalcanti are considered *the* maestros of Monzù cookery, sharing and interpreting the culinary ways of Monzù chefs for home cooks. The Monzùs, whose name may have come from a mispronunciation of the French "mister" (i.e., monsieur), combined their haute cuisine artistry with local ingredients. In the process, they united the different strands of Neapolitan food life. Monzù elegance added a layer of richness to the simple, rustic cuisine. Still revered by modern chefs, Cavalcanti and Corrado also are honored occasionally, such as the banquet that took place in December 2016 at Naples's il Palazzo Salerno, which celebrated the culinary art of the Bourbon table.

So many of Naples's iconic dishes surprise in their aristocratic provenance, as they are so much a part of traditional Neapolitan cooking.

La parmigiana, a baked layering of eggplant, came from the Monzù kitchen. *La salsa Genovese*, a long-simmered sauce of meat and masses of onions, is what most Neapolitans grew up eating on Sundays (when they weren't eating *'o raù/ il ragù Napoletano*). It smells like home. But it came from the Monzù tradition—most likely a Genovese cook made the dish in one of the aristocratic houses. When people would ask, "What is this dish?" the reply would be "It's what the Genovese cook makes." Yet he likely borrowed it from the French tradition, as it is basically a thick onion soup that became a pasta sauce, then a culinary icon.

The fancy *timballo* likely started as a French *timbale*, a mold of vegetables and meats held together with béchamel. In the Neapolitan kitchens, local pasta was used to line the baking pan and that became classic. Or *sartu*, an elaborate rice mold or individual molds, filled with saucy meats and then baked.

ICONIC DISHES

La Parmigiana di Melanzane

Just one forkful of the melting eggplant, tomato, and cheese (known as *mulignane a parmigiana* in the Neapolitan language) evokes a happy nostalgia for Neapolitans, Sicilians, and anyone in between. It's odd, though, that such a southern dish's name refers to Parma, the town, or possibly Parmigiano, the cheese. Odder still is that it isn't terribly popular in Parma. Oddest of all is that this dish of consummate southern ingredients—eggplant, olive oil, and tomatoes—screams *il Mezzogiorno* (the south), though most agree that it probably came from the Monzù kitchen.

Basically, the dish is sliced eggplant fried in olive oil, layered in a pan, and baked. It predates the tomato (even today, sometimes it is made *en bianco*, without tomato). Some cooks dip the eggplant slices in batter or egg before frying, some just fry it plain, many flour it first and then fry, and some simply brush the eggplant with olive oil and grill (which is actually the old Neapolitan way). Layered into a casserole with tomato sauce, mozzarella cheese, Parmigiano cheese, basil, and sometimes hard-boiled eggs, it is baked until crusty and melty and irresistible.

Since Parmigiano cheese is not native to Campania, it might seem that the dish did not originate there. But southern Italy has been importing this hard, grating cheese since at least the fourteenth century. Even then it was easy to transport and keep, and it became an ingredient in many southern classics.

Would it have been called eggplant parmigiana because of the cheese, though? Unlikely, since Parmigiano isn't even a crucial part of the recipe. Far more plausible is that the dish originated in the south, since that is where eggplant itself first appeared in what is now Italy, flourishing in the hot sun. Any dish of eggplant and tomatoes is far more likely to have come from Campania than from Parma. Olive oil, too, speaks of the south; in Parma, it would have been butter.

Many cookbook authors suggest that the name comes from the Sicilian *palmigiana*, the wooden slats of louvered shutters that the layered eggplant slices are said to resemble. Others suggest that it may have been from Palermo (Palermitiana, the "el" sound hard to pronounce outside of Sicily) or even *parmiciana*, Sicilian dialect for "Persian," but I think this is a bit of a reach.

The two Monzù chef-authors, Corrado and Cavalcanti, give recipes for it. Corrado's eggplant is sliced; layered with vegetables; baked "in the Parma way" with butter, herbs, cinnamon and spices, and grated Parmigiano cheese; and covered with an egg yolk–enriched cream sauce before being baked. As you can see, the Parmigiano cheese is negligible in terms of importance.

Cavalcanti's recipe came much later. His included tomatoes, which would seem to point to the dish having evolved somewhere in the Campania countryside, as that was the first place chefs began falling in love with them.

The modern classic is said to follow these rules: Slice eggplant thinly (peeled or unpeeled according to taste), flour it, dip it into beaten egg, and fry in olive oil. Then layer in a baking dish with tomato sauce, buffalo mozzarella, a little grating of dry, hard cheese, and a few leaves of fresh basil here and there.

In the old Neapolitan way, the eggplant was fried but not dipped and floured. Other variations include pecorino in place of Parmigiano, *fior di latte*, or even fresh provola (smoked mozzarella) in place of buffalo mozzarella. Hard-boiled eggs have always been an option, but sometimes, instead of both breading and hard-boiled eggs, raw, beaten eggs are poured over the top before baking.

The tomato sauce is whichever one you love the best, but a variation of pureed intense tomatoes, or passata, is best, no onions required. Recently a Neapolitan friend confided that she always simmered a sausage or two in her tomato sauce for *la parmigiana*. The definitive recipe appears to have only one requirement, expressed in this Neapolitan saying: "*A parmigiana e' mulignane ca se fa a' Napule è semp'a meglio!*" (The eggplant Parmesan that is made in Naples is always the best!) It is close to the Neapolitan heart.

I was at a gathering near Naples where we drank wine, ate this, ate that, and when the next platter appeared, we ate that, too. Chef brought out his *candele* and Nonna's ragù, and everyone oooohed and ahhhhhed. Then came platters of exquisite buffalo cheeses. By then we were scattered relaxed on couches and big chairs throughout the room. Digesting.

Just when I thought it might be time to go home, a buzz started at one end of the room, spreading through the crowd. People sat up and started getting excited. "What's going on?" I asked. "*La parmigiana di melanzane* is here!" was the cry of the suddenly animated crowd. And it is such a beloved dish that no one, absolutely no one, sat back and said, "No, thank you. I'm full." We were *all* full; yet we *all* needed a bite—or two.

In his 1858 cookbook *Usi e cosumi di Napoli e Contorni* (The Uses and Customs of Naples and Her Surrounding Area), Swiss-born, Neapolitan-by-choice Francesco De Bourcard addresses the local dishes—the ragù, macaroni, tomato—that in the not-too-distant future became beloved culinary symbols of his adopted land. It includes what is likely the first published recipe for pizza Margherita; his instructions, however, include pounding the dough with a rolling pin (a modern-day no-no).

Although an Italian cookbook and not specifically Neapolitan, Pellegrino Artusi's *La Scienza in Cucina e l'Arte di Mangier Bene* ("The Science and Art of Eating Well"), published in 1891, remains a valued cookbook locally and is still referred to. It provides a portrait of the culinary era, and its 790 recipes came from each region of the newly unified nation. The idea of putting all of these far-flung recipes together must have felt daring, heady, exciting—revolutionary, even—it was the first recipe book to do so. The specialties of all of the former city-states, nations, towns, and regions were united at the table under one flag: Italian.

In its pages, Artusi describes the wide variety of vegetables of the (now-unified) Italian table, reviling many as "Jewish." As unpleasant as his opinions may be, it is a record that we can refer to centuries later to see where certain foods came from, making it an important historical document.

Artusi was from the north, Emilia-Romagna, but spent much of his life in Firenze until his death in 1910. Despite writing his massive cooking tome, Artusi did not cook; his faithful servant, referred to only as "Morietta," did.

Sfogliatelle

Sfogliatella is a love-at-first bite food, equally adored by those who have been eating it their entire lives. Its citrus-scented ricotta is wrapped in either a multitude of crisp pastry layers (*riccia*) or a shortcrust-like crust (*frolla*). (A lesser-known *sfogliatelle* Santa Rosa is filled with custard and amarena cherries, and there's also a lobster tail–shaped *sfogliatella* filled with whipped cream.)

Sometimes *sfogliatelle* are filled with savory fillings, especially in the winter, like the sausage and *friarielli* of Sfogliatelle Mary, or the mini *sfogliatelle* filled with oniony, meaty Genovese sauce, like at Di Martino Pasta Bar. The savory ones are as lovable as the sweet.

It is said that *sfogliatelle* originated in the kitchens of the Croce di Lucca Monastery during the 1700s. There are records of them being made by the cloistered nuns at the Santa Rosa Convent on the Amalfi Coast. For many, many years they were unseen outside the convent, prepared by the silent nuns.

But even if the nuns weren't talking, it's hard to keep this stuff secret. In 1818, the pastries appear in Napoli at the pastry shop Pintauro on Via Toledo, prepared by Pasquale Pintauro. Customers couldn't get enough. Their popularity spread throughout Napoli, then throughout the entire region. Other bakeries began making them, too, and soon they became the icon they are today. And Pintauro Bakery? It is still there, making its exquisite pastries.

The website www.visitnaples.eu/en has a good short video of preparing *sfogliatella*, with a musical background, a cha-cha-cha!

Nick Malgieri's *Sfogliatelle Napoletane*

Makes 12–18 pastries

This recipe is courtesy of master pastry chef and author Nick Malgieri, who adds, "There is probably no more quintessentially Neapolitan sweet than *sfogliatelle* (sfo-lya-TELL-lay). Rich, flaky pastry made with lard encloses a semolina and ricotta filling scented with cinnamon and candied peel. Best warm from the oven (in Naples, bakeries keep them in warmers)."

I've left the double measurements in, to stay faithful to his recipe.

DOUGH

3 cups (400 grams) bread flour or high gluten flour

1 teaspoon (6 grams) fine sea salt

1 cup (225 grams) warm water, plus more if necessary

2 ounces (55 grams) unsalted butter

2 ounces (55 grams) leaf lard

FILLING

1 cup (225 grams) water

½ cup (100 grams) sugar

⅔ cup (115 grams) granular semolina

1½ cups (340 grams) thick ricotta, strained

2 large egg yolks

2 teaspoons vanilla extract

¼ teaspoon ground cinnamon or 2 drops oil of cinnamon

⅓ cup (75 grams) candied orange peel or a mix of orange peel and citron, diced

A pasta machine and 2 jelly roll pans covered with parchment or foil

For the dough, combine the flour and salt in a mixing bowl and stir in the water. The dough will be very dry. Scrape the contents of the bowl onto the work surface and press and knead the dough together so that all the dry bits

Nick Malgieri's *Sfogliatelle Napoletane* (continued)

are incorporated. Press or roll the dough about ⅓-inch thick and pass repeatedly through the widest setting of the pasta machine to work the dough smooth. Fold the dough in half every time after passing it through the machine and change the direction of inserting the dough occasionally. After passing the dough through about twelve or fifteen times, it should be smooth. Knead the dough into a ball, wrap in plastic, and allow to rest in the refrigerator about 2 hours.

For the filling, combine the water and sugar in a saucepan. Bring to a boil and sift the semolina over the boiling water gradually, stirring constantly to avoid lumps. Lower the heat and cook for a minute or two, stirring often, until very smooth and thick. Press the ricotta through a fine sieve and stir into the cooked semolina mixture. Cook several minutes longer, stirring often. Remove from the heat and stir in the yolks, vanilla, cinnamon, and candied orange peel. Scrape the filling into a shallow bowl or glass pie pan and press plastic wrap against the surface. Refrigerate until cold. The filling will become very firm.

Combine the lard and butter in a bowl and beat by machine until well mixed and soft. Flour the dough and divide it into four pieces. Flour each piece of dough and pass through the pasta machine at the widest setting. Make sure the dough emerges in a neat, rectangular strip as wide as the opening of the machine. If the dough is uneven, fold it over on itself so that it is as wide as the opening and pass through again. Continue to roll the dough in this manner, passing through every other setting on the machine, ending with the next-to-last setting. Repeat the process with the three remaining pieces of dough.

Place one of the strips of dough on a lightly floured surface and brush it with the lard and butter. Begin rolling the dough into a tight cylinder from one of the short ends, stretching the dough gently in width to make the cylinder about two inches wider. Paint another strip of dough with the fats and position the rolled piece on it so that the end of the first strip meets the beginning of the second and continue to roll up. Proceed with the third and fourth strips in the same way. Reserve the remaining lard and butter mixture covered, in the refrigerator, for baking the *sfogliatelle*. The dough should form a tight cylinder about two and a half inches in diameter and ten inches long. Wrap in plastic and chill several hours until firm. The dough may be frozen at this point; defrost it in the refrigerator overnight before proceeding.

Preheat the oven to 400°F and set a rack in the middle level. Remove the roll of dough from the refrigerator, place it on a cutting board, and trim the ends straight. Cut the roll into 12 to 18 slices, each about ⅓-inch thick. Place the filling in a pastry bag that has a ¾-inch opening; a tip is not necessary. To form the pastries, take one slice of the dough at a time and flatten it from the center outward in all directions. Form it into a cone by sliding the layers away from each other with the thumbs underneath the slice of dough and the first two

Nick Malgieri's *Sfogliatelle Napoletane* (continued)

fingers of each hand on top, manipulating the piece of dough from the center outward. Holding the cone of dough on the palm of one hand, and the pastry bag with the other, squeeze in the filling, so that the pastry is full and plump. There is no need to seal the open end; the filling is too firm to run during baking. Position the formed and filled *sfogliatelle* on the paper-lined pans and brush the outside of each with the remaining fats.

Bake the *sfogliatelle* at 400°F for about twenty to twenty-five minutes, basting once or twice with the remaining fats, until they are deep golden. Remove from pans to racks to cool. Serve the *sfogliatelle* warm on the day they are baked. To reheat, place on paper-lined pan and heat at 350°F for about ten minutes.

Variation: Sfogliatella Frolla
Instead of the pastry recipe above, use a sweet shortcrust to encase the filling. You can, of course, vary the size: they should look something like large, round ravioli.

The Cook's Decameron: A Study in Taste appeared in 1901. Written by a Mrs. W. G. Waters and published by the Alexandria Library, it is a fascinating little narration about nothing in particular. You also could say the opposite—that it is about everything; the important thing is that it eventually all comes down to meals.

The book describes a group of British travelers who are sharing a residence in Rome, which includes sharing the table. For some of the group, it means pleasures; for others, complaints about foreign food. Most passages end describing the meals taken that day. Our heroine and narrator, Mrs. W. G. Waters, loves Italian food. At the local marketplace, she unearths a Neapolitan cookbook with a bright yellow cover that becomes her personal connection to the food of Italy. It is, in a way, her ticket to falling in love with her surroundings. In its pages, you can sense her excitement as she describes a dish of macaroni with sausage and tomatoes, which she adores. When she is extolling the virtues of garlic, one can only imagine how radical (and difficult) it was for her British dining companions.

Talismano della felicità by Ada Boni was published in 1928 and republished over and over until eventually it was translated into English in 1950. It was the leading Italian cookbook in America for decades. I have the copy my mother used in my childhood. In its original Italian, it was an all-purpose cookbook, 866 pages and two thousand recipes (of which at least half were not Italian). Translated into English, the international dishes were snipped out, and it became an Italian recipe compendium.

Babà

Tender little yeast-risen, rum-soaked cakes: you might know them from elegant French patisseries, along with eclairs, tartlets, *mille-feuilles*, and the like, but when you go to Naples, expect to be amazed—it's babà, babà, and more babà.

Gaze into any pastry shop or *caffè* window and sigh at their beauty. Stuffed with whipped cream and wild strawberries, glazed with tutti-frutti, awash in limoncello—sometimes so alcoholic that you need to lie down afterward. Babàs can even be shaped like Vesuvio, surrounded by tiny babàs.

In France, a small babà is a babà, with a large one called savarin, but in Napoli it's always babà—a whole food category unto itself—and size knows no limits! From teeny, one-bite morsels (at most, two) to big, big babà for twenty people, there's one for every occasion and meal: breakfast, an afternoon *merenda*, dessert, or coffee break.

Though this Neapolitan food icon shares pastry presence with Paris, it is believed that babà originated in Poland—hence its name, *babà*, an Eastern European word for "grandma."

Legend tells us this: Louis XV's Polish father-in-law, Stanislaw I, adored cake, but it often got disappointingly dry. His patissier, Nicolas Stohrer, thought that soaking it in sweet wine might help (perhaps inspired by Ottoman cuisine?). Stanislaw loved it.

Stohrer moved from Poland to Paris and opened a patisserie on rue Montorgueil in 1730. It's still there, still beautiful and delicious. Strangely, his shop didn't begin selling the soaked cakes until they were firmly ensconced in palace baking, about a hundred years later.

Most likely it was the French chefs employed by aristocratic Neapolitan families who brought these exquisite pastries in their recipe repertoires. A February 27, 1897, court reception lunch in the Naples palace residence for Umberto I of the House of Savoy lists babà as its own special course, right before dessert.

When babà arrived in Naples, like so many other things (and people), it was embraced. It became Neapolitan: gone were the raisins—who needed dried fruit when you had juicy fresh local fruits in season? And while rum is delicious, sometimes a babà might like a different alcoholic bath: cognac, grappa, limoncello, Strega. Its unique spongy-yet-airy texture soaks up the syrup greedily so that each morsel drips an exquisitely light, strongly alcoholic, syrup. (As realists, we must pay attention to our babà's alcohol level if driving. This is my public service announcement. Each bite is so delicious that you might not realize the punch it packs.)

If you have the chance to purchase a babà from Antonio Mennella of Torre del Greco, don't pass up the opportunity. It is divine: light, springy, and filled with cream and wild strawberries. Sfogliatella Mary, on the corner of Galleria

Umberto I and Via Toledo, has an awe-inspiring array of babàs, as well as *sfogliatelle* and even cannoli. Scaturchio also has beautiful babà—and beautiful *sfogliatelle*, and a beautiful outdoor setting. Babàs are even sold in jars. *Agriturismi*, country shops, and restaurants sell them. In a jar? Can they really be fantastic in a jar? Yes—they can be delectable.

Chef and cookbook author Jeanne Caròla Francesconi (1903–1995) was considered the most important Neapolitan food authority after Cavalcanti. Her masterwork, *La Cucina Napoletana* (1965), has been referred to as the "bible" of Neapolitan cuisine. In it are Neapolitan classics, more than 480 of them, including seventy-seven for pasta, thirty-seven for vegetable soups, and five different versions of the Monzù rice dish *sartu di riso*. Occasionally she fashions a twist on tradition, such as adding curly-headed endive to her *insalata di rinforzo* (Christmas salad of marinated cauliflower and pickled vegetables) or using fish instead of meat for her *sartu di riso*.

The recipe list unfurls: ten recipes for salt cod, or *baccalà*, six frittatas, endless seafood dishes, and seventy pages on vegetables. There is recipe upon recipe for homemade pizzas, *pizzette*, calzones, taralli, and all the *fritti* so beloved by Neapolitans. The desserts are, of course, excessive: pastries, gelati, and homemade liqueurs. She includes a good recipe for the Ravello specialty *melanzane al cioccolato* (eggplant with chocolate), which sounds strange but is delicious. As modern as it sounds, eggplant as a dessert has been around since historical times.

Her next book, *La Vera Cucina di Napoli*, continued her mission of preserving local dishes while freshening and sometimes reinventing them. She wanted to leave a legacy, and she does: a lovingly written elegy to Parthenopean culture. Vignettes of history and personal stories embellish nearly each page, saluting the ragù, *minestra maritata*, Genovese, *soffritto Napoletano*.

In English, Claudia Roden extoles Francesconi's contribution to the culinary excellence of Naples in the Campania chapter of her book, *The Food of Italy*, and American food writer Arthur Schwartz pays tribute to her in his excellent book, *Naples at Table*.

Francesconi is remembered for hosting legendary meals for Naples's upper echelons, for her devotion to feeding family and friends, and for writing down recipe upon recipe to pass along. All of this she did joyously, feeling it the most important thing in her life.

A Napoli si Mangia Così ("In Naples We Eat Like This") is both a proverb and the title of a 343-page cookbook by Vittorio and Lydia Gleijeses published in 1977. A Neapolitan author and journalist, Vittorio specialized in all things Naples: history, culture, geography, and occasionally food—the delicious unifying force of the place. Born in the early twentieth century, he died in 2009. Lydia was his wife.

The covers of both editions portray Pulcinella eating spaghetti with his hands. The 1977 edition included classic dishes on the cover, such as rice with Savoy cabbage from Ischia. On the 1990 cover, Pulcinella is still eating spaghetti with his hands, but the other dishes are gone, and Pulcinella himself is looking far more elegant than in 1977, when it appeared that he was too immersed in pasta joy to pay attention to his style.

La Vera Antica Cucina Napoletana by Guglielmon Limatora is a heartfelt book. Though it appears traditional and of the ancient ways, *280 Ricette della Tradizione Partenopea, con la Smorfia Gastronomica* ("280 Recipes of Traditional Partenopea and its Gastronomic Ways") was published in 1998. Publishers Lito-Rama collaborated with the restaurant Lo Scoglio di Frisio di Mario Romagnolo. It is a compendium of traditional Neapolitan recipes in Italian language with subtitles in Neapolitan dialect.

Though not available in English, a small amount of Italian and a dictionary can get you through recipes you didn't know you needed until the very moment you look. It was in this book that I realized how much love a Neapolitan has for *sugna* (lard).

Once again (as is so often the case in food boos about Naples), the masked Pulcinella adorns the cover, this time along with *parmigiana di melanzane, linguine alla puttanesca*, pizza with clams and seafood, and a mound of caramel-covered pastry balls—in other words, the basics.

The recipes are not innovative, nor are they stylish. They are the traditional dishes at the heart of the Neapolitan table. Pick up a recipe, go into the kitchen, and make it your own.

'O Raù (in Neapolitan)/**Ragù** (or *Sugo*) *di Carne* (in Italian)

Whether it's ragù Napoletano "*classico*" or "*leggero*," this richly flavored sauce is a perfect example of traditional, long, slow food, the sort of memory-filled dish that makes all Neapolitans, rich or poor, remember their childhood and their nonnas with just a bite or even a sniff of the bubbling sauce.

It needs to be looked after, slowly simmered, attention paid so that it doesn't burn or scorch, as that scorched flavor will ruin the entire potful. Though now it is consummate family food, it no doubt came from the Monzù kitchens—who else would have had such an abundance of meat and the attention to give to cooking? Such a sauce would have been beyond the means of the city's poorer inhabitants, which meant most of the population. Its name also shows a French influence: *ragù* is likely from the French *ragout*, or saucy stew. The Neapolitan *'o raù*/ragù is exactly that, but with a lot of tomato, unlike the ragù of other Italian regions, which are a thick, chunky sauce of chopped meats and vegetables.

Il ragù Napoletano tells the story of Naples after unification. As nobility declined after a republic replaced French rule, food traditions and class differentiations changed; the chefs who once worked for the aristocracy now worked in restaurants or ordinary homes. Their traditions and specialties began to reach everyone's table, not just those of the rich. Meanwhile, ordinary people began to eat better; the tradition of Sunday lunch was usually cooked by Nonna, and her influence on culinary culture usurped that of the fancy chefs.

Ragù is one of the hallmarks of the Neapolitan table; it is a dish that says Nonna, Mamma, whoever is making this for you, loves you. A ragù takes a long, slow simmer. Mothers and nonnas used to awaken at the crack of dawn to put up the ragù for its five or six hours of cooking. Sometimes they'd stretch the process over several days. The first day, they'd put it up and bring it to a boil; the second day, they'd simmer; and on the third day, they'd take the meat off the bones and serve it: sauce on pasta, meat as its own course. At various times during cooking, it might need a little water, broth, or wine to loosen it up and keep the bottom from burning.

'O Raù/Il Ragù Napoletano

To the rest of Italy, a ragù is a thick sauce of finely chopped meat, wine, aromatics, and maybe a little tomato. In Campania, ragù is quite different. Here, it is a tomato sauce full of meaty essence (because a large chunk of meat such as brisket, eye of round, or pork roast is cooked in it for hours and hours and hours) but not chunky like a northern ragù (or *sugo*, as it's sometimes called).

The meat gives a huge umami layering to the sauce, then it is taken out and eaten as a second course or saved for the next day's dinner. The sauce is tossed with pasta and eaten for Sunday lunch. Sometimes a small slice of the meat is served on top.

The ragù itself remains a tomato and wine sauce made savory with the juices of the meats that have simmered in it. It's frugal: two courses for the effort and cost of one. Also, it's sleek and unique, poaching a bit of meat in a tomato sauce is similar to how the Japanese simmer kombu and bonito in water to make dashi.

Basically a rich, red-brown tomato and meat sauce simmered with a big chunk of beef or pork and a few other meaty enrichments: a whole fresh sausage or two (especially with fennel), the heel end of a salame, a hunk of pancetta or *guanciale*, or *braciola di cotica* (*cutica* or *codica*). The last item, pork skin rolled around aromatics, is something that I had noted wasn't included in modern cookbooks or food magazines, specifically American (or UK) ones. So when I saw the rolls of by now translucent, simmering pork skin bobbing up and down in the sauce, I asked the chefs what it was. "*Braciola di cotica*," they answered, "pork skin wrapped around aromatics." Then they all smiled: "It's what our nonnas

'O Raù/Il Ragù Napoletano (continued)

did." And though Nonna did not use garlic in her ragù—no one does!—a little bit rolled up into the skin or into thin pieces of meat is illusorily delicious.

The long-simmered sauce has an audio component as well: the sound of the *pippiare*, or the bubbles bursting when they gently reach the top of the sauce. The sauce should be very thick, so the *pippiare* is a sign that it is nearly the perfect thick consistency and ready to be eaten. This warns you to watch the temperature, to monitor the sauce, to take care the bottom doesn't burn. A burnt bottom ruins all the sauce. Only when the meats slip from the bone, the meat is butter tender, and a bit of the pork skin roll melts in your mouth at first bite is the ragù ready.

The pork rolled up around chopped aromatics is the key to the dish. Most foreign recipes don't include it, but in Napoli Nonna wouldn't make a ragù without it. As for the pasta, big, thick, long tubes—*candele*—are broken into pieces. Giuseppe Di Martino of Pastificio Di Martino and past president of Consorzio di Tutela della Pasta di Gragnano explained this local tradition to me: "Long ago, purchased dry pasta was made in long big pieces to be broken up as needed. That way, you could break it at any size you wished—rigatoni, penne, ziti, or other fat, shortish tubes—and the broken pieces with their irregular edges gave a variety of textures to the dish as well as helped thicken the sauce."

If *candele* are not available, use any pasta shape you like: ragù Napoletano is good with them all. My personal favorite is *paccheri*.

2 onions, finely chopped

3–4 tablespoons extra virgin olive oil

2–3 ounces fatty cured pork, such as pancetta, in a whole piece/chunk

2½–3 pounds beef or pork roast, tied together with a string (or both a small beef roast, such as brisket, and a pound or two of lean pork spareribs or other pork with bones)

Several rolls of *braciole di cotica* (pork skin rolled around chopped parsley and garlic—just a tiny bit)

2–3 cups red wine or white wine (as much of the bottle as you wish to contribute, but save yourself a glass to sip when your work is done and the ragù begins to cook)

2 cups tomato passata or 1 large can San Marzano tomatoes (1 pound, 12 ounces), broken up with your hands (Nonna squishes them through her hands and fingers), plus the juices

2–3 tablespoons tomato paste, as needed

Chop the onions finely, and then sauté over low heat in the olive oil in a heavy casserole or pot until the onions are translucent.

Add the pancetta, whatever meat you are using, and a few *braciole di cotica* to a tablespoon or two of the olive oil, and cook together gently, covered, stirring from time to time, over low heat for about an hour.

'O Raù/Il Ragù Napoletano (continued)

Uncover and pour in a little wine; then raise the heat and let it evaporate, repeating this once or twice. Add the rest of the wine and continue to cook another fifteen minutes or so.

Add the tomato passata or canned tomatoes and a cup or two of water to keep the sauce from becoming too thick and burning. Keep your ears alert—the sound that a good Neapolitan ragù makes when it is cooking properly is a gentle bubbling and plopping sound. It is said that it "spits" or "sputters," which is called *pippiare*.

Continue cooking over very low heat, on the stove or in the oven, until the meat is very tender, adding more water as needed. You can do this over two days if you like.

When the meat is cooked, remove it from the sauce and set it aside for another course or meal.

Variation: While much of the meat will fall apart into the sauce, the big pieces may be, as traditionally done, removed and served as a second course, or eaten the next day. Or you might just coarsely chop all the meat and make a dense, chunky, meaty ragu. A ragu you can eat from a bowl, and instead of pasta, with bread to dunk in.

Cucina Napoletana by Arturo Iengo, in conjunction with the Naples Chamber of Commerce and Manuela Barzan, published in both the United States and the United Kingdom, was nominated for a World Gourmand Cookbook Award. Chef and sommelier Iengo is not Neapolitan born, but Campania has been his home since 1975. His love of his adopted land's food resonates in the dishes he prepares for his Benevento restaurant, Pascalucci, and in the professional chefs' classes he teaches.

The book contains gorgeous photos of city and landscapes, mysterious black-and-white portraits, and snapshots of enticing dishes. They show that *cucina Napoletana* isn't out to impress you with fanciness; it is all about taste (and heritage). Side passages explain Neapolitan gastronomical life—its vivacious flavors, evocative atmosphere, and soulful inhabitants.

Frijenno Magnanno by Luciano de Crescenzo, published in 1997, contains a wide variety—1,001—of recipes for contemporary Neapolitan dishes.

Inventing the Pizzeria: A History of Pizza Made in Naples by Antonio Mattozzi (with a delightful foreword by Ken Albala, the commissioning editor for the book you are reading) was published in 2009. It is everything you've ever wanted to know about the history of Naples pizza. At once a scholarly observation of politics and social and agricultural history, it tells the story of how the pizzeria came into being from the eighteenth through the nineteenth century. The effort that Mattozzi has put into *Inventing the Pizzeria* is no surprise. I have long been a fan of his restaurant and his dedication to his craft, family, and beautiful pizza dough. His restaurant, Mattozzi's L'Europeo, is full of pizza, mozzarella, *pasta con patate*, *friarielli*, and Mattozzi's marvelous meatballs. I have a photo somewhere of the two of us, his arm around me, big smile on his face after popping out of the kitchen to say hello. Reading his book about pizza warms my heart.

In his 2015 book, *La Cucina Aristocratico Napoletano* ("The Cuisine of the Neapolitan Aristocrats"; written in Italian), Franco di Torpino Santasilia offers a culinary homage to the past cuisine of nobility and the kitchen heritage they passed along: seventy-four traditional recipes with French aristocratic influences, such as raviolini filled with sole, tossed in butter and sage or curry powder added to meat stews such Genovese. We might think such additions strange and foreign, but it was typical of the chefs of aristocratic Naples.

Chef Rosanna Marziale is one of a brigade of southern Italy's new young chefs who, having worked with modern chefs in other parts of Europe, have returned home to cook, reuniting, in deep reverence, with local food heritage.

Marziale now cooks at Le Colonne, her family's restaurant in Caserta. And since it's Caserta, is it a surprise that Marziale is known as the queen of mozzarella? She is devoted to buffalo mozzarella and claims that it sparks her creativity and encourages her urge to cook. Her mozzarella creations are so imaginative: she manipulates the cheese, she kneads it, she achieves a variety of textures and consistencies without losing its fresh taste. She wraps mozzarella around a poached egg, bakes it into tender cakes, and even pairs it with seafood! Recently she has been making *la pizza al contrario*, contrary pizza, which isn't a pizza at all: fresh mozzarella—kneaded into a thick, billowy base—takes the place of crust. It is filled with tomato sauce and crisped and melted with a blowtorch until charred on the outside, melty within. Besides being author of two cookbooks, she is also the author of two children's books and the voice of a character in an animated television series.

Insalata Caprese

The Caprese, as this salad is affectionately known, became chic among the jet set in 1950s Capri when artists, aristocrats, royalty, film stars, and celebrities of all kinds sat in *caffes* in the piazza once or twice a day.

According to the Naples Chamber of Commerce, in its beautiful booklet "The Flavor of Capri," the combination of mozzarella, or *fior di latte*, with tomato and basil first became known at the dinners that the leader of the Futurist movement,

Filippo Marinetti, gave at the historic Hotel Quisisana toward the end of the 1920s. The Naples Chamber of Commerce also notes that Egypt's King Farouk helped spread its popularity when he was served a plate of tomatoes, mozzarella, and oregano stuffed into a roll. He loved it and served it often to visitors.

However, Costanzo and Titina Vuotto, proprietors of CapriFlavors, which offers products for sale, cooking classes, and many other tastes of Capri, claim on their website that it was Titina's mother, Margherita, who invented the dish. She wanted to serve something light so that the beautiful people could "have a nice lunch but still fit into their bikinis."

I'm not convinced that any of the stories are definitive origin of *insalata Caprese*, though I am sure that all accounts are correct and true. Recently I was assured that the salad was popular in the early twentieth century, as early as 1910. One thing, though, has bothered me: There are no buffalo on Capri, so how did the mozzarella (made in Caserta and around Salerno) become *the* major ingredient of one of Capri's iconic dishes? Since Capri makes cow's milk mozzarella (*fior di latte*), perhaps the original was made with this? Or was the salad prepared with fresh buffalo mozzarella brought in by the daily ferries? No one really knows—and no one I spoke with seemed to care. The important thing, all agree, is that it is delicious and local and a perfect, edible, portrait of life in the summer sun of the island.

Ripe Tomatoes, Fresh Mozzarella, and Sweet Basil, Known the World Over as *Insalata Caprese*

There are endless ways to prepare *insalata Caprese*. Most, unless you are in Campania, are so awful they should be called criminal.

Arrange your tomatoes and mozzarella on a plate, enjoying the artistic pleasure. Scatter with a few whole leaves of beautiful basil, enjoying the fragrance. The red tomatoes, white cheese, and bright green basil leaves, together on your plate, are so beautiful that it is almost romantic. Forget an elaborate dressing, and don't even think of marinating—it obscures the fresh flavor. All you want is a splash of excellent olive oil and a sprinkling of salt. If anyone begs for vinegar, okay—they can have balsamic if they wish. But really, it is best without!

The most amazing *insalata Caprese* I once ate was in Vietri sul Mare, overlooking the sea, up the hill from Salerno: a plate of tiny, quartered sweet cherry tomatoes, a few basil leaves, and a fat ball of fresh mozzarella, whole and unsliced, sitting in the middle. If I close my eyes, I can feel the warm air of late summer around my shoulders, the sweet scent of tomato, the springy bites of mozzarella. I wanted to hold on tightly to the wonderful sensations—the warmth of the sun, the kindness of Neapolitans—as I chewed my way slowly, thoughtfully, through that salad.

CLASSES: THE BEST WAY TO LEARN IS WITH A TEACHER

The Associazione Verace Pizza Napoletana's Pizza-Making Courses
www.pizzanapoletana.org/it/corsi

The Associazione Verace Pizza Napoletana offers training courses for various levels of professionalism, a residential program with a faculty of many of Naples's finest pizza makers.

Pizza Consulting by Enzo Coccia
www.pizzaconsulting.com

Maestro *pizzaiolo* Enzo Coccia of La Notizie Pizzeria offers three courses of pizza-making knowledge: a week for amateurs, a master class for professional pizza makers, and a twenty-day class for those who wish to become professionals.

Mamma Agata: A Legend on the Amalfi Coast
www.mammaagata.com/cooking-class.aspx

They called her "Baby Agata" once upon a time because she was still so young when she seriously devoted herself to the art of cooking. In the summers of 1950s and 1960s, she worked in the kitchen of a wealthy American, feeding illustrious personalities of the era, becoming personal chef to many.

She always remembered the guests' favorites. Anita Eckberg loved her pasta e fagioli; Humphrey Bogart loved her fried anchovies and ate them thoughtfully, gazing out to sea. Jacqueline Kennedy adored fresh mozzarella with tomatoes, eaten outside, next to the pool in Ravello. Richard Burton and Liz Taylor, Federico Fellini (another fan of pasta e fagioli), Marcello Mastroianni, and Fred Astaire— they all came, they all ate. When Fred Astaire visited, *spaghetti alla puttanesca* was on the menu, and afterward he waltzed the hostess's elderly mother around the courtyard.

These days Mamma Agata's cooking course takes place in her private Ravello home, high on a clifftop overlooking the Amalfi Coast. Terraces of lemon and fruit trees, flowers, and vegetables surround the house; she feeds most of her family and the school with it.

In her book, *Mamma Agata (Simple and Genuine)* (written with Chiara Lima, her daughter), the recipes tell the story of her culinary life. The dishes come from her garden and heart, and there are so many beautiful Amalfi lemons involved.

Sitting at Mamma Agata's—high up in the clouds, overlooking the small town of Ravello—might feel unreal, the view is that beautiful. You'll probably be surrounded by others happily chattering away to each other, to you, enjoying the view, the morsels, the moments, the blue sea, the sweet air.

These days Mamma Agata teaches the classes, while her daughter, Chiara, and Gennaro, a great cook, AIS-certified sommelier, and professional cheese taster (*maestro degustatore di formaggio*), run the hotel and restaurant. In the huge vegetable and fruit gardens, they save seeds to protect local biodiversity.

Mamma Agata's attitude has always been that every meal must be prepared with the love and respect it deserves, whether a lavish banquet for hundreds or a small picnic on the beach. And rather than the overly prevalent fancy-pants dishes in chic establishments, she still prefers the local ones made with devoted tradition and of regional ingredients.

Buffalo, Mozzarella, and "Old Tastes": Tenuta Azienda Agriturismo Seliano

Only five kilometers from the archeological ruins of Paestum, the *agriturismo* Seliano is run by Baronessa Cecilia Belelli Baratta, along with her family. The farm has been in the family since 1806, when the king granted the land and title of baron to Gaetano Baratta. Degas painted the family portrait (which hangs in the Musee d'Orsay), but these days they are less fancy, devoting themselves to their *agriturismo* farm.

They breed buffalo, horses, and the local Podolica cows, run a restaurant, rent out rooms, and offer cooking classes. Cooking classes usually take place in spring and autumn unless there's a special request (like when cookbook author Arthur Schwartz brings a group of his students for a week of cooking and exploring). The dishes taught lean toward local traditional influenced by both Greek and Roman kitchens, which the family refers to as "the art of the old tastes." In other words, what makes *la cucina* its unique self.

Classes include visits to mozzarella dairies, wine cellars, and traditional oil mills.

Mediterranean Cuisine of Don Alfonso

The kitchen of the legendary hotel Don Alfonso 1890 offers cooking lessons of its Mediterranean cuisine for its guests. To arrange classes, get in touch with them directly.

The Consortium of Gragnano Pasta

If you would like a cooking class in pasta, why not go to the experts? The Consortium of Gragnano Pasta can arrange a special cooking class for you with a local chef or cook. Email info@consorziogragnanocittadellapasta.it.

Academia Gustarosso

www.gustarosso.academy

Academia Gustarosso recently opened its doors in Sarno, a place to gather for classes and tastings of prized local ingredients. It offers classes in pizza making and peasant cuisine, as well as various guided tastings with knowledgeable chefs. Master *pizzaiolo* Gennaro Salvo worked with Gustarosso to develop the pizza-making project, referred to as Pomodoria. Gustarosso also has recently opened a bed-and-breakfast with five rooms, each named (and color-coordinated) for a type of vegetable grown there: Lucariello, Crovarese, Friarielli, Spunzillo, and San Marzano.

Gastronomical Trekking

When gathering edible wild greens, you must always be certain that what you harvest is not poisonous. Most are fine and safe and healthy; a few are not, such as the attractive, lacy leaves that look so much like the greens of wild carrots (which they often grow near): hemlock. Poison hemlock. Deadly poisonous. In other words, you need a knowledgeable guide.

You can ask the *agriturismo* or hotel clerk for help in locating someone who leads foraging walks. I recently noticed a gastronomical trekking program located in the hills overlooking Positano called Metafarm. It starts with a hike to pick wild things with an experienced wild food guide and is followed with a cooking class to prepare a meal of what was gathered. The Gastronomic Trekking website (www .gastronomictrekking.com/english) describes its focus on sustainability, not only in the realm of the edible and culinary but also in the psychological and social benefits of gathering together and being closely in touch with the Earth.

Learning Videos: If You Don't Have a Neapolitan Nonna or Nonno, Not to Worry—You Have YouTube!

No matter how far away we might be, we can click ourselves into a kitchen with a Neapolitan family who isn't our own but who is cooking all the classic dishes, and we are welcome to join them. Many of the online videos are in Italian, not English, but you can learn by watching and maybe pick up a little Italian in the process.

Marinella Penta de Peppo has a series on YouTube in which she makes the classic Neapolitan dishes. Often described as a modern-day Francescone, Marinella is slender, blonde, nicely dressed, and enthusiastic about *la cucina Napoletana*. She must be into her eighties; yet she is seriously dedicated to sharing the dishes of Campania on YouTube.

Mimmo Corcione is another dedicated YouTube cook. He loves his food, his cuisine, his culture. His eyes sparkle, and he is not ashamed to smack his lips. He makes sauce, frittata, and pasta, and you can always see how much he loves cooking.

The website Brigata di Cucina (www.brigatadicucina.it) offers excellent videos for making *pane cafone*. It takes a while, maybe a month or two, but it is worth it.

On a video posted on YouTube (www.youtube.com/watch?v=UMAvcH5b8Eg), Carlo Frigente, a San Marzano farmer, speaks with Beatrice Ughi of Gustiamo. You don't need to understand Italian to tell that he's imbued with the love of growing these tomatoes. In that part of Italy, growing tomatoes is almost a religion in the farmers' devotion to and belief in their importance.

Casa Surace's website (www.casasurace.com) posts absolutely hilarious videos that capture the very food-loving, food-obsessed Italian south. Many are only in Italian, but English subtitles are beginning to emerge. Titles include "How to Make Coffee (Italy vs. World)," with similar treatments for themes such as pasta, mothering, and eating together. Absolutely enchanting, the company's videos tell you all you need to know to be Neapolitan.

8

How to Eat Like a Neapolitan

In *Craig Claiborne's Favorites from the New York Times*, Claiborne describes the Neapolitan food at his local trattoria as "a trifle more robust" than that of northern Italy. I chuckled—oh, did I chuckle: one of *la cucina Napoletana*'s most defining characteristics is its vibrant robustness! If you want light and delicate, don't eat in Naples!

Eating well is important in Napoli and Campania. Cooks possess the knowledge of what foods go together, how something should taste, what is in season next, and how best to serve the mozzarella. The spirit of those who eat the food is often as robust as the food itself. Or perhaps it is vice versa—the food has become lively because of the people who create and consume it. You can taste the emotion.

And it is never far from Nonna, Mamma, even Uncle Vito. It is food—even the fancy stuff—that feels like it was made for you, personally, with love. Because it was.

Eating in Naples is more a celebration of the senses than simply eating to fuel your body. Why have just a meal when you can have a party? When I got to Naples and found a whole culture that felt the way I do about food, I felt like the luckiest person ever. Sometimes in Campania I look at a plate before me, and it is so enticing that I want to shriek with glee.

To understand *la cucina Napoletana*, it is not enough to eat in Naples or cook Neapolitan recipes. To fully appreciate Neapolitan food, one must eat like a Neapolitan. When I say "must," of course, I don't mean it's mandatory, only that you'll enjoy it more, that you'll "get it" in the same way that knowing about art or music amplifies your pleasure of them.

I understood this when asked once in Naples whether I was Italian American by heritage, because I loved the area so. "Alas, no," I answered, going on to say that I wished I was, as it would be a tangible connection. My friend looked at me kindly; then he said, "Never mind, because you can come here anytime and eat with us, and when you do, you are Napoletana for real."

He wasn't just being polite. Spending time at the Neapolitan table is to be at one with their culture, to understand their passion for the pleasures of the table and their emotion for their own unique cuisine. Eating with the Neapolitans, you are practically blood relatives.

Yesterday, while I was waiting for a train, I had a coffee at the *caffè* bar next door. After regaling everyone there with stories in damaged Italian (they were amazed I knew so much about cooking—and about *their* cooking), the train arrived. As I left to catch my train, they all called out, "You are family now!"

It is true, of course, that in much of Italy, attention to high-quality food is paramount. Speaking about and sharing enjoyment of food is *normale* and of crucial importance in life. People talk about it, spend endless time shopping for it, preparing it, feeding those they love, and feeding themselves. Each meal is another opportunity for a little adventure in taste sensations, a vignette of life's possibilities for pleasure.

What about "healthy eating"? Pastry for breakfast? Pasta every day? Yet, in general, the culture manages a sensible, almost intuitive way of eating. For instance, if you eat too much for a few days, do as Napoletana Sonia Carbone exclaims: "Now I will just eat salad."

A few years ago, I was visiting a family olive farm in Caserta. On the table was perhaps every specialty of the Casertan countryside, all lovingly prepared by the family: frittata di pasta, bitter greens pie, bean stew over crunchy toast, platters of cured meats and cheeses, stuffed peppers, a bowl of meatballs, and who can remember exactly what else there was, but it was spectacular. The grandfather, Nonno, face and hands weathered from a lifetime of sun, was munching his way through a nice heaping plate of—everything! Gesturing to the table of rich food that he was enjoying so thoroughly, he commented, "We don't eat like this every day; usually we eat vegetables, beans, a little wine, pasta. Only every so often do we eat like this." Paolo Ruggiero of Sarno, in a touching Facebook post, urges us to remember the way the farmer families traditionally ate: nearly completely the food of their land, always in season, nothing industrial or commercial. Bread was made in the communal oven, maybe every three days or so (or even once a week), to grow stale and become the backbone of so many dishes that would sustain the family, along with the seasonal vegetables, and always the olive oil (Paolo Ruggiero, Facebook, June 27, 2018).

Occasional long, sensual meals are lavished with care and attention; so, too, are small nibbles, a snack of mozzarella, bite of *sfogliatella*—this several-times-a-day joy is a crucial part of the culture, and vitally important to a happy life. How should they eat, if not like this?

AS A NAPOLETANO, YOU KNOW WHEN TO EAT WHAT

Breakfast (*colazione*) is coffee, with milk if you like (because you won't be allowed milk with your coffee after 11:00 am). It's not exactly the law—you won't go to prison—but it is a cultural norm. Cakes, pastries, and *cornetto* (lighter, brioche-like croissants) are all considered breakfast food. Every Napoletano knows that baked goods are for breakfast: gentle sweetness with which to start the day. Though starting the day with pastries or simple cakes is breakfast throughout Italy, in Naples, eating pastries for breakfast surpasses *Italianismo*, becoming an almost patriotic Neapolitan thing to do. And here you have *sfogliatella*, *cornetto* filled with custard and cherry jam or chocolate cream, fruit tarts, all sorts of simple sliced cakes. And if you have more than one? It's normal. What I still don't understand, however, are the "toasts"—the packaged rusk-like things that are dry and bland. They might be an acquired taste. However, taralli (the crisp, cracker-like savory cookies usually eaten with wine) are also good for breakfast if you prefer savory over sweet.

Though meal structures and traditions change, especially in recent decades and even little Naples feels the lure of fast food, lunch (*pranzo*) is traditionally the biggest, most important meal of the day. Of course, you have eaten only coffee and pastry so far today, so you are ready for a good meal. Lunch starts anywhere between 1:00 and 4:00, but since you'll need to be ready for an *aperitivo* around 6:00, it's best not to wait too long.

Cena, dinner, rolls by around 8:30 or 9:00 pm. That might sound late, but it's on southern Italy time. Don't go to a restaurant early thinking you'll beat the rush. It won't be open yet. Even if a restaurant seems open before 12:30 pm (for lunch) or 7:30 pm (for dinner), usually they are still setting up and won't open until 1:00 pm for lunch or maybe 8:00 pm for dinner.

At odd times of the day, coffee is imperative. You know that, as a Napoletano/Napoletana, that shot of hot, strong fragrant coffee is something you are entitled to as many times a day as needed. You also know that *caffè sospeso* is your civic duty. No one should be without that reviving moment of pleasure that is a cup of coffee, and you can help ensure that someone who can't afford it can have one anyway. If that sounds like a lot of coffee, remember that *caffè Napoletano* is a tiny little cup of espresso. The joy in that tiny cup of coffee is part of Napoli's appreciation of life's small things.

In the afternoon, a snack is called *merenda*. You can get a pastry at a *caffè* with your coffee, especially in the afternoon when you are flagging. There's sweet pastry—but what about savory? I usually point to a slab of escarole-stuffed bread. If the weather is hot, a granita cools you down. Icy, cooling slushy granita is so "sensible" in the heat. When it's hot, I often skip lunch in favor of gelato if I'm near a favorite gelateria.

So many things change, even if so much stays the same, but what surprises me is how pastry has changed in recent years. The *sfogliatelle* there, for instance, used to be tiny, but now there are also taller and longer ones. No one knows why, but aficionados agree: it's new, it's different, it's good, so why not? Also, there's the presence of pistachios and cannoli. Suddenly cannoli is everywhere, with pistachios, both a Sicilian influence. But, of course, Sicily and Campania share a history as the Kingdom of the Two Sicilies.

Lunch and dinner are similar, though, in a sit-down restaurant, pizza is likely to appear only in the evening. The basic structure of a meal includes antipasto, a small one or a crazy-big one, depending on the situation. Lovely vegetables, some grilled, some fried, some lightly pickled; walking into a restaurant and seeing a table with platters of vegetable antipasti is so inviting. You could have only a ball of mozzarella, maybe a handful of arugula, or an *insalata Caprese*. Then there are *gli affettati*, or "the slices," meaning a plate of sliced salame and cheeses. Sitting and eating this plateful of salty cured treasures gives me shivers of joy.

If you're going deep into antipasto land, consider hot, freshly fried fritters: seaweed, baby fish, soaked *baccalà*, peas and pasta, mini *arancini* (rice balls), or a parade of pizza-like stuffed breads, in appetizer portions.

Then comes *il primo*, the first course. Even if you are feeling a little bit full, you must have the pasta course. As a waiter recently said to me, "Pasta is required; the rest is as you wish." So you could have antipasti and pasta. But you might like a little *secondo*; we'll get to that in a minute.

Pasta has been described to me so often as the soul of Neapolitan food—the food that speaks to all Neapolitans. The plates of spaghetti, *paccheri*, linguine, macaroni, all sauced and tossed, are full of local flavor. Seafood, vegetables, meats, Naples has a pasta dish for every day of the year, and then some.

The *secondo*, second course, is what we would think of as the main course: a tiny piece of meat, a plate of seafood, roasted fish, though it could be a dish with eggs and cheese, such as *la parmigiana di melanzane*. Not a lot of meat is eaten in Napoli, but meatballs and sausage are fantastic, a result of *cucina povera*, in which small amounts of tough meats are chopped and formed into something super delicious. (I had some mediocre meatballs last week, and I'm still angry. To make matters worse, the next day at a tomato harvest festival, I missed the meatball station and afterward heard everyone swooning over them.) Meatballs are taken seriously in Campania—and I take them seriously, too.

After a big meal, or, let's say, after a Neapolitan meal, dessert would be wasted—best to save it for when you are hungry enough to pay attention to its beauty (like at breakfast). At the end of a meal, maybe some sliced pineapple? A few strawberries or slices of melon? Of course, *caffè*—espresso, short and strong—is on its way. And, okay, a small chocolate or cookie might appear on the saucer; it is perfect.

Some things in Naples are as in the rest of Italy, but many things are not and are unique to Campania. For instance, in the rest of Italy, you will have grated cheese showered over your spaghetti with tomatoes. In Napoli, your *spaghetti al pomodoro* is simply this: spaghetti and some form of tomatoes—sautéed, fresh, canned, chunks or pureed, as desired—plus olive oil and a leaf or two of basil. Sometimes it includes garlic, maybe a pinch of red chile flakes, sometimes not. Neapolitans know that in the rest of the country—and, indeed, the rest of the world—people enjoy grated cheese on their tomato-sauced pasta; therefore, they might even offer it. But if you look in your waiter's eyes, you may see a haze of sadness. The tomatoes of Campania are so special, so full of their own taste—why would one add grated cheese? When you refuse his offer of cheese, you might hear a sigh of relief from the waiter and the response, "It's better that way."

On the subject of pasta, I have a theory: Everyone is more beautiful when they are eating spaghetti! I came to this after years of observing Neapolitans eating pasta. It's the emotional content, the pureness of joy that infuses the person who is eating, putting radiance into his or her face. Eating spaghetti brings happy memories of seasons, of loved ones, of events. Neapolitans eat so much pasta—so many days and meals of pasta in their lives—that each plateful is viewed as another opportunity to visit this magic place.

Think of Sophia Loren eating spaghetti, gesturing to herself up and down: "Everything you see I owe to spaghetti." Or photos from the 1950s of starlets lined up at the table, their mouths joyously full of spaghetti, or the legend of Pulcinella, or the legendary actor, Totò, almost ecstatically eating spaghetti. When it comes to pasta, it's not just a plate of food—it's a whole culture and life, concentrated into one delicious sustaining plateful.

TO EAT LIKE A NAPOLETANO . . .

You always seek quality. It goes without saying. Why would you want less?

You understand that not only is cooking an act of poetry, but eating is also an act of grace.

And you know deep in your heart of hearts that *la cucina Napoletana* is best. You know that even though there are fabulous cuisines all over the world (including throughout the rest of Italy), none sustains you physically and emotionally as does Neapolitan food. When you travel, you've got olive oil, pasta, and even canned tomatoes in your suitcase. When you are abroad, you seek out restaurants where the chef/owner is from Napoli. I have heard some Napoletanos say that the only place they can travel to is Spain, because where else is there such good olive oil, fish, and vegetables (tomatoes!)? You *never* cut up your spaghetti (well, no Italian would), and you *never* use a spoon to help roll the strands of pasta onto your fork. Just don't do it. And have pity for whomever you see blaspheming the poor pasta this way.

To be a Napoletano in the kitchen, you do know that long pasta needs to be twirled it into a "nest" before being placed on an individual plate. This circular form conserves the heat, looks tidy on the plate, and provides a perfect place right on top to arrange something lovely as a garnish: a few extra spoonfuls of sauce, a large prawn, a tiny *scallopina*, or a leaf of basil.

You know that there are classic and traditional dishes, but you also know that they are a starting point only. Pasta with beans is delicious studded with mussels or clams, pasta with seafood is fabulous with seasonal vegetables, and a crock of seafood pasta or soup may be topped with pizza or bread dough, then baked quickly to form a crisp lid topping the dish. When cut into, the fragrant steam is heady, quite exciting, like opening a gift-wrapped present.

A Napoletano knows not to eat bread with pasta. No! *But*—there is always a but—you may use a piece of the bread to make *la scarpetta*, wiping the last of the delicious sauce off the plate and popping it into your mouth. There is nothing like a chunk of bread rubbed with ragù to finish your plate of pasta!

Neapolitans shop at the open market and relish the social interaction; if they find a bargain, it's even better.

As a Neapolitan, you sit down to a meal with great relish and deliberation, taking delight in what you are about to enjoy.

A true Napoletana in the kitchen knows not to put too many flavors into a dish. It is important to let the taste of the ingredients themselves shine through. Neapolitans use far fewer ingredients in each dish, so the flavors remain clean, and you can taste everything that is there. According to the Neapolitans I have canvassed on the subject, other cuisines add *troppi sapori*: too many ingredients, too many flavors! Other cuisines, even other Italian cuisines, start with carrots, celery, and a crushed garlic clove or a little bit of chopped onion, adding the other ingredients for a sauce, soup, or meaty braise. Naples uses garlic or onion, occasionally a little celery, and a pinch of red chile flakes—very streamlined so that the main ingredient, whatever comes next, can shine through clearly, brightly, deliciously.

Pizza sauce is a good example. For the best pizza sauce, just puree canned tomatoes—San Marzano or other high-quality tomatoes are best—or, if in season, lightly chop fresh tomatoes and cook them down a little bit to intensify the taste; a little salt is good. Other things—oregano, garlic, peperoncini, and so forth—you can sprinkle on top of the pizza. With a simple sauce, you can taste the tomatoes rather than the stuff added to canned sauces.

Neapolitan food is not all about garlic—quite the opposite! Some places in the world put garlic into everything, it is true, but not Naples. The popularity of garlic rose and waned depending on who was ruling the area. The ancient Greeks did not like garlic at all. Their heirs in the eastern Mediterranean, the Byzantines, loved it both raw and cooked; the Romans who ruled over much of Campania were partial to garlic as well. Emperor Nero loved garlic so much he was said to have created the first aioli, a pounded raw garlic sauce. However, the priestesses of Cybele forbade anyone who smelled of garlic to enter the temple in Rome.

To this day, the garlicky aspects of *la cucina Napoletana* vary widely. Sometimes a dish has garlic—lots of it, even; sometimes none at all; sometimes the garlic is added to the oil, fried until lightly golden, and then removed.

Onions might not be used to season most sauces, as they are in other places, but they often are the star of the dish rather than just a supporting ingredient. For instance, local onions are thinly sliced, softly fried until golden, and then made into a frittata. Just the thought of an onion frittata can bring a smile to many a Neapolitan's face.

Onion and garlic are seldom used together in large quantities, and certainly not as the base of every dish, as they might be elsewhere (America, Poland, Greece, and other parts of Italy), but if you are from Benevento, you add both. In most of Campania, they are used together in small amounts, with one dominant. If the foods are cooked with onion, they might include a little garlic in some part of the dish—say, for example, rolled into *braciola*, thinly sliced meat, or simmered in the ragù. Another way to vary the garlic taste is to add just a tiny bit, raw, chopped, at the end of cooking. Adding the onions and garlic at different times provides depth of flavor and allows each aspect of the dish to maintain its own flavor. But really, too much garlic is looked down on.

Last-minute additions to a dish—say, garlic, fresh herbs, or black pepper—give the dish a fresh accent, almost like tasty adjectives in a lovely sentence.

Likewise, sometimes neither onions *nor* garlic are included in a dish.

Still, many Italian Americans (and thus, Americans) persevere in their belief that Neapolitan food, Italian food, the food from the old country, starts with a generous amount of onions and garlic. Why? Most likely because so many Italian immigrants to America came from the area around Benevento, which is the exception to the rule. There, both onions and garlic go into everything!

And sometimes, sometimes, Neapolitans throw garlic into the pot with abandon, and you smell its deliciousness in the street, wafting through the air. And really, is there anything better? When Neapolitans say, "Oh, no, we don't use much garlic!" I think, *Why not?* Because the garlic in Naples is beautiful.

One of my favorite garlic moments is biting into the marinara pizza at Pizza a Portafoglio di Gennaro Salvo. Without cheese, a marinara's glory is the tomato and the savory accents such as oregano, sea salt, and a whisper of olive oil. But its *true* glory always seems to be that one chunk of garlic that's thrown raw onto the pizza before the oven. I always know it's there, perfuming the dish, but when I find it in my mouth, I chew with glee. I thought that perhaps it was only me because I love garlic so much. But then the pizza girl behind the counter looked at me as I was burbling on about how good it was and said, "That piece of garlic!" She said it with such affection and enthusiasm, I began to think that this girl might be my sister.

Garlic is sold in shops, outdoors markets, all the places one would expect, but you'll also find stalls set up in unexpected places by their growers: along country roads or on the sidewalk of a street market with a little handwritten sign that says "*aglio è buono*" (garlic is good for you). And chilies are sold in strands with a similar sign, this time reading "Viagra *naturale*" (nature's Viagra).

TO BE A NAPOLETANO AT THE TABLE MEANS . . .

When something is incredibly delicious, instead of exclaiming so (perhaps your mouth is full?), you gesture with your hands, forefinger poking into your cheek, with the rest of your hand sort of twisting back and forth. Your lips are perhaps pursed, and your face has a blissful expression of having exquisite morsels in your mouth.

You watch others, especially an older someone, eat: carefully, thoughtfully, with attention. You realize its importance, that it is a devotion.

You discuss food at the table. And emotions run high! It's like a food fight; it's like a food love-fest! And when you inquire whether it is always like this, the answer is "*è normale*" ("of course, for us it is normal").

You know that a selection of antipasti—fried tidbits, raw fish, leaves of salad—is a great way to start a pizza dinner, and you also know that if you ask to take home leftover pizza, you will get strange looks. (There's a belief that the cheese, once heated and then cooled, is so undigestible as to create terrible indigestion. Or *worse.*)

You know that ordering a cappuccino after a meal is a social blunder of colossal proportions. Cappuccino is a breakfast drink. You also know that *latte* is plain milk, not the milk-and-espresso drink. For this, ask for a *caffè latte*—but only in the morning!

You have the deep confidence in what is on your table, knowing that the foods you choose to eat are good. Possibly the best thing I ever ate was a plate of cantaloupe and wild strawberries. Or a plate of ripe tomatoes and mozzarella: no cooking, nothing else added. It is sensational.

Being Neapolitan means being sociable—so sociable, especially at the table. "It's bad luck to eat alone!" you might hear if you are indeed eating alone. Suddenly you'll find your chair being carried over to a larger group, with a glass of wine being poured for you.

Eating like a Napoletano means that you know the ins and outs of the mysteries of ragù. When you smell ragù Napoletano cooking, you think of your Nonna and your Mamma. You know that unlike the rich sauce of chopped meats ladled over tagliatelle in the north, a ragù Napoletana is a big pot of meat (whole roasts or large chunks) long braised (at least three hours) in either tomatoes (ragù Napoletano) or onions and wine (Genovese), or with rabbit: *coniglio all'Ischitana* (rabbit from the island of Ischia). The unique aspect is that this one pot cooks the meat so tenderly while the meat flavors the sauce. Often it's eaten in two courses: the sauce with pasta for the first course, the meat as a second (or held aside and served the next day).

Dressing a salad in Napoli means that you don't understand bottled salad dressing. You simply shake good extra virgin olive oil onto your leaves and add a little vinegar—if you don't like vinegar, splash on local lemon instead—along with salt and pepper.

A Napoletano knows who makes his or her favorite mozzarella and understands that big ball of milky cheese is one of life's glories. By simply being Neapolitan, it is meant for you.

On the subject of mozzarella, the long-held notion of fish not combining with cheese does not apply to mozzarella. For instance, mozzarella and anchovies: the cheese so mild, the anchovy salty; together it is beautiful. You see it in pizza, *mozzarella in carrozza*, or the salty anchovy sauce, *colatura*, which is sprinkled over *mozzarella di bufala* as a salad or antipasto. Sometimes mozzarella is added to a cold seafood antipasto platter, while mozzarella with smoked salmon is a "thing," often as a separate course for a fancy-schmancy sit-down meal. Popularized in recent years in Cetara and spreading around the world, the pizza with lemon, anchovies, and mozzarella is life affirming, and I am sure it will convert anchovy haters immediately.

Neapolitans are very specific about how to eat spaghetti with tomatoes: *very* specific. In other words, no cheese! It interferes with the goodness of the pasta and tomatoes. They will offer cheese to you, make no mistake, because they are infinitely hospitable people, and they understand that foreigners (i.e., anyone from outside of Campania) likes grated cheese with their spaghetti and tomato sauce. But, as stated earlier, if you eschew the cheese, you will see relief on your waiter or waitress's face, and he or she will utter something to the effect of "Oh, good. It's better this way."

You have a favorite trattoria (or several) and are vociferous about where to find the best pizza. You are particular about who makes the best babà. I like Mennella, in Torre del Greco. Filled with cream and wild strawberries, the spongy, light cake is doused so generously with rum and syrup that you can become giddy just thinking about it. It is said that Mennella makes three babàs each week for the Vatican. But Scaturchio is magnificent, too, and right in the center of town; then there's Sfogliatella Mary at the corner of the Galleria on Via Toledo.

If you are invited to someone's home and wonder what to bring, go to your favorite pastry shop. They have a *vassoio* (tray of assorted pastries) ready. You'll leave with a big box tied with a string, wrapped like a present. It is exactly the right thing to bring. That doesn't mean your hosts won't have already baked a cake—or two—which is fine; everyone will end up tasting it all! (With joy, no guilt, because it's Napoli, it's Campania!)

Finally, if you are a smoker—and oh so many are, at least socially—you know that during the break between courses at a restaurant, everyone jumps up and goes outside to smoke. They puff and chat and joke around, then head back in for the next course and glass of wine. Once people stayed at the table to smoke, but when that became illegal, parading outside to sociably smoke became an added dimension to the meal. Everyone is having so much fun that sometimes I wonder if that doesn't encourage people to take up smoking, though nothing prevents them from socializing outside with the smokers or from moving around the table from this seat to the next, chatting with a variety of people you are not sitting near. And you won't be alone—the nonsmokers will be doing exactly that.

TO BE A NEAPOLITAN IN THE KITCHEN . . .

As a Neapolitan, you know that coarse black pepper has a strong flavor that muddies as it cooks. Red chile flakes or finely ground white pepper is best during cooking. Then coarsely ground black pepper is added at the end, for its deep flavor and warmth.

When adding basil to a sauce, add a sprig or two at the start to let it cook in (you can fish it out before serving). At the end, you serve the finished dish with a sprinkling of fresh, raw basil leaves. So fresh and aromatic! (Dried basil? What are you thinking? You must not be a Neapolitan!)

As a Neapolitan, when you see a perfectly ripe, sweet, juicy peach, you think, where is the red wine to soak them in? Ditto for fragrant strawberries.

Neapolitans feel deeply about tomatoes. They know the practicalities: big, long, ripe tomatoes (San Marzanos, if you are lucky) are for making sauce, tiny ripe tomatoes for cutting up onto a plate with mozzarella, and slightly green tomatoes for salads and sandwiches, or to make a fresh, bright sauce (especially if they are quite green).

In Campania, people know things about tomatoes that no one else has ever thought about, unless, like me, you are obsessed with tomatoes. For instance, tomatoes are not always best freshly picked; they often improve by sitting in the sunshine for a few days, concentrating their flavors. And sometimes they are at their best slightly green, tart and refreshing.

In the tomato-growing regions at the foot of Vesuvio, I was told by a local woman that small tomatoes that will be eaten fresh (raw or cooked) should be strung together in a bunch and left outside. This way, they keep a long, long time after harvest. "However," she warned me, "very important, do not leave your tomatoes outside during the full moon. Bring them in. You can return them outside when the moon begins to wane." No explanations were given. She said that her mother did it and was very adamant about it, but she didn't know why, either. She just said that the tomatoes were divine!

I have even heard of some Vesuvio-area farmers who play music to their tomato plants as a sort of music therapy, but I doubt that is limited to Campania tomato growers, instead applying to anyone obsessed with their garden.

When tomatoes are in season, someone you know will be drying them, maybe even you (the *pomodorini* Crovarese are like tiny San Marzanos, particularly meaty, fleshy, and tasty dried). To dry them, cut them in half lengthwise, lay them out on a large board, cut side up, and sprinkle with salt. Turn them regularly, and the hot sun should dry them before too long, giving you preserved tomatoes that can last for months and months. Super savory and chewy, dried tomatoes can be enjoyed as is or added to sauces. Anchovies are similarly salted and dried, not only a delicious preserved food but also a culinary heirloom from the time of Magna Grecia.

As a Neapolitan, you know that to get the most juice from a lemon, you must roll it hard, pushing with all your might, on a countertop or other hard surface. This breaks down the cell walls and thus releases far more juice than if you hadn't rolled it (alternatively, nuke the lemon: thirty seconds to a minute).

You don't look askance at crumbling a small amount of bouillon cube (*dado*, singular, or *dadi*, plural) into a sauce or soup that needs a little extra savor. Most home kitchens have a small piece of bouillon cube, partially wrapped in its foil, sitting on the shelf ready to be broken off as needed. (I particularly like the porcini bouillon cubes to oomph up the taste of a dish with mushrooms or *funghi* or to add a little unidentified flash of savory, almost as a Japanese cook would add dashi.) A pinch of bouillon cube is, in a way, an extension of the traditions of the "old days," in which there was always a pot of concentrated *sugo* or other strong meat sauce simmering on the back burner, ready for the cook to dip into and season whatever was being cooked at that moment.

Traditionally, though, Neapolitans don't eat much meat. Instead of starting a meaty sauce with lots of meat, add a tiny bit (either cured or fresh) to a tomato sauce as it cooks. You're not making a meat sauce per se, but the small piece of meat flavors the sauce. Each portion of pasta gets topped with a small bit of the meat, really no more than a bite or a garnish: dry, cured meat like prosciutto or pancetta, a few thickish slices of salame, or even a slice of beef, veal, pork, any sort of meat.

And you know not to waste: the bone from prosciutto, the last slice of sausage, the end of the salame. Tidbits that might be discarded in other places will, in Naples, become a precious ingredient.

If you come from the coast, you eat fish. If you come from inland, you eat pheasant or wild boar. Maybe someone you know hunts, and if you are the hunter, there are weather forecasts online for *la caccia*, the hunter. Still, hunting is not as big a deal in Campania as it is in Sardinia or Tuscany. (Except for Irpinia—it has truffles, which are always worth hunting for, in my opinion.)

Being a Napoletana means that you always have a package of pasta on your shelf, along with good olive oil, a head of garlic, and perhaps a few anchovies or chile peppers, and are therefore always ready to whip up an emergency *pasta di mezzanotte* (midnight pasta) or *fare una spaghettata* (make a spaghetti party). You get together, you make a big pot of spaghetti, and that is your evening entertainment. Even if you do not cook a lot, you know that as long as there is pasta on your shelf, you can sit down to a delicious bowlful within minutes.

The most important thing to know about pasta Napoli style is that al dente is overcooked! For a Neapolitan, pasta should be cooked *fujenni*—not yet al dente. If it's your first time eating pasta this way, you might think it underdone—even other

Italians from outside Campania do. But try it once, twice, and see whether you don't start loving your pasta this way: just past crunchy, almost al dente, a super-satisfying texture with sauce cloaking each strand or chunk intimately. When pasta is cooked like this, it feels lighter to eat, and so do you afterward.

Being a Napoletana, you know that pasta is not a recipe—it is a way of life. Here are the basics: cook it half done, maybe two thirds of the way to al dente, lightly drain (reserving some of the water), and finish cooking in its sauce with a little cooking water added for a few minutes over medium-low heat. The pasta and sauce meld into one.

The secret ingredient for such perfection? The cooking water.

To make beautiful pasta, watch the Neapolitans. See them salt the water to the taste of the sea, never adding oil to the cooking water. Watch them get animated and excited, draining the pasta, and then adding it to the sauce and letting it finish cooking there, adding some of the cooking water to create a liaison between sauce and pasta. To quote pasta maestro Giuseppe Di Martino, "You must *love* pasta in your heart to make it wonderful."

A Neapolitan knows to cook pasta in as wide a pot as possible—even a deep frying pan—so that the long spaghetti hits the boiling water all at once rather than partially hanging out of the pot before it softens enough to fall in. This is essential for even pasta cooking, but you are Neapolitan, so you already know this!

The quality of the dried pasta is important so that it holds its shape and doesn't get gummy or flaccid when you finish cooking it with the sauce. Remember Gragnano!

You might not knit, but you have a couple of knitting needles in the kitchen for when you make fresh pasta, rolling the flour-and-water dough around the knitting needles for the original fusilli shape and for making macaroni.

As you know, not all pastas need grated Parmigiano or pecorino; some pasta dishes want other cheeses—or no cheese at all. You also know that there is a wide variety of cheeses that are amazing on pasta. Indeed, knowing when and what kind of cheese to use is almost a code in Napoli. And once you have broken it, you are ready to expand your pasta-cooking creativity.

And if you don't want cheese, but rather crunchy crumbs, look toward the bag of taralli instead of breadcrumbs. Crush up a handful, and then sprinkle them onto your pasta.

Speaking of taralli, it is the crisp nibble of choice to accompany wine. They go together so well that there's a saying when things turn out especially well that everything has turned out "*tarallucci e vino*"—like taralli and wine.

Spaghetti Is So Emotional

A few years ago, when I was suffering family sadness and headed toward inevitable loss, I spent time in Sorrento with a group of colleagues. It was during a major soccer/football event, and the streets were lined with huge Italian flags, red, white, and green hung from every window.

As we were walking down a cobbled street toward dinner, a large flag billowed gently through the air like a leaf falling from the sky, landing at my feet. My friends picked it up and put it over my shoulders, wrapping it around me like a shawl, and ushered me toward a trattoria. It was an artistic, surreal, beautiful moment, like being in a film. (So much of life in Campania is like being in a film.)

But I was still so sad that when the pasta arrived, tears began to stream from my eyes and down my cheeks. Yet the pasta was so good, its tomatoey steam rising from the plate to lift my spirits. It was perfect, of course, and the basil leaves on top were soothingly sweet and fragrant. But I could not stop silently crying, even as I put fork to mouth. Though I might be very sad, I was eating this beautiful pasta while it was hot!

Alarmed, the owner came over immediately and patted me comfortingly. His dark eyes looked into mine with understanding. "It is very emotional to eat pasta. Sometimes I eat this spaghetti and I also cry."

And then, of course, being Neapolitan, he tried to make me smile. And I did smile, at his caring, at my friends wrapping me in red, white, and green stripes, at the streets alive with celebration. And especially at the honesty and caring of another human being who also cries when he eats spaghetti.

FOOD LIFE, ACCORDING TO MY NAPOLETANA MENTOR, SONIA CARBONE

"You know that bread is vital for any Neapolitan. Fresh bread must be bought every day—typically *il palatone* and *pane cafone*." Stale leftover bread becomes crumbs for meatballs, stuffings, or a base to ladle *zuppa* over, but fresh bread will be bought to eat for the meal.

"Neapolitans can be very superstitious about bread. You should never put it on the table upside down. It's bad luck. Also, some say that if you put the bread upside down, the baker will have terrible abdominal pains. Many of the older generation consider it sacrilegious to serve bread upside down, an act that can bring about misfortune for one of the diners. Some believe it may even mean famine for the whole area!

"And you should never ask somebody at the table to pass you the salt. Better to get it yourself with your own hands, even if it is miles away from you. If you drop some salt on the table, it is very bad luck. Then there is oil: Dropping oil on the table or onto the ground leads to mischief. Not everyone is superstitious, but the feeling is that it may not be true, but maybe doing it protects you anyway."

Not all superstition is grim. A little spilled wine? No problem—dip your finger into the wine and dab a little behind your ear, as if it were perfume, to bring you good luck.

Sunday lunch is a high point of Neapolitan family life: "A Neapolitan Sunday lunch would never start before 2:00 pm because Neapolitans wake up calmly and, just after the morning/midday walk and visit to relatives, they get comfortable and ready for lunch. If a Neapolitan doctor on such a sacred day of the week had to have lunch before this time, there is only one reason: it means he or she is tending an emergency, because only at the hospital is lunch served so early." So 2:00 or 3:00 is when you probably will gather for Sunday lunch.

When you see your Nonna, your grandmother, she feeds you. She worries that you are starving! Even if you are not related, she feeds you until she is reassured that you are out of danger (and cannot eat another bite). A joke about how much Nonna loves to feed: "Well, it is true that there is hunger in this world, but it's because our Italian grandmas are afraid to fly!"

"Sunday is not Sunday without *le pastarelle* (pastries). After walking around, visiting the relatives, or going to the church, the pastry shop is obligatory. On Sundays, sweets are fundamental. You could have eaten tons of ragù, kilos of bread to make the *scarpetta* [the bread that mops up the last of the sauce on your plate], but a space in your stomach for the pastry should always be there. Pastries on Sunday is not a choice; it is your duty to enjoy."

E' Purpett ca Sarz

Polpette al Ragù! Il Vero Napoletano! (The Real Neapolitan Meatball!)

Serves 4–6

Tender, savory, a mixture of beef, veal, and pork enriched with local cheese and cooked in tomato sauce, Neapolitan meatballs are one of the most wonderful things you will ever eat. The pine nuts and raisins (or currants) are a Sicilian duo, no doubt a relic from when Napoli and Sicily were part of the same kingdom and influenced by the mutual Arab and Jewish fondness for the combination.

E' Purpett ca Sarz (continued)

2–3 thick slices (about 2–2½ ounces) stale, rustic bread
Mixture of half water and half milk to cover the bread
½ pound each: ground/minced beef, pork, and veal (1½ pounds total)
4–5 heaped tablespoons freshly grated Parmesan or pecorino
2 cloves garlic, grated (I use a ginger grater)
2 eggs
2 tablespoons untoasted pine nuts
2 tablespoons currants or raisins
Salt and pepper
Flour for dusting the meatballs
Olive oil for sautéing
½ onion, chopped
1 can (about 14 ounces) tomato passata or diced tomatoes and their juice or about 2 pounds fresh tomatoes, diced
½ cup dry white wine
Pinch of sugar
Chopped flat-leaf parsley

Place the bread in a bowl and pour enough milk and water over it to cover. Let soften for a few minutes, and then squeeze the excess liquid out.

Place meat mixture in a bowl along with the soaked and squeezed bread, the cheese, garlic, eggs, pine nuts, and currants or raisins. Mix well and shape into meatballs about the size of a ripe lemon (or however large you prefer).

Dust/roll the meatballs in flour; then brown them in extra virgin olive oil in a heavy pan, turning several times. You want to lightly brown them and firm them up so that they won't fall apart, but don't cook them through, as they finish cooking in the sauce.

When the meatballs are browned, remove to a plate, and add the chopped onion to the pan, cooking for a few moments until it softens. Then add the tomatoes and wine and cook over high heat until it reduces a bit. Season with salt, pepper, sugar, and chopped parsley.

Return the meatballs to the pan with the sauce, and reduce heat to low, letting the meatballs simmer gently, covered, until they are cooked through. Do not stir or you risk breaking the meatballs apart.

Serve on a plate with love in your heart.

9

Regions and Their Food Ways

It might be a united republic, but modern Italy is not exactly a homogenous nation, especially with regard to food and culture, and *most* especially not when it involves the south and the north. Let's put it this way: Napoli (and Campania) is Italy, but Italy is not Napoli. Its temperament, food, culture, and way of life is, as some say, a world of its own (it *was* once its own kingdom).

Anywhere in the world, if you ask, "What is Italian food?" you will hear, "Pizza! Spaghetti! Mozzarella!" Yet they are not really Italian at all—they are delicious gifts from Naples.

The city itself is intense, crowded, aristocratic and squalid both, endlessly convivial—but the city is only one part. Campania is made up of five provinces. The Province of Naples includes its namesake city, the surrounding area, and islands. The other provinces—Benevento (also known as Il Sannio), Avellino (also known as Irpinia), and the two buffalo cheese capitals of the world: Caserta and Salerno—each reflect its own character, heritage, and geography. Even when the foods are the same, they may be prepared differently or called by a different name. For instance, in Salerno, as an homage to how much the Neapolitans love their marinara pizza, it is known not as a marinara but as a Napoletano.

Campania has 217 miles of coastline along its mainland and islands: beautiful vistas, wild nature, luxury, clear water, gulfs and inlets, some accessible only by boat. On the coast of Campania, people love fish, fish, and more fish (and seafood). *Paranza*, sold for frying, along with tiny anchovies, red mullet, branzino, cod, prawns, lobsters, crabs, mussels, clams, squid, and an abalone-like creature that is called *scungilli* in Neapolitan dialect—the seafood is spectacular.

The islands—Capri, Ischia, and Procida—are a quick (and beautiful) ferry ride away from the city. Once there, you are in another world: breathtaking vistas, clear azure water, tiny walkways snaking through towns and villages. Ancient buildings hang onto sheer cliffs, with tiled steps leading up and down the hills, often in place of paved roads. Here's my public service announcement: Don't go to Capri in high season unless you like crowds.

Down the coast from Naples is Sorrento—charming, charming Sorrento—whose culinary traditions reflect both Naples and Salerno, which is reasonable since it is located between the two. You might think it's all seafood there, but Sorrento revels in its exquisite dairy products from nearby Mount Lattari and, of course, the juicy, local lemons that grow on surrounding terraced hillsides.

Inland, fresh fish has never been a part of the diet. In the mountains of Benevento and Avellino, it was seldom seen before modern refrigeration and transportation; the only fish eaten was preserved. Without fish, locals eat more vegetables, beans, cheese, and nuts. Growing seasons there are not as forgiving as the more temperate coast. Rural Campania is famous for creating delicacies from very little.

The specialties of each area reflect its history, as it does geography and climate. The food of Ravello, with its grand villas and hotels, not to mention stuffed crepes such *crespolini* filled with sheep's milk ricotta and *sofficiatinni* (spinach), reminds you that the great Monzù chefs once cooked there.

Traditionally, chicken specialties are few throughout Campania, though in recent years chicken has been sneaking onto the menu. It's healthy, it's tasty, it makes great soup—who doesn't love chicken? But traditional? No.

For one thing, it was historically expensive. There are so many other meats, and if you kill the chicken, where will the eggs come from? (Campania loves its frittatas and the like.) Today, gorgeous chickens revolve juicily on the spit at most takeouts and *roticcerias.* You'll find them pan-roasted with potatoes and lemons in the occasional trattoria, and on the beach in Ischia you might find people baking them in their "sand ovens." You're unlikely, however, to find them atop your pizza or tossed with pasta. (You might find a juicy chicken burger on a pub menu, however.)

Everywhere in Campania has a sweet specialty; biscotti di Castellammare, *delizie al limone* of the coasts and islands, *sospiri* ("sighs," also known as *Zizz'e Monache,* "nuns' breasts"), the lemon ricotta–filled ravioli of Positano. Sorrento and Amalfi have endless lemon-based pastries. Small, pale, dome-shaped pastries from Maiori and Minori on the Amalfi Coast are filled with lemon cream. Then there is the chocolate-eggplant concoction of Ravello. Delicious. Odd. Both.

ANDIAMO A NAPOLI

This big crazy city, the third largest in Italy (and fourth largest in Europe), is home to both beauty and grime, a city with its own personality so strong that it feels almost like a person. One interacts with Naples as one does with a human: Naples seems to require it. And we need this interaction to navigate Naples.

One way of describing how things in Naples came to be is that legend of unusual sea currents that flow only toward Naples, bringing to her great spirit, mysterious happenings, and abundant richness. In other words, no one knows; it's unexplainable magic.

The Naples Quartet by Elena Ferrante has captivated hearts and minds worldwide at least in part for its portrayal of the city; it is almost a main character. In Elizabeth Gilbert's *Eat, Pray, Love* (and the resultant movie starring Julia Roberts), Neapolitan pizza was part of her cosmic enlightenment.

Smaller shops are more typical than huge when shopping in Naples. Sometimes it's hard to believe that such a small shop could offer such an array of goodies but check out the cheese and cured meat counter: the big, fat, balls of mozzarella rest in a vat of brine, mortadella is studded with green pistachios, and the *pane cafone* at the bread counter could not be better. Maybe only two types of olives—one green, one black—but ladle out some of each. They are exceptional. And the pasta—a grand wall of Gragnano's best in more shapes and sizes than you ever thought possible—takes up the rear of the shop.

Of course, there are inexpensive discount supermarkets, a bargain (if not a pleasure). And in the street, vendors offer knockoffs of luxury brands. If it's raining, umbrellas will be for sale. Perhaps the cutest bright yellow umbrella you have ever seen will be available for 5 euros. Okay, mine broke within minutes, but maybe yours won't.

To walk the street markets such as Pignasecca, Sant-Antonio, Porta Nolana, and Buvero is to discover what people are eating and, sometimes, how to make it. Most vendors have advice for you. La Pignasecca, one of Naples's oldest markets for food, turns off at an angle from Via Toledo. It's lined with stalls and shops selling fruit, vegetables, cheeses, fish, kitchenwares, shoes, and children's toys. Along the way are countless tripe and offal stalls gaily decorated with golden, yellow lemons. They are beautiful and uniquely Napoli. On my last trip to Pignasecca, a woman stood outside a mozzarella shop offering samples of fresh mozzarella. Even though I protested, "No! no! I've already had some!" (which I had, many times, each time I passed by), she just smiled a big smile and handed me another milky, chewy chunk of mozzarella. Across the way in a small piazza, a downhearted man with a basket was nearly crying because no one was buying his garlic. "I grew it myself, such hard work!" It was a heat wave, too. As a kindness, I bought two huge bunches, but when I tasted it later, I wished I had bought it all; it was exquisite.

Il Mercato di Sant-Antonio and Il Mercato di Porta Nolana are amazing for fish and seafood—a whole sea of creatures, so fresh, so varied, so abundant, laid out in boxes of ice in the stalls. Shops open onto the streets, vendors sell from tables, jars offer capers in salt, more types of olives than you ever thought possible. An old man glares and snarls menacingly when I ask to take a photo. A sweet man sees this, poses for a selfie with me, and hands me—free—a bunch of basil. The fruit, the vegetables, the chaos—it's pretty hard core.

And because Naples is Naples, you must eat pastry. Sometimes just standing in front of a pastry window gazing at all of the babà, *sfogliatelle*, and *pastiera* could make you crazy. What to eat—I mean, what to eat *first*? The two most iconic pastries of Naples are the *sfogliatelle* (both *riccia*, curly, and *frolla*, smooth) and the babà. No two pastries (well, three, since both *sfogliatelle* are quite different, though they contain the same filling) could be more different.

Here is a guided bite tour: The *riccia sfogliatella* is shaped like a clamshell (or sometimes large, like a lobster tail), made of crisp multilayered pastry. Take a bite. It's okay to close your eyes; you'll probably want to. It will have the delicate crispness of baklava but without the sweetness. The sweetness comes when you reach the candied fruit–studded ricotta inside. The *sfogliatella frolla* is the same, but with a shortbread type of crust. And the babà? Sigh. How can one describe babà? Fragrance, syrup, but, most of all, a spongy, airy texture unlike anything you've probably ever eaten. Since most babà makers stuff the cakes with whipped cream and endless seasonal fruits, you have another flavor to look forward to. And the alcohol leaves a little buzz.

Once I interviewed the owner of Gambrinus for an article about *caffè sospeso*—it was created at Gambrinus. He told story after story after story; then, just when we got up to go, he exclaimed, "Where are you going? Now you must taste everything!" Oh, it was good. I tried my best—a tiny spoonful here, a bigger spoonful there—and soon it became a pastry party, the table covered with plates of half-eaten pastries, and all around me people laughing with joy, with glee. It was the kind of crazy hospitality that tells you the world is a good place after all.

Artisanal chocolate is a Neapolitan tradition. Exquisite shops, much like jewelers, display arrays of handcrafted confections. Easter bunnies couldn't be more elegant, and once I saw rows of little San Gennaros called *i gennarini*. I regret not buying one. Naples's Gay-Odin tells a love story with its chocolate. Opened in 1894, the original store (there are other locations in Napoli, Rome, and Milan) is still located on Via Toledo. Its founder, Isidore Odin, a chocolate maker from

Piemonte, fell in love with his chocolate-making assistant, Onorina Gay of Switzerland. Marrying, they took both names for the shop and became a Naples icon.

The energy of the city is as intoxicating to locals as it is exhausting for the outsider. I think the natives build up a tolerance. Doing anything in Naples requires a level of interaction that would cause most introverts to flee in horror.

But there is the sea, ever present, rippling delicately at the city's edge, bringing beauty to the vistas seen from so many vantage points. A walk along the *lungomare* is a place to leave behind the frenzy and to breathe salty air. Or a stroll along the Mergellina, poised between city and sea, offers an escape from the urban cacophony—with a gelato in your hand, of course. Gazing across the bay is more soothing than a bucketful of antidepressants.

Zuppa Forte/Zuppa e Suffritto ("Strong Soup")

This rustic stew, a dish local to Naples, arouses gastronomical nostalgia in some—and horror in others. Its name means "strong," and strongly flavored it is: a mixture of pork lungs, trachea, heart, spleen, windpipe, and so on. In Napoli the mixture is called *campanale* or *cavetto* and is available in butcher shops. The mixture is cooked in an intense sauce of red wine, tomatoes, olive oil, with a sprig of rosemary and a pinch of red chile flakes, and then ladled over toasted stale *pane cafone*. It seems quite local to Naples, as Caprese friends said they had never tasted it until a Neapolitan friend fed it to them; yet an elderly friend who grew up on the Amalfi Coast said he grew up eating it. He added that before refrigeration, the *zuppa* was prepared, strained, and cooked down to concentrate it. It could be kept on hand for a fairly long time to use as a seasoning for other dishes or even to dilute with hot water, like instant soup.

NAPLES TO CASERTA

From the tip of Naples's Posillipo Hill to the acropolis at Cuma and Capo Miseno, the unspoiled area known as Campi Flegrei is rich with archeological sites, lakes, and treasures. Its beauty grabbed me unexpectedly—everyone speaks of other places in Campania; Campi Flegrei is far less known. The amphitheater in Pozzuoli is stunning, and imagining the Piscina Mirabilis during the time of Vesuvio's eruption felt emotionally transportive. I felt incredibly privileged to be there. The ancient Greek colony of Baiae is now submerged, but a glass-bottomed boat can float you over the underwater ghost town.

I thought I knew Campania until I spent an afternoon with my friend, Indian food writer Mridula Baljekar on a houseboat/bar, Roof & Sky, drifting on Lake Miseno. We sat upstairs on the open deck, gazing at the lake, the shore, the water rocking the boat gently. The sun felt gently warm in midwinter, and every so often a delicious little *aperitivo* morsel would appear from the galley below. Each evening, at 10:00 pm, the boat unmoors and putter-floats itself out to the middle of the lake, bar and *aperitivi* going strong. A favorite *aperitivo* snack in the area comes from the fishermen: raw seafood with a squirt of lemon and a piece of bread.

Local wines still follow planting directions from the ancient Romans, the favorite grapes still the indignous Piedirosso and Falanghina. Falanghina takes its name from the Roman word *falanghae*, referring to the wooden stakes used to support the vines, a system still used locally today. You can see the tall vines in the countryside, pickers standing on ladders to harvest.

Further along the coast are some nondescript towns with long, straight streets. "Not so interesting," my hosts said. Then I saw *this*: the long boring main street of town was lined with makeshift stands and people selling wild mushrooms. The mushrooms were set out and piled up in wooden boxes and baskets. The sellers definitely looked like they spent time in the forest. I thought they should rename the street "Road of Foraged Porcini."

And even in the most nondescript restaurant, somewhat empty, off-season, on the beach, past some ramshackle housing, you could find your next great meal. You just never know. I'll always think fondly of Mondragone for just this reason, just that meal.

At the border with Lazio is the ancient town of Gaeta, once famous for its important naval position, now most famous for its olives. Smallish, wrinkled, and black, they are held in deserving esteem: full of flavor with nicely chewy (yet tender) flesh.

As gloriously sun-drenched and chic as the coastline and islands, inland is a different world. Caserta, lying between Naples and Rome, is a land of buffalo, palaces, ruins, and well-kept medieval sites. The magnificent La Reggia di Caserta, built by the famous architect Vanvitelli, is considered the eighth wonder of the world, with exquisitely painted rooms, walls, and ceilings and park-like grounds. Huge waterfalls, lakes, and fountains tumble down the hillside. Lesser known is the English garden, leafy and secluded, with its Bath of Venus.

The province was once known as Campania Felix. Though it sounds like Happy Campania, *felix* refers not to mere happiness but to the gentle climate and fertility of the land. And the buffalo are happy there, too. Caserta is the main region for buffalo mozzarella, producing about 60 percent of the *mozzarella di bufala* DOP (the rest is divided between Salerno and a few pockets around Napoli, Lazio, and, of course, Puglia). Buffalo farms and cheesemakers dot the area, especially around Capua. Many accept visitors (call ahead); others do not. Most have a shop attached where you can buy their cheeses in the most perfect of condition. Along the roads, you see herds of buffalo, and if you are lucky, they will be bathing in their happy place: mud.

The mozzarella you buy here must be eaten immediately. It is chewy, milky, protein rich, dense as well as light: it is magic. How to decide which is your favorite? By tasting. Stay in an *agriturismo* and spend each day trying out cheeses, though there is also hiking, biking, swimming, and touring, of course. But, cheese.

In Benevento (Il Sannio), vines cover rolling hills and moody prairie-like fields stretch endlessly; yet right around the bend is almost always an old village or town, a thermal spa, and really good food. If you think the food tastes different in Benevento, you are right. One reason is their attitude to garlic and onions—whereas the rest of Campania uses onions *or* garlic, and quite abstemiously, Benevento starts most dishes with onions *and* garlic.

Hearty fare: stuffed lamb intestines, *ammugliatielli*, and, in season, wild thistle—something between an artichoke and cardoon—are made into a soup with mutton. The *scarpariello* pasta, which was created on the Sorrentine coast, is now happily part of Benevento cuisine for the way that it combines with the local rustic sauces, especially lamb or pheasant.

Torrone is a specialty at Christmastime, an ancient Samnite treat. The nougat of local nuts and honey seems even more luscious for its festive, brightly colored wrapping papers. It lifts my spirits just to look at them.

The complex, herbal liqueur known as Strega is luscious to sip as a *digestivo* or to enjoy as part of a dessert: in zeppole, torta Caprese, *chiacchiera*, or simply spooned over ice cream.

Avellino, also known as Irpinia, is rural and unspoiled—nothing like the picture-postcard scenes of lemons, glamorous coastline, azure sea, or lively, glittery Naples. Avellino, especially in the mountains, is a land filled with castles, churches, and cathedrals, surrounded by nature, with hillsides dotted with sheep. Hazelnuts grow in such profusion that one of the names for the nut, *avellana*, is said to be the namesake of Avellino (the other word for hazelnut is *nocciola*). Sometimes chopped hazelnuts are butter-toasted and tossed with cheese-stuffed pasta—*buono*.

Life has always been arduous here, food scarce, religion strong. Customs and traditions are held tightly, sometimes they were the only things that they could hold on to.

In 1980, a terrible earthquake shook the area, destroying villages and towns. More than three thousand died and forty-five thousand were left homeless. People who had fled to the north or abroad in search of fortune and future returned to re-build. In an odd way, this catastrophe helped revitalize the region—its spirit nour-ished by those who had returned. They appreciated the culture and area that they once fled and once again considered it home. Many stayed, opening businesses (often restaurants), bringing influences and ideas from afar, and modernizing tradi-tional foods and the way that they served them.

And here is something special about Irpinia: it has truffles—a black truffle, *tartufo nero di Bagnoli*, and a summer truffle, *tartufo estivo*. During their fleeting season, they are shaved over a cheese ravioli similar to that from Capri. More often, they are preserved in small jars as savory pates and spreads. Less fancy-schmancy but equally delicious is another specialty of Bagnoli: the local ricotta salata (eaten, intriguingly, with smoked fish and hot red pepper flakes).

NAPLES AND VESUVIO, THEN ON TO THE ISLANDS

Vesuvio looms majestically over the Bay of Naples, reminding all of its power, history, and destructive capability. Yet the tragedy of the volcano's eruption is what made the soil so rich. First the lava flow decimated the land, then revitalized it, enriching the soil with minerals, especially potassium. At the mountain's base are small towns, its slopes lined with farms and vineyards. Higher still is a national park where one can hike the crater and peer down—if you are brave.

Who can visit Pompeii and not be moved? (The tile portrait of a dog with his collar has always touched me.) It's a snapshot of life as it was, preserved in a lava encasement: people going about their daily routines, caught in the poisonous gas, and then covered with lava and ash, preserved as statues. In recent years, new, less destructive techniques have helped locate and excavate more Pompeiian ruins. So much of what we know about how people ate, historically, comes from Pompeii. Nearby Herculaneum is home to a modern, interactive museum, a virtual visit to its past: the colors, art, structures, and, of course, the kitchens.

Whatever grows on Vesuvio develops an intensity of fragrance and taste not found elsewhere. I think of the little baker who fed me bread and tomatoes (at a bread and tomato party, of course), pointing toward Vesuvio, saying that though he grew the tomatoes, it was Vesuvio that made them so delicious. (The tomatoes of Vesuvio include the famous pointed-tip *piennolo* or *spongillo*; tied in bunches and hung in a well-ventilated place, they last until the winter, concentrating their flavor over time.)

Inland, on the far side of Vesuvio, is a tomato paradise: Sarno, home to the San Marzano DOP, and Striano, famous for tasty tomatoes of many types. In this region, the tomato is almost a cult, though one could say that about the whole of Campania.

Apricots—grown here since the time of Nero—have been cultivated since the sixteenth century. Today the *albicocca Vesuviana* refers to more than forty different biotypes. And artichokes, such as the *carciofi di Schito*, which grows near Castellammare, a town known for its lovely beach. Castellammare is famous for its biscotti flavored with anise and enjoyed with a glass of Acqua della Madonna.

The town of Gragnano is nearby, epicenter for pasta making since Roman times. The grains grown there are hard wheat, perfect for making—and drying—pasta. It once was a communal activity, rows upon rows of drying racks set out in the town square, terraces, courtyards, piazzas, along the streets. In the early twentieth century, pasta made a huge leap into the industrial scale, though still based on the legacy of traditional artisanal methods. Recently, Conde Nast declared Gragnano a tourist designation.

The archipelago of Naples's islands are Ischia, Procida, and Capri (pronounced CAH-pri), each a distinctive geography, landscape, and style. Ischia is largest, then comes Capri, then tiny Procida. As an archipelago, one would think that all of the islands would be related, broken off from the same part of the mainland, but, in fact, Ischia and Procida were once part the Flegrean Fields (Campi Flegrei), whereas Capri separated from the Sorrento Peninsula following an earthquake.

Today it takes only thirty minutes by ferry from the Port of Naples, but Capri has lured visitors with its beauty and charm since people were capable of sailing there. Colonized by Greeks from Acarnania, then the Romans, it was Augustus who, in 29 BCE, having received "a good omen," decided he needed the island. Negotiating with the Greek city that is now Naples, he traded Ischia for his coveted Capri. There, he built luxurious settlements, establishing its reputation for pleasure. Of Capri, Augustus Caesar famously said, "*la citta del dolce far niente*" (it is a town for doing sweet nothings). Tiberius, his successor, spent his last years on Capri, ruling the empire from one of his many villas. Like so many, Tiberius was fond of the local wines. In more recent times, Lenin, an Anacapri houseguest of Gorky, was known to enjoy the island wine, calling it a consolation for his lack of success at fishing (he went out every morning to fish but usually came back empty-handed).

Go fishing, drink wine, become blissfully overwhelmed by the views—this is Capri life. Gaze out over the breathtaking vistas, the blue, blue water, the greenery of the hills, the little ferries sailing from Napoli and Sorrento, the shops and cafes and Italians. Absorb the atmosphere.

Though not culinary, all emotional experiences affect our food lives, so you must go to the Blue Grotto. A friend told me that growing up, she swam in it. Entering is not as easy as you might think: In your little boat, you must duck your head to clear the top of the cave. Then you and boat burst into the grotto, bobbing on the water, bathing in the otherworldly blue light streaming into the darkness. The experience is unworldly. There is, apparently, a smaller, green grotto, where the light that floods into the cave glows emerald.

As international as it is Italian, Capri remains itself, inspiring artists and writers to keep coming. Claude Debussy stayed in nearby Anacapri around 1919 and was inspired to write a prelude dedicated to the surrounding hills. According to the Naples Chamber of Commerce, Debussy's favorite dish was ravioli alla Caprese, a cheese-filled handmade ravioli served with tomatoes and marjoram. (It's one of my favorites, too.) Sometimes they might be sauced with lemon and olive oil, or with butter and either sage or marjoram, and sometimes crushed, toasted nuts.

In the 1930s, Capri's Quisisana Hotel was the location of a gathering held by Filippo Marinetti, founder of Futurism. The meeting was called regarding a manifesto of what to eat for the new era, optimum health, and both physical and mental strength. He decreed that "modern man" needed different food for the challenges of a new world. Pasta was stupid and heavy and should be replaced by meals in which the senses are stimulated with strangely colored foods and aspects of whimsy designed to provoke thought and creativity. (Preaching is easier than practicing, however; Marinetti was discovered eating a huge bowl of pasta in a Milano restaurant.)

Norman O. Douglas was another of Capri's great characters. An English aristocrat turned outrageous hedonist, he feuded with D. H. Lawrence, got arrested in London, divorced in Posillipo, hung out with his close friend Graham Greene, and reported for London publications. He was most famous for his depravity, however, referring to himself as "pagan to the core." He cast Capri as the setting of his fictional Nepenthe in the book *South Wind*. Capri made him a citizen in 1946. His last book, published in 1952, was called, appropriately, *A Footnote on Capri*. In 1951, a friend, food writer Elizabeth David, came to visit. British food was still dreary; on Capri, the food was so colorful, so fresh that one felt alive eating it. Lemons! Olive oil! Tomatoes! (A collection of David's writings, published in 2006 by David R. Godine, was titled *South Wind through the Kitchen*.) The sun-drenched inspirations that David published in postwar London impacted the way the British have eaten ever since.

It was a wild and fabulous time in Capri in the 1950s. The chic and glamorous were everywhere: hanging out at the piazza, visiting the farmer's market, buying the scorpion-fish/*scorfano* soup with pasta from the fishermen's wives in Marina Grande (few could resist).

Among the many films made on Capri during this time was Jean-Luc Goddard's *Contempt* in 1953, starring Brigitte Bardot. Locals still remember that Goddard loved squid, fishing for it and eating it, especially the local stew with squid and potatoes.

Totani con Patate (Humble Fishermen's Classic: Squid Simmered with Potatoes)

Serves 4 as a moderate portion or a starter; may be doubled for a main course.

Squid, simmered with wine, potatoes, and tomatoes: it's not fancy, not difficult, and really not very pretty, either. But oh, it is truly a comfort dish from the *cucina povera* tradition.

3–4 cloves garlic, chopped

1 onion, preferably a shallot or other fresh onion, such as the bottoms of green onions

About ¼ fresh hot pepper, not too hot, sliced very thinly

3–4 tablespoons extra virgin olive oil

½ pound squid, cleaned into tubes and tentacles

½–¾ cup dry white wine

3 small- to medium-sized tomatoes, diced (or about half of a 14 ounce can of diced tomatoes)

4 medium-sized all-purpose potatoes, peeled and cut into a large dice or small chunks

Salt to taste

Chopped flat leaf parsley

Lightly sauté the garlic, onion, and hot pepper in the olive oil until softened and lightly browned here and there, five to seven minutes over medium-low heat.

Add the squid, stirring through the fragrant mixture for a minute or two; then pour in the wine, continuing to cook five to ten minutes until the wine reduces.

Add the tomatoes and a little water and cook about ten minutes. Add the potatoes, plus a pinch or two of salt; then cover and cook another fifteen minutes or so over low heat or until the potatoes are tender.

The long cooking should make the squid tender, too. Taste for seasoning—it might need more salt—then serve sprinkled with parsley.

Variation: Squid and Potato Soup
Add extra liquid (fish stock or white wine mixed with water, until you have a soupy rather than saucy consistency).

Naples' beloved comedian, Totò, fell in love with the island when filming *The Emperor of Capri*. He was often found, elegantly dressed, sitting in the Piazzetta Umberto reading the paper, drinking coffee, meeting friends, and eating pasta and seafood soup.

Where did the name Capri come from? Was it the goats (from the Latin *capreae*), or was it the boars, the wild pigs (from the Greek *kapros*) that roamed the countryside then (and still do now)? Experts lean toward the wild boars, based on fossil remains.

The island is divided by the steep mountain, Monte Solaro, into two basic parts and two separate towns: Capri, at sea level, and Anacapri, up the mountain. If you are afraid of heights, hairpin turns, and sheer drops when driving, have someone else at the wheel and keep your eyes closed. If you are brave enough take a peek, it is the most beautiful view imaginable. If, however, you are like me, you might be hyperventilating. There is also a famous hairpin-turned footpath, tiled and absolutely gorgeous, or you can take the funicular. The important thing is to just get up to the top, because Anacapri is a lovely little place.

Up a few stairs is Capri Palace Hotel. Turn right, and you are on an un-touristy road in Anacapri, a sort of main road with shops and restaurants. Dart down the side streets and wander sweet streets and bougainvillea-covered houses.

Torta Caprese (Chocolate and Ground Almond Cake from the Island of Capri)

Serves 8–10

So many famous dishes bear the name of Capri, such as *insalata Caprese* and the dark chocolate cake made with ground almonds called *torta Caprese* (there is also a lemon and white chocolate version). *Torta Caprese* is said to have been brought to Capri by a family of Russians whose cook once baked it for the officers of Napoleon's army during the Russian campaign.

5 ounces unsalted butter
5 ounces dark or bittersweet chocolate (approx. 55 percent cocoa solids), broken or cut up into small pieces
4 medium-large eggs, separated
⅔ cup sugar

2–3 tablespoons coffee liqueur
A few drops almond extract (up to ⅛ teaspoon)
A pinch of salt
3 heaping tablespoons cocoa
8 ounces finely ground almonds or almond meal

Prepare a round cake pan, about ten inches in diameter and two and a half to three inches deep, by buttering (or oiling with olive oil) and then adding a few spoonfuls of flour and tossing around until it coats most of the inside of the pan, especially the bottom.

Heat the oven to 350°F.

Place butter in a glass bowl and microwave until it is melted. Add the chocolate, and microwave perhaps another thirty seconds. Set aside to allow the chocolate to melt completely in the hot butter. If you prefer to heat it on the stove, melt the butter in a saucepan without letting it brown; then add the chocolate, set aside, and let the chocolate melt in the hot butter. Set aside to cool while you prepare the rest of the recipe.

Torta Caprese (Chocolate and Ground Almond Cake from the Island of Capri) (*continued*)

Meanwhile, place the egg yolks in a bowl with the sugar, coffee liqueur, almond extract, and cocoa, and whip until creamy. When it is creamy, whip in the almond meal.

Place the egg whites in a clean bowl, add a pinch of salt, and whip, using clean beaters, until the egg whites have formed peaks somewhere between soft and firm: "firmish."

Stir together the melted but no longer hot butter and chocolate, combining well, then add to the egg yolk mixture until well combined. Lighten the mixture by folding in about a third of the beaten egg whites. When it is fluffy and lightened a bit, repeat until the egg whites are gone, folding as one would a souffle.

Pour into the prepared cake pan, gently so as not to remove the air from the batter.

Put cake in oven and lower heat to 325°F. Bake for forty minutes or until a skewer comes out clean from the center of the cake. The edges will bake to doneness first.

It's touching to realize that even in such a glamorous place where life can be luxurious and gilded, food traditions hold fast. For instance, in Anacapri one eats *zuppa di cicerchie*, a thick, rustic soup of the small, chickpea-like legume known as the grass pea, which is unique to the region and grown on the island.

So many dishes on Capri are vibrant: pasta with fish sauce, spaghetti with sea urchin, chickpeas with squid, fried anchovies, braised rabbit with pancetta and wild herbs. *Pesce all'acqua pazza* is a roasted fish served in a sort of soup/sauce of wine, tomatoes, and sometimes potatoes that is shared with much of the area, especially Naples. And one wouldn't expect such a sleek place to cherish offal stew ladled over stale, toasted bread; yet it is a beloved specialty cherished from days when food was scarce and eating an act of grateful sustenance.

When Capri got too crowded, film studios discovered that Ischia and Procida also could be dazzling backdrops to almost any story. *The Talented Mr. Ripley* was made on Procida, and *Il Postino* was filmed on Ischia. Ask the locals—they will happily tell you about it.

Like Capri, the islands have been inhabited since ancient times. In the eighth century BCE, Greeks from Euboea settled Ischia. Because of its strategic position in the sea, everyone has stopped there since. Though there are vestiges of their presence in buildings here and there, Ischia has little ancient architecture to reflect its past. Seismic incidents have destroyed so much. The island itself is basically the remains of an extinct volcano, Mount Epomea.

A huge seismic catastrophe took place July 28, 1883, a beautiful day when all of Ischia's citizens were enjoying themselves on the streets and in the piazzas. Suddenly a massive *terremoto* (earthquake) struck; of the island's population of twenty-six thousand, five thousand people were killed and thousands were left homeless. It was observed with tears of lamentation that no one had been safe: nobles, convicts, children, priests, aristocrats, and street sweepers died. (Recently, in August 2017, a small earthquake killed several and injured many.)

But the power responsible for so much destruction is what creates the bubbling mineral baths and therapeutic mud that lures people to the island.

Like Vesuvio, Ischia's soil is mineral rich, its fruit and vegetables lush. Figs, citrus, apples, pears, peaches, and apricots grow; olives give oil; bees make honey; ancient grapes make modern DOC wines. The hills are carpeted with wild herbs: arugula, mint, borage, rosemary, lemon balm, marjoram, and delicate spindly asparagus. Small tomatoes are tied together in bunches to air dry and intensify in flavor like Vesuvio's *piennolo*.

The seaside areas are fish rich and chef chic. In the mountainous inland areas, it is rustic and meat based. Cows, pigs, and sheep are raised, and goats wander the hills as they have done for centuries. Wild boar roam—vicious and delicious. You might find a trendy little wine bar in the hills at once stylish and rustic, candlelit for diners sipping local wines and noshing small bites of delicious tradition such as *lardo* draped over garlic-rubbed crostini or local goat or sheep's milk cheese.

Ischia's most famous specialty is *coniglio all'Ischitana* (Ischian-style rabbit), a savory braise of rabbit, wine, and tomatoes, its sauce tossed with a chunky pasta such as bucatini for the first course, and the sauce-braised rabbit in its terra-cotta casserole as a second course. The number of Mediterranean islands that I have visited where the specialty is rabbit has often made me wonder whether it's coincidence.

On Ischia, I asked a local and got this answer: "In ancient times, Phoenician traders sailed the Mediterranean from island to island, staying awhile before moving on. They needed a reliable source of food when they returned, and since rabbits breed so prolifically, ships would leave live rabbits of both sexes on the islands." There it was: the rabbits multiplied. And multiplied.

Anyone who has ever gardened knows that rabbits are crazily destructive. So islanders developed a unique way of raising them. Called *fossa*, meaning "hole," it's a series of narrow tunnels and trenches beneath the ground's surface, which allows the rabbits to live in an almost natural environment, no cage or hutch, yet be contained in an area in which they cannot ravage the landscape.

Rabbits bred with this method are called *conigli di fossa*. Their meat is firmer and healthier from the exercise, and they are happier rabbits, too, as the trenches

are very much like the rabbit warrens in the wild. It is a more humane way of raising rabbits than hutches, and many animal husbandry associations are trying to
revive it.

If you like fat, juicy sandwiches, Ischia has one for you. Called *zingara* ("gypsy
woman"), it is a large flattish roll based on artisanal *levain* baked in a wood oven.
Cut open, spread with mayonnaise, and then stuff with salame, cheeses, oil and
vinegar, and maybe a pickled pepper or two. You can have one of spicy soppressata and provola with pickled pepper pesto, or one of tomato, basil, and a little
preserved fish and/or olives. It seems like a distant relative of every sub, hero,
muffuletta, and big-roll sandwich of America.

Cooking in the Hot Sands on the Island of Ischia

Because of its underground volcanic activity, Ischia is rife with hot mineral baths,
hot mud, hot rocks, hot sand. Ischians have developed a unique cooking tradition: cooking in the hot springs that lie beneath the surface of the sand.

Though the beach appears normal, look more closely and you'll see openings
like tiny geysers of scalding steam scattered around the sand. Called fumaroles,
they can reach temperatures up to 240°F.

For centuries, on warm summer nights, locals (and tourists alike) have flocked
to Spiaggia delle Fumarole beach, on the western side of the island in the Bay
of Maronti to cook. Whether you make a snack (say baked potatoes) or a meal
(chicken or fish), it's like a campfire, but instead of fire, your food cooks in boiling sand.

To make your sand oven, dig—very carefully, the steam is hot!—near the
fumaroles. A small hoe is useful for this.

Place your ingredients—whole potatoes in their skins with sprigs of rosemary,
fish covered in a salt paste, chicken with herbs and lemon—into a heavy container. (I like clay.) Then wrap the container into a *cartoccio* (package) made
of heavy-duty foil. Next, tie a rope around it and lower it into the hole. Cover
with boiling sand. Whole eggs in their shells cook nicely, taking only about half
an hour.

While you wait for your food to cook, open a bottle of wine, light a couple
of candles, enjoy the flames flickering in the dark, and listen to the sound of the
waves washing against the shore.

To retrieve your food, pull up your parcel by the rope. Open it carefully:
steam is hot. Then inhale the enticing aromas. A plate of ripe, juicy tomatoes
and aromatic basil leaves is the classic accompaniment, and hopefully you have
brought bread to eat along with it all.

As locals say, "Only at the Spiaggia delle Fumarole, only on Ischia!"

Procida is tiny (about two and a half miles), its pretty little hillsides and harbors dotted with brightly colored houses with cobbled streets leading up the hills. It's hard to believe that in such an exquisite spot, everyday ordinary life exists. Wouldn't you need to be rich and famous to live there? But no, ordinary people do live there; some commute to work by ferry to nearby Naples.

Its name is said come from the word *prochyta*, meaning abundance, reflecting how lavishly its fruit and vegetables have always grown. Vegetables have always been a mainstay of daily meals: savory pies filled with leafy greens and a soup filled with eggplant, zucchini, potatoes, and basil called *bobba*. And the artichokes, oh, the artichokes! Procida artichokes are legendary. If you love them, you must get yourself there during their season, usually early May, when the locals also hold a *sagra*. The main grape is Aglianico, which is made into both red and white wines.

Procida's lemons are special: huge, golden orbs usually enjoyed as salads, unusual to outsiders but beloved to locals. The flesh and its abundant, delicate pith are cut up and dressed with olive oil and a drop or two of vinegar (perhaps). On sweltering days, it is deeply reviving. Of course, everyone has his or her own recipe, and it is the correct one. Bring the subject up for discussion at your own peril—the only thing people seem to agree on is lashings of olive oil, fresh mint, and garlic. Onions may come and go, *vino cotto* (similar to a sweet, aged balsamic vinegar) may be tossed in, and most add a pinch (at the least) of chile flakes.

There's a sad aspect to the dish, however; during the days of great hunger, locals ate lemon salad as their main meal, and they ate it often. Sometimes they ate it with smoked herring; sometimes lemon salad was all they had. A whole generation remembers these times.

The little island rests in a big sea of fish, and although fish stocks have declined, they are still plentiful; efforts toward sustainability are fully engaged. Each day a dozen or so fishing boats go out, bringing back shellfish, crustaceans, sea bass, octopus, prawns, and my favorite: anchovies. If you are not yet a fan of the local, fresh anchovies, you will be.

Served fresh, raw, splashed with a little lemon and slathered in olive oil, raw anchovy fillets are so elegant, so delicious, so pure. If you can, find an *agriturismo* in which the Mamma makes her anchovies from the morning's catch. And if it is a lemon farm as well, so much the better.

Some fish are expensive, some cheap. There is a mixture of small fish for frying called *Mazzamma* and a special dish for "those who can't even afford the cheapest fish." Called *pesce fjiuto*, it means "the fish that got away." Crushed ripe tomatoes, herbs, oil, garlic, and chile pepper are poured over rustic toast—in other words, it's fish soup with everything but the fish!

Being Campania, Procida loves its sweets. Besides the usual pastries, cakes, and frozen treats, there is a tongue-shaped pastry puff called *lingua* that's filled with custard.

La tarantella—the dance of the *contadina*—is said to have originated in Procida, inspired by the energetic stamping of feet against the imagined tarantula. Food fairs and celebrations are a good place to catch tarantella dancing.

The two tiny Flegrean islands—Nisida and Vivara—are closed to visitors. Nisida, now a refuge of flora and fauna, was famous in ancient Greece for its delicious wild asparagus. Vivara has been a prison, army base, and now a juvenile detention facility.

Insalata di Limone/Piatto di Limone (Lemon Salad)

The *limoni pane*, also known as "bread lemon," is the star of the salad, as its tree is the star of Capri (and grown on Ischia, too). Almost everyone has at least one tree, though, sadly, they are dying off in favor of the juicier lemons. Locals are making an effort to preserve the trees so that they are not lost to history.

1–2 large *limoni pane*, the Procida lemons with abundant pith and small amount of juicy flesh
Vino cotto or balsamic vinegar to taste
Salt to taste

1–2 garlic cloves, grated
Dried chile flakes to taste
Onions, if desired, thinly sliced
Handful of fresh mint leaves, torn
Olive oil, drizzled in abundance

Shave the zest/peel off the lemon. If it is very fragrant—and it should be—this is a good excuse to make limoncello.

Take the whole peeled lemon with its abundant pith and cut it into bite-sized cubes. Toss with the vino cotto or balsamic vinegar and salt. Allow to marinate for about ten minutes.

Dress with the garlic, chile flakes, onions, mint, and lots of olive oil.

Serve right away or chill until ready to eat.

Variation: To eat *piatto di limone* as a cool, refreshing salad/soup, add a small amount of cool water—perhaps a few tablespoons per plate—to the salad before you let it absorb the other ingredients.

Variation: Similar lemon salads are made in Sorrento and Salerno, but in Sorrento no garlic is added, and the salad is dressed with wine vinegar, fresh chile, and chopped flat-leaf parsley.

ALONG THE SORRENTO COAST

When you leave the grit and grime of Naples, drive through the tunnel and emerge on the other side, you are suddenly surrounded by beauty sandwiched between hills and sea. As gray as it was before the tunnel, life is beautiful now, only minutes later.

Homer described Sorrento as "land of the Sirens," those beautiful mermaids who basked on the rocks and frolicked in the waters. Sorrento is just the first of a long string of jewel-like towns that dot the coastline.

When the rich Romans under the rule of Emperor Tiberius felt that Capri was too crowded, they moved across the water to the Sorrentine Coast, building magnificent villas perched high atop cliffs. Since then, Sorrento's sparkle has not dulled. Goethe, Byron, Dumas, Verdi, Britain's royal family, the Rockefellers, and Jacqueline Onassis were all drawn to its beauty and atmosphere. (It is still crawling with celebs these days, though I seldom know who they are.)

One night I was sitting on the balcony of the Hotel Tramontano, gazing out at the sea. The moon was shining on the dark water like a nightlight. It was so beautiful. I was drinking wine. And then, as the song "Retorno a Sorrento" ("Torna a Surriento" in dialect) was playing, I was nearly overcome with emotion (aren't we all, during those just-like-a-movie moments?).

Reality snapped me back when I heard a voice speaking to me. It was the waiter: "You do know that the song was written exactly where you are sitting, early in the twentieth century?" I didn't, but I will always think of the balcony when I hear the song.

Sorrento, the town, is charming, small, and touristy. Even so, there is quite a bit to it culturally, culinarily, and agriculturally. Climb the hills, wander around the country roads with their vineyards and orchards, perhaps examining their unique way of growing lemon and olive trees together (at two different height levels, supported by wooden stakes and nets).

Make your way down to the water. Eat at a beach restaurant, such as Bikini. Walk through the town; have a gelato; pretend that the paparazzi are trying to snap *you* instead of that gorgeous creature next to you. Meander the cobbled streets. The shops are touristy, but they sell a lot of nice things: hot peppers, lemon soap, ceramics. Produce shops sell local fruit and vegetables. I always like to walk past and observe the "working men's" social club: retired guys sitting on the terrace, sipping, chatting, and hanging out.

Being a tourist destination, I expected the food to be mediocre (at best). But in Sorrento I've only had good—really, really good—food, as if restaurants believe that everyone, even tourists, deserve it. Once I was led into a huge place catering to large groups passing through. My heart sank, as it always does, at the prospect of a disappointing meal. And I was shocked—absolutely shocked. I forget its name, I forget our menu, but I do remember that it was all delicious!

Once in an ordinary hotel I ate the most glorious cantaloupe heaped with sweet, fragrant strawberries. I tell you this in case you ever consider passing such a dish by, thinking, well, how good could it be? Don't ask—just eat. In season, of course.

Fruit and vegetable stands sell locally grown lemons, artichokes, tomatoes, and oranges, as well as hot peperoncini, fresh and dried, laughingly referred to as "Italian Viagra."

Sorrento dishes often feature cheese—in the hills behind the town is Mount Lattari ("milk mountain"). Cows, sheep, and goats graze while cheesemakers produce lovely local *fior di latte* and *provolone del Monaco*.

Sorrento's famous gnocchi alla Sorrentina is a casserole of gnocchi sauced with tomato and layered with masses of melty cheese. Its joy is in its lack of restraint. To make, simply layer the tomato-dressed gnocchi with lots of chunks of cheese. Individual casseroles are the most delightful way to do it, but one big one is fine. Heat it until the cheese is molten; then serve with a basil leaf or two on top.

Of course, Sorrento is a summer destination—bikinis on the beach, parties by the pool, drinks on the terrace. Sorrento is a wedding destination, and one often sees brides and grooms in the streets, next to fountains, the sea, and grand buildings posing for the camera, almost Fellini-esque in their wedding garb.

Locals are friendly, especially considering that they are faced with an endless parade of tourists and foreigners passing through. It is their livelihood as well. But after summer fades and the tourists leave comes an intimate time for Sorrentines. With the runup to Christmas, it becomes a time for pleasing oneself rather than hoards of visitors. Streets are strung with tiny lights, reflecting on the wet stones of the cobbled streets, and sparkly stars decorate most shops. Each evening the whole population of Sorrento enjoys a *passegiata*, greeting friends and family, peering into shop windows. During summer they were busy working; now they take back the town.

Like all of the lemon-drenched coastline, Sorrentines sip limoncello—homemade or produced commercially. Many factory/workshops welcome visitors, but you'll need to contact them ahead of time. I am particularly fond of the magnificent Villa Massa, with its lemon groves overlooking the sea in Piano di Sorrento. A family summer residence for generations, it is a beautiful venue for weddings.

Lemon dances through the whole menu, though, not just dessert: lemon pasta, risotto, meatballs, chicken, fish stuffed with lemon and lemon leaves, cheese and lemon pizza. The desserts include *delizie al limone*, a sponge cake filled with lemon custard and covered with lemon cream, often served two on a plate with a morsel of candied lemon on top, resembling plump, lemony breasts. Or babà limoncello! A local snack is the ancient, rustic *follarielli* or *passolini*, golden raisins or figs wrapped in lemon (or orange) leaves, then dried. Sometimes restaurants offer an all-lemon meal. If you love lemon as much as I do, treat yourself.

Not long ago I was on a private boat sailing between Ischia and Capri on the way to a party, when I began speaking with an elegantly dressed American man in an Italian suit. He was gazing toward Sorrento. "My grandparents were from there," he said, gesturing across the water. "They were so poor—they fled starvation and poverty, never to return. I've been around the world but never there." We were so close to Sorrento—ten, maybe twenty, minutes away by boat, although a much longer swim. I wanted, more than anything, at that moment to take his hand, dive into the water, and paddle to the shore. I wanted him to discover the beautiful place that was in his DNA. I think of him always when I am in Sorrento and hope that he has now returned to his grandparents' land.

From Sorrento to Amalfi, the road hugs cliffs, overlooking and sharply dropping to the sea. Beaches, resorts, and towns are at road level. On the other side of the street, tiny roads lead off into the hills, passing villages, hamlets, and tiny towns. It's a lovely place to dine along the way or to plop yourself down and stay. The enchanting Fattoria Terranova, "*sospesa tra terra e mare*" (suspended between the earth and the sea), in Massa Lubrense serves delicious food, grown in its garden, and wines from its vineyard, and it overlooks the sea.

If you're driving the coastal road, though, you'll find yourself transported along the towns and hamlets for which the Costiera Amalfi is famous. Positano, Ravello, Amalfi, Atrani, Minori, Cetara, Vietro sul Mare. I would be insincere, however, if I didn't tell you that this road scares me to death. Perhaps you are less skittish than I. There is a guardrail, so, really, you'll be okay. But me? I chewed fingernails and popped anti-anxiety meds. But I will do it again, any time, at the drop of a hat, because the sea, sky, mountains, and little towns are each more enchanting than the next.

Linguine alla Nerano [though we ate it in Positano] (Pasta with Zucchini, Delicate Buttery Cheese Sauce, and Basil)

Serves 4

A few years ago, I helped organize a trip of writers, chefs, and mixologists to the Amalfi Coast. Descending narrow walkways, down stone steps, and toward the sea, I felt disheartened by tourist shop after tourist shop. And then the cobbled walkway ended at a tiny, sandy beach, and at that moment I never

Linguine alla Nerano [though we ate it in Positano] (Pasta with Zucchini, Delicate Buttery Cheese Sauce, and Basil) (*continued*)

wanted to leave. Straight ahead, the water lapped against the sand, behind us the town perched high, clinging to cliffs. Whichever direction I looked was beautiful: the beach, cliffs, cafes, little boats moored near the shore. I looked at that water, sparkling and blue, the clear crisp sky and felt the strong sun. I asked a few passersby; the answer was "yes, it's suitable for swimming."

With Los Angeles beer expert and mixologist Lisa Witkowski, we pulled large beach coverups over our clothes and underneath them shimmied and squirmed out of our street clothes and into swimsuits. There! In public, right on the beach! It felt daring, but of course no one cared. They just saw two women shaking around under big coverups. Most of the women on the beach wore little more than a string or two. Within moments, dressed in our swimsuits, we donned sunglasses and sun hats and felt as if we were immersed in a 1960s technicolor movie about a couple of clueless gals who were suddenly in love with the Amalfi Coast.

The water was shockingly cold, so salty that I could taste it through my skin. The sandy sea bed dipped fast, suddenly giving way to the deep. I lost my footing and, after a moment of terror, launched myself into swimming. Tiny brightly colored boats bobbed up and down in the water, and we swam around them, laughing as we did so. It wasn't an ocean swim; it was a sea dip. And when we got out, it was time for lunch.

This was November 2008; the whole world was in love with Barack Obama. When we walked into the restaurant, damp and salty from the sea, the owner beamed at us with joy and ran into the back room. In moments, he came running out wearing his Obama T-shirt. He kept patting us as if we were miracles, not just for the United States but also for the whole world. We felt so hopeful; the world was going to be wonderful.

But now I need to tell you about the pasta we ate, because it *was* wonderful. The dish was creamy, the zucchini so sweet and fresh, they were no doubt grown nearby and harvested maybe a few minutes ago? And butter! A little finishing with butter! It was all so indulgently beautiful and beautifully indulgent. The dish is named after the town of Nerano, just down the coast.

About 2–2½ pounds zucchini/
   courgettes, trimmed and
   cut into julienne strips or
   thin slices
Olive oil for browning
1 clove garlic, cut into thin
   slivers (optional)
Salt as desired

3½–4 ounces freshly grated Parmigiano cheese
4 ounces white melting cheese such as
   provolone, white cheddar, a tasty
   Monterey Jack, soft, fresh pecorino,
   Jarlsberg, fontina, Gruyere, whatever cheese you are able to find
   where you live, diced

Linguine alla Nerano [though we ate it in Positano] (Pasta with Zucchini, Delicate Buttery Cheese Sauce, and Basil) (*continued*)

6–8 tablespoons unsalted butter
3–4 tablespoons basil leaves, torn,
  or small ones that don't need
  to be torn

1 pound linguine, a slightly wider
  long ribbon of pasta, spaghetti,
  or vermicelli

Sprinkle the zucchini with a little salt and toss well. Leave for ten to fifteen minutes. (Alternatively, as suggested for *zucchini alla scapece*, you could leave the zucchini, covered with a cloth, in the sun for several hours.)

Heat a few tablespoons olive oil in a frying pan and add the zucchini, cooking until they are lightly browned and softened. Halfway through, add the garlic. When tender, set aside. You can do this ahead of time, even up to a day or two.

Bring a large pot of water to a boil, and then add salt to taste.

Meanwhile, place the Parmigiano, diced white cheese, and butter in a bowl. Set aside.

Add the pasta to the boiling water, stirring to separate the strands, and boil until they are just al dente. Ladle out two cups of the cooking liquid and set it aside; then drain the pasta and return it to the hot pot.

Add the cheese, butter, and reserved zucchini to the pasta, along with a little bit of the reserved liquid. You may use all of the liquid depending on how the sauce forms.

Over medium-low heat, toss the pasta, adding a little of the water as you go, letting the cheese melt with the water to form a small amount of sauce.

Serve immediately, sprinkled with basil.

Postitano may be rich and glitzy, but in the hills high above, it is an unspoiled area of nature. Rich with mineral springs, pure, clean water bubbles down from the mountains in small creeks. Along paths are shrines, statues, and various spots from which to drink. In these villages, Italian is not even spoken; residents still speak only dialect.

Further along the coast, Cetara is one of the most exquisite of the tiny water villages. It is said to have been named for tuna because of its abundant fish. It is home to *colatura di alici* (also made in nearby Marina di Piscotta), the modern equivalent of the Roman *garum*, or the Western equivalent of the Southeast Asian fish sauce. It's eaten on pasta, mozzarella, almost everything. When wild fennel is growing, it is combined with the anchovies, sardines, and tuna of Cetara.

Spaghetti alla Cetarese (Spaghetti with an Anchovy Pesto)

The tiny fishing town of Cetara has one industry: preserving fish. Its most famous preserved fish product is *colatura di alici*.

Likely the descendant of the ancient Roman condiment *garum*, *colatura* is made by layering raw anchovies and salt in a large container with a spigot at the bottom, topping it with a heavy weight to weigh it down. As it ferments, the liquid called *colatura* is created. The liquid is harvested from the spigot at the bottom.

A *colatura* workshop is fascinating and smelly. The boats with their fish come nearly to the door of the little factory. The fish are salted immediately; then they begin fermenting. A huge amount of fermenting fish smells exactly as you imagine it does.

But, like so many smelly things, *colatura* is delicious—subtle and not overwhelmingly fishy. You know what happens with anchovies: Cook them with meat, pasta, or fish, and they disappear into a savory haze. Though you don't taste fish or anchovies, you taste something incredibly savory that enhances the rest of the dish.

Although I am calling this a pesto, it is not the smooth green sauce but a hand-chopped near-relish, with flecks of herbs bound to the chopped anchovy, fish sauce, olive oil, capers, and garlic. It's the kind of delicious paste that sidesteps the objections of people who don't like anchovies (or capers)—it's just so appealing. Hand chopping is best for a paste that has texture; yet each ingredient is married to the other by virtue of being chopped together. Neapolitans do a lot of hand chopping.

1 ounce pine nuts
2-ounce tin of anchovies in olive oil,
 plus their oil
1 big clove of garlic or 2 smaller ones
½ bunch parsley or 1 smallish bunch
½ bunch basil or 1 smallish bunch

1 tablespoon capers (in brine or
 salted and drained)
½ teaspoon *colaratura di alici* of Cetara
 (or Southeast Asian fish sauce)
2–3 tablespoons extra virgin olive oil
1 pound spaghetti

Using a large knife, on a cutting board, chop the pine nuts. Add the anchovies to the pine nuts, chopping them together. You might need to wash the handle of the knife so that your hand doesn't slip as you continue to chop. Chop in the garlic, then the parsley, then the basil, and the capers. Continue chopping it all together until you reach a thick, chunky consistency. Place in a bowl.

Stir in the *colatura* and olive oil. Cover and refrigerate until ready to serve.

Cook the spaghetti in boiling, salted water until not quite al dente; then drain, reserving about a cup of the cooking water. Into a heavy frying pan, place about half the pesto, then the pasta, heating them through a minute or two; then add about half the water, and cook together, tossing. You may need to add more water; you may not. See how it goes. Add the rest of the pesto, and serve right away with a little extra olive oil drizzled over it all.

Amalfi may be a small, charming tourist town now, but once it was a great sea-faring nation. It has gorgeous *caffes*, chic shops, and tour buses parked nearby. But do the tourists spoil it? Hard to answer—because, even overwhelmed by crowds, it is still a wonderful place, with wonderful food and atmosphere.

Sfogliatelle can be found in Italian bakeries worldwide, but the Santa Rosa version, with a dollop of cream and a black cherry, are found in two places: the annual *sfogliatelle* feast on August 25 in Conca dei Marini, and also at Amalfi's Andrea Pansa, a *pasticceria* dating from 1830. Situated directly next to the cathedral of Amalfi, it's practically a museum of local pastry.

In the hills above the town are groves of trees and springs of pure water that are excellent for pasta making and also for paper making. Amalfi was once famous for its paper, made not from wood mash like papyrus but from a mash of worn-out white cloth (the everyday clothing of the people) mixed with spring water. A little museum at the top of the main street not only tells the story but also, when I was there, allowed visitors to make their own paper.

If overcrowding threatens in Amalfi, go to Atrani instead; to get there, turn off the road just before Amalfi. You will find yourself in a tiny seafaring town without a tourist in sight. Soon you are likely to be gathered around a big table, eating pizza.

On such a coastline with its exquisite beaches accessible only by sea, one can sail along the coast, much as Odysseus did, stopping in coves and former smugglers' caves. You will need a boat; private boats and yachts can be hired. Flying Charter is the oldest yacht charter company in Italy, based in the area.

One expects to eat things like lemon, fish, and seafood as traditional dishes. One unexpected specialty is a chocolate and eggplant dessert special from Ravello. Peeled eggplant slices are fried, then layered with dark chocolate, dried fruit, and nuts. Though it seems odd to outsiders, eggplant has been eaten with chocolate for centuries, since the exchange of New World foods. There are many versions of this dish in Ravello, from simple to elaborate, no doubt reflecting once again its Monzù heritage.

If you like bright colors and beautiful plates and views to take your breath away, go to Vietri sul Mare. Perched high on a cliff overlooking the sea (to which you can descend and swim), this little town is famous for the brightly painted pottery that probably is what comes to mind when you think of Italian ceramics. In the little town of Vietri, everything is ceramic. On one side of the road is a massive museum of ceramics, and on the other side, Vietri itself. The town's benches are ceramic; walls, signs, pots with flowers that sit on the wall overlooking the sea: all ceramic. The tables, doorways, businesses of all sorts, each and everything is basically decorated with tiles and ceramics.

Just past Vietri sul Mare and down the hill is the town and port of Salerno; past that, Paestum and the Cilento. It is the second area for raising buffalo and making mozzarella, ricotta, and the like. Salerno makes a wider selection of cheeses that differs subtly from Caserta, reflecting its own terroir: diet, temperature, humidity, and so on.

The Greek and Roman ruins of Paestum are breathtaking monuments to ancient Greece and Rome; yet there is still so much unknown. Since 1991 they have been part of the Parco Nazionale del Cilento e Vallo di Diano e Alburnia, now granted UNESCO status, created to protect the region from mass development.

Monzù heritage from the wealthy aristocrats whose estates dotted the area gave a layer of richness and finesse to the otherwise rustic region. Cannelloni is a favorite, stuffed either with cheese and baked in tomatoes or with spinach and cod and baked in cream. Local *cucina povera*, by contrast, is made to sustain and please rather than to impress, handed down mother to child with loving frugality. *Sfrionzola* is a great example from Ottati in Salerno, made with scraps of leftover meat braised with fresh and/or pickled peppers (and sometimes potatoes). *Buonissima.*

The care for eating and of feeding others is taken seriously; one could even say it is holy. Not long ago I was at a crowded festival in a nondescript town feeling irritated. My (local) friends said, "Let's go for dinner."

Instead of a restaurant, however, we pulled up in front of a modest church. I must have looked confused because I was told that it *was* a restaurant in the evening, but midday for *pranzo* (the main meal) it was a restaurant without cost—in other words, a soup kitchen. The community had been moved by the plight of migrants who struggled to get to Italy and then struggled to feed their families. When I asked the priest what sort of dishes they served, he described them proudly: "All the local specialties, vegetables in season." His pink cheeks and abundant belly clearly reflected his own love of the table. "The only thing we do not serve is pork. Many of our guests are Muslim. We want them to enjoy the food unafraid."

A Food Festival

A while back I went to a festival of artisanal foods from Italy's south. I was told it would be "fun." Well, "fun" doesn't even come close—it was hysterical fabulous noshing, hella-fun.

Taking place in a huge white tent set up next to the Port of Naples, the exposition included stalls, samples, workshops, lectures, local costumes, and demonstrations. Extra virgin olive oils, wines, limoncello and other liqueurs, incomparable tomatoes, vegetables, fruits, cheeses, "the white arts" of pastries,

A Food Festival (*continued*)

pizza, and breads, fresh and dried hot chilies, and pastas all under one big, rambling tent, all waiting to be tasted.

Neapolitan Barbara Castaldo Lajvnas was my guide and translator. Tall, willowy, with flashing dark eyes and long tapering fingers, she was much like Sophia Loren in her heyday. Her mission, she claimed, was to make sure I didn't miss anything vital, especially in the mozzarella realm. She was also keen to taste as much the *mozzarella di bufala* as was humanly possible. In this spirit of shared gastronomical greediness—I mean, cultural exploration—we set out to see the fair.

Sponsored by the regional board for agricultural development of Campania, it billed itself as "Flavors, Sounds, and Colors of the Mediterranean." After our first hour of wandering and sampling, however, I subtitled it in my mind: "the best county fair you've ever gone to where there are so many delicious things to taste you could scream."

At the agricultural display a health campaign was under way: "Cinque Colori del Benessere" (the five colors of wellness), Italy's answer to eating more fruits and vegetables. We looked at the chart and matched the colors to the vegetables and fruits, like the children were doing: red peppers, dark leafy greens, gleaming purple eggplant, creamy colored onions, pumpkin the color of the bright autumn leaves. The crowd was nearly giddy with color, and how healthful it all was! "Try this pepper—*molto buono!*"

After much admiring and nibbling and reflecting on the benefits of vegetables, we moved on to the salame and cheesemakers, who probably made up the largest group at the fair. Large salame, small salame, cheeses in great varieties, all local, starting with the animals.

I got into a discussion with a pecorino-making woman about her fat-tailed sheep and how their particular metabolism created a cheese that is very light, very low fat (the tail attracts all the fat) and particularly delicious. It was, of course. I could have stayed there and eaten her cheese, admiring her wonderful sheep photos forever, except I smelled something that was pulling me in a different direction: truffles.

A slightly taciturn couple from the mountains of Irpinia were spreading inky black truffle paste lavishly onto bread, urging us to eat. This wasn't a sample size; this was a truffle sandwich. They told me of a truffle fest to be held a week later. (I was going to miss it and for a few moments felt inconsolable.)

But in Naples, especially at the festival of all things Neapolitan, I couldn't stay depressed for too long. A minute or two later, there was something else wonderful to explore. Within minutes I was smacking a tambourine and leaping about to the tarantella. A crowd had gathered, we were surrounded by music, and life was good again.

A Food Festival (*continued*)

Mozzarella people were everywhere. A photo of a big, fat baby eating a big, fat mozzarella, milky goodness spilling out everywhere, says it all: sweet, fresh milk, purity, delicate nourishment. I felt like that baby when I took my first bite. There were, of course, many more bites to follow. Every so often throughout the afternoon, Barbara and I would look at each other, eyes alight, and she would say, "Shall we go have another mozzarella? Let's go!" with no shame at all! And it was back to our *bufala*.

Every two hours, a different chef prepared a different pasta. Navigating the crowds for this was brutal. Working in partnership was helpful. We ate a bowl of spaghetti with chickpeas in a tomato-tinged sauce studded with bits of prosciutto—or was it pancetta?—served in rustic earthenware bowls. It was the best pasta with chickpeas I've ever eaten, before or after, no doubt due to the quality of the locally grown chickpeas and the pasta, of course, always in Napoli, the pasta.

When we went out for a breath of fresh air, we found a pizza truck parked in a little alleyway outside the gates of the festival, tables and chairs set out for everyone—and I do mean everyone. From gossiping grannies to chic young things to bouncing babies, all eventually stopped, sat, and ate some pizza. Was it fancy? No. You could have either Margherita or marinara. Was it stylish? No. Was it wonderful? There, on a wobbly folding chair in a parking lot next to a pizza truck, watching the ferries bustle in and out of the harbor, the pizza was, indeed, completely wonderful.

10

The Tradition of Going Out to Eat

Pleasure, Sustenance, and Sociability

Eating in restaurants in Campania is, at once, functional, luxurious, practical, affordable, wildly expensive, chic, traditional, innovative, and modern in surroundings that can veer from a terrace overlooking the sea and the lights of the villages to Formica-topped tables on a side street of cobbled stones, with *motorini* whizzing by every few minutes. It's all of these things.

In other words, eating out is so varied and so much a part of life that it feels like what you are meant to do. In Campania, a restaurant—say, a trattoria or osteria—is like home, making the dishes that Mamma and Nonna fed you. A restaurant might also make specialties that you don't eat at home.

It reminds me of Paris: eating out is normal; everyone deserves it. Choosing a restaurant, sharing discoveries, meeting your friends—it's part of life, with Paris's bistros much like Naples's trattorie: informal, homey, and welcoming. Of course, the tradition is different, and Paris's crisply ironed and refined haute cuisine exists in its own stratosphere, but even then the food reflects the culture, and everyone is entitled to partake. Of course, if you have money, you go to expensive places more often; if you have less, you go to the cheaper ones. But it is likely that you still go. People love to go out to eat, as cultural an act as it is gastronomical.

THE IMPORTANCE OF RESTAURANTS

In a place where home food is so important, where family and friends still gather for traditional lunch on Sunday, why would restaurants be important?

Wouldn't people just eat at home, or at their Mamma's? Wouldn't they just cook for each other?

For one thing, restaurants are fun. A home away from home if the restaurant is your local trattoria, run by a Mamma and Pappa who aren't yours but who seem to love you and feed you very well. Most likely their food is really good. You're tired after the day at work, or it's lunch time and you are out and about, or maybe you simply wish to eat out. Restaurants serve you; they aim to please (hopefully); you can watch the other eaters; and there is plenty of space for a gathering. It is sociable—and Neapolitans are nothing if not sociable.

Dining is not only about eating and being fed but also about the social interactions in which problems are solved (or argued about), exclamations accompany each dish, and small children are admired. I once saw a babe-in-arms passed around a long restaurant table to be cooed at and cuddled with. Elders are watched to make sure they are eating—and eating happily—people laugh, and someone might get upset and then just as quickly settle down, because it's time for dessert.

I once queried my friend, Duly Torricilla Peckmann, about the percentage of restaurants in Napoli and its surroundings that are good, excellent, and mediocre or bad. Duly thought for a moment: "I think that 50 percent of the restaurants are good; 25 percent are excellent, and 25 percent are not good at all; you could call them bad." She continued, "People here love to eat well and know the difference between good and not. They wouldn't put up with less than delicious. A meal is to be enjoyed, not something to get out of the way."

Many Neapolitan restaurants have their origins in a Mamma: a warm, hardworking woman who cooks beautifully, who is moved to feed people, and who views it almost as a calling. I would say that most Neapolitan restaurant owners are like this—even the men! As Duly says, "The best restaurants here are the ones run by a couple or a family rather than a business model or a chain. They come from the heart."

Running a restaurant, indeed, is taking part in the ancient tradition of hospitality. It is almost holy. This tradition includes the Mamma who proudly held up the empty pasta plate of her favorite guest (sadly, it wasn't me; no one doubts that I will finish my pasta), and the grandma who owns a trattoria and still insists on cutting up the vegetables when she becomes bedridden.

Good cooking is considered an art, a gift. Hospitality is an opportunity to make life more pleasurable, even if just for an hour or for one person. In Napoli, you get the feeling that it's not only a business transaction—they *want* to feed you.

THE RESTAURANTS: WHERE ARE YOU GOING TO EAT?
WHERE AM I GOING TO EAT?

You're going out to eat. First, let's have a nice walk: the *passeggiata*. Though not exclusively Neapolitan—all of Italy loves its *passeggiata*—the evening stroll through town is a citywide socially active walk. It takes place each evening around 7:00 pm or so, depending on the season and weather. The streets suddenly fill with men, women, young, and old, dressed smartly, strolling the streets, hanging in the piazza, milling about. They join arms; run into friends and relatives, kissing each other in greeting; and meander their way through this lovely time of day. In the summer, especially, as the unbearable oppression of heat begins to lift, it is exquisite relief when the day cools enough to be outside enjoying the fresh air. The *passeggiata* is the best prelude to an evening meal, wherever you decide to dine.

Il caffè bar is a cafe/hangout offering classic espresso drinks, cold drinks, juices, hot chocolate, beer, and various teas, wines, and cocktails (both with and without alcohol). Many are also pastry shops—important if you are stopping for breakfast, since Neapolitan breakfasts are basically milky coffee (cappuccino) and perhaps a pastry such as a beautiful *sfogliatelle*, simple cake, or fruit tart. It might not seem like much of a start to the day, but remember, the Italian, the Neapolitan, has many eating opportunities throughout the day and must be ready for them!

Later in the day *caffes* might serve stuffed panini—sandwiches that make them the perfect places for a little *merenda* (more than an afternoon snack, less than a meal). On summer days, the *caffes* have their granita machines swirling the icy mixture around to a sweet slush. Sometimes they are set outside to tempt you as you walk past. Lemon, almond, cherry, mint, coffee, pomegranate, watermelon, cantaloupe, strawberry, orange—during summer's heat waves, they are literally lifesavers.

For wine, an *aperitivo*, and a small and savory nibble to go with it, a wine bar or *enoteca* is very much part of Neapolitan life these days. *Aperitivi* drinks are usually bitter and sweet: Campari, Cinzano, Punt e Mes, and Cynar (based on artichokes), usually mixed with soda, bitter lemon, or tonic. Aperol is another bittersweet *aperitivo* with an alcohol level about half that of Campari. The bitterness of the *aperitivi* kindles the appetite, luring you to your next meal. With the drinks usually come small plates of potato chips (sometimes homemade), olives, or crisp nuts. Lately, especially in the city of Naples, early evening cocktails with little plates of savory goodies are becoming dinner itself.

They are a new sort of thing, a place to hang out, to sit outside if weather permits. Usually they have a well-chosen assortment of wine by the glass. Sometimes it may be a wine shop, other times a complete restaurant. Some serve tapas-like offerings or one or two dishes scrawled on a chalkboard, like eggplant parmigiana or local cheeses and cured meats. Some offer informal foods, such as a *panuozzo* (a hefty panino on a flat, chewy roll, hot and melty), while others, such as Capalice, serve interesting, inventive dishes and are devoted to local wines, both local to Italy and local to Campania.

Maybe you'll go to a pizzeria; after all, you're in Naples. All *pizzerie* have wood-burning ovens and most also act as a *friggitoria* (i.e., a "place that fries foods like an artist"). Sometimes it may be a ristorante as well, serving pasta, fish, antipasti, meat—all of the beautiful Neapolitan specialties. If you're in a pizzeria restaurant with friends for a celebration dinner—every dinner is a celebration—don't even think of skipping the antipasti. Recently my pre-pizza antipasti included marinated sundried tomatoes, stuffed eggplant, balls of mozzarella with arugula, crispy fried zucchini blossoms, fried seaweed balls, fried fish, raw fish, raw sea urchin, and a plate of cheese and salame. I feel happy reliving the memory as I tap this out.

Gastropub bar-restaurants specialize in the new craze of craft beers, accompanied by the Neapolitan perception of pub grub, but sometimes it's the traditional that wins out, such as Neapolitan tripe, cold, with lemon and a cold glass of craft beer.

Translated literally, *sfizioseria* means something so tempting that it urges you to eat it; in reality, it refers to a snack bar.

Once upon a time, the type of restaurant meant something and one would choose it by its title. Osteria meant spaghetti and wine, a trattoria specialized in hearty peasant fare, and the ristorante was all about white tablecloth formality (i.e., fancy).

Now, it doesn't matter—you can't tell the type of restaurant by its name. A fancy restaurant might call itself a trattoria to create a feeling of charming rusticity; a trendy spot might call itself an osteria to convey an image of simple and chic, whereas an inexpensive place might call itself a ristorante to enhance its prestige. Even the French term *bistro* is used these days, such as the Anemos Winebar Bistrot in Vomero, an *enoteca* that prides itself on big sandwiches. At its origin—that is, in France—a bistro is not a sandwich bar, but none of that really matters. What matters is the spirit of the kitchen and the hospitality of the hosts. That is the Neapolitan way.

Giulia Cannada Bartoli's book *Guida alle Trattorie di Napoli: Storie, Luoghi e Ricette della Tradizione* is a guide and history of Naples's trattorias. It is useful to have, even if you don't understand Italian. Bartoli also has a blog that I recommend: *Le Officine Gourmet* (http://officinegourmet.blogspot.com).

Another website/blog for excellent trustworthy advice and recommendations is *Luciano Pignatoro Wine and Food Blog* (www.lucianopignataro.it). Both of these are in Italian, but at times are translated partially into English, and some computer programs can do the translation for you.

How to Order

It used to be that the progression of an Italian meal was sacrosanct, or at least expected: an optional antipasto, a primo (usually pasta), then a secondo (usually fish or seafood, sometimes meat). A *contorno* or two filled the table and filled out the contours of the meal (hence its name). Then, maybe, dessert—perhaps a piece of fruit with a fork and knife to cut it up and peel it as you eat.

If you are entertaining or it's in any way a special meal, antipasti are called for—like tapas, or meze, or big party—it's all there, an array of Neapolitan goodies from fried tidbits to pizza-like crostini, fresh mozzarella, raw fish, pizza stuffed with bitter greens, tiny seafood kebabs, octopus and fennel salad, tiny fish and baby squid fried to a crisp, baby fish that look like shredded celery root, mussels cooked with black pepper, razor clams, round clams, and a virtual sea full of clams. After antipasti, it takes a will of steel to move on to the next course. One must leave room in one's appetite for it.

These days restaurant meals are looser, more individualized. Also, this is Napoli. What you want, what you need, that's what you need to order. Except for pasta: "The pasta course you must have," said my waiter not long ago. "Everything else is optional."

Menus do exist: sometimes printed on paper (or scrawled on a board), sometimes even in English, which doesn't necessarily signal a tourist trap. Neapolitans like to please guests; translating a menu *can* be an act of hospitality. Of course, it can also be a ploy to grab tourists and feed them what they think a tourist wants, which is probably not what you really want.

Even if there is a menu, go ahead and ask for something that isn't on it—some things, such as pasta with tomatoes, can *always* be made for you.

But if you really want to feel the joy, eschew the menu completely (you can look at it first if you like) and put yourself in the hands of your waiter/waitress, who really, really wants to be a part of your dining experience. Together you will have discussions; you'll speak of the sea, of land, of the air, of what is freshest in the kitchen and what the chef loves cooking best. In the end, you will have a meal far more memorable than anything on the menu. If you don't speak Italian, bring along a translating device or use hand gestures, or show an interest in your meal and in the culture it comes from: somehow let the waiter know that you are open to being delighted.

I admire waiters and waitresses in Campania. I see how hard they work, and I see how eager they are to ensure that my dining experience is good. Sometimes they are formal, other times down to earth. Not long ago in a formal, white-tablecloth restaurant perched on the cliffs high above the sea on the Amalfi Coast, our handsome, hunky, tuxedoed waiter, after we ate our artfully arranged plates of pasta, returned to the table with a big platter of seconds. Still hunky and handsome, his presence had transformed into Mamma, looking eager to serve us more! More! More! Everyone said yes, of course

Definitely ask for help in choosing the wine. There are so many good local wines, and your waiter knows what is best with what you are eating. Many house wines are great, especially if you are having only a glassful. Or two.

Every restaurant throughout Napoli, throughout Campania, has its own source of mozzarella. Some are more or less salty or chewy, each with the flavors and aroma that come from the diet of the buffalo, the fermenting agents used, the artistry of the cheesemakers. More often than not, I find myself choosing a restaurant based on memories of the mozzarella: this one is perfect, that one I'm less fond of, that one I can't wait to eat again. Because eating mozzarella is the one thing I know that will happen that night (or afternoon, if it is lunch).

But not all restaurants offer mozzarella. Some offer a plate of cured meats and various local cheeses instead (*gli affettati*, "the slices").

Even fine dining tells the story on the plate: history, tradition, agriculture, local culture, and sensuality of taste brought together in a way that is so bright that it might be seen as brash. Each bite screams at you, "Taste me! Me next!"

When chefs know traditional flavor but are trained in starred restaurants, they are able to take the flavors and emotions they conjure up and reinterpret them in a way that tastes fresh. It might prod the eater intellectually, artistically, gastronomically; yet its character remains uniquely, distinctly Neapolitan. I'm not going to say that a contemporary food outlook always works: I've had some dire and bizarre meals not only in Naples but also throughout Italy. Soy sauce, curry, or avocados might appear without reason, but take a chance—it might surprise you. Usually, though, the modern face of *la cucina Napoletana* is more in the restructuring rather than in the obliterating of traditional flavors.

Here are a few contemporary dishes I've picked up (and put in my mouth) lately: a bitter orange tart with fresh almonds; olives and anchovies with a hit of curry in the oil; artichokes and candied lemon added to lobster *taglierini*; fish wrapped in fried eggplant sitting in a sauce of tomato and ricotta! (Fish and cheese? Yes.) Ravioli filled with eggplant parmigiana, foie gras with red onion sorbet and raspberries, babà with candied tomato.

These days many pizza makers are—like that other unsung hero, the barista—true chefs and artists. Their pizzas are their creations, their artistic expression that becomes part of you when you bite into it. Even sandwiches can be art; for instance, *pizzaiolo* Enzo Coccia, in his highly esteemed La Notizia pizzeria, makes sandwiches on the bread he bakes in his pizza oven. "I want people to experience a different way to enjoy pizza," he has been known to say. He slices a flattish bread roll, filling it with ingredients like mortadella with pistachio pesto. It is a thing of beauty because of the thought put into making it and because of his dough—that dough is magic.

A SNAPSHOT OF SOME OF MY FAVORITE RESTAURANTS INSIDE THE CITY

Rosiello

Rosiello, one of Naples's most famous and esteemed restaurants, evolved from a home kitchen with Mamma at the stove to a restaurant with celebrity clientele. No one bats an eyelid, because it is the most unpretentious, real, and delicious restaurant you could want.

The restaurant sits on a cliff overlooking the sea, its entrance a plain doorway in a sort of wooden fence on the street without a hint of what lies inside. Open the door, walk through a courtyard, and you are overlooking the Bay of Naples. Not too far in the distance is Capri. I was once there when the night sky over the sea flashed brightly colored fireworks. It took our breath away. (Turned out to be June 29, the feast day of the Apostles Saint Peter and Saint Paul.)

In 1933, Gelsomina Rosiello opened a small trattoria. It was a few tables and chairs set under a wisteria pergola (which is still there), where Gelsomina served homey dishes and meaty soups and stews with vegetables (escarole, broccoli, borage, and cabbage) from her garden. Pumpkin flower soup was one of her specialties, as was linguini with octopus (without tomato).

Currently, owner Salvatore Varriale presides over what is old-school unpretentious, slightly formal, a restaurant of respected excellence. Salvatore is likely to be the one to show you the whole fish, fresh from the sea, that you have ordered. He'll hold it up for you to see, and if you approve, the next time you see it is when it's beautifully roasted, laying on a platter.

For all the times I've visited Rosiello, I have never seen a menu. There's a discussion, and before you know it, food appears. The antipasto pizza stuffed with bitter greens, the *spaghetti alle vongole*, the pasta with garden vegetables, and—oh!—the tiny seaweed fritters: slightly salty, full of warm, yeasty air with a hint of the sea, like savory doughnut holes.

Gelsomina's garden down the hill is still there, and the vineyard is doing beautifully with grapes such as Falanghina, Fiano, Cacamosca, Sanguinella, and Per' e' palumm. Ask Salvatore which to choose with your meal.

Hosteria Toledo

Hosteria Toledo is a smallish, old-fashioned trattoria festooned with postcards, photographs of famous visitors, photographs of the owner's husband (a former professional boxer), dark wood, small tables, and the most delicious smells. It's a bit like a movie set about a Neapolitan trattoria. Hosteria Toledo started in 1951 in a little alleyway in the Spanish Quarter with Mamma dishing out spaghetti. Photos of her hands tossing the pasta festoon the menu. It still feels the same. I loved that the waitstaff was all women, how smooth and professional the service, how warm and caring the attitude. By my second visit I was greeted like an old friend, my waitress and I took selfies together, and I met her little daughter, who came to say goodnight before bedtime.

Tourists walk in slightly bemused. Apparently it is in many guidebooks. It doesn't matter! Everyone is welcomed warmly. I recognized locals, including the greengrocer who had saved me the last of the white peaches earlier in the day; he gave me a big smile. My friend Judy Witts Francini once brought a group of chefs to the restaurant. "My chefs *loved* this place," she said. So did I, and so, it seemed, did everyone else eating there.

When you enter, you pass a table of vegetable antipasto: grilled, marinated, braised, a whole balance of tangy, spicy, garlicky, soft, and crisp—a symphony of tastes and textures of the vegetables in season right this moment, without repetition. It is my favorite—simple, fresh, and cozy. The waitress and I agreed: *la parmigiana alla melanzane* is "something special." There is fish! Scallopini! *Pasta alla puveriello* is even on the menu—the old-fashioned "dish of poverty," which is served with a fried egg. And while we're on the pasta, it is so properly undercooked I wanted to laugh with glee at first bite. The house wine by the glass is delightful. But here is the thing: in Hosteria Toledo, I felt loved.

Europeo di Mattozzi, Ristorante e Pizzeria

Europeo de Mattozzi is both a traditional trattoria and a pizzeria. There are other restaurants called Mattozzi, but this is the one you want: old-school, walls lined with plaques, awards, hand-painted crockery, and framed photos. Businesspeople and politicos go for a traditional lunch; tourists and celebrities are there at any and all times.

The owner, Antonio, tells me proudly that the restaurant is now sixth-generation family owned. He has written a book about his family's heritage working in food (i.e., pizza), which was published by Slow Food. Motioning proudly toward his little son, helping around the restaurant, Antonio's face says it all: "the next generation of Mattozzi!"

A pizza tasting is recommended—each one baked with a different topping or baked blind, and then topped with a different ingredient that gently melts in—and don't forget the calzone with bitter greens and provola cheese. By the time you finish, you feel as though you have completed a master's thesis on what it means to be a pizza in Naples. Don't miss Mattozzi's meatballs, but remember, in Naples meatballs don't come on spaghetti: they come on a plate with a puddle of tomatoey sauce (to make *la scarpetta* with).

Mattozzi's was the first place I ate *pasta con patate* (pasta with potatoes)! It looked like the stodgiest thing I had ever seen, but it tasted like I might want to eat it (happily) forever. In the winter they serve *paccheri* pasta with Genovese sauce; in summer, it's with tiny sweet tomatoes. All the local specialties are there: octopus salad, pasta with clams and broccoli, bean soup with tripe, sausages with *friarielli*.

Timpani e Tempura

As its name suggests, Timpani e Tempura embraces East as well as West and in the process is utterly Neapolitan: tiny, packed with diners, full of good things to eat. Really enjoying—and respecting—the pleasures of the table is the most Neapolitan tradition of all.

Antonio and Lucio Tubelli started with a serious restaurant, Pozzo. Supporters of Slow Food loved it and held tastings and gatherings there. But the brothers liked the idea of a takeout shop selling house-prepared traditional dishes and switched from restaurant to tiny shop near Piazza del Gesu. When people came and bought arancini, mozzarella, vegetable fritters, slabs of pasta *timbale, parmigiana di melanzane*, and *rustici* (small country cakes), they wanted to eat right there. (Their selection of cheeses, both imported and local, is also excellent.) So they put a few tables and chairs out, and soon it was filled to bursting each afternoon—a modern take on the traditional the *tavola calda*.

Luciano Pignataro, on his wonderful wine blog, referred to Antonio Tubelli as "the last Monzù" for collecting and reinterpreting the foods of the Monzù era. Tubelli treats cuisine with immense respect, eschewing too much tomato, salt, or oil. He believes that no matter how much we might love them, they can overpower and spoil our tastes for more subtle flavors and textures.

Speaking with Tubelli about food, I could feel his excitement bubble up when he spoke of food and cooking and how seriously he values his culinary heritage. He has, at times, been feted and honored by Neapolitan culinary societies and given lectures and special dinners at various historical dining societies. One thing you will notice: people sitting at the tables are excited about eating and pay attention to the food, which is absolutely wonderful.

Sea Front Di Martino Pasta Bar: All Pasta, All the Time

Located at the seafront, Sea Front Pasta Bar is a stylish, innovative take on the most traditional of Neapolitan foods: pasta. Its location evokes ships sailing in and out of the harbor, fishermen bringing their daily catch to shore, Neapolitan citizens eating pasta in the streets. Across the way from the Castel Nuovo, where Naples's early kings ruled, it is next to the Piazza Municipio, with its exquisite fountain, which is brilliantly lit at night. People happily gather around it at almost any hour day or night (it's also a great place to eat the spaghetti to go).

The business consists of three parts: Downstairs is a shop selling a wide variety of Di Martino pasta, chic little aprons (it recently paired with Dolce & Gabbana), and metal pasta containers, all with the vintage logos. Around the corner is the takeout spaghetti: the old-school streets-of-Napoli way. Though it was once traditional to eat pasta in the streets of Naples, in recent times pizza and even international burgers have taken over. Where is the pasta? It's there, a takeout counter dispensing the tomato-sauced spaghetti that makes every Neapolitan's heart give a happy bounce. Buy a carton and eat at the fountain across the way. (Sitting at the fountain, a few droplets of tomato sauce on my chin, I felt as if I had been dropped into someone else's glamorous emotional life—perhaps Sophia Loren's.) They do give you a fork, but I'm never against eating it with my fingers. I have a photograph of Chef Pierpaolo Giorgio doing just that.

Upstairs is the elegant little restaurant, set up like a sushi bar, but with pasta chefs instead of sushi (though there is plenty of raw fish—crudo—a traditional delicacy of the area). Each course on the menu incorporates pasta of some sort, dancing between the traditional and the innovative. The idea is the brainchild of Giuseppe Di Martino of Di Martino Pasta and Peppe Guida, chef-owner of L'Antica Osteria di Nonna Rossa in Vico Equense. (Guida won my heart with his modern sensibility, yet reverence for the traditional, such as his grandmother's spaghetti cooked in lemon water with *provolone del Monaco*.) Chef Giorgio's dishes are traditional, yet with a different eye and attitude. The traditional pasta with mussels, for instance—he purees half the mussels with some of their cooking liquid and uses it as a sauce for the pasta along with the remaining whole mussels. He makes his shrimp pasta by sprinkling crustacean powder over lemon-buttered fettuccine—same ingredients, new attitude. I've tasted *le candele*, broken unevenly, with squid and squid ink crumble, but my favorite dish was the *fettuccelle*, a thickish fettuccine sauced with little more than its cooking water, parsley, olive oil, and a thin line that looked like gray dust sprinkled across the plate. The gray dust was crushed Darjeeling tea leaves, which gave fragrance and a tiny hit of bitterness to each bite.

Sometimes chefs come to hang out, cooking in the little kitchen with owner Giuseppe Di Martino—it's like a party. Sadly, I missed the night that Albert Sapere, elegant mozzarella man and gastronome, made *pasta cacio e pepe*, tossing it together in a cloth napkin and serving it in the cloth for the diner to eat with the hands.

If you order coffee at the end of the meal, it comes in your own tiny Moka espresso pot.

L'ebbrezza di Noe

With the trend toward wine bars and restaurants with a more relaxed, less formal structure of meals yet with a high standard of gastronomy, I give you Napoli's L'ebbrezza di Noe, an *enoteca, vineria, e degustazioni* (a wine shop, wine tasting, and the delicious things to go with it). Named in appreciative homage after the most famous of Michelangelo Buonarotti's frescos, the Sistine Chapel, it is, by day, a wine shop and, in the evening, a restaurant (or, as they term it, *tavola calma*—calm table—a pun on the traditional *tavola calda*, or hot table, which refers to prepared dishes to eat at one of a few tables in the corner of the shop or to take out).

Burger Joints

Now I'm going to say something that might shock you: hamburger. I know; it *is* shocking. But these are not fast food burgers. I'm talking about a big creative thing in a bun made with the care taken with other foods. Hand-chopped beef is to be counted on, and perhaps a fat, juicy ground chicken patty. You never know when a ball of mozzarella might show up. Burgers in Campania are far more Neapolitan than they are American.

Opened by three Neapolitans, 12 Morsi and Friends has an amazing array of local meats: local pork, *chianina* and wagyu-type beef, plump golden yellow chickens. It's a restaurant, not street food, so I wasn't sure where it would fit into the portrait of what and how Campania eats. Mr. Han serves his burger with zucchini and a sort of Parmigiano layer.

At Old Horse Pub, burgers are served with *provalone del Monaco*, yellow tomatoes (*pomodorini gialli*), and San Daniel ham. The pork burger is topped with arugula, bacon, cheddar fonduta, cherry tomatoes, and shards of grana padana on a big fat bun.

Sciue il Panino Vesuviano is a pub and burger bar with crazy, wild burgers located in Pomigliano d'arco, a municipality in the city area of Naples, north of Vesuvio. The area itself is a mix of housing and the auto and aerospace industries; its fame is "The Burger Store," also known as Scuie il panino Vesuviano, subtitled

Casa del Gusto (House of Taste). The burgers are often named for neighborhoods of Naples—the Spaccanapoli, the Vesuvio, and so forth—all with varying combinations of such things as *porchetta*, peppers, pancetta, cheeses, tiny balls of mozzarella, anchovies, arugula, and pistachios.

OUTSIDE THE CITY

The whole of the countryside, towns, regions, and islands are dotted with wonderful dining opportunities. There are also some truly terrible places. You can never tell what a restaurant is like unless it has been recommended, or until you sniff the air and just *know*.

There is a charming countryside tradition—especially in Ischia—of restaurants open only for requests. You ring ahead and ask, "Can we come today [or tonight, or whenever]?" They are usually amazing. Many *agriturismi* offer lunch and dinner not just for their guests but also to outside customers, like any restaurant. An *agriturismo* prepares the local foods of the season, often produced on their farm.

Here is a little snapshot of where I've been, what I've eaten, and perhaps what to expect.

Ristorante Pascalucci

Ristorante Pascalucci is located near Benevento—a no-frills, old-fashioned, hearty food ristorante. At its helm is chef, cooking teacher, and author Arturo Iengo. The dishes are hearty inland food rather than delicate seaside fare, and you can end your meal with some of the local Strega and Torrone. It is an abundant place, a place of conviviality. I also remember a particularly lovely dish of grilled meat.

Gran Telese

Gran Telese is a once-glamorous spa resort, its rambling, graceful grounds, manicured lawns, and curving driveway hinting at the old-time splendor of its past. Once upon a dolce vita, film stars and celebrities flocked there, posing for the paparazzi, taking the waters. Named for Terme Telese, the hot spring that bubbled up in the year 300 AD following an earthquake, its sulfuric waters are said to be very healthy—they are even bottled and sold. Its swimming pool is gorgeous and huge.

Eating there has always been a delight of old-fashioned elegant goodness. Traditional dishes with finesse but not somersaults and fireworks. I can't single out a specific dish to extole—everything has always been good—and with regard to food, good in Campania means really good.

What I remember from my last visit is the waiter—the saddest, most depressed waiter in the world. Our waiter was depressed as only a Neapolitan could be: he was so fully depressed that he was practically exuberant in his depression. He was so dedicated to it, so creative with it, that it was no longer depressing. It was art. Each time he made his way to our table and around it, we got further reports as to why he hated Italy and why he wanted to go back to the United Kingdom, where he once lived. We were staying at the spa for a few days, so we got a full dose of his life and his trials and tribulations. "Why, oh, why did I have to come home to Naples?" he cried. He dismissed the sunshine as a taunt by nature: "How can there be such beautiful sunshine when I am so depressed? I prefer the gray of England." At mention of the beautiful food of Campania, he would say, "But I love fish and chips! I like baked beans!" Toward the end, I began to think he wasn't sad at all, but rather enjoying having an audience for his complaints. And, to be honest, he was as wonderful a waiter as he was an entertainer.

Historia Birreria

Behind Talese Terme is Mount Pugliano, down from the castle, and in the little town of Puglianello are two restaurants, one devoted to wine and one to beer. Across from the castle, Historia Birreria is a very cool craft beer pub that serves artisanal handcrafted beers along with its interpretation of pub grub. Its website says it best: "We do not want to please our guests but amaze them." Personally, I *was* amazed. The setting is warm and charming, woody with a welcoming bar staff, like pubs should be, and the food was far more exciting that any pub where I've eaten. It referenced UK pub style with Campania food style: smoked buffalo mozzarella and eggplant and Neapolitan meatballs with cheddar and truffles. There is tripe fried in a rice-flour batter and served with ginger gelee, herb salad, wasabi mayo, and freeze-dried vegetable bits.

Steak is served with smoked salt, salmon eggs, pickled eggs, and small droplets of geleed truffle essence. Burgers are cut in half and each half topped differently: the first with lardo, caramelized onions, red pepper pate, and a local cheese; the second half with homemade tomato chutney, spreadable buffalo mozzarella, and smoked anchovies. Bread and chocolate is on the menu as dessert, and the menu of the day includes "a surprise."

Osteria d'Entroterra il Foro dei Baroni

At Osteria d'Entroterra il Foro dei Baroni, wine, not beer, is the focus, and the menu is devoted to celebrating the local foods of il Sannio, also known as Benevento province. Pheasant ravioli with herbs of the fields, smoked eggplant with a basil mousse, and a tomato salad of sliced San Marzanos dressed with celery-onion gelee, crisp bits of fried breadcrumbs, and a scattering of marinated white beans. The *tagliata* is of buffalo, and the traditional stuffed red pepper is served in a pool of silky truffled potato sauce (truffles are local to Irpinia). The one dessert that stays in my mind is a sphere of airy almond cake filled with lemon cream, little bits of different taste and texture sensations such as crumble, salt flakes, and extra virgin olive oil. Their wine selection—sigh. Put yourself in their hands.

La Casa del Nonno 13

La Casa del Nonno 13 in Salerno is a collection of three restaurants. One is gastronomical, with both Michelin stars and the aim of providing intellectual and sensual stimulation with each bite. Sometimes I like to visit the website menus and daydream (cue daydream music): ravioli stuffed with *la parmigiana di melanzane*, or a tiny pizza of salt cod with fennel, cucumber, orange, capers, and savory olive powder. Caramelized sweetbreads with tomato carpaccio came with a slow-cooked egg yolk, tarallo-crumb *gomasio* and kimchi sauce, while confit cod with Neapolitan vegetables brings us right back to Campania terra firma. The dessert of crunchy flax with ricotta cream, orange jam, and carrot cake sounds like something I might be thrilled with, as does the *sfogliatella* with buffalo ricotta, pear sauce, and licorice (the plants grow locally). The gastronomical restaurant is in the Mercato Sant' Eustachio, along with the osteria in San Severino.

At the osteria, chef Assunta Rispoli is in the kitchen. As the Neapolitan saying goes, "The best food is always the food of home," and Assunta's cooking captures that food-made-just-for-you essence. There's spaghetti with tomatoes, thick, rare grilled *fiorentina* steak, and local products such as the onions Assunta is especially fond of.

The Salumeria+Cucina is in Salerno in a cave-like dwelling that started as a wine cellar and was used as a hiding place during World War II. Here, now, chef Giovanni Mellone combines his chef's skills and visions with fine artisanal cheeses and cured meats. The cheese list is amazing, with goat, cow, sheep, buffalo, and even donkey milk cheese on the menu.

Agriturismo Al Celone

Agriturismo Al Celone is located near Foggia. Go there, and don't miss the antipasti. The cheese, the salame, the warm hospitality—just do it.

La Trattoria O Romana

You might not think of traveling to the tomato fields of Sarno, but if you do, it is a revelation how many good restaurants there are. People expect no less. The more I tasted, the more I spoke with people, the more I saw how pure their love of good food was.

If you were making a film about a trattoria, you could choose no better restaurant than this: it looks the part, it *feels* the part, and the food it serves come straight from the heart, reflecting the local specialties. Indeed, if you were to write a book about the local specialties, you could choose no better restaurant than O Romana in Sarno. The menu celebrates everything local, in season, ancient traditions interpreted by the chef, often with innovations. The food is so traditional and local that it seems to have existed before the tradition even developed.

Reginella

At the Pomadoro San Marzano Day tomato festival in Sarno, I flitted through the crowds in the sweltering sun. I passed the shack ladling out alcoholic tomato cocktails, a tent frying pizza (and all the classic *fritti*), a couple of guys making fresh mozzarella, a bruschetta table, and, at the end, a sort of pizza/pasta celebration. Along the way I stopped at the classic pizzeria Reginella for a slice of Margherita. The crowds took pity on me, seeing that I had no pizza in my hands, and rushed me to the front, where, halfway there, someone rushed a pizza slice to me. I took a bite, swooned, and said, "I have never had pizza this good." I was told, "Yes, maybe this is true for you, but for us, here, this is the way good pizza should always be."

Another time, while waiting for a train in Sarno, I stopped for a coffee at a *caffè-gelateria* next to the station. As I downed my espresso, everyone in the *caffè* wanted to speak with me (okay, maybe it was to poke fun at the huge coffees of Starbucks compared with the tiny shots of espresso right there in the little ceramic cup). I like to think that they were admiring my Neapolitan coffee-drinking skills. The owner told me about how she makes her gelato, by hand with a big whisk and wooden paddle, and before you know it, I'm in the back room with her peeking into containers of her fresh ingredients: mashed peaches, chocolate, lemons from her garden. The *caffè* is owned by two sisters; in fact, that is its name: Sisters' Caffè and Gelateria. One of the sisters told me that their brother owns a pizzeria down the piazza and that it's very good. I've got Sarno on my schedule next tomato—and gelato—season.

Granita al Pomadoro (Tomato Granita)

Innovative rather than traditional, and so refreshing during tomato season.

¼ cup sugar
2 tablespoons water
1 can San Marzano whole
   tomatoes, broken up, plus their
   juices

2 ripe raw tomatoes, chopped
   coarsely (skinned if you like; I'm
   lazy that way and seldom do)
Juice of ½ lemon
Several drops of vanilla extract
A pinch of salt

In a saucepan, stir to combine the sugar and the water. Heat together over medium to medium-low heat, stirring a few times until the sugar melts; then cook a few minutes until the mixture bubbles and boils.

Add the canned tomatoes all at once, taking care not to splash. Stir until well combined. Remove from heat and add the raw tomatoes, lemon juice, vanilla, and salt. Taste, and if the mixture seems too strong, add a little bit—say, half a cup—of water.

Pour into a wide bowl or casserole dish and freeze. As the granules of ice freeze around the edges of the bowl, scrape them up as you do with any granita. Scrape every so often, every thirty minutes or so, until frozen.

Variation: Three Tomatoes Filled with Their Own Granita

For a unique presentation, choose three smallish tomatoes of different colors— yellow, green, orange; the different colors increase visual delight and offer a variety of flavors. Cut off the tops and spoon out the flesh. Freeze the hollowed-out tomatoes on a baking sheet.

Omit the raw tomatoes from the basic recipe, dividing the canned tomato mixture among three bowls. Add the tomato pulp from each tomato to one of the bowls of canned tomatoes. Freeze, scraping the bowls every thirty minutes or so. When the granitas are all frozen, match the granita to its corresponding tomato, stuff it with the mixture, and return stuffed tomatoes to the freezer until ready to serve.

Not far from Naples in the town of Palma, "local boy" Pietro Parisi has returned home from his years of cooking with star chefs in glittering, international temples to gastronomy. In 2005, he opened his own restaurant, Era Ora, meaning "it's about time." Here, in this modern adaptation of an osteria-pizzeria, he has distilled the techniques and precision of great chefs and focused it on the cuisine of his home. Indeed, he calls himself the "peasant chef" because the specialties and foods of the region are so close to his heart. The restaurant is affiliated with Slow Food;

one might even call it a holistic restaurant due to how Parisi eschews waste and celebrates the local heritage, along with the farmers who grow the ingredients. One of Chef Parisi's most famous dishes is eggplant parmigiana steamed in a glass jar. It's hard to explain how wonderful this dish is—for one thing, to me part of the huge joy of *la parmigiana* is its crusty topping, but in the jar it is delicate, light, soft, and tender. It is exceptional. The menu is so exciting and down-to-earth that simply reading it nearly makes me giddy with excitement.

Also in the shadow of Vesuvius, in the town of San' Anastasia on Mount Somma, is a beloved restaurant known as 'E Curti. Its curious name translates from the Neapolitan to English as "Dwarves." Two dwarf brothers opened it as a tavern 1952, calling it O Monaco (The Monk) in honor of their uncle, who decided to leave the priesthood and devote himself to having a good time running the tavern. They served meals, and the two brothers were devoted to rediscovering local culinary heritage and reimagining old dishes, especially from the pages of Cavalcanti and Corrado.

Today's 'E Curti is run by descendants of the two dwarves, famous for their beautiful renditions of local home cooking and also for their bottled Nucillo, a walnut liqueur. Local tradition insists that the unripe walnuts be harvested only on June 24; the bottles that 'E Curti produces has written on the label the trees from which the walnuts were picked.

SORRENTO

Antica Trattoria was opened in 1930 as a salted cod and stockfish shop. Owner Carmela Ioviero began to offer dishes prepared with these ingredients. In 1975 they began serving typical local dishes, and by 1980 they were stretching to embrace a slightly more gastronomical level of cooking. Today the kitchen mixes tradition with creativity, stuffing ravioli with ricotta and lemon and served with seafood and offering local lamb with a sauce of *provolone del Monaco* cheese and soups filled with sea creatures and fish roasted in salt or poached in *aqua pazza*.

If you want a pizza, La Pizzeria Fortuna alla Duchesca is the hometown of Naples's legendary *pizzaiolo*, Enzo Coccia. He grew up in this pizzeria. Today two of his brothers run the place, as dedicated to pizza as Enzo.

Another place for pizza is L'Antico Forno a legna Da Franco, which also serves the typical saltimbocca, a sandwich made with pizza dough and stuffed with *fiordilatte* cheese from Agerola and raw ham. Take your saltimbocca across the street to the Fondo L'Agrumaio, a two-hundred-year-old citrus garden, and sit on a wooden bench under the trees to enjoy your sandwich with the air scented by fruit trees.

Enjoy an *aperitif* at the famous Fauno bar in Torquato Tasso square, whose origins trace back to the 1950s. Have a dessert at the Primavero Bar; the lemon *delizie*, sponge cake filled with lemon cream, is pretty great.

Da Filippo has served traditional cuisine for more than twenty-five years. Outside the center of Sorrento, it is renowned especially for its homemade desserts such as fig tart with Sorrento hazelnuts, Sorrento lemon tart, *pastiera*, sorbets, and ice creams.

In Campania, in fact, throughout Italy, the legendary hotel Don Alfonso 1890 is mentioned in hushed, respectful, yet affectionate tones. A food colleague remarked recently that she nearly cried when she ate there; it was emotional, beautiful, inspiring.

Located in Sant Agata sui Due Golfi, up a long winding drive from Sorrento and overlooking the Bay of Nerano on the Amalfi side, the genteel Don Alfonso 1890 was established that year, when its founder returned from America and opened the hotel. The Iaccarino family has run it since then. It wasn't until the economic boom in the north sent the newly wealthy middle class on vacations to the south that the hotel added a fancy restaurant. It served the nouveau riche with plates of (mostly international, as expected) luxury.

Then came the 1960s and 1970s, and with the changing times came new ways of thinking: Anything is possible! Follow your dreams! The dream of the Iaccarinos' younger generation, Livia and Alfonso, was to translate the idea of luxury to their traditional food culture. They imagined a cuisine reflecting the goodness of this sun-drenched land: traditional, yet lighter and more creative. They dreamed of a kitchen, stimulating both gastronomically and emotionally.

They were truly pioneers. Believing strongly that the quality of a cuisine begins in the garden, they planted eight hectares of fruits and vegetables and began to feature dishes that used lemons, tomatoes, olive oil, and local fish. It formed the basis of their new culinary style, innovation combined with respect for the local culture of both the Sorrentine and the Amalfitano coasts, where it is located.

The wine cellar is an extraordinary collection of more than twenty-five thousand bottles, carefully stored in an ancient nook carved out of a pre-Roman tunnel, many stone steps into the earth. There is also an aging cave for cheeses.

Some of the dishes on the menu might include marinated lobster with zucchini flowers, a summery salad with a vegetable ravioli and tomato sorbet, or fried cod with buffalo yogurt ice cream, padrone peppers, sweet-sour lemon compote, and crisp lemon chips. Red mullet is served with lemon gnocchi, capers, and three contrasting sauces. The cuisine is exquisitely sophisticated, ambitious, yet still the essence of the Mediterranean.

Don Alfonso's attention to detail and celebration of local ways have elevated it to high esteem, leading the way for other restaurants throughout the area. The chefs and sommeliers who have trained there have often gone on to spread this particular beautiful finesse.

Lo Stuzzichino in Massa Lubrenese, Sant Agata sui Due Golfi, serves typical local foods prepared extraordinarily well. It's a family-run restaurant with a warm heart and delicious food. From the greens and the fish come antipasto and *fritto misto*. Or try the *parmigiana di melanzane*. There is *scialatielli*, the handmade pasta with clams, zucchini, and lemon; *paccheri di Gragnano con pomodorino del Vesuvio*; and the traditional *cannellone alla Sorrentina*. But maybe they have prepared a warming soup for you: *maritata* or savory cabbage with chestnuts.

It's a wonderful area for cheeses, and if you decide on dessert, there's ricotta and pear torte, a simple cake, and *la delizie al limone*, a lemon specialty cakelet of the area.

In the touristy town of Amalfi, Da Gemma offers food to make you swoon: fish and pasta and traditional local dishes prepared with open-mindedness, curiosity, and great generosity. On a hot day, I went there with a group. In the procession of extraordinary dishes (yet ordinary dishes for Amalfi), I picked up a gorgeous lemon, and in the act of sniffing it absentmindedly, I swear I found my spiritual center.

La Caravella at Amalfi first opened in 1959 in the historical center and rose through the heady 1960s, enchanting visitors and earning Michelin star status. Its cuisine evokes its maritime past, linking flavors of East and West, products of sea and land. Old Amalfi recipes are envisaged for modern times, often in tasting menus of small, exciting dishes. The restaurant is also an *enoteca* and a museum, housing a collection of Amalfi Coast ceramics dating from 1800 to the present. This past summer, typical dishes included red shrimp tartare with buffalo ricotta, cream of pumpkin soup, and squid with fried bread. For dessert, there is a parfait of almonds with lemon sauce, coffee, chocolate, and sponge cake.

As touristy as Amalfi is, just a few kilometers away is the quiet cove-like town of Atrani. No crowds, the streets were quiet. I remember having a lovely meal, typical local food in what looked like it was once a fisherman's hut. I don't remember what we ate—it was good and local—but I do remember a feeling of peacefulness. It was like visiting your aunt and uncle who ran away to a fishing village and now were welcoming you to their table.

In Massa Lubrense, on the Amalfi Coast, Lo Scoglio da Tommaso is one of those casual places whose menu exists not to impress but to delight. A wide array of vegetables is offered as an antipasto, the garden gives fresh vegetables such as favas, seafood is utterly fresh (and sometimes crisply fried), and pasta is served with tomatoes, or zucchini and basil, or clams, or lobster. No delicate jellies here—just fresh food with bright, clear flavors.

Since 2012, Tenuta Antica Braceria has been serving pizza and grilled meats with a modern sensibility—traditional flavors with occasional far-flung ones. (In Campania, deliciousness is most important; if it tastes wonderful, that is the tradition!) It is located in the countryside between Amalfi Coast and Salerno near Cava de'Terreni.

Not long ago I came upon one of its menus for Christmas lunch. I love its balance between traditional and international, rustic and sophisticated:

A soup of barley, pumpkin, porcini, and truffle
Fonduta di mozzarella with cima di rape/rapini, and a pork meatball
Risotto enriched with dry provolone
Grilled rare steak with potatoes and chimichurri sauce
Desserts [unspecified]

In the seaside town/village of Cetara, the restaurant Il Convento became famous for many reasons, one of which was a visit by Anthony Bourdain's television show, *No Reservations*. When I went to Cetara to visit the anchovy, tuna, and *colatura* workshops, however, it had yet to be discovered by the media. After visiting the fish-preserving workshops, Il Convento set out a specially prepared meal in the shade near the tiny dock. Each dish—pasta, mozzarella, vegetables—featured the fish sauce *colatura*. It was the chef's enthusiastic tribute to the tiny fish at Cetara's heart. The luscious lemon, anchovy, and mozzarella pizza whose charm has spread far and wide was created first at Il Convento.

On Ischia, there's an absolutely charming little wine-bar trattoria, right on the harbor of Ischia Porto, called Un Attino Di Vino. This translates to "A Moment of Wine," or, alternatively, "Divine Moment," and captures the spirit of its owner-chef Raimundo Triolo. In the evenings there is often live music, with Raimundo joining in.

Originally from Sicily, trained in Paris, and an islander by marriage, he is truly an original. His most inspiring quality is his sincerity—how intensely happy he seems with every movement he makes, every fish he scales. Sometimes, when I am far away and perhaps feeling down, my spirits lift just thinking that someone like him can exist, creating his small but perfect vision.

There are tables outside on the lovely sea-edge port for sipping wine and nibbling bruschetta. Small boats pull up regularly offering their freshest catch to Raimundo. He loves fish, he loves pasta, and he loves wine, so these are the things you will eat: crudo with pesto, pasta with zucchini flowers, *paccheri* with seafood, and fish with fresh mint and a layer of thinly sliced potatoes. I want to try his mullet with orange, bay leaves, cherry tomatoes, pine nuts, and Sicilian extra virgin olive oil.

I had been to Da Paolina on the island of Capri several times before I realized it was called anything other than "the lemon garden." At the end of a rural (read: dirt) road in a lemon grove: that is Da Paolina. Its courtyard terrace is filled with lemon trees that have grown together to form a canopy of lemons and leaves over the dining tables. Try the antipasto table or anything with lemons and pasta and seafood. I'm issuing a warning right now about the dessert/*dolce* table: It is lavish and abundant, and you can taste anything and everything you like. One of my dining buddies turned to me and said, "It's like being at an orgy. I don't know what to try next!"

As homey and informal as Da Paolina is, Il Riccio is opposite on the elegance spectrum: clean design, light and airy, with a menu devoted to the sea (especially its namesake sea urchin). Pasta, *risotti*, all the dishes they serve with seafood are so beautifully rich, but even dishes without any seafood at all, only vegetables, are wonderful. Il Riccio also has a cool pastry room with a dessert bar in which I spent a few sugar-induced moments of delicious madness trying to decide what to taste.

Located in the charming Pozzuoli's main harbor area of restaurants, Ristaurante Bobo is at first the very picture of a tourist restaurant, perhaps a tourist restaurant with a sign that says, "We are a tourist restaurant!" So, yes, I was initially put off. But when Bobo himself appeared, followed by the food, I was won over. He fusses over his guests, popping up here and there with what seems like superhuman energy. Most of all, Bobo adores fish. It is his passion. On his website it says, "*il pesce fresco preferisce essere cucinato da Bobo!*" Translation: "The fish *want* to be cooked by Bobo!" I think the pasta does as well.

Il Cibo di Strada

Naples's Street Food Inheritance: An Ancient Tradition

Buying, selling, and eating food in the streets of Campania is an ancient tradition, probably with origins in Roman *thermopolium* (food stalls, as we have seen from ancient ruins such as Pompeii), though it could be earlier.

Pasta was first eaten in the street (with the hands!), as was pizza. They were cheap and nutritious, and many didn't have their own kitchens. At one point, anything that could be sold and eaten on the street was: soup poured over bread, marinated vegetables, granita, and coffee.

These days, the delight and quality of street food seems to be having a renaissance. Walk down the street, especially in the *centro storico*, and peer into the glass cases of the shops that line the streets: pizza-like pies filled with bitter greens, focaccia topped with tomatoes or potatoes, pastries filled with cheese, ham, and vegetables, winter *sfogliatelle* stuffed with savory rather than sweet

Il Cibo di Strada (continued)

(Genovese or sausage-*friarielli*). Pizza is famously sold in the street, pizza *a libretto* or *portafoglio*, found especially in pizzerias in via dei Tribunali, port'Alba, and piazza Cavour. Most markets have a pizza window nearby for the crowds' midday break.

From Mergellina to via Caracciolo, there are still several little shops selling *taralli nzogna e pepe* (salty rusks with pork fat and black pepper). Street shops used to sell *'o spassatiempo*, a mix of baked hazelnuts, pumpkin seeds, toasted chickpeas, and lupinos in brine. Now, not so much. Other street foods that are rarely seen these days include *nervetti* (cartilage from veal and pork feet, cooked until tender, pressed into a loaf, then sliced); *maruzzelle*—snails—cooked in tomato sauce; *O'brok e purp*, or octopus soup; and frog soup, which was fed to babies.

But if some of the old things are disappearing, new things keep popping up. The richness of noshing opportunities in the street matches Naples's frenzy for walking. Walking around and discovering new things is my happiest pastime. The little things that appear when you walk the same places each day, the life of the street, are so stimulating. And walking makes you hungry. So convenient!

Some things you might find and eat in the streets:

Panini Napoletani are sandwiches on crusty rolls filled with typical Neapolitan foods—bitter greens and sausages (*salsicce e friarielli*), ragù, mozzarella, prosciutto, sautéed mushrooms or eggplant slices in olive oil with red chile flakes—whatever is available and irresistible.

Panuozzo is a sandwich of local ingredients stuffed into a pizza-like flatbread.

Grilled, whole *caciocavallo* cheeses hang over a charcoal grill at just the right height for the heat of the flames to soften and melt the cheese, which is then scraped off and plopped onto a piece of country bread, which is toasted on the same grill.

'O Pere e Musso—cow tripe, heads, feet, and various offal—is sold from stalls that are draped not only with the meats but also with lemons. You can identify them at a distance by the sunny yellow lemons hanging everywhere. (The first time I saw one, I thought they were selling lemon granita and was hugely disappointed when I realized they were selling innards instead.)

Pizza *a portafoglio*, or pizza to go, is folded into quarters somewhat like a wallet, so that it can be eaten while you walk without the melty cheese and tomato inside falling out. Eating a pizza *a portafoglio* is a different experience from eating a flat pizza in a restaurant with a knife and fork. For one thing, the restaurant pizza has a larger variety of toppings from which to choose, and it's served with a knife and fork, which feels different from eating with your hands. It's more formal and complex, whereas a pizza *a portafoglio* is handed to you, its toppings closed up against each other,

Il Cibo di Strada (continued)

the whole thing wrapped in paper. You hold it, biting in gingerly, carefully (since it's hot, hot, hot!), feeling the soft and chewy crust in your teeth with its bright tomatoey topping.

Crisp, crunchy, utterly Neapolitan (also Pugliese), taralli are a cross between crackers and grissini/breadsticks. Some are studded with almonds, fennel, chile flakes, or black pepper. I've even had some with bitter greens kneaded in before baking. There are small taralli, big taralli, rough-textured taralli, and smooth taralli, all delicious whether you are munching as you walk or sitting down to sip a glass of wine.

Carcio arustat—artichokes—can be found roasting over open fires in season. When you find them, eat one, and please eat one for me—I might miss the season. They are so good.

A world of fried things (*fritti*) is sold in *friggitoria* (vendors of fried goodies), with the admonition, *frienn' magnann'*, in the local dialect ("from the fryer to your plate!"—in other words, freshly made, eat while it's hot!). Pizzerie also sell fried things. *Palle 'e Riso* is the Neapolitan version of arancini, croquettes of risotto stuffed with something delicious such as cheese, which melts and makes you oh so happy. Artichokes, zucchini, cauliflower, ricotta, cow's brain, and chunks of liver are all offered in the frying frenzy that is Naples. Why not get a *cuoppo* or a *cuppetiello*, a paper cone filled with an assortment of fried delicacies?

One of the most beguiling deep-fried goodies imaginable—so enticing it could make me scream—and worth eating, even if it takes several days to digest, is the *frittatina di maccheroni*: crisp patties or croquettes of macaroni with cheese, ham, peas, and sometimes a layer of braised beef and onions in the middle. One evening at Pizza a Portafoglio on Via Toledo, the young woman behind the counter and I bonded over food talk. Soon she was sharing the secret of their *frittatine* (they only use Di Martino bucatini broken into four lengths). They stuff the insides with Genovese sauce in addition to creamy béchamel, cheese, ham, little green polka dots of peas, all encased in batter and fried to crispness. I bought one, meaning to eat just a little bit, but once I started, I couldn't stop. One more bite turned into the whole thing. The next day, I was still digesting. Sometimes I think I am still digesting—two months later. But happily so: *frittatine* may not be light, but they are comfortingly delicious.

Krapfen, also known as Graffe, are light, fluffy, raised doughnuts, often made with potatoes. A long-ago transplant from Vienna are now a beloved street treat: plain with a sprinkle of sugar or filled with Nutella or lemon. These days the krapfen are filled after they are fried, but traditionally they are filled before frying.

Il Cibo di Strada (continued)

Mozzarella in Carrozza is a sandwich of fresh mozzarella (and often anchovy or another highly flavorful ingredient) dipped in flour and egg or batter, then fried until the bread crisps and the cheese melts.

Pagnottiello is a hefty, savory pastry/roll that makes a brilliant breakfast if you are not one for sweet things. It is a soft dough stuffed with ham, cheese, black pepper, and eggs, then baked until crisp and melty and irresistible. It's much like a casatiello, except prepared in individual rolls rather than large loaves.

GELATO

One thing you can be sure of in Napoli is that you are never far from a gelato—in a cone, cup, or brioche. All gelati are not of the same excellence, however. To start with, look for the term *artiginale*; it means "artisanal" but not in a hipster way—it really *is* artisanal. Of course, something can be artisan made and still be disappointing. That's why I've been hitting the streets of Napoli eating gelato, just for you.

I was on my way to a recommended *gelateria*, but it was so hot, and I was tired and wanted a gelato right away, not after a long walk as planned. I sat down on a bench and probably kvetched to myself for a moment. When I looked up, in front of me was a bright white-and-blue storefront with the logo of a lovely cow: Il Gelato Mennella. People gathered around it munching ice cream.

Once I fought my way through the crowd, I was licking a crisp, slightly caramelized shop-made cone filled with gelato—a scoop each of dark chocolate and almond milk. It was melting fast in the sweltering sunshine and I was doing my best to keep up. Sitting on the bench in Piazza Carità, feeling the breeze, loving that gelato, I was thinking, *Are these life's best moments?* Also, *What flavor will I get tomorrow?* My future in gelato tasting felt limitless.

Then I mused about the name: Mennella. Not an uncommon name in the area, surely it couldn't be the same Mennella as my favorite babà bakery, the one I wrote about for *Saveur Magazine* once upon a time. The same Mennella of delicate, spongy, light babà soaked in rum, filled with whipped cream and wild strawberries? It is a common name; I'm sure they're not related.

The next day I found another Mennella gelateria, and then another—in total, four—so I checked the website and found that, yes, the gelato is indeed the same family, the brainchild of the Mennella sons. My world felt smaller and cozier immediately.

I tried the pistachio, which was too gritty and nutty for my taste, I wasn't a fan, but, oh, the cantaloupe, peach, *fior di latte*, and apricot joined the dark chocolate and almond milk in my gelato hall of fame. As I finished a brioche filled with gelato, a friend—Judy Witts Francini again—messaged me: "Go to the *gelateria*, you know the one—with the monkey." She couldn't think of its name. In the meantime, as I walked the city, I tried other gelati. They were okay, but I was now devoted to Mennella. Then Judy remembered the name: Gelateria della Scimmia (the monkey part of the logo). I got there almost immediately—I can't bear to think of life if I had missed it. I had its namesake banana ice cream pop covered with dark chocolate.

Since 1933, when the current owner's grandfather set up shop, the family has been making artisanal gelato, sorbettos, ice cream molds, and delicious frozen delicacies, only in season. They are also famous for their *zuccottini* (tiny individual bombes of thinly sliced, rum-soaked cake filled with gelato), as well as spumone.

Spumone (plural: spumoni), darling of Italian American restaurants during my California childhood, is not an Italian thing. If you've ever indulged in a gelato-eating jaunt through Italy and not found spumone, here is the reason: It isn't Italian at all; it is Neapolitan. The name comes from the world *spuma*, which means foam, and *-one*, used as a suffix meaning "big." So spumone is a kind of "big foam." Usually molded, it has three layers of ice cream—chocolate, pistachio, and cherry—with whipped cream and candied fruit, pistachios and/or almonds, rum, vanilla, and cinnamon. It is not a subtle creation—it is as wildly flavored as Naples itself. Spumone can be served in individual molds, in scoops, or in slabs cut from a loaf-shaped mold.

It is said that the American and UK ice cream flavor, Neapolitan, came from the layering of spumone's three different colors and flavors. Chocolate, strawberry, and vanilla were less challenging flavors for local taste. *Tortoni*, *zuccotti*, all sorts of molded frozen desserts crossed the Atlantic, but Neapolitan ice cream is the only one with staying power.

I had tragic gelato tastings as well. There was a time at a famous *gelateria* that I didn't even finish my cone. Luckily, though, I discovered Vincenzo Bellavia pastry shop, established in 1925, whose care and attention to their pastries is, frankly, beautiful. My first bite of their *sfogliatelle* was exhilarating. I didn't know whether to laugh or cry with happiness. However, I made the mistake of not trying the gelato until the last day of my last trip. But you won't make that mistake now that I've advised you, right?

And then there is granita. In the summer when it is so very hot, granita will save your life. They are sold everywhere, often outside cafes but also from their own stalls. The flavors vary in both variety and quality—some artisan made, others a neon-glowing color that doesn't auger well for their quality. Last summer's heat wave prompted this personal research and review of granitas: espresso, to die for; cantaloupe, so brightly colored, so fresh tasting; watermelon, too sweet and flat and pink. You could taste lemon granitas from all over town, and each would be slightly different: some sweeter, some more sour, some with the hit of bitter peel. On a hot day, nothing refreshes you quite as well. *Ghiacciate* is the Neapolitan version of a snow cone; if you come upon one and the weather is hot, it could be a good idea.

TROUBLE IN GASTRONOMICAL PARADISE: PUBLIC SERVICE ANNOUNCEMENT

After eating in so many excellent restaurants, I had forgotten that on the first night I had returned to Napoli (on my second trip), our dinner of classic dishes was miserable: stale, tasteless, pathetic, depressing. (Though the spaghetti was properly al dente, the tomatoes delicious, and no cheese served on it, as Neapolitan spaghetti with tomatoes should be served. But the rest? Even the *sfogliatelle* for dessert was stale.)

Even though I knew intellectually that it was possible—because of others telling me about their own decidedly un-delicious experiences—I had forgotten that food could be terrible in Naples and Campania. Throughout the years that I had been coming to Naples, a long parade of fabulous meals followed that really bad meal, and I had forgotten it.

So one night on Ischia, I let my guard down. Ischia is the island that boasts some of my favorite restaurants; yet I bowed to the wishes of my traveling companions. They didn't want to make reservations, they didn't want to travel too far, they didn't want to make a big deal of it. I couldn't understand; if you're in Campania, why *not* make a big deal of every eating opportunity that comes along? But I was in the minority, so I headed with them to the most tourist of tourist roads.

And it was the worst food ever: stale bread (and a huge amount of it!), fish fried in bad oil, gloppy risotto. Little was even edible—except the stale bread, with which I filled my handbag (stale bread always comes in handy). As for my dining companions—well, they come from a culture and nation that values drinking over eating well. They drank, so they were happy. However, my first glass of unexceptional wine saw me grow angrier and angrier inside. Every platter the waiter brought to our table was more disappointing than the last, until I thought I might explode like hot lava from Vesuvio. *How can they not be bothered by this? How can they be satisfied with this slop? How can an island of such good food serve this?* I still feel annoyed when I think of that night, that terrible meal. What really makes me angry is that I was the only one angry! Everyone else was satisfied with the wine, so the food didn't matter.

I'm telling you this as a warning: Don't allow yourself to be lulled into a sense of false security regarding all the wonderful food. There are some truly awful meals out there. You could be the next victim.

And, as long as I'm ranting, there was a ragù and Genovese that tasted dubious and gave me heartburn, and a local red wine sorbetto from a lovely little *caffè* along the waterfront on Procida. Don't make my mistake, people: sweet, flat, and terrible, it tasted of cough medicine. I still feel like throwing my cone violently to the ground when I think about what should have been a wonderful red wine sorbetto and my disappointment in its terrible, fakey, frozen reality. (If you would like a beautiful red wine sorbetto with berries, boil a bottle of a light red wine, adding more sugar than you think is wise—maybe half a cup?—for about five to ten minutes until the alcohol has dissipated. When it cools, add some pureed berries and freeze. It won't freeze completely, so it will be more of a slush. Add fresh whole berries and return to the freezer.)

Even if the menu lists Neapolitan specialties and rings every bell of authenticity, it can still be—thankfully not often, but it's possible—mediocre. You can't really tell by the location, either, though some are obviously devoted to undiscerning tourists—fair enough, those are the ones to avoid whenever possible. If you ask locally, you will usually get good advice.

Bad restaurant meals, revolting ragù, terrible ice creams—I want you all to be safe from the unpleasantness of being surrounded by delectable food, yet eating mediocrity.

Bibliography

Adamson, Melitta Wiess, and Francine Sagan. *Entertaining from Ancient Rome to the Super Bowl: An Encyclopedia in Two Volumes*. Greenwood Press, 2008.

Amandonico, Nikko, Natalia Borri, and Ewa-Marie Rundquist. *La Pizza: The True Story from Naples*. Mitchell Beazley, 2001.

Arellano, Gustavo. "In Praise of Flour Tortillas, an Unsung Jewel of the U.S.-Mexico Borderlands." *New Yorker*, January 13, 2018. www.newyorker.com/culture/annals-of-gastronomy/in-praise-of-flour-tortillas-an-unsung-jewel-of-the-us-mexico-borderlands.

Artusi, Pellegrino. *La Scienza in Cucina e L'arte di Mangiar Bene*. N.d.

Barenbaum, Rose Levy. *The Bread Bible*. W. W. Norton, 2003.

Barilla. *Pasta: History, Technologies, and Secrets of Italian Tradition*. Barilla, 2000.

Bernadin, Tom. *Ellis Island Immigrant Cookbook*. Toma Bernadin, 1991.

Black, William. *Al Dente*. Corgi Books, 2004.

Boni, Ada. *The Talisman Cookbook*. Crown Publishers, 1950. (*The Talisman Cookbook*, *Talismano della Felicita*, in Italian, first published in 1928 with many subsequent printings—recognized as *the* national cookbook.)

Boxer, Arabella. *Mediterranean Cookbook*. J. M Dent and Sons, 1981.

"Campania: A Land as Clear as Daylight." Regione Campania Assessianto di turismo e ai Bene Culturali, n.d.

Capalbo, Carla. *Food and Wine Guide to Naples and Campania*. Pallas Athene, 2005.

Carluccio, Antonio. *Italia*. Quadrille, 2005.

Carluccio, Antonio and Priscilla. *Complete Italian Food*. Index Books, 1997.

Cato, Marcus Porcius. "The First History of Rome." In *Entertaining from Ancient Rome to the Super Bowl*, by Melitta Weiss Adamson and Francine Sagan. Greenwood Press, 2008.

Cavalcanti, Ippolito. *Cucina Casareccia* (Home Cooking). Il Polifilo, 2005. First published 1839.

———. *Cucina Teorico, Pratica* (Cooking: Theory and Practice). Grimaldi, 2002. First published 1852.

Claiborne, Craig. *Craig Claiborne's Favorite Recipes from the New York Times*. Vol. 3. Warner Books, 1977.

Clark, Maxine. *Trattoria*. Ryland, Peters and Small, 2004.

Corrado, Vincenzo. *Pranzi Giornalieri Variati*. 3rd ed. Grimaldi, 2001. First published 1832.

———. *Il cuoco galante* (The Gallant Cook). 3rd ed. Forni, 1990. First published 1786.

Costantino, Rosetta, with Janet Fletcher. *My Calabria*. Norton, 2010.

David, Elizabeth. *An Omelette and a Glass of Wine*. Grub Street, 2009.

Del Conte, Anna, and Val Archer. *The Painter, the Cook, and l'Arte di Sacla*. Conran Octopus, 2007.

Della Croce, Julia. *Pasta*. Dorling Kindersley, 2000.

Esposito, Gaetano. *L'Arte Della Pizza*. Edizioni Napoli d'Oc, 1998.

Ferrante, Elena. *The Story of the Lost Child*. Edizioni E/O, 2015.

———. *Those Who Leave and Those Who Stay*. Edizioni E/O, 2014.

———. *The Story of a New Name*. Edizioni E/O, 2013.

———. *My Brilliant Friend*. Edizioni E/O, 2012.

Ferrigno, Ursula. *Italy: Sea to Sky*. Mitchell Beazely Books, 2003.

———. *Truly Italian*. Mitchell Beazely Books, 1999.

"Flavor of Capri." Ente Provinceiale Per Il Turismo ACS Turismo Isole di Capri, 2002.

Fort, Matthew. *Voyages on a Vespa*. Fourth Estate, 2004.

Gilbert, Elizabeth. *Eat, Pray, Love*. Bloomsbury, 2007.

Goldstein, Joyce. *Cucina Ebraica*. Chronicle Books, 1999.

Gransden, K. W., and S. J. Harrison. *Student Guide to Virgil*. Cambridge University, 2004.

Grey, Rose, and Ruth Rogers. *The River Cafe*. Random House, 1995.

Grossman, Loyd. *Italian Food Journey*. Vermillion Books, 1994.

Harris, Robert. *Pompeii*. Arrow Books, 2004.

Harris, Valentina. *Recipes from an Italian Terrace*. Cassell Illustrated, 2004.

———. *Valentina Harris Cooks Italian.* BBC Books Worldwide, 1996.

Hazan, Marcella. *The Classic Italian Cookbook.* MacMillan, 1973.

Hazzard, Shirley, and Francis Steegmuller. *The Ancient Shore: Dispatches from Naples.* University of Chicago Press, 2008.

Hengel, Livia. "Meet the Female Pizza Makers Shaking up Naples' Food Scene." *The Independent.* May 31, 2017. www.independent.co.uk/travel/europe/naples-female-pizza-makers-pizzaiola-italy-women-isabella-de-cham-teresa-iorio-a7765261.html.

Iengo, Arturo, in association with IRVAT (Naples Chamber of Commerce). *Cucina Napoletana.* Interlink Publishers, 2008.

Jenkins, Nancy Harmon, and Sara Jenkins. *The Four Seasons of Pasta.* Avery Press, 2015.

Kumer, Corby. "Random Acts of Coffee." *The Atlantic.* December 25, 2014. www.theatlantic.com/business/archive/2014/12/random-acts-of-coffee/384056.

Limatora, Guglielmo. *Antica Cucina Napoletana.* Lito-Rama-S.A.S., 1998.

Locatelli, Giorgio. *Made in Italy.* Fourth Estate Books, 2007.

Lonely Planet Food Lover's Guide to the World. Lonely Planet Publishers, September 2014.

López-Alt, J. Kenji. "The Serious Eats Guide to Pizza in Naples." Serious Eats. 2013. https://slice.seriouseats.com/2013/01/serious-eats-guide-to-eating-pizza-in-naples-napoli-italy-neapolitan-pizza.html.

Loren, Sophia. *Eat with Me.* Doubleday, 1972.

———. *In Cucina con Amore.* Rizzoli Editore, 1971.

Luard, Elizabeth. *European Festival Food.* Bantam Press, 1990.

Marks, Gil. *The World of Jewish Cooking.* Fireside Books, 1996.

Mengozzi, Barbara, Assunta di Maruo, Giuseppe Pesapane, and Italo Santangelo. *Campania terra dell 'ortofrutta* (Campania: Land of Fruit and Vegetables). Trans. Jane Upchurch. Regione Campania, 2003.

Miseria e Nobilita. *The History of Neapolitan Cuisine.* TempoLungo, 1999.

Mozzarella di Bufala Campania. *History, Traditions, and Imaginings of a Cheese Created in the Fabled Lands of Magna Grecia.* Consorzio Tutela, 2007.

Naples and the Amalfi Coast. Dorling Kindersley, 1998.

Naples Chamber of Commerce. "Capri, Ischia, Procida." COMTUR/Naples Chamber of Commerce Special Organisation for Tourism, 2010.

"Napoli, Le Perle del Golfo" (Naples: Pearls of the Bay). Naples Chamber of Commerce, n.d.

Pandolfi, Keith. "The Gold of Naples." *Saveur.* May 2, 2013. www.saveur.com/article/Travels/The-Gold-of-Naples.

Pascalucci Restaurant. "Il Sannio nei piatti/ingredienti e vini di questa cena." Pascalucci Restaurant/Iannassi, n.d.

Passigli, Patrizia, and Lorenza Da'Medici. *Italy: The Beautiful Cookbook*. Williams Sonoma, 1989.

Pastificio Di Martino. *100 Years of Pasta*. Giusseppe Di Martino and Family/ Pastificio Di Martino, 2012.

Pirozzi, Nico. *Mozzarella di Bufala Campana*. Consorio per la Tutela del Formaggio Mozzarella di bufala Campana, 2007.

Plotkin, Fred. *Italy for the Gourmet Traveler*. Kyle Cathie, 1997.

Roddy, Rachel. *Two Kitchens: Family Recipes from Sicily and Rome*. Headline Publishing, 2017.

Roden, Claudia. *The Book of Jewish Food*. Penguin Group, 1997.

Root, Waverly. *The Cooking of Italy*. Foods of the World Series. Time Life Publications, 1978.

Schwartz, Arthur. *The Southern Italian Kitchen*. Clarkson Potter, 2009.

———. *Naples at Table*. HarperCollins, 1998.

Scott, Jack Denton. *The Complete Book of Pasta*. Bantam Books, 1968.

Sorrentino, Lejla Mancusi. *I Dodici Capolavori della Cucina Napoletana* (The Twelve Masterpieces of Neapolitan Cooking). Intra Moenia, 1999.

Spieler, Marlena. *Yummy Potatoes*. Chronicle Books, 2007.

———. *Olio di Oliva* (Cooking with the Olive and Its Sweet Oil). Apple Press, 1998.

Tannahill, Reay. *Food in History*, Broadway Books 1995.

Toussaint-Samat, Maguelonne. *A History of Food*. Wile-Blackwell, 1987.

Wilde, Mary Poulos. *The Best of Ethnic Home Cooking*. Tarcher, 1981.

Williams-Sonoma. *A Taste of the World*. Ed. Thy Tran. Gold Street Press, 2008.

Weinzweig, Ari. "Pasta Showdown: Artisan vs. Industry." *The Atlantic*, January 7, 2010. https://www.theatlantic.com/health/archive/2010/01/pasta-showdown -artisan-vs-industry/33127/?utm_source=fbb.

Young, Daniel. *Where to Eat Pizza: A Worldwide Guide*. Phaidon Press, 2016.

———. *Coffee Love*. John Wiley and Sons, 2009.

OTHER RESOURCES

A good personal trip-planning service is Insider's Italy. Through their blog (www .insidersitaly.com), they share their love and knowledge of Italy. The company offers a bespoke service for any type of Italian travel you might desire.

An excellent online resource is the gastronomic library whose books date back to the sixteenth century, available at www.academiabarilla.com.

If you are a fan of Elena Ferrante's Naples quartet, Sophia Seymour runs a tour of Naples (www.lookingforlila.com) covering the rough streets behind the railway station, Rione Luzzatti, and all the spots highlighted in the novels.

To verify your San Marzano tomatoes, visit https://gustiblog.gustiamo.com/san-marzano-2.

For an excellent schedule of food marketplaces and antiques/flea markets throughout the region, visit www.initaly.com/regions/campania/markets.htm.

USEFUL WEBSITES

https://afoodobsessionblog.wordpress.com
www.amoitaly.com/napoli/index.html
www.annamariavolpi.com/public_html
www.arrangiarsifilm.com
https://charlesscicolone.wordpress.com
https://coochinando.com
www.ecampania.it/food
www.elizabethminchilli.com/
https://ericademane.com
http://theespressobreak.blogspot.com
https://flavorofitaly.com/aboutus
https://grandenapoli.it
www.greatitalianchefs.com
www.gustiamo.com
www.illy.com/en-us/company/coffee/how-prepare-napoletana-coffee
www.insidersitaly.com/marjories-blog
www.ischiareview.com
http://juliadellacroce.com
www.lifeinitaly.com
www.lucianopignataro.it
www.mangiabenepasta.com
http://memoriediangelina.com

www.mozzarelladop.it/index.php?section=notiziario&filter=news
www.napolitoday.it/blog/napoli-food-porn
www.napoliunplugged.com
http://pancrostata.blogspot.com
www.regione.campania.it
www.sorrentoinfo.it
www.spaghettitaliani.com/index.php
www.timeout.com/travel/features/438/italys-best-eating-and-drinking-destinations
www.visitnaples.eu/en
www.vocedinapoli.it

Index

Lightning Source UK Ltd.
Milton Keynes UK
UKHW010355101118
332105UK00008B/219/P